MAMMALS
of
WASHINGTON
and OREGON

Tamara Eder

Lone Pine Publishing

The Publisher: Lone Pine Publishing

10145 – 81 Avenue	1901 Raymond Avenue SW, Suite C
Edmonton, AB, Canada	Renton, WA, USA
T6E 1W9	98055

Website: www.lonepinepublishing.com

National Library of Canada Cataloguing in Publication Data
Eder, Tamara, (date)
 Mammals of Washington and Oregon

 Includes index.
 ISBN 1-55105-337-3

 1. Mammals—Washington (State)—Identification.
2. Mammals—Oregon—Identification. I. Title.
QL719.W2E33 2002   599'.09797   C2002-910557-9

Editorial Director: Nancy Foulds
Project Editor: Lee Craig
Editorial: Volker Bodegom, Lee Craig
Illustrations Coordinator: Carol Woo
Technical Review: Richard Forbes
Track Terminology: Mark Elbroch
Production Coordinator: Jennifer Fafard
Book Design: Heather Markham
Layout & Production: Ian Dawe
Cover Design: Gerry Dotto
Cover Photo: Black-tailed (Mule) Deer buck
(© Darrell Gulin/CORBIS/MAGMA)
Map Work: Ian Dawe, Roland Lines, Lee Craig
Scanning, Separations & Film: Elite Lithographers Co.

The publisher and author thank Chris C. Fisher and Don Pattie for their previous contributions to the Mammal series.

Photograph and Illustration Credits
All photos are by Terry Parker, except as follows: Ken Balcomb, pp. 70–71; Corel Corporation (photos by Eric Stoops), pp. 82–83, 86–87; Renee DeMartin/West Stock, pp. 74–75, 78–79, 140; Leslie Degner, p. 110; Mark Degner, pp. 120, 124; Tamara Eder, p. 132; Eyewire, p. 150; Wayne Lynch, pp. 128, 176–77, 180.

All illustrations are by Gary Ross, except as follows: Ian Sheldon, all track illustrations and animal illustrations on pp. 68–69, 72–73, 76–77, 80–81, 84–85, 145, 149, 153, 340; Kindrie Grove, animal illustrations on pp. 208, 220, 222, 267, 317, 325.

The photographs in this book are reproduced with the generous permission of their copyright holders.

We acknowledge the financial support of the Government of Canada through the Book Publishing Industry Development Program (BPIDP) for our publishing activities.

PC: 04

Contents

HOOFED MAMMALS

Mountain Goat
p. 28

Bighorn Sheep
p. 32

Pronghorn
p. 36

Elk
p. 40

Mule Deer
p. 44

White-tailed Deer
p. 48

Moose
p. 52

Caribou
p. 56

Feral Pig
p. 60

Feral Horse
p. 62

WHALES

Gray Whale
p. 66

Humpback Whale
p. 72

Orca
p. 76

Pacific White-sided
Dolphin, p. 80

Dall's Porpoise
p. 84

Mountain Lion
p. 90

Canada Lynx
p. 94

Bobcat
p. 98

Western Spotted
Skunk, p. 102

Striped Skunk
p. 104

American Marten
p. 106

Fisher
p. 108

Short-tailed Weasel
p. 112

Long-tailed Weasel
p. 114

American Mink
p. 116

Wolverine
p. 118

American Badger
p. 122

CARNIVORES

Northern River
Otter, p. 126

Sea Otter
p. 130

Ringtail
p. 134

Northern Raccoon
p. 136

Harbor Seal
p. 140

Northern Elephant
Seal, p. 144

Northern Fur Seal
p. 146

Northern Sea-Lion
p. 148

California Sea-Lion
p. 152

American Black
Bear, p. 154

Grizzly Bear
p. 158

Coyote
p. 162

Gray Wolf
p. 166

Red Fox
p. 170

Kit Fox
p. 174

Common Gray Fox
p. 178

RODENTS

Nutria
p. 184

North American
Porcupine, p. 186

Western Jumping
Mouse, p. 190

Pacific Jumping
Mouse, p. 191

Western Harvest
Mouse, p. 192

Northwestern Deer
Mouse, p. 193

Deer Mouse
p. 194

Canyon Mouse
p. 196

Pinyon Mouse
p. 197

Northern
Grasshopper Mouse
p. 198

Desert Woodrat
p. 200

Dusky-footed
Woodrat, p. 201

Bushy-tailed
Woodrat, p. 202

Norway Rat
p. 204

Black Rat
p. 205

House Mouse
p. 206

7

Southern
Red-backed Vole
p. 208

Western
Red-backed Vole
p. 209

White-footed Vole
p. 210

Red Tree Vole
p. 211

Western Heather
Vole, p. 212

Meadow Vole
p. 213

Water Vole
p. 214

Montane Vole
p. 216

Gray-tailed Vole
p. 217

California Vole
p. 218

Townsend's Vole
p. 219

Long-tailed Vole
p. 220

Creeping Vole
p. 221

Sagebrush Vole
p. 222

Northern Bog
Lemming, p. 223

Common Muskrat
p. 224

American Beaver
p. 226

Great Basin Pocket
Mouse, p. 230

Little Pocket Mouse
p. 232

Dark Kangaroo
Mouse, p. 233

Ord's Kangaroo Rat
p. 234

Chisel-toothed
Kangaroo Rat
p. 236

California
Kangaroo Rat
p. 237

Northern Pocket
Gopher, p. 238

Western Pocket
Gopher, p. 240

Camas Pocket
Gopher, p. 241

Botta's Pocket
Gopher, p. 242

Townsend's Pocket
Gopher, p. 243

Yellow-pine
Chipmunk, p. 244

Least Chipmunk
p. 246

Allen's Chipmunk
p. 247

Townsend's
Chipmunk, p. 248

Siskiyou Chipmunk
p. 250

Red-tailed
Chipmunk, p. 251

Woodchuck
p. 252

Yellow-bellied
Marmot, p. 254

Hoary Marmot
p. 256

Olympic Marmot
p. 258

White-tailed
Antelope Squirrel
p. 260

Townsend's Ground
Squirrel, p. 261

Columbian Ground
Squirrel, p. 262

Merriam's Ground
Squirrel, p. 264

Piute Ground
Squirrel, p. 265

Washington Ground
Squirrel, p. 266

Wyoming Ground
Squirrel, p. 267

California Ground
Squirrel, p. 268

Belding's Ground
Squirrel, p. 270

Cascade Golden-
mantled Ground
Squirrel, p. 271

Golden-mantled
Ground Squirrel
p. 272

Western Gray
Squirrel, p. 274

Eastern Gray
Squirrel, p. 276

Eastern Fox Squirrel
p. 276

Douglas' Squirrel
p. 277

Red Squirrel
p. 278

Northern Flying
Squirrel, p. 280

Mountain Beaver
p. 282

Pygmy Rabbit
p. 285

Brush Rabbit
p. 286

Eastern
Cottontail
p. 287

Mountain
Cottontail
p. 288

Snowshoe Hare
p. 290

Black-tailed
Jackrabbit, p. 292

White-tailed
Jackrabbit, p. 294

European Rabbit
p. 295

American Pika
p. 296

BATS

Brazilian Free-tailed
Bat, p. 299

Fringed Bat
p. 300

Long-eared Bat
p. 301

Keen's Bat
p. 302

California Bat
p. 303

Little Brown Bat
p. 304

Western
Small-footed bat
p. 306

Yuma Bat
p. 307

Long-legged Bat
p. 308

Western Red Bat
p. 309

Hoary Bat
p. 310

Silver-haired Bat
p. 312

Big Brown Bat
p. 313

Western
Pipistrelle
p. 314

Spotted Bat
p. 316

Pallid Bat
p. 317

Townsend's
Big-eared Bat
p. 318

American Shrew
Mole, p. 321

Townsend's Mole
p. 322

Coast Mole
p. 323

Broad-footed Mole
p. 324

Masked Shrew
p. 325

Preble's Shrew
p. 326

Vagrant Shrew
p. 327

Montane Shrew
p. 328

Fog Shrew
p. 329

Baird's Shrew
p. 330

Pacific Shrew
p. 331

Water Shrew
p. 332

Marsh Shrew
p. 334

Trowbridge's
Shrew, p. 335

Merriam's
Shrew, p. 336

Pygmy Shrew
p. 337

Virginia
Opossum
p. 338

BEST SITES FOR MAMMAL WATCHING

1. Olympic National Park
2. Cape Flattery
3. San Juan Island
4. North Cascades National Park
5. Mountain Loop Highway
6. Flume Creek Mountain Goat Viewing Area
7. Palouse Falls State Park
8. Lone Butte Wildlife Emphasis Area
9. Highway 101
10. Denman Wildlife Area
11. Klamath Marsh National Wildlife Refuge
12. Hart Mountain National Antelope Refuge
13. Rimrock Springs Wildlife Area
14. Elkhorn Wildlife Area
15. Wallowa Lake State Park

Introduction

Few things characterize wilderness as well as wild animals, and few animals are more recognizable than our fellow mammals. In fact, many people use the term "animal" when they really mean "mammal"—they forget that birds, reptiles, amphibians, fish and all the many kinds of invertebrates are animals, too.

Mammals come in a wide variety of colors, shapes and sizes, but they share two characteristics that distinguish them from the other vertebrates: only mammals have real hair, and only mammals nurse their young with milk from mammary glands (the feature that gives this group its name). Three other, less well-known features are unique to mammals as well: a muscular diaphragm, which separates the lower abdominal cavity from the cavity that contains the heart and lungs; a two-point connection between the skull and the first vertebra—a bird's or reptile's skull has only one point of contact, which is what allows birds to turn their heads so far around; and a lower jaw that is composed of a single bone on each side—the left and right dentary bones—whereas most other jawed vertebrates have five or six bones in their lower jaws. As well as setting mammals apart from all other kinds of life, these characteristics also identify humans as part of the mammalian group.

The natural regions of Washington and Oregon provide spectacular mammal-watching opportunities, whether you are viewing a beaver swim in the evening light, watching a Humpback Whale as it breaches, or listening to the haunting sound of an Elk's bugle. Much has changed over the last 150 years, but the coast and the interior of Washington and Oregon remain internationally recognized destinations for visitors who are interested in rewarding natural experiences. This book is intended to provide readers with the knowledge needed to appreciate the rich variety of mammals in the region. Whether you are a naturalist, a photographer, a wildlife enthusiast or all three, you will find terrific opportunities in Washington and Oregon that will satisfy your greatest wilderness expectations.

American Beaver

15

The Washington and Oregon Region

Although Washington and Oregon represent only a small portion of the United States, they are extremely biologically diverse. Pristine coastal zones, rugged coastal mountains, temperate rainforests, wild backcountry, arid grasslands and clear blue lakes all contribute to the scenic beauty and ecological uniqueness of this region.

Significant areas of these states, especially in the mountains, have been protected, and the value of that foresight is easily seen in the wealth of wildlife encounters possible for all visitors here. Even outside of protected areas, these states include areas of wilderness, and wildlife is never far. Coyotes, deer and foxes can be seen in some of our largest cities, while in more remote areas, you can see and hear Elk, Moose and maybe even a Gray Wolf. In the bays and inlets around our coastal cities, we are frequently delighted by passing whales and other marine mammals. Those of us lucky enough to live in or visit Washington and Oregon may be just minutes away from some of the most thrilling wildlife encounters in North America.

Washington and Oregon are extremely varied in their biogeography. For simplification, this book divides the two states into eight different ecozones: Olympic Peninsula; Puget Trough and Willamette Valley; Pacific Coast and Coastal Mountain Range; Cascade Mountains; northeastern Washington and Selkirk Mountains; Columbia Basin; Harney Basin; and Blue Mountains and Columbia Plateau. Looking at these natural regions in detail can lead to a better understanding of the mammals here and how they interact with each other.

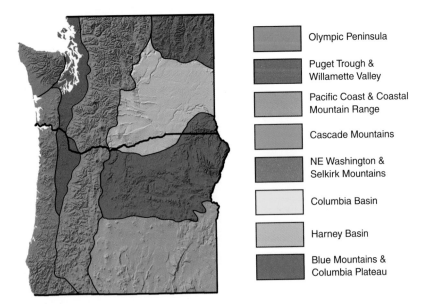

- Olympic Peninsula
- Puget Trough & Willamette Valley
- Pacific Coast & Coastal Mountain Range
- Cascade Mountains
- NE Washington & Selkirk Mountains
- Columbia Basin
- Harney Basin
- Blue Mountains & Columbia Plateau

Olympic Peninsula

This lush region receives the highest annual rainfall of any of the lower 48 states. The result is a moist temperate rainforest of Douglas-fir, western hemlock and western red cedar. Scenic mountain peaks rise above the forest over much of the peninsula, and some of this mountainous area, such as Olympic National Park, is protected. The peninsula is home to large variety of mammals, including the endemic and endangered Olympic Marmot. The open coastline is an excellent place to see Sea Otters and migrating Gray Whales.

Puget Trough and Willamette Valley

The sheltered waters of Puget Sound are a unique biogeographical feature of Washington. Puget Sound alone has more than 1000 mi. of coastline and boasts a wealth of marine life. Many species of marine mammals can be found here, such as seals, sea-lions, Orcas and Dall's Porpoises. Geologically and physiographically, the lowlands of the Puget Trough continue as far south as the Willamette Valley in Oregon. This valley has been extensively converted to agriculture, but some of the native oak savannas, grasslands and wetlands remain. The American Beaver, Black-tailed Deer, American Mink, Northern River Otter, Coyote, Red Fox and even the occasional Black Bear are seen in these lowlands.

Pacific Coast and Coastal Mountain Range

The rocky Pacific coastline with sandy beaches and nutrient-rich estuaries is bordered by open ocean on one side and high coastal mountains covered in lush temperate forests on the other. The resulting landscape is dramatic in its beauty and its wildlife assemblage. Numerous small cities occur along the coast, and a good balance exists between the cities and the surrounding wilderness. In this unique ecozone you can find Gray Whales, migrating Humpback Whales, Black Bears, Mountain Lions and Roosevelt Elk. As well, the endangered Columbian Deer can be seen in the Julia Butler Hanson National Wildlife Refuge on the Washington side of the lower Columbia River.

Cascade Mountains

The high mountains of the Cascade Range pass through both Washington and Oregon and parallel to the coastline. Formed from volcanic processes, many of the high peaks bear the distinct conical shape of a dormant volcano. Volcanic events have had a dramatic effect on the geological and ecological make-up of the region. Most peaks are between 7000 ft. and 9000 ft.; the highest is Mount Rainier, in Washington, at 14,410 ft. The mammals of the Cascade Mountains are diverse; look for Mountain Lions, Black Bears, Bobcats, Wolverines, deer and Cascade Golden-mantled Ground Squirrels.

Northeastern Washington and Selkirk Mountains

The high, densely forested northeastern interior of Washington lacks the moderating influence of the ocean, and its winters are colder than elsewhere in the state. Animals from further north, which are adapted to cold climates, can be found here. In the very northeast corner of the state are the Selkirk Mountains. The Selkirk Mountains are actually part of the much more extensive Rocky Mountains, and it is in the Selkirks that you might encounter the elusive Caribou. The Caribou in this area number only about 100, and this population is considered endangered. In addition to Caribou, the Selkirks have the only stable population of Grizzly Bears and Moose in either Washington or Oregon. Grizzly Bears are reported in the northern Cascades, but their numbers are probably very small.

Columbia Basin

Compared to the coastal areas, the Columbia Basin is warm and dry. This open region is strongly affected by the rainshadow effect of both the Olympic and Cascade mountains. Geologically, this basin was formed from glaciers during the ice age, though the Columbia River and some major flooding events have eroded and reshaped much of the landscape. The region is characterized by shrubby vegetation and is bespeckled by numerous small lakes and marshes. Many mammals are found throughout the basin region, including Bobcats, Coyotes, American Badgers and Yellow-bellied Marmots.

Harney Basin

The Harney Basin of south-central and southeastern Oregon is bordered to the north by the Columbia Basin. Like the Columbia Basin, it was formed primarily by glacial activity during the most recent ice age. Today, the landscape is exhilarating in its sweeping vistas and long horizons. Although the basin region appears stark by comparison to the lush forests in western Oregon, it boasts a unique environment of arid sagebrush flats interspersed with clear ponds and nutrient-rich marshes. Birds are abundant here, and some of the mammals you might encounter include ground squirrels, Black-tailed Jackrabbits, Mule Deer, Coyotes, Common Muskrats and even the majestic Bighorn Sheep. Some mammals—such as the Dark Kangaroo Mouse, Little Pocket Mouse and Kit Fox—that are more common in drier desert regions farther south reach their northern limit here.

Blue Mountains and Columbia Plateau

The Blue Mountains in the southeast corner of Washington and most of northeast Oregon encompass rugged peaks, low valleys, arid grasslands, lush marshes and pristine lakes. This varied environment has the dramatic appeal of true backcountry wilderness. Winters in this region are tougher than in the warmer areas to the west, but they are not harsh as in the mountains to the north. East of the Blue Mountains are the Wallowa Mountains; this small range is biologically more similar to the Rocky Mountains than are the Blue Mountains. The animals and plants that live in the Blue Mountains and Columbia Plateau are well adapted to a variety of climatic situations, including aridity, summer heat and winter cold. In this area, look for Pronghorns, Rocky Mountain Elk, Bighorn Sheep, American Mink, Northern River Otters and American Beavers.

Human-Altered Landscapes

The impact of human activity on natural environments is visible throughout Washington and Oregon. Cities, roadways, agricultural areas and forestry and mining sites are just a few of the ways we have altered the land. Many of the most common plants and animals that are found in these landscapes did not occur before the arrival of Europeans and modern transportation. House Mice, Norway Rats, Black Rats and, most recently, Nutrias are some of the highly successful exotics that were introduced to North America from Europe and Asia.

Black Rat

Seasonality

The seasons of Washington and Oregon greatly influence the lives of mammals. Aside from bats and marine mammals, most species are confined to relatively slow forms of terrestrial travel. As a result, they have limited geographic ranges and must cope in various ways with the changing seasons.

With rising temperatures, reduced snow or rain and the greening of the landscape, spring brings renewal. It is at this time of year that many mammals bear their young. The abundance of food cycles through the food chain: lush new growth provides ample food for herbivores, and the numerous herbivore young become easy prey for the carnivorous mammals. While some small mammals, particularly the shrews and rodents, mature within weeks, offspring of the larger mammals depend on their parents for much longer periods.

During the warmest time of the year, the animals' bodies have recovered from the strain of the previous winter's food scarcity and spring's reproductive efforts, but summer is not a time of relaxation. To prepare yet again for the upcoming fall and winter, some animals must eat vast quantities of food to build up fat reserves, while others work furiously to stockpile food caches in safe places. For some of the more charismatic species, such as the bugling bull Elk—which demonstrates extremes of aggression and vigilance—the fall is the time for mating. Some small mammals, such as voles and mice, mate every few months or even all year-round.

Winter differs in intensity and duration throughout different regions of these states. In coastal and southern areas, winters are mild and not too stressful. In the mountain and northern regions, winter can be an arduous, life-threatening challenge for many mammals. For herbivores, high-energy foods are difficult to find, often requiring more energy to locate than they provide in return. This negative energy budget gradually weakens most herbivores through winter. Those herbivores not sufficiently fit at the onset of winter end up feeding the equally needy carnivores, which ironically find an ally in winter's severity. Voles and mice also find advantages in the season—an insulating layer of snow buffers their elaborate trails from the worst of winter's cold. Food, shelter and warmth are all found in the thin layer between the snow and the ground surface, and the months devoted to food storage now pay off.

An important aspect of seasonality is its effect on species composition. When you visit the interior or mountainous regions in winter, for example, you will see a different group of mammals than in summer. Many species, such as ground squirrels and bears, are dormant in winter. Conversely, many ungulates may be more visible in winter because they enter lowland meadows to find edible vegetation.

Long-tailed Weasel, winter coat

Watching Mammals

Many types of mammals are most active at night, so the best times for viewing are during the "wildlife hours" at dawn and at dusk. At these times of day, mammals are out from their daytime hideouts, moving through areas where they are more easily encountered. During winter, hunger may force certain mammals to be more active during midday. Conversely, when conditions are more favorable during spring and summer, some mammals may become less active.

Within the national parks of Washington and Oregon, many of the larger mammals can be viewed easily from the safety of a vehicle along the many roadways that cut through the parks. If you walk backcountry trails or hike through temperate rainforests, however, you can find yourself right in the homes of certain mammals.

Although people have become more conscious of the need to protect wildlife, the pressures of increased human visitation have nevertheless damaged critical habitats, and some species have experienced frequent harassment. Modern wildlife viewing demands courtesy and common sense. Some of the mammals that are encountered in Washington and Oregon appear easy to approach, but it is important to respect your own safety as much as the safety of the animal being viewed. This advice seems obvious for the larger species—it is ignorantly dismissed in some instances—but it applies equally to small mammals. Honor both the encounter and the animal by demonstrating a respect appropriate to the occasion. Here are some points to remember for ethical wildlife watching in the field:

- Confine your movements to designated trails and roads wherever provided. Doing so allows animals to adapt to human use in the area and also minimizes your impact on the habitat.
- Avoid dens and resting sites, and never touch or feed wild animals. Baby animals are seldom orphaned or abandoned, and it is against the law to take them away.
- Because stress is harmful to wildlife, never chase or flush animals from cover. Use binoculars and keep a respectful distance, for the animal's sake and also your own.
- Leave the environment, including both flora and fauna, unchanged by your visits. Take home only pictures and memories.
- Pets are a hindrance to wildlife viewing. They may chase, injure or kill other animals, so control your pets or leave them at home.
- Take the time to learn about the wildlife and the behavior and sensitivity of each species.

Caribou

Top Mammal-Watching Sites

Washington

Olympic National Park

The world-famous Olympic National Park contains some of the most beautiful and pristine temperate rainforest in the world. Numerous trails offer excellent opportunities to see the indigenous flora and fauna of the region. Throughout the park, look for Olympic Marmots, Mountain Lions, Bobcats, Black Bears, Black-tailed Deer and squirrels. The park includes a small, isolated portion on the coast, south of Cape Flattery, where you may see Gray Whales, albino deer, Sea Otters, Harbor Seals and California Sea-Lions.

Cape Flattery

Cape Flattery offers excellent opportunities to experience local natural and cultural history. The coastline boasts abundant marine life and dramatic scenery. Several trails along the coast provide ample chances to see wildlife firsthand. The area is the best place in Washington to see Sea Otters, but also keep your eyes open for Gray Whales and other marine mammals as well.

San Juan Island

Remote and beautiful, San Juan Island is the perfect place for viewing marine mammals. Several sites on this island, such as Lime Kiln Point State Park and Cattle Point, offer you the best chances of seeing Minke Whales and Orcas. Other mammals to look for include Dall's Porpoises, Harbor Porpoises, Harbor Seals and Northern River Otters.

North Cascades National Park

North Cascades National Park offers exceptional opportunities for wildlife viewing amidst dramatic mountain scenery. Grizzly Bears and Gray Wolves are infrequently reported here, but your chances of seeing either are low. The most likely mammals to see include Cascade Golden-mantled Ground Squirrels, Hoary Marmots, other squirrels and chipmunks, Coyotes, Mule Deer, Elk and Black Bears.

Mountain Loop Highway

For those people who prefer wildlife encounters from the safety of their vehicle, driving the Mountain Loop Highway is an excellent way to see the local wildlife. The trip lasts about three hours and takes you through riparian zones, mountain forests and alpine habitat. Keep your eyes open for Mule Deer, Coyotes, squirrels and Mountain Goats. If you take to the trails along this route, you may have the chance to see beavers, Northern River Otters and Red Foxes.

Sea Otter

21

Flume Creek Mountain Goat Viewing Area

Perhaps the best place in Washington for viewing hoofed mammals, Flume Creek provides outstanding chances to see wildlife found nowhere else in Washington. The forests, high-elevation grassy plateaus and wetlands are prime habitat for Moose, White-tailed Deer and Mule Deer. Mountain Goats are frequently seen in the rockier areas, as are Bighorn Sheep. Flume Creek also has the only resident population of Caribou in the state. Look for these elegant northern animals in high meadows.

Palouse Falls State Park

Palouse Falls may not offer the best chances for seeing the charismatic mammal species, such as carnivores and hoofed mammals, but the sheer dramatic beauty of this waterfall makes up for it. The spectacular basin and waterfall were formed during violent flooding events about 12,000 years ago. Look for Yellow-bellied Marmots, Mountain Cottontails, White-tailed Jackrabbits and the occasional White-tailed Deer.

Lone Butte Wildlife Emphasis Area

The meadows and mixed forests of Lone Butte are good places for peaceful wildlife viewing. Several trails in the area expose visitors to the riparian forests and mixed coniferous forests that characterize much of the area. The luckiest visitors here may see Black Bears, Northern River Otters, Coyotes, Red Foxes, Mule Deer and American Beavers.

Oregon

Highway 101

All along the Oregon portion of Highway 101 are world-class state parks and wildlife refuges where you can see the abundant coastal flora and fauna of Oregon. The highway parallels the coast, as do migrating Gray and Humpback whales. In March, April and May watch for whales from the headlands. Few other spots in the world offer such outstanding opportunities to see marine mammals from land. The tidepool life along this route is exceptional, but remember that most state parks prohibit collecting and touching of tidepool life, and in some places trespassing is also prohibited. On coastal rocks and rocky islets look for sea-lions and Harbor Seals. Along the length of

Yellow-bellied Marmot

the highway and its numerous walking trails, watch for Black-tailed Deer, Roosevelt Elk, Black Bears, Northern Raccoons, Northern River Otters, Brush Rabbits and Mountain Beavers. In the south of Oregon along this route at night you might even see a Ringtail.

Denman Wildlife Area
The excellent wetlands and lush forests of the Denman Wildlife Area are home to a wide variety of birds, reptiles and amphibians. Birdwatchers are richly rewarded here because of this region's habitat diversity. The mammals are also diverse in this wildlife area, but most mammals tend to be more secretive than birds. Along the trails and open areas of this park, look for American Beavers, Common Muskrats, Northern River Otters, Western Gray Squirrels, Black-tailed Jackrabbits and deer.

Klamath Marsh National Wildlife Refuge
This wildlife refuge encompasses extensive wetlands, meadow and forest habitat. Such a mixed habitat is home for a wide diversity of birds, amphibians and mammals. Along with the dozens of bird species here, look for Yellow-pine Chipmunks, Mountain Cottontails, Northern River Otters, Northern Raccoons, Mule Deer and Rocky Mountain Elk.

Hart Mountain National Antelope Refuge
As its name suggests, this wildlife refuge was developed to protect the habitat of the Pronghorn and ensure a stable population. Of course, animals that live in the same habitat enjoy the protection that this refuge offers. This area encompasses wetlands, sagebrush flats, grasslands, rugged canyons and aspen groves. In addition to Pronghorn, you have a good chance of seeing ground squirrels, Black-tailed Jackrabbits, Coyotes, Mule Deer and Bighorn Sheep along the trails and roads of this refuge.

Rimrock Springs Wildlife Area
A wide variety of plants and animals make their home in the protected habitats of the Rimrock Springs Wildlife Area. This area includes marshlands, grasslands, sagebrush flats and riparian zones. Birds are abundant and diverse here, as are mammals. Visitors to this wildlife area frequently see Yellow-pine Chipmunks, Mountain Cottontails, North American Porcupines, American Beavers, Coyotes, Mule Deer and Pronghorn.

Elkhorn Wildlife Area
Some of the best opportunities to see Rocky Mountain Elk in Oregon can be found in the Elkhorn Wildlife Area. This protected area was intended to serve as a feeding range for Elk during the winter months. Because agricultural land has taken over so much of the native grasslands, Elk were previously relying on agricultural forage to survive the winter. The Elkhorn area boasts a high concentration of Elk, and visitors are rewarded with excellent sightings of this elegant animal. In the fall, you may even hear the haunting calls of a bugling bull Elk. Another mammal to watch for is the Western Spotted Skunk, a handsome, if smelly, resident.

Wallowa Lake State Park
Located in northeastern Oregon, the Wallowa Lake State Park is situated in the scenic Blue Mountains. The region encompasses beautiful mountain wilderness, lakes and thick forests. The trails and campground are good places for viewing the abundant wildlife. Watch for Golden-mantled Ground Squirrels, Red Squirrels, Northern Raccoons, Striped Skunks, North American Porcupines, American Mink, Rocky Mountain Elk and Mule Deer. Meadows in this region may also be home to Columbian Ground Squirrels.

About This Book

This guide describes 158 species of wild and feral mammals that have been reported in Washington and Oregon. Domestic farm animals, such as cattle, sheep and llamas, are not described here. Although many whales, dolphins and porpoises are known to occur in the waters off Washington and Oregon, only those that are most common and most likely to be encountered near shore are included. Humans, a member of the order Primates, have lived in this region since at least the end of the last Pleistocene glaciation, but the relationship between our species and the natural world is well beyond the scope of this book.

Organization

Biologists divide mammals (class Mammalia) into a number of subgroups, called orders, which form the basis for the organization of this book. Nine mammalian orders have wild or feral representatives in Washington and Oregon: even-toed hoofed mammals (Artiodactyla); odd-toed hoofed mammals (Perissodactyla); carnivores (Carnivora); whales, dolphins and porpoises (Cetacea); rodents (Rodentia); rabbits, hares and pikas (Lagomorpha); bats (Chiroptera); insectivores (Insectivora); and opossums (Didelphimorphia). In turn, each order is subdivided into families, which group together the more closely related species. For example, within the carnivores, the Wolverine and the American Mink, which are both in the weasel family, are more closely related to each other than either is to the Striped Skunk, which is in its own family.

Mammal Names

Although the international zoological community closely monitors the use of scientific names for animals, common names—which change with time, local language and usage—are more difficult to standardize. In the case of birds, the American Ornithologists' Union has been very effective in standardizing the common names used by professionals and recreational naturalists alike. As yet, no similar organization exists to oversee and approve the common names of mammals in North America, and this situation can lead to some confusion.

For example, many people apply the name "mole" to pocket gophers. These burrowing mammals leave loose cores of dirt in fields and reminded early settlers of the moles they knew in the East and in Europe. To add to the confusion, most people use the name "gopher" to refer not to pocket gophers, but to the ubiquitous ground squirrels. If you consider non-mammalian species, it would get even worse. The name "gopher" is used in many parts of North America to denote a species of snake and even a tortoise!

You may think that such confusion is limited to the less charismatic species of animals, but even some of the best-known mammals are victims of human inconsistency. Most people clearly know the identities of the Moose and the Elk, but these names can cause great confusion for European visitors. The species that we know as the Elk, *Cervus elaphus*, is called the "Red Deer" in Europe, while "Elk" is the name Europeans use for *Alces alces* ("elk" and *alces* come from the same root), which is known as the Moose in North America. The blame for this confusion falls on the early European settlers, who misapplied the name "Elk" to populations of *Cervus elaphus*. In an as-yet-unsuccessful attempt to resolve the confusion, many naturalists use the name "Wapiti" for the species *Cervus elaphus* in North America.

Despite the lack of an "official" list of mammal common names, there are some widely accepted standards, such as the "Revised checklist of North American mammals north of Mexico, 1997" (Jones et al. 1997, Occasional Papers, Museum of Texas Tech University, No. 173) and *The Smithsonian Book of North American Mammals* (Wilson, D.E., and Sue Ruff, 1999). This book follows these sources for the scientific names of mammals and, for the most part, for common names as well.

Range Maps

Mapping the range of a species is a problematic endeavor: mammal populations fluctuate, distributions expand and shrink, and dispersing individuals are occasionally encountered in unexpected areas. The range maps included in this book are intended to show the distribution of breeding, sustaining populations in the region, and not the extent of individual specimen records. Full-color intensity on the map indicates a species' presence; pale areas indicate its absence. For species with especially small ranges, arrows are used to highlight the range, and triangles indicate isolated specimen records. A question mark is used to indicate uncertainty about the presence of a species.

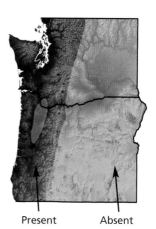

Present   Absent

Similar Species

Before you finalize your decision on the species identity of a mammal, check the "Similar Species" section of the account; it briefly describes other mammals that could be mistakenly identified as the species you are considering. By concentrating on the most relevant field marks, the subtle differences between species can be reduced to easily identifiable traits. As you become more experienced at identifying mammals, you might find you can immediately shortlist an animal to a few possible species. By consulting this section, you can quickly glean the most relevant field marks to distinguish between those species, thereby simplifying the identification process.

Canada Lynx   Bobcat

HOOFED MAMMALS

These mammals are the "megaherbivores" of Washington and Oregon, so called because they fall into the largest size class of terrestrial mammals and because most of them eat plants exclusively. Nearly all hoofed mammals are strict herbivores; the only exception in Washington and Oregon is the Feral Pig, which is omnivorous.

All of the native hoofed mammals in the region and the introduced Feral Pig, which can be found in scattered populations in the United States, belong to the order Artiodactyla (even-toed hoofed mammals). The even-toed hoofed mammals all have either two or four toes on each limb. If there are four toes, the outer two, which are called dewclaws, are always smaller and higher on the leg, touching the ground only in soft mud or snow. The Feral Horse, which was introduced to North America, belongs to the order Perissodactyla (odd-toed hoofed mammals) and has just a single toe on each foot.

Another difference between the two orders of hoofed mammals is in the structure of their ankle bones. The ankle bones of all the even-toed hoofed mammals are grooved on both their upper and lower surfaces, which enables these animals, such as Moose and deer, to rise from a reclined position with their hindquarters first. This ability means that the large hindleg muscles are available for fight or flight more quickly than in the odd-toed hoofed mammals, such as Feral Horses, which must rise front first. Additionally, the native even-toed hoofed mammals have incisors only on the lower jaw; they have a cartilaginous pad at the front of the upper jaw instead of teeth. The exception is the introduced Feral Pig, which has upper incisors and canines.

In Washington and Oregon, several of the native hoofed mammals are divided into well-known subspecies. The Elk and Mule Deer, for example, are better known in western Washington and Oregon as the Roosevelt Elk and the Black-tailed Deer, respectively. Even though these subspecies are quite well defined, they are not considered distinct because they are capable of interbreeding with others of the same species found elsewhere.

Cattle Family (Bovidae)

Native bovids are distinguished by the presence of true horns in both the male and female. The horns are never shed, nor are they branched, and they grow throughout the animal's life. They consist of a keratinous sheath (keratin is the main type of protein in our fingernails and hair) over a bony core that grows from the frontal bones of the skull. Like the deer and allies, bovids are cud chewers, and they have complex, four-chambered stomachs to digest their meals.

Bighorn Sheep

Pronghorn Family (Antilocapridae)

This exclusively North American family contains just the one species. The Pronghorn has only two toes (no dewclaws), and, like the other native artiodactyls, it lacks upper canine teeth (as well as upper incisors). Both sexes have true horns, but, unlike bovids, the Pronghorn sheds and regrows the keratinous sheath each year (the bony core is not shed). The darkly colored sheath—but not the bony core—is branched, hence the name "*prong*horn."

Pronghorn

Deer Family (Cervidae)

All adult male cervids and female Caribou have antlers, which are bony outgrowths of the frontal skull bones and are shed and regrown annually. In males with an adequate diet, the antlers generally get larger each year. New antlers are soft and tender, and they are covered with "velvet," a layer of skin with short, fine hairs and a network of blood vessels to nourish the growing antlers. The antlers stop growing in late summer, and as the velvet dries up the deer rubs it off. Cervids are also distinguished by the presence of scent glands in pits just in front of the eyes. Like all native artiodactyls, their lower canine teeth look like incisors, so there appear to be four pairs of lower incisors.

White-tailed Deer

Swine Family (Suidae)

The Swine Family includes eight species that originated in Eurasia and Africa. Most of them are restricted to their native ranges, but the Domestic Pig (*Sus scrofa*) has been widely introduced in most areas of human habitation. Despite its name, the Domestic Pig now ranges free in many parts of North America, and these feral populations can become quite large. These free-ranging pigs are now called Feral Pigs. The European Wild Boar is another wild form of *Sus scrofa* that was also introduced to North America, and these two varieties of swine sometimes hybridize. Feral Pigs are the only artiodactyls in Washington and Oregon to have upper incisors and upper canines. The canines are modified into tusks.

Feral Pig

Horse Family (Equidae)

All members of this family, which also includes zebras and donkeys, have a single toe on each limb, a bushy dorsal mane and a long, well-haired tail. Although horse-like animals were once native to North America, they disappeared from our continent more than 10,000 years ago. The herds of Feral Horses that are now found in several places throughout the western United States are descended from domestic horses.

Feral Horse

27

Mountain Goat

Oreamnos americanus

Acrophobia—the fear of heights—is unknown to the Mountain Goat. This nimble bovid is at home on rocky cliffs, so the very heights that instill fear in many people are comfortable and easily navigable for this animal.

The Mountain Goat has several physical characteristics that help it live in such precarious surroundings. The hard outer ring of each hoof surrounds a softer, spongy central area that provides a good grip on rocky surfaces. The dewclaws are long enough to touch the ground on soft surfaces, and they provide greater "flotation" on weaker snow crusts. To keep the Mountain Goat relatively comfortable in the subzero temperatures and strong winter winds that sweep along mountain faces, its winter coat consists of a thick, fleecy undercoat topped by guard hairs more than 6 in. long. By the time spring arrives, the goats begin to shed "blankets" of thick hair, which fall in pieces, often in their dusting pits dug high on the sides of mountains. At this time Mountain Goats are not in their picturesque prime. Their short, neat, white summer coat comes in by June, and it continues to grow to form the thick winter coat.

The steep relief of their rocky home offers significant protection for Mountain Goats, but the ever-present risk of avalanches and rockslides is an expensive trade-off. Snow and rock slides are a major cause of death among most populations of Mountain Goats, particularly during late winter and spring. These unfortunate incidents are not without benefit, however, because recently awakened, winter-starved bears and other hungry carnivores scavenge along spring slides for dead Mountain Goats.

DESCRIPTION: The coat of this stocky, hump-shouldered animal is white and usually shaggy, with a longer series of guard hairs over a dense fleecy undercoat. The lips, nose, eyes and hooves are black. Both sexes may sport a noticeable "beard," which is longer in winter. The short legs often look like they are clothed in breeches in winter, because the hair of the lower leg is much shorter than that of the upper leg. The tail is short, and the ears are relatively long. Both sexes have narrow, black horns. A billy's horns are thicker and curve backward along a constant arc. A nanny's horns are narrower and tend to rise straight from the skull and then bend sharply to the rear near their tips. A Mountain Goat kid is also white, with a gray-brown stripe along its back.

RANGE: The Mountain Goat's natural range extends from southern Alaska and the eastern Yukon south through the Coast Mountains into Washington's Cascade and Olympic mountains and southeast through the Rockies into Idaho and Montana. It has been introduced successfully to several other states, including Oregon.

Total Length: 4–5 ft.
Shoulder Height: 3–4 ft.
Tail Length: 3¹⁄₂–5¹⁄₂ in.
Weight: 100–300 lb.

male

HABITAT: The Mountain Goat generally occupies steep slopes and rocky cliffs in alpine or subalpine areas, where low temperatures and deep snow are common. Although it typically inhabits treeless areas, the Mountain Goat may travel through dense subalpine or montane forests going to and from salt licks. In summer, it tends to be seen more frequently at lower elevations, especially in flower-filled meadows close to the escape shelter of cliffs. It moves to the highest windswept ledges in winter to find vegetation that is free of snowcover.

FOOD: This adaptable herbivore varies its diet according to its environment. In some areas it may eat shrubs almost exclusively, with the balance of the diet coming from mosses, lichens and forbs; in other areas only a small portion of the diet may be shrubs and the rest is grasses, sedges and rushes. The Mountain Goat's winter feeding areas are generally separate from its summer areas. At about the same time as the spring molt, the Mountain Goat has a strong need for salt, and it may travel long distances to find outcrops of mineral-rich soil.

DID YOU KNOW?

The Mountain Goat's skeleton is arranged so that all four hooves can fit on a ledge as small as 6 in. long and 2 in. wide—smaller than this book. A goat can even rear up and turn around on such a tiny foothold.

hoofprint

DEN: Mountain Goats bed down in shallow depressions scraped out in shale or dirt at the bases of cliffs. Clumps of the goats' white hair are often scattered in the vicinity of the scrapes. In early summer, goats dig dusting pits in which they may lie and rub themselves or sit and rest. Nannies will often evict billies from their dusting sites, indicating their dominant status.

YOUNG: In May, after a gestation of five to six months, a nanny bears a single kid (75 percent of the time) or twins, weighing $6^1/_2$–$8^1/_2$ lb. The kids are precocial and can follow their mother within hours. After a few days, the kids start eating grasses and forbs, but they are not weaned until they are about six weeks old. The young are very playful, and they leap, jump and eagerly scale boulders as they learn the art of rock climbing. Both sexes become sexually mature after about $2^1/_2$ years. Nannies mate every other year.

walking trail

Bighorn Sheep

SIMILAR SPECIES: The **Bighorn Sheep** (p. 32) has brown upperparts and a whitish rump patch. Its brown horns are either massive and thick at the base (in rams) or flattened (in ewes), but they are never black, round, thin and stiletto-like, as a Mountain Goat's horns are.

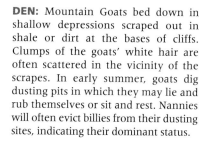

Bighorn Sheep
Ovis canadensis

No matter where you travel in North America, the mountains of the Pacific Northwest simply cannot be beaten for their diversity of hoofed mammals. It seems fitting, therefore, that one of the most recognizable and revered ungulates, the Bighorn Sheep, is a favorite symbol of mountain wilderness. Although the Bighorn Sheep has a well-developed sense of balance and is at home on steep slopes and rocky ledges, it is also common along roadsides in mountain parks and wildlife areas. The subspecies seen in Washington and Oregon is the California Bighorn (ssp. *californiana*).

Bighorn Sheep were once eliminated from Washington and parts of Oregon because of problems with disease transmission to domestic cattle. Recently, successful introductions have developed a stable population in both these states. Sightings of Bighorn Sheep increase each year. Provided that people are unobtrusive and non-aggressive, they can be rewarded with glimpses of these mammals' natural behavior amidst the beautiful mountain scenery. As friendly and quiet as Bighorn Sheep appear, however, always remember that they are wild animals and should be treated as such.

Bighorn lambs that are too young and too small to have mastered the sanctuary of cliffs are particularly vulnerable to predation by carnivores. Newborn lambs occasionally become prey for eagles, Mountain Lions (p. 90) and Bobcats (p. 98). Provided they survive their first year, most Bighorns live long lives—few of their natural predators can match Bighorn Sheep's sure-footedness and vertical agility.

The magnificent courtship battles between Bighorn rams have made these animals favorites of TV wildlife specials and corporate advertising. During October and November, adult rams establish a breeding hierarchy that is based on the relative sizes of their horns and the outcomes of their impressive head-to-head combats. In battle, opposing rams rise on their hindlegs, run a few steps toward one another and smash their horns together with a magnificent bang. Once the breeding hierarchy has been established, mating takes place, after which the rams and ewes tend to split into separate herds. For the most part, the rams abandon their head blows until the next fall, but broken horns and ribs are reminders of their hormone-induced clashes.

ALSO CALLED: Mountain Sheep.

DESCRIPTION: This robust, brownish sheep has a bobbed tail and a large,

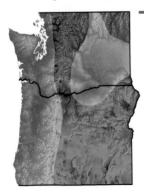

RANGE: From the Rocky Mountains of Alberta and west-central British Columbia, the Bighorn Sheep's range extends east to the Dakotas and south through California and New Mexico into northern Mexico.

Total Length: 5–6 ft.
Shoulder Height: 30–45 in.
Tail Length: 3¼–5 in.
Weight: 120–340 lb.

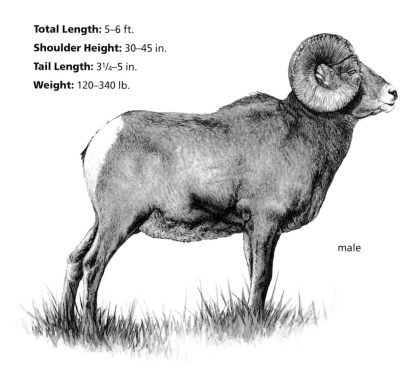

male

white rump patch. The belly, the insides of the legs and the end of the muzzle are also white. The brown coat is darkest in fall, gradually fading with winter wear. It looks motley in June while the new coat grows in. "Bighorn" is a well-deserved name, because the circumference of a ram's horns can be as much as 18 in. at the base. The curled horns can be over 43 in. long and spread 26 in. from tip to tip. Heavy ridges run transversely across the horn. A deep groove forms each winter, which makes it possible to determine a sheep's age from its horns. A ewe's horns are shorter and noticeably more flattened from side to side than a ram's. Also, a ewe's horns never curl around to form even a half circle, whereas an older ram's horns may form a full curl or more.

HABITAT: Although it is most common in non-forested, mountainous areas where cliffs provide easy escape routes, the Bighorn Sheep can thrive outside the mountains. Some populations live along steep riverbanks and even in the gullied badlands of more arid environments.

FOOD: The diet consists primarily of broad-leaved, non-woody plants and grasses. Exposed, dry grasses on windswept slopes provide much of the winter food. The Bighorn Sheep exhibits a ruminant's appetite for salt. To fulfill this need, herds may travel

DID YOU KNOW?

Bighorn rams occasionally interbreed with domestic ewes. The hybrids, which have the economically inferior, coarse hair of Bighorns, are a concern to wool ranchers as well as conservationists.

hoofprint

walking trail

miles, even through dense forests, to reach natural salt licks. They often eat soil along highways for the road salt that is applied during winter. This activity increases the number of collisions with vehicles.

DEN: A Bighorn Sheep typically beds down for the night in a depression that is about 4 ft. wide and up to 1 ft. deep. The depression usually smells of urine and is almost always edged with the sheep's tiny droppings.

YOUNG: Typically, a ewe gives birth to a single precocial lamb in seclusion on a remote rocky ledge in late May or early June, after a gestation of about six months. The ewe and her lamb rejoin the herd within a few days. Initially, the lamb nurses every half hour; as it matures, it nurses less frequently, until it is weaned at about six months. Lambs are extremely agile and playful: they jump and run about, scale small cliffs, engage in mock fights and even leap over one another. These activities prepare them for escaping predators later in life.

SIMILAR SPECIES: The **Mule Deer** (p. 44) also has a large, whitish rump patch and an overall brown color, but bucks have branched antlers, and does lack antlers entirely. The **Mountain Goat** (p. 28), which sometimes shares habitat with the Bighorn Sheep, is white, not brown, and its horns are black and stiletto-like.

Mule Deer

Pronghorn
Antilocapra americana

Through the blurred, heat-shimmered light of a grassland afternoon, the shape of a Pronghorn emerges from the brown landscape to stand and stare. Just as suddenly, it turns and retreats into the open plains. The Pronghorn superficially resembles a deer, and it is often called an antelope, but it has no close living relatives—it is the sole member of an ancient family of hoofed mammals that dates back 20 million years. This animal's unique, pronged horns are neither antlers nor true horns; only the outer keratin sheath is shed each year, not the bony core.

In open landscape, the Pronghorn's phenomenal eyesight serves it well in detecting predators. The Pronghorn's large eyes protrude so far out from the sides of its head that it has stereoscopic vision to the rear as well as in the front. A Pronghorn is rarely seen first.

Should danger press, a Pronghorn will erect the hairs of its white rump patch to produce a mirror-like flash that is visible at a great distance. Speed, which comes easily and quickly to the Pronghorn, is this animal's chief defense, and even three-day-old fawns are quite capable of outrunning a human. The Pronghorn is the swiftest of North America's land mammals, and it is among the fastest in the world. With its efficient metabolism, powered by an extremely large heart and lungs for its body size, the Pronghorn can run at about 55 m.p.h. for several minutes at a time. Its lack of dewclaws is also thought to be a result of its adaptation for speed.

For all its speed, the Pronghorn is a poor jumper, and its numbers declined rapidly with the fencing of rangelands throughout the West. In the 1800s Pronghorns were believed to have numbered in the millions, but by the early 1900s the total population in the United States was about 20,000. This decline was a combination of restricted movement from fences and over-hunting. Pronghorn are still considered a game animal, and some hunting occurs. Fortunately, the efforts of government and private programs have helped increase their numbers.

The fences still remain on rangeland, but many people now construct fences suitable for a Pronghorn to fit underneath. Running Pronghorns surprise many passing motorists when, one after another, they hardly break stride to deftly dip beneath the lowest strand of barbed wire in a fence.

DESCRIPTION: The upperparts, legs and tail are generally tan. The belly, lower

RANGE: The Pronghorn is found through much of western North America, from southern Alberta and Saskatchewan southwest into Oregon and south through California and western Texas into northern Mexico.

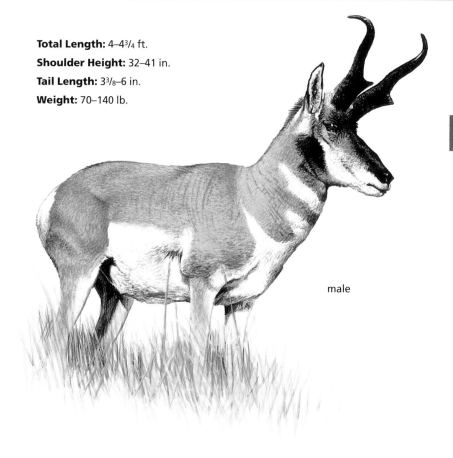

Total Length: 4–4³/₄ ft.
Shoulder Height: 32–41 in.
Tail Length: 3³/₈–6 in.
Weight: 70–140 lb.

male

sides and lower jaw are white; two broad, white bands run across the throat; and the rump has a large, white patch. A short, black-tipped mane is on the nape of the neck. The legs have no dewclaws. Both sexes may have horns, but those of the doe are never as long as her ears and they do not have the ivory-colored tips occasionally seen on the buck's. The buck's horns are straight near the base, and then bear a short branch or "prong" before they usually curve backward or inward to sharp tips. The muzzle is black, and on the buck the black extends over the face to the horn bases. The buck also has a broad black stripe running from the ear base to behind the lower jaw.

HABITAT: The Pronghorn is a staunch resident of relatively treeless areas. It inhabits open, often arid grasslands, grassy brushlands and semi-deserts and avoids woodlands.

FOOD: The winter diet is composed almost exclusively of sagebrush, bitterbrush and other woody shrubs. In

DID YOU KNOW?

Although Pronghorns typically give humans a wide berth, they can display an extreme curiosity, and a piece of plastic or a rag caught on a fence and waving in the breeze can often entice individuals to approach.

hoofprint

walking trail

spring, the diet switches: snowbrush, snowberry, rabbitbrush and sagebrush constitute 67 percent of the intake; forbs make up 17 percent; alfalfa and crops make up about 15 percent; and grasses only 1 percent.

DEN: Because it is a roaming animal that remains active day and night—it alternates short naps with watchful feeding—the Pronghorn does not maintain a home bed.

YOUNG: Forty percent of does bear a single fawn with their first pregnancies, but 60 percent of first pregnancies and nearly all subsequent pregnancies result in the birth of twins. In June, a doe finds a secluded grassy spot to give birth, following a gestation period of $7^1/_2$ to 8 months. The precocial fawns lie hidden in the grass at first, and their mothers return to nurse them about every $1^1/_2$ hours. The does gradually reduce the frequency of nursings, and when a fawn is about two weeks old and capable of outrunning most potential predators, mother and young rejoin the herd. Some does may breed during the short, mid- to late September breeding season of their first year, but most do not breed until their second year.

SIMILAR SPECIES: The **Mule Deer** (p. 44) has a white rump, but it is larger, and the bucks have antlers, not black horns. The **White-tailed Deer** (p. 48) does not have a white rump. Neither deer has the white throat bands or white lower sides of the Pronghorn.

Mule Deer

Elk

Cervus elaphus

The pitched bugle of the bull Elk is, in parts of the northwest, as much a symbol of fall as the first frost, golden leaves and migrating geese. The Elk has likely always held some form of fascination for humans, as evidenced by native hunting and lore, but it is another of North America's large mammals that suffered widespread extirpation during the time of settlement and agricultural expansion across the continent.

The dramatic decline of Elk in North America during the 19th century prompted wide-scale conservation efforts for remnant populations and far-reaching reintroduction programs to form new herds. Even the great numbers of Elk currently seen in mountain parks owe their presence to mitigative human efforts.

In Washington and Oregon there are two well-known subspecies of Elk, the Roosevelt Elk and the Rocky Mountain Elk. The Roosevelt Elk (ssp. *roosevelti*) is usually darker in color, and the males tend to develop a "cup" on the royal tine of their antlers. This cup gives the tip of the antlers a slightly palmate appearance. The Roosevelt Elk inhabits the region west of the crest of the Cascades; look for it in deciduous and mixed-wood rainforest in Olympic National Park and surrounding areas. The Rocky Mountain Elk (ssp. *nelsoni*) inhabits the areas east of the Cascades in Washington and Oregon.

Elk form breeding harems to a greater degree than most other deer. A bull Elk that is a harem master expends a considerable amount of energy during the fall rut—his fierce battles with rival bulls and the upkeep of cows in his harem demand more work than time permits—and he frequently starts winter in a weakened state. Once the rut is over, however, bulls fatten up by as much as a pound a day. Cows and young Elk, on the other hand, usually see the first frost while they are fat and healthy. This disparity makes sense in evolutionary terms: many cows enter winter pregnant with the next generation of the Elk population, whereas, once winter arrives, the older bulls' major contributions are past.

Fortunately for Elk, much of their inhabited areas in Washington and Oregon have become more accessible to grazing, even during winter. Artificially lush golf courses and agricultural fields supply high-quality forage throughout the year, while roads, townsites and other human activity have eliminated most major predators—except, of course, humans. In wilder areas, Elk are typically most active during the daytime, particularly near dawn and dusk,

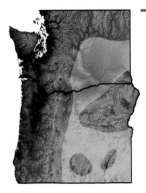

RANGE: Holarctic in its distribution, the Elk occupies an enormous belt of chiefly upland forests and grasslands. In North America, it occurs from northeastern British Columbia southeast to southern Manitoba, south to southern Arizona and New Mexico and along the Pacific Coast from Vancouver Island to northern California. It has been introduced as a game species and as ranch livestock in many areas.

Total Length: 6½–8½ ft.
Shoulder Height: 4–5 ft.
Tail Length: 4¾–7 in.
Weight: 400–1100 lb.

Rocky Mountain
Elk, male

but they often become nocturnal in areas of high human activity where hunting occurs.

ALSO CALLED: Wapiti.

DESCRIPTION: The summer coat is generally golden brown. The winter coat is longer and grayish brown. Year-round, the head, neck and legs are darker brown, and a large, yellowish to orangish rump patch is bordered by black or dark brown fur. The oval metatarsal glands on the outside of the hocks are outlined by stiff, yellowish hairs. A bull Elk has a dark brown throat mane, and he starts growing antlers in his second year. By his fourth year, the bull's antlers typically bear six points to a side, but considerable variation will occur both in the number of points a bull will have and the age when he acquires the full complement of six. A bull rarely has seven or eight points. The antlers are usually shed in March. New ones begin to grow in late April, becoming mature in August.

HABITAT: Although the Elk prefers upland forests and grasslands, it sometimes ranges into alpine tundra, coniferous forests or brushlands. In Washington and Oregon, the Elk tends to move to higher elevations in spring

DID YOU KNOW?

By the end of the 1800s, Elk had disappeared from eastern North America, and two subspecies became extinct. From an estimated low of perhaps 41,000 for the entire continent, the species has since recovered to probably over 1 million. Elk are popular animals for game ranching, so their numbers may increase still more, and they are being reintroduced to some areas in the East.

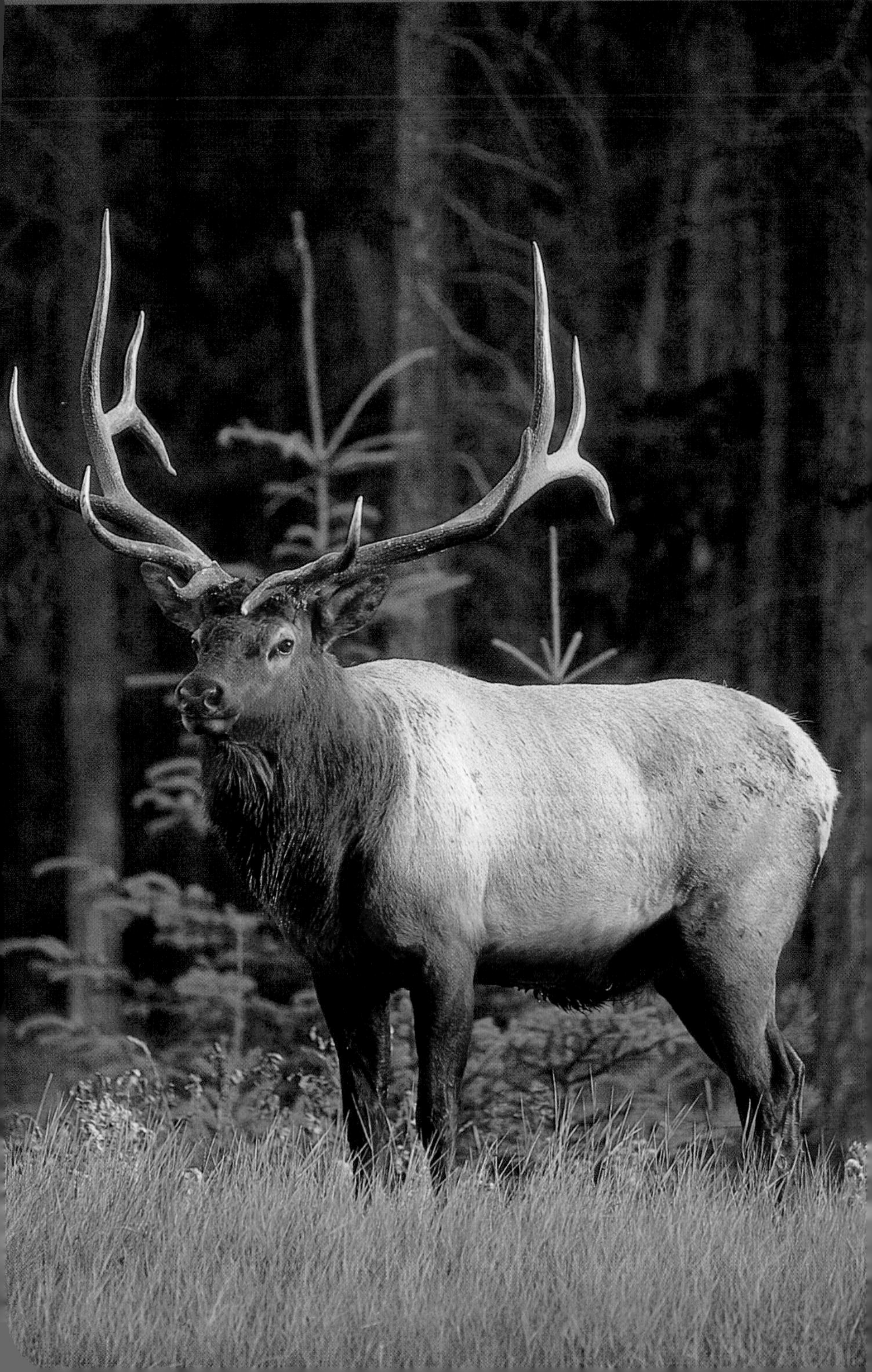

hoofprint

walking trail

and lower elevations in fall. The coastal populations enjoy the lush forests and do not exhibit such pronounced altitudinal migrations.

FOOD: Elk are some of the most adaptable grazers. Woody plants and fallen leaves frequently form much of their winter and fall diet. Sedges and grasses frequently make up 80 to 90 percent of the diet in spring and summer. Salt is a necessary dietary component for all animals that chew their cud, and Elk may travel vast distances to devour salt-rich soil.

DEN: The Elk does not keep a permanent den, but it often leaves flattened areas of grass or snow where it has bedded down during the day.

YOUNG: A cow Elk gives birth to a single precocial calf between late May and early June, following an $8^1/2$-month gestation. The young stand and nurse within an hour, and within two to four weeks the cow and calf rejoin the herd. The calf is weaned in fall.

Moose

SIMILAR SPECIES: The **Moose** (p. 52) is darker and taller, has palmate antlers (males) and has lighter lower hindlegs. The **Mule Deer** (p. 44) has a whitish, rather than yellowish or brownish, rump patch and is smaller. Both the **White-tailed Deer** (p. 48) and Mule Deer bucks have smaller racks of antlers.

Mule Deer
Odocoileus hemionus

The Mule Deer, an inhabitant of this region since prehistoric times, continues to thrive in the mountains and in fragmented landscapes. If you want an intimate encounter with a large deer in the wild, no better candidate than the Mule Deer exists. It tends to frequent open areas in parks and other protected areas, and it can be bold, conspicuous and quite tolerant of human visitors.

One of the Mule Deer's best-known characteristics is its bouncing gait, which is known as "stotting" or "pronking." When it stots, a Mule Deer bounds and lands with all four legs simultaneously, so that it looks like it's using a pogo stick. This fascinating gait allows the deer to move safely and rapidly across and over the many obstructions it encounters in the complex brush and hillside areas it typically inhabits. Although stotting is characteristic of the Mule Deer, this animal also walks, trots and gallops perfectly well. When disturbed, a retreating Mule Deer will often stop for a last look at whatever disturbed it before it disappears completely from view.

Mule Deer feed at dawn, at dusk and well into the night. They have great difficulty traveling through snow that is more than knee deep, so they are unable to occupy most high mountainous areas of Washington and Oregon in winter. To avoid the snow, they migrate to lower elevations at the onset of winter, often into townsites, which have buried grasses and dormant ornamentals that are much to their liking.

During the mating season, Mule Deer bucks compete for the does that are in estrus. Two bucks will tangle with their antlers, trying to force each other's head lower than their own. The weaker of the two eventually surrenders and usually leaves the area. Rarely, the antlers of two bucks become locked during these competitions, and if they are unable to free themselves, both bucks inevitably perish from starvation, predation or battle wounds.

In regions where both the Mule Deer and White-tailed Deer (p. 48) occur, they do hybridize on occasion. Hybrid male offspring are sterile, and though hybrid females are fertile, all hybrids seem to have higher mortality rates than the pure species, which may be why hybrids are rarely seen.

There are two subspecies of Mule Deer found in Washington and Oregon: the Black-tailed or Columbian Deer (ssp. *columbianus*) is found in coastal regions, and the Rocky Mountain Mule Deer (ssp. *hemionus*) is found east of the

RANGE: Widely distributed through western North America, the Mule Deer ranges from the southern Yukon southeast to Minnesota and south through California and western Texas into northern Mexico.

Total Length: 4½–5½ ft.
Shoulder Height: 35–41 in.
Tail Length: 4¾–8¾ in.
Weight: 68–470 lb.

Rocky Mountain
Mule Deer, male

Cascade crest, through the Rockies and most of the plains.

DESCRIPTION: The Mule Deer gets its name from its large, mule-like ears. It has a large, whitish rump patch that is divided by a short, black-tipped tail. (The Black-tailed Deer has a smaller white rump patch and an almost fully black tail.) The dark forehead contrasts with both the face and upperparts, which are tan in summer and dark gray in winter. A dark spot is on each side of the nose. The throat and insides of the legs are white all year-round. A buck has fairly heavy, upswept antlers that are equally branched into forked tines. The metatarsal glands on the outside of the lower hindlegs are 4–6 in. long.

HABITAT: This deer's summer habitats vary from dry brushlands to alpine tundra. Bucks tend to move to the tundra edge at higher elevations, where they form small bands; does and fawns remain at lower elevations. In drier regions, both sexes are often found in streamside situations. The Mule Deer thrives in the early successional stages of forests, so it is often found where fire

DID YOU KNOW?

Although the Mule Deer is usually silent, it can snort, grunt, cough, roar and whistle. A fawn will sometimes bleat. Even people who have observed deer extensively may be surprised to encounter one that is vocalizing.

hoofprint

walking trail

or logging removed the canopy a few years before.

FOOD: Grasses and forbs form most of the summer diet. In fall, the Mule Deer consumes both the foliage and twigs of shrubs. The winter diet makes increasing use of twigs and woody vegetation. Grazing occurs in hayfields adjacent to cover.

DEN: The Mule Deer leaves oval depressions in grass, moss, leaves or snow where it lies down to rest or chew its cud. It typically urinates upon rising. A doe usually steps to one side first, but a buck will urinate in the middle of the bed before leaving.

YOUNG: Following a gestation of $6^{1}/_{2}$ to 7 months, a doe gives birth to one to three (usually two) fawns in May or June. The birth weight is $7^{3}/_{4}$–$8^{1}/_{2}$ lb. A fawn is born with light dorsal spots, which it retains until the fall molt in August. The fawn is weaned when it is four to five months old. It becomes sexually mature at $1^{1}/_{2}$ years.

SIMILAR SPECIES: The **White-tailed Deer** (p. 48) has a much smaller rump patch, and it shows the white undersurface of its larger tail when it runs. A White-tail buck's antlers consist of a main beam with typically unbranched, rather than equally forked, tines. The **Elk** (p. 40) is much larger, has a dark mane on the throat and has a yellowish or orangish rump patch. The **Bighorn Sheep** (p. 32) has large, curled horns. The **Pronghorn** (p. 36) has black "horns" and two white bands around its neck.

White-tailed Deer

White-tailed Deer
Odocoileus virginianus

Given the current status of the White-tailed Deer in Washington and Oregon, it is hard to imagine that before the arrival of Europeans this graceful animal was only found in small, isolated populations. Historically, this deer was rather uncommon (except along the Columbia River and some western valleys), but with the spread of agricultural development and forest fragmentation, the White-tailed Deer has become quite widespread. In some parts of the two states, the White-tailed Deer is now more common than the Mule Deer (p. 44).

The White-tailed Deer is a master at avoiding detection, so it can be frustratingly difficult to observe. It is very secretive during daylight hours, when it tends to remain concealed in thick shrubs or forest patches. Once the sun begins to set, however, the White-tailed Deer leaves its daytime resting spot to travel to a foraging site. The White-tailed Deer moves gracefully, weaving an intricate path through dense shrubs and over fallen trees. Indeed, a White-tailed Deer in prime form seems uncatchable in its own habitat. The animal itself clearly does not share this view—its nose and ears continually twitch, aware that any shadow could conceal a predator. Wolves, Mountain Lions and humans are the major threats to this deer, although fawns and old or sick individuals may be easy prey for Coyotes, Bobcats, Canada Lynx and Wolverine.

Speed and agility are effective defenses against most of the White-tail's predators, but all deer are vulnerable to severe winters in the colder, mountainous parts of Washington and Oregon. Snow and a scarcity of high-energy food leave the deer with a negative energy budget from the time of the first deep snowfalls until the green vegetation emerges in spring. In spite of their adaptations to winter, some deer still starve before spring arrives; these victims of winter provide food for scavengers.

In the national parks and wildlife areas, White-tailed Deer may become habituated to the presence of humans, and they can sometimes be closely approached. Doing so can be perilous, however, especially when it comes to does protecting their young or bucks in the rutting season. These deer can rear up and strike down with their forelegs with enough force to kill. Although there is a real danger in approaching any wild animal too closely, reports that White-tailed Deer are responsible for far more human fatalities annually than all North American bears misrepresents

RANGE: From the southern third of Canada, the White-tailed Deer ranges south into the northern quarter of South America. It is largely absent from Nevada, Utah and California. It has been introduced to New Zealand, Finland, Prince Edward Island and Anticosti Island.

Total Length: 4½–7 ft.
Shoulder Height: 27–45 in.
Tail Length: 8¼–14 in.
Weight: 110–440 lb.

male

their demeanor. While true, these statistics include human fatalities resulting from vehicle collisions with deer. Each year, several hundred thousand deer are involved in accidents on North American roads.

ALSO CALLED: Flag-tailed Deer.

DESCRIPTION: The upperparts are generally reddish brown in summer and grayish brown in winter. The belly, throat, chin and underside of the tail are white. A narrow, white ring extends around the eye, and a white band encircles the muzzle. A buck starts growing antlers in his second year. The antlers first appear as unbranched "spike-horns"; later, generally unbranched tines grow off from the main beam. The main beams, when viewed from above, are usually heart-shaped, though the terminal tines end just before the apex. The metatarsal gland on the outside of the lower hindleg is about 1 in. long.

HABITAT: The optimum habitat for a White-tailed Deer is rolling country with a mixture of open areas near cover. This deer frequents valleys and stream courses, woodlands, meadows and abandoned farmsteads with tangled shelterbelts. Areas cleared for roads, parking lots, summer homes, logging

DID YOU KNOW?

The White-tailed Deer is named for the bright white underside of its tail. This deer raises, or "flags," its tail when it is alarmed. The white flash of the tail communicates danger to nearby deer and provides a guiding signal for following individuals.

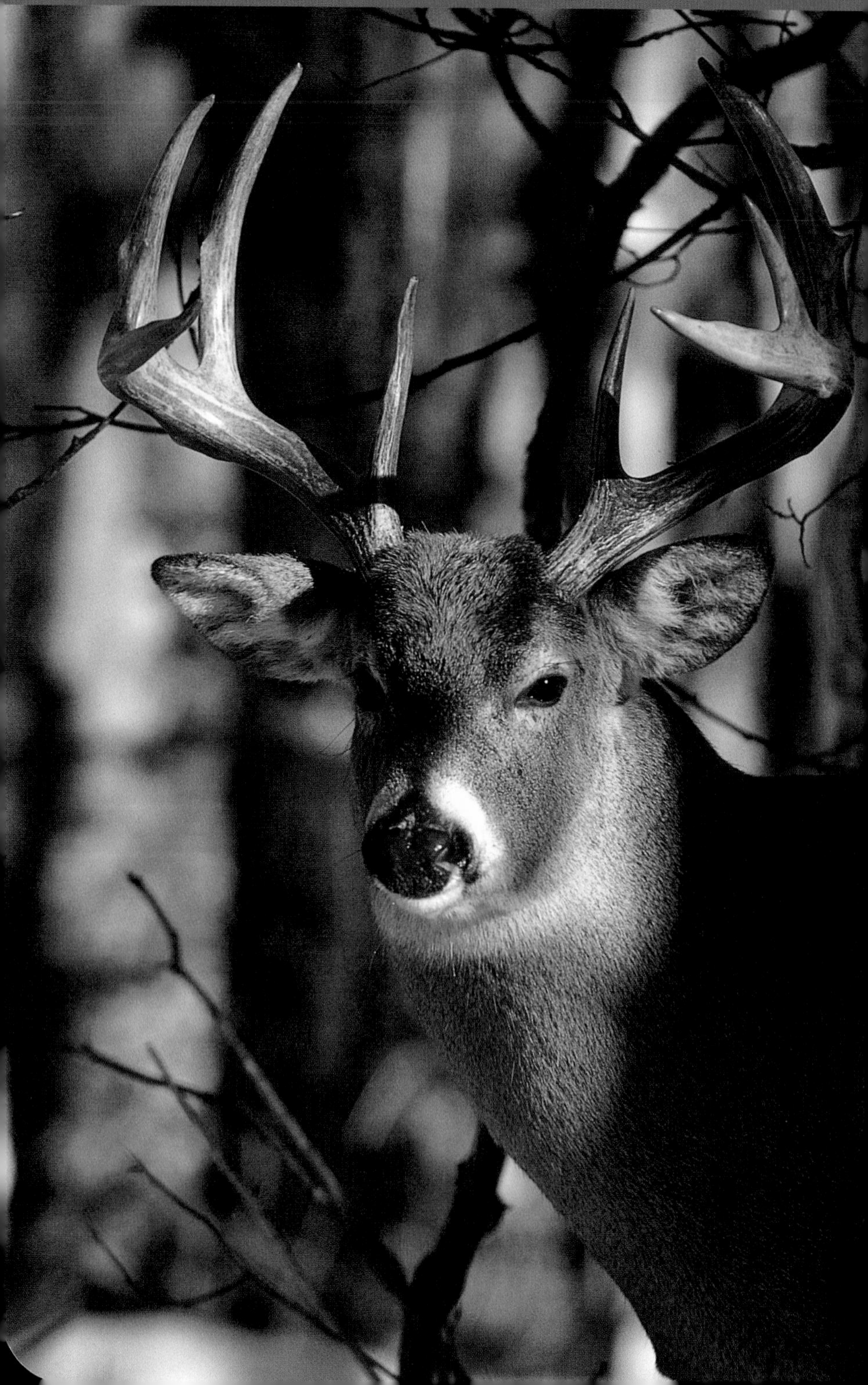

hoofprint

walking trail

and mines support much of the vegetation on which the White-tailed Deer thrives.

FOOD: During winter, the leaves and twigs of evergreens, deciduous trees and brush make up most of the diet. In early spring and summer, the diet shifts to forbs, grasses and even mushrooms. On average, a White-tailed Deer eats $4^1/_2$–11 lb. of food a day.

DEN: A deer's bed is simply a shallow, oval, body-sized depression in leaves or snow. Favored bedding areas will have an accumulation of new and old beds. These areas are often in secluded spots with good all-around visibility where inactive deer can remain safe.

YOUNG: A White-tailed doe gives birth to one to three fawns in late May or June, after a gestation of $6^1/_2$ to 7 months. At birth, a fawn weighs about $6^1/_2$ lb., and its coat is tan with white spots. The fawn can stand and suckle shortly after birth, but it spends most of the first month lying quietly under the cover of vegetation. It is weaned at about four months. A few well-nourished females may mate as fall fawns, but most will wait until their second year.

Mule Deer

SIMILAR SPECIES: The **Mule Deer** (p. 44) looks very similar, but it lacks the large tail with a prominent white underside, and it has a whitish rump patch and much longer metatarsal glands. As well the male Mule Deer has antlers with forked tines. The **Pronghorn** (p. 36) has black "horns" and two white bands around its neck. **Elk** (p. 40) are much larger and have larger antlers and darker brown heads.

Moose

Alces alces

The monarch of mountain forests and lush wetlands, the Moose is a handsome animal that provides a thrilling sight for both tourists and wildlife enthusiasts alike. People who know it only from TV cartoon characterizations may not have such feelings for the Moose, but those who have followed its trails through snow and mosquito-ridden bogs respect its abilities. This great animal is not common in the region—it is found only in northeastern Washington—but recent studies indicate it may be increasing in numbers in the Selkirk Mountains and southward to Spokane. Admirers of the Moose should try Washington's Sherman Creek–Growden Heritage Site, Big Meadow Lake or Little Pend Oreille Wildlife Refuge for the best viewing opportunities. Only one subspecies of moose is found here; it is the British Columbia Moose (ssp. *andersoni*).

The Moose's long legs, short neck, humped shoulders and big, bulbous nose may lend it an awkward appearance, but they all serve it well in its environment. With its long legs, the Moose can easily step over downed logs and forest debris and cross streams. Snow, which seriously impedes the progress of predators, is no obstacle for the Moose, which lifts its legs straight up and down to create very little snow drag. The Moose has a huge battery of upper and lower cheek teeth, which are perfectly suited for nipping and chewing the twigs that make up most of its winter diet. The big bulbous nose and lips hold the twigs in place so the lower incisors can rip them off.

Winter ticks are often a problem for the Moose. A single Moose can carry more than 200,000 ticks, and their irritation causes the Moose to rub against trees for relief. With excessive rubbing, Moose will lose much of their guard hair, resulting in the pale gray "ghost" Moose that are sometimes seen in late winter. Winter Moose deaths are often the result of blood loss to the ticks, rather than starvation—the twigs, buds and bark of deciduous trees and shrubs that form the bulk of their winter diet are rarely in short supply. The Moose's common name can also be traced to this feeding habit: the Algonquian called it *moz*, which means "twig eater." The summer diet of aquatic vegetation and other greenery seems quite palatable and varied, but even then, more than half the intake is woody material.

DESCRIPTION: The Moose is the largest living deer in North America. The dark, rich brown upperparts fade to lighter,

RANGE: In North America, this holarctic species ranges through most of Canada and Alaska. Its range has southward extensions through the Rocky and Selkirk mountains, into the northern Midwest states and into New England and the northern Appalachians. The Moose is expanding into the farmlands of North Dakota, South Dakota, Alberta and Saskatchewan, from which it was absent for many decades.

Total Length: 8–10 ft.
Shoulder Height: 5½–7 ft.
Tail Length: 3½–7½ in.
Weight: 500–1180 lb.

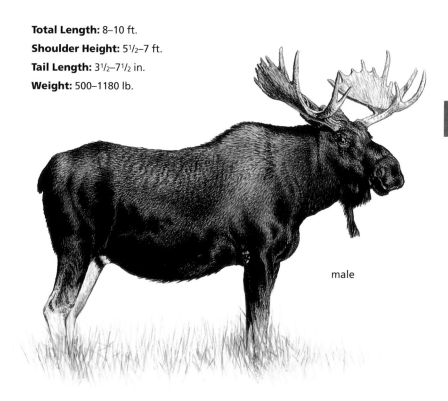

male

often grayish tones on the lower legs. The head is long and almost horse-like. It has a humped nose, and the upper lip markedly overhangs the lower lip. In winter, a mane of hair as long as 6 in. develops along the spine over the humped shoulders and along the nape of the neck. In summer, the mane is much shorter. Both sexes usually have a large dewlap, or "bell," hanging from the throat. Only bull Moose have antlers. Unlike the antlers of other deer, the Moose's antlers emerge laterally, and many of the tines are merged throughout much of their length, giving the antler a shovel-like appearance. Elk-like antlers are common in young bulls (and they are the only type seen in Eurasian individuals today). A cow Moose has a distinct light patch around

the vulva. A calf Moose is light brown or grayish red during its first summer.

HABITAT: Typically associated with the northern coniferous forest, the Moose is most numerous in the early successional stages of willows and poplars. In less-forested foothills and lowlands, it frequents streamside or brushy areas with abundant young, deciduous, woody plants. In summer, it may range

DID YOU KNOW?

The Moose is an impressive athlete: individuals have been known to run as fast as 35 m.p.h., swim continuously for several hours, dive to depths of 20 ft. and remain submerged for up to a minute.

hoofprint

walking trail

well up into the subalpine or tundra areas of the mountains.

FOOD: About 80 percent of the Moose's diet is woody matter, mostly twigs and branches. It prefers deciduous trees and shrubs over conifers. In summer, it also feeds on submerged vegetation. Sometimes a moose sinks completely below the surface of the water to acquire the succulent aquatics, but these never make up a large part of the diet.

DEN: The Moose makes its daytime bed in a sheltered area, much like other members of the deer family, and it leaves ovals of flattened grass from its weight. Other signs around the bed include tracks, large oval droppings and browsed vegetation.

YOUNG: In May or June, after a gestation of about eight months, a cow bears one to three (usually two) unspotted calves, each weighing 22–35 lb. The calves begin to follow their mother on her daily routine when they are about two weeks old. A few cows breed in their second year, but most will wait until their third year.

Feral Horse

SIMILAR SPECIES: With its large size and long head, the Moose resembles a bay or black **Feral Horse** (p. 62) more than any native mammal. The **Elk** (p. 40) and the **Caribou** (p. 56) are both lighter in color, and the bulls of both species do not have the lateral, palmate antlers of a bull Moose.

Caribou

Rangifer tarandus

The Caribou carves out a living in the deep snows and blackfly fens where most other species of deer do not venture. It appears to do best in areas of expansive wilderness that allow it to undergo seasonal migrations between its summer and winter feeding grounds. This specialist is better adapted to cold climates than other deer—even the Caribou's nose is completely furred. Caribou are not common in the lower 48 states, and the only Caribou population is in the Selkirk Mountains of northeastern Washington. The total population may be fewer than 100, and at one time, in the 1980s, only 25 were left. Reintroductions of Canadian Caribou have helped build this endangered population.

The Caribou's winter coat has hollow guard hairs up to 4 in. long, which top a fine, fleecy, insulating undercoat. These hollow guard hairs provide excellent flotation, as well as insulation, when the animal is swimming across rivers and lakes during its migrations. The Caribou's broad hooves serve it well over rough terrain, or when it digs through snow to expose edible lichens. The bristle-like hairs that cover a Caribou's feet in winter may help prevent the snow from abrading the skin when the animal digs. This feeding strategy has been one of the Caribou's best-known characteristics for centuries—its name comes from eastern Canada, from the Micmac name *halibu*, which means "pawer" or "scratcher."

Unlike all other North American cervids, both sexes of the Caribou grow antlers. Not all Caribou shed their antlers at the same time: mature bulls shed their large sweeping racks in December; younger bulls retain theirs until February; and cows keeps theirs until April (within a month they are growing a new set). After losing their antlers, the bulls become subordinate to the still-antlered cows, which are then better equipped to defend desirable feeding sites.

The fragmentation of Caribou populations is of serious concern to resource managers, biologists and naturalists. Few places exist where you can be certain of seeing this threatened animal, and seasonality greatly influences their whereabouts. In general, Caribou spend summers at high elevations to avoid the heat and the flies, and, in spring and fall, they migrate between the mountains and the foothill forests. There is also a latitudinal migration. In winter they are more frequently seen in the southern parts of their range.

The seasonal movements of Caribou in the Selkirks hardly compare to the

RANGE: The North American range of this holarctic animal extends across most of Alaska and northern Canada, from the Arctic Islands south into the boreal forest. Its range extends south through the Canadian Rocky, Columbia and Selkirk mountains.

Total Length: 5½–8 ft.
Shoulder Height: 3–5½ ft.
Tail Length: 5–9 in.
Weight: 200–240 lb.

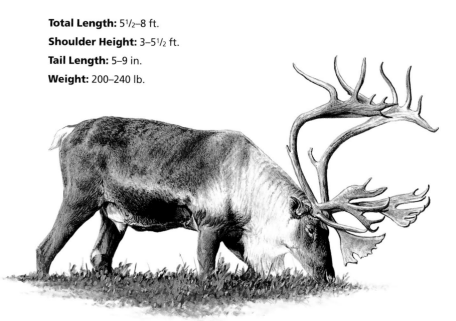

incredible migrations of Caribou in the Arctic. Previously, the Caribou of North America were considered four separate species, but now all the North American Caribou and the Reindeer of Eurasia are classified as one species.

DESCRIPTION: In summer, a Caribou's coat is brown or grayish brown above and lighter below, with white along the lower side of the tail and hoof edges. The winter coat is much lighter, with dark brown or grayish-brown areas on the upper part of the head, the back and the front of the limbs. Both males and females have antlers, but a bull's are much larger. Two tines come off the front of each main antler beam; one lower "brow" tine is palmate near the tip and may be used to push snow to the side as the Caribou feeds. All other tines come off the back of the main beam, an arrangement that is unique to the Caribou.

HABITAT: Most of the Caribou in the Selkirks tend to remain in forests of spruce, fir, pine and aspen much of the year, but in summer they move into alpine meadows and the adjacent sub-alpine forest.

FOOD: Grasses, sedges, mosses, forbs, mushrooms and terrestrial and arboreal lichens make up the summer diet. In winter, a Caribou eats the buds, leaves and bark of both deciduous and ever-green shrubs, together with primarily arboreal lichens. This restless feeder takes only a few mouthfuls before

DID YOU KNOW?

Lichens, the Caribou's favorite winter food, grow very slowly and are frequently restricted to older spruce and fir forests, but a herd's erratic movements typically prevent it from overgrazing one particular area.

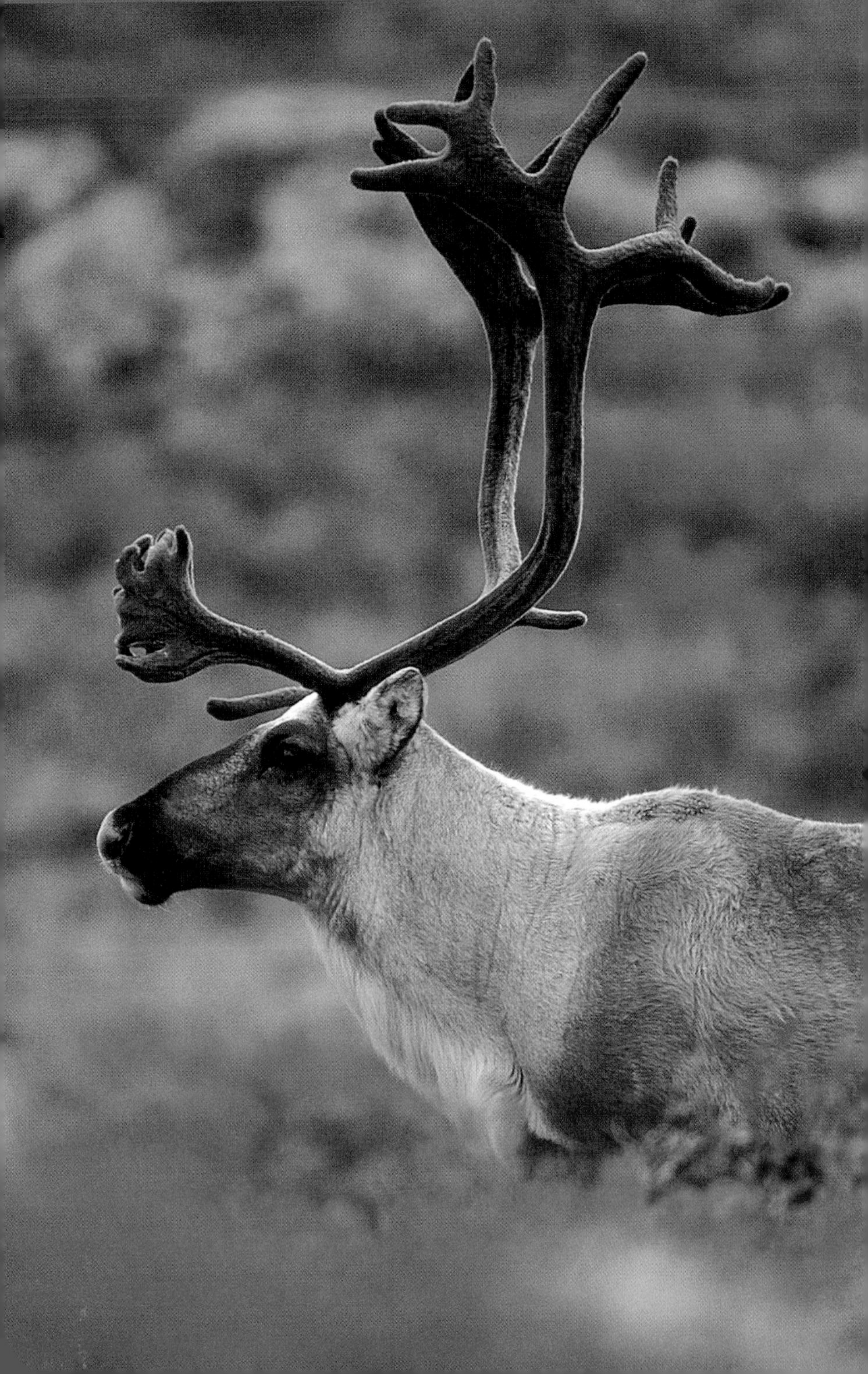

hoofprint

walking trail

walking ahead, pausing for a few more bites and then walking on again.

DEN: Like other cervids, the Caribou's bed is a simple, shallow, body-sized depression, often in a late-lying snowbank in summer. In winter, it usually lies with its body at right angles to the sun on exposed frozen lakes. It may absorb more solar energy that way. Entire herds will sometimes lie in the same orientation.

YOUNG: Calving occurs in late May or June after a gestation of about $7^1/2$ months. The unspotted calf, usually born singly (rarely as twins), weighs about 11 lb. at birth. Within hours of birth, it often follows its mother, and it begins grazing when it's two weeks old. A calf may be weaned after a month, but some continue to nurse into winter. A cow usually first mates when she is $1^1/2$ years old; most males do not get a chance to mate until they are at least three to four years old.

SIMILAR SPECIES: The rectangular head and heavy body of the Caribou distinguish it from the other members of the deer family, which have more triangular heads and less stocky bodies. The **Moose** (p. 52) is darker brown and much larger. Both male and female Caribou bear antlers, and even calves may bear spikes, a feature that distinguishes them from females or young of the other deer species. Also, a Caribou's feet produce clicking sounds when the animal is moving.

Moose

Feral Pig
Sus scrofa

When we enter wildlife areas and national parks and think of the potentially dangerous animals therein, the first animals that conjure up some fear in us are bears and Mountain Lions (p. 90). Oddly enough, we should be thinking of the Feral Pig, which is one of the most ferocious animals when wounded, cornered or with young. If you see distinctive patches of torn-up earth where a pig has been rooting around, be cautious because the pig may still be in the vicinity. Feral Pigs do not have good eyesight, but their hearing is acute and they will know of your presence long before you know of theirs.

The Feral Pigs that are found in North America are descended from escaped domestic pigs; from European Wild Boars introduced for hunting; or from hybrids of the two. The wild, pure-blood boar (European Wild Boar) is different in appearance to the farm-raised variety, but they are able to interbreed. When these boars were introduced into North America from Europe, they were first contained in preserves for hunting purposes. Many individuals escaped and cross-bred with existing domestic varieties. As a result, many populations are entirely hybrids, but a few pure-blooded lines of boar are well established in the southern and western states. The Feral Pig populations in Oregon are likely all hybrids, while some of the ones in California are the pure-blooded line that is native to Europe and Asia.

ALSO CALLED: Wild Boar, Wild Pig, Wild Hog.

DESCRIPTION: The Feral Pig is a medium-sized hoofed mammal, just slightly smaller in height than the Mule Deer (p. 44). Like domestic pigs, it has a sensitive, flexible disk at the end of the snout. The Feral Pig has coarse, dense fur, and in winter it has a thick undercoat. Usually, it is gray, brown or black in color, but some individuals may be mottled with white. Along the ridge of the back are long, dark, bristly hairs. The tail is sparsely furred and hangs straight down. The Feral Pig has tusks, or modified canines, that continue growing throughout its life. The upper tusks curl out and up over the mouth, and they may be up to 9 in. long. The lower tusks are much smaller and curl slightly outward from the mouth. Unlike the native artiodactyls, the Feral Pig has both upper and lower incisors.

HABITAT: The Feral Pig inhabits a variety of regions, such as forested moun-

RANGE: Wild varieties of the boar occur in many southern and coastal states. Feral populations of the domestic pig are more common in the south-central states. Many nature or hunting preserves support large populations of boar.

Total Length: 4¹/₂–6 ft.
Tail Length: up to 12 in.
Weight: males 165–440 lb.; females 77–330 lb.

tain areas, brushy areas, marshes or swamps, and ravines or ridges.

FOOD: Feral Pigs eat like domestic pigs—that is, they are omnivores and eat almost anything. In nut-bearing forests in fall, they dine heavily on acorns, walnuts and pecans. At other times of the year—or in other habitats—they eat green vegetation, roots, tubers, fruit, crayfish, frogs, salamanders, eggs, fledgling birds, rabbits, newborn fawns and carrion.

DEN: At night, pigs sleep in hollowed-out depressions or places of trampled vegetation. Pregnant sows hollow out a shallow "nest" in the ground and line it with grass.

YOUNG: Mating occurs throughout the year, but there are two seasonal peaks. Dominant males mate first, followed by young and subordinate males. Gestation is 16 weeks, whereupon females give birth to a litter of 3 to 12 young. Young are born in a grass-lined depression made by the sow. The piglets have

several longitudinal stripes along each side, but they lose these by the time they are six weeks old. The young are weaned when they are three months old. A sow and her young often feed together as a family group, and, in some places, families join and form herds of up to 50 individuals.

SIMILAR SPECIES: Wild pigs from domestic stocks tend to have finer fur, rounder bodies and shorter legs, and they lack tusks. Hybrids of the two varieties (wild boar and domestic pig) have intergrading characteristics.

DID YOU KNOW?

Feral Pigs have an extremely well-developed sense of smell. For this reason, pigs are famous for their ability to "sniff-out" truffles, a fungal delicacy that grows underground. The pigs that are used to find truffles are muzzled, so they can locate the truffle but not eat it.

Feral Horse
Equus caballus

Feral Horses in North America are descended from domesticated populations, and they have lived in the West for centuries. These Feral Horses can usually be distinguished from their domestic kin by their much longer manes and tails and their patterns of behavior. Most of North America's Feral Horses live in the Great Basin, but a few populations live in parts of southeastern Oregon.

Horse herds can have a different assortment of males and females, depending on the herd type. An accumulation of young bachelors is one type of herd. Males, usually over the age of two, leave their parent herd and may band together for a while, because no herd stallion—the dominant male—will permit them near his mares. These young males stay together until either they find mares of their own, or they are strong enough to steal mares from older stallions.

A second type of herd is the mixed herd, in which a number of mares, a single adult stallion, a few young males and foals live and forage together. The mares in a herd like this type are closely guarded by the stallion and are not free to come and go, but they are the ones that decide the herd's daily activities.

Another type of herd has two stallions, a number of subordinate mares and perhaps a few foals. In this grouping, the subdominant, usually younger, stallion exhibits "champing" behavior, in which it approaches the dominant stallion nose to nose with its ears forward in a gesture of friendly respect. The subdominant stallion is usually the offspring of one of the mares in the harem. As he matures and becomes the dominant stallion's equal, this "champing" behavior may become more threatening. Ultimately, a duel occurs. The two stallions face each other with their ears back, necks arched and tails high. They fight standing side-by-side, biting, kicking and pushing each other off balance. Eventually, one stallion is beaten and runs off, possibly to find other mares to make a new harem. The mares of the harem stay together and accept the control of the victorious stallion. Only very rarely does a mare leave a harem to join a different herd.

A Feral Horse uses its teeth to groom the mane, neck and withers of another horse, which helps develop and maintain the bonds between herd members. Biting flies seem to be a serious irritant to the Feral Horse, and after too many bites a horse may be in a state of extreme distress. To rid itself of the flies, the Feral Horse may walk into thick foliage to scrape the flies off, roll in mud

RANGE: Feral Horses occur in pockets along the Rocky Mountains from Grand Cache in Alberta through Montana, Wyoming, Utah and Colorado. Much larger populations occur in the Great Basin, and other local herds occur in the southwest and into Oregon. Most Feral Horse populations in the U.S. are being managed and herd sizes controlled.

Total Length: up to 7 ft.
Shoulder Height: 3¹/₂–5¹/₂ ft.
Tail Length: up to 3 ft.
Weight: 590–860 lb.

to cover and soothe the skin, or submerge itself in water.

ALSO CALLED: Mustang.

DESCRIPTION: Feral Horses are extremely variable in size and color because of their domestic roots. They may be a solid color, ranging from black to white, or they may be spotted or bay or have various other color patterns. White markings, such as a star or blaze, are often on the face. Horses have both upper and lower incisors and small (if any) canines. They generally have a long mane and a long tail. Their hooves are semi-circular and uncloven, and they lack dewclaws.

HABITAT: Feral Horses prefer areas of abundant vegetation beside watercourses, but they are so adaptable that they may be found from deserts to alpine tundra. In southeastern Oregon,

they are found in woodland areas, foothills, dry ridges, brushlands and even marshy plateaus.

FOOD: As grazers, Feral Horses spend as much as 80 percent of daytime hours grazing. Even at night they sleep only about 50 percent of the time—the rest of the night they are still grazing. These horses are herbivores, and they consume mainly grasses and forbs during the summer months. In winter, they eat woodier vegetation, such as the twigs or the bark of shrubs.

DID YOU KNOW?

Because of selective breeding, domestic horse breeds vary greatly in size. The smallest are considerably less than 2 ft. high at the shoulders, while the largest work horses are up to 6 ft. tall. Feral Horses are usually medium to large sized.

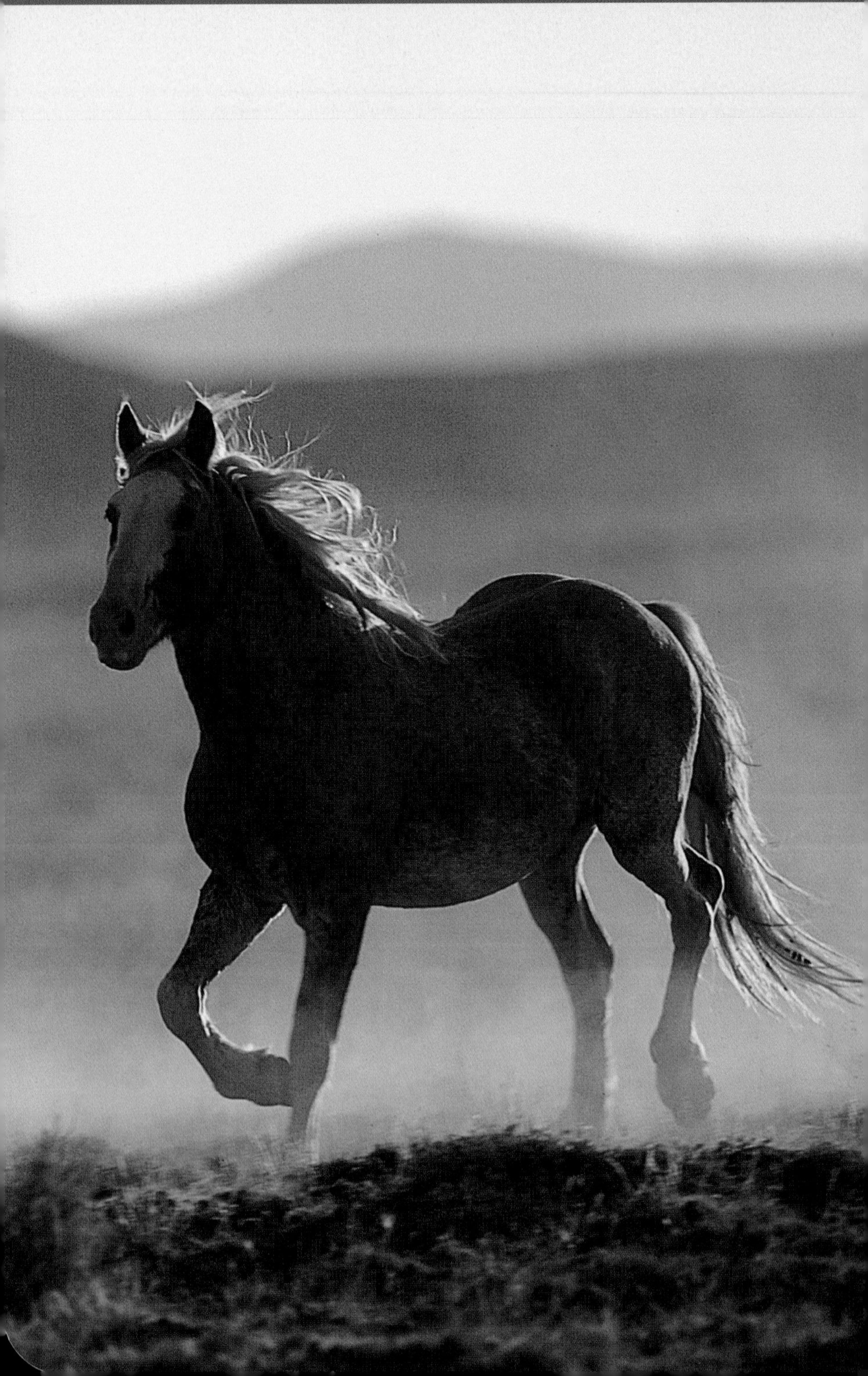

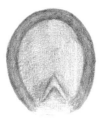

hoofprint

walking trail

DEN: Feral Horses make no den for sleeping, but if they lie down a "bed" is visible where the grass was flattened. Although Feral Horses can lie down, they usually sleep standing up. While standing, the horse closes its eyes and falls asleep. As soon as it slips into sleep, a highly specialized tendon in each leg locks the knee and prevents the leg from collapsing. As soon as the horse wakes, the tendon is released and it can move. This mechanism evolved as a defensive strategy. As soon as the animal detects danger and is awakened, it is able to run, rather than having to take the time to rise from a prone position.

YOUNG: A mare gives birth to one foal a year after a gestation of 11 months. Mating may occur during spring, summer or fall, often just a few days after a mare delivers her foal. The foal is precocious, and within a few hours of birth it is able to run with its mother and the rest of the herd. The foal is weaned shortly before the next foal is born. If a mare is weak, or if food is scarce, she may have a foal only every second year.

Moose

SIMILAR SPECIES: Although a large dark-colored Feral Horse may be mistaken for a **Moose** (p. 52) from a distance, the resemblance is restricted to the general size and color. No other animal has the same combination of a long-haired mane and tail and a single, uncloven hoof on each foot. Unlike the native ungulates, Feral Horses have neither antlers nor horns.

WHALES, DOLPHINS & PORPOISES

All whales belong to the order Cetacea, and they are distinguished from other mammals by their nearly hairless bodies, blowholes on the tops of their heads, paddle-like forelimbs, lack of hindlimbs, fusiform bodies and powerful tail flukes. At least 80 species occur worldwide, and they are classified into two suborders according to whether they have teeth (suborder Odontoceti) or baleen (suborder Mysticeti). The toothed whales are far more numerous and diverse, with some 70 species worldwide: the porpoises, dolphins, sperm whales, beaked whales, Narwhals and Belugas. There are only 11 species of baleen whales worldwide, but this group contains the largest cetaceans: the rorquals, Gray Whales, Bowhead Whales and right whales.

The coast of Washington and Oregon has some of the best whale-watching areas in North America. About 25 species regularly occur in these waters, of which 18 are odontocetes and 7 are mysticetes. The most well-known and commonly seen cetaceans in the region are Gray Whales, Humpback Whales, Orcas and Pacific White-sided Dolphins. The little Dall's Porpoise is less frequently seen, but sightings of schools of it are delightful, memorable events. With luck, and in the right locations, these five species can be viewed from land while they feed in bays and inlets or pass by on their annual migrations. For this reason, only these five cetaceans are included here. Less common species may be encountered unexpectedly at any time, especially if you take a boat trip into open waters.

While whale-watching, you may be lucky enough to see any of a number of whale displays. In a "breach," some or all of the whale's body rises out of the water and splashes back in. "Lob-tailing" refers to a whale forcefully slapping its tail flukes on the surface of the water—not to be confused with "fluking," which refers to the flukes rising clear above the water before a dive. Whales are "spy-hopping" when they rise almost vertically out of the water, just far enough to have a look around. "Logging" is a form of rest; individuals float at the surface alone or in a close group, all facing the same direction.

Gray Whale Family (Eschrichtiidae)

The unique Gray Whale is the sole member of this family. This whale shares some characteristics with the rorqual whales, but it is dissimilar enough to be classified on its own. Like the rorquals, the Gray Whale has throat pleats that expand when food-rich water is drawn into the mouth, but the Gray's throat pleats are fewer (only two to four) and much less effective. Each Gray Whale typically has at least two pleats, although three to seven are not uncommon. Gray Whales have a heavy appearance, an arched mouth, yellowish-brown baleen and two distinct blowholes. The species is believed to carry more creatures, such as barnacles and whale lice, than any other whale.

Gray Whale

Rorqual Family (Balaenopteridae)

Rorqual whales, numbering only a few species worldwide, represent some of the largest whales on earth—including the Blue Whale, the largest animal on this planet. The name "rorqual" is derived from the Norwegian word *rorhval*, meaning "furrow," and refers to the numerous pleats or folds in the skin of the throat. These pleats unfold and allow the throat to distend to an enormous balloon-like shape when the whale gulps a massive volume of food-rich water into its mouth.

Rorquals are easily identified by their pointed snouts, flattened heads, long, slender bodies and relatively small dorsal fins that protrude about two-thirds down the length of their body. When a rorqual's mouth is open, the short, black baleen, which is continuous around the forward point of the jaw, is visible. All of the rorquals have two distinct blowholes.

Humpback Whale

Ocean Dolphin Family (Delphinidae)

This family includes some of the most well-loved cetaceans. Aquariums, movies and anecdotal accounts have made Bottlenose Dolphins (*Tursiops truncatus*) and Orcas world famous. Although many people call the Orca a whale, it is actually the largest dolphin in the world. All delphinids have a sleek fusiform shape and are generally free of callosities and barnacles. Many delphinids exhibit high brain to body size ratios (encephalization quotients) and are considered the most intelligent of the cetaceans. Bottlenose Dolphins top the scales with the highest "encephalization quotient"—a ratio similar to that of chimpanzees. All toothed whales (including porpoises) have only one external blowhole.

Pacific White-sided Dolphin

Porpoise Family (Phocoenidae)

The porpoises, which number only six species worldwide, are often mistakenly referred to as small dolphins, which they superficially resemble. The largest porpoise rarely reaches more than 6$^1/_2$ ft. in length, and the smallest (the Vaquita, *Phocoena sinus*) is just less than 5 ft., making it one of the smallest cetaceans in the world. Unlike dolphins, which have conical teeth for holding and biting prey, the porpoises have flattened, spade-shaped teeth that slice their prey. They do not have a distinct beak, and their heads are quite rounded. Their body shape is a bit more robust than the streamlined dolphins—from the ocean dolphin family—and their flippers are typically small and stubby. Viewing porpoises in the wild can be a challenge because they are generally shy and timid. When they surface for air, they rise only long enough for a quick breath and then roll rapidly back in.

Dall's Porpoise

Gray Whale

Eschrichtius robustus

Gray Whales, some of the most frequently observed whales, are famous for their extensive migrations—among the longest of any mammal. In their voyages, these whales travel back and forth between the cold Arctic seas where they spend summers and the warm Mexican waters where they spend winters. Each year, almost the entire world population of Gray Whales performs this cycle, amounting to over 12,400 mi. of travel along the western coast of North America.

During their summers in Arctic or near-Arctic seas, Grays feed on the abundant bottom-dwelling crustaceans known as "amphipods." These whales eat enormous quantities of food during their five to six months in the North. During their migration and especially their stay in southern waters, they eat very little and may even fast completely. Having lost as much as 30 percent of their body weight, they are slim and hungry when they return to the rich Arctic waters.

The Gray Whales' journey to winter waters takes approximately 2 to 2½ months: they leave the Arctic waters by late September and arrive in the warm waters off California and Mexico by late December. This southward migration coincides with the reproductive activity of the whales, and once in warm waters, a female either mates or gives birth. If she mates, her journey south the next year will be to give birth because gestation is about 13½ months. Conversely, if she gives birth, she will court and mate the next year.

By late February or March, Gray Whales begin their return to northern waters. Mothers with new calves may postpone their journey a bit longer to ensure the young have the strength for the journey. The whales arrive in the Arctic again by May or June.

The best time to view migrating Gray Whales in Washington and Oregon is between March and April (sometimes as late as May) and again from October through December. Many whale-watching sites are found along the coast of Oregon.

Gray Whales, which once inhabited both the Atlantic and Pacific oceans,

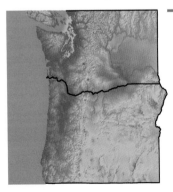

RANGE: Gray Whales are now found only in the coastal waters of the North Pacific, mainly on the North American side. A small population spends summers in the Sea of Okhotsk off Siberia and migrates to the southern tip of Korea for winter.

Total Length: up to 50 ft.; average 45 ft.

Total Weight: up to 45 tons; average 35 tons

Birth Length: about 15 ft.

Birth Weight: 1000 lb.

have been close to extinction at least twice in history and now live only in Pacific waters. Grays are particularly vulnerable to whalers because they live mainly in shallow waters. As a result of many years of protection, these whales now number some 21,000 in the eastern Pacific.

Aside from humans, the only predator of Gray Whales is the Orca, which might take young or weak individuals.

ALSO CALLED: Devilfish, Scrag Whale, Mussel-digger.

DESCRIPTION: The Gray Whale is easily distinguished from other whales by its mottled gray appearance and narrow, triangular head. Between the eye and the tip of the snout, the head is slightly arched; the jaw line usually has a similar arch. Many yellow, orange or whitish patches of barnacles and "whale lice" (actually a crustacean, not true lice) are over most of the body; these patches are especially prominent on the head. There is no dorsal fin, but this whale does have one bump where the dorsal fin should be, and then a series of smaller bumps or "knuckles" continuing along the dorsal ridge to the tail. In a dive, these bumps are visible, as are the distinctly notched tail and pointed flukes. The small flippers are wide at the base, but they taper to a pointed tip. Female Grays are typically 3 to 4 ft. longer than males.

BLOW: When seen from the front or the rear, the blow of Gray Whales appears bushy and heart-shaped and can be up to 15 ft. high. The blow looks V-shaped in some cases. From the side, the blow appears bushy but not distinctive.

OTHER DISPLAYS: Gray Whales exhibit breaching, spy-hopping and fluking.

DID YOU KNOW?

Gray Whales are favorites among whale-watchers because they can be very friendly and may even approach boats. In extraordinary encounters, Grays seem to enjoy the occasional back rub from willing admirers.

They will breach anywhere in their range, but most often in breeding lagoons in the south. They rise nearly vertically out of the water, come down with an enormous splash and then repeat the breach two or three times in a row. Spy-hopping is also common, and these whales may keep their heads out of the water for 30 seconds or more. In shallow water they may "cheat" and rest their flukes on the bottom so they can keep their heads above water with minimal effort. Before a deep dive, they raise their flukes clear above the surface of the water.

GROUP SIZE: Generally, these whales are seen in groups of only one to three individuals. They may migrate in groups of up to 15, and food-rich areas in the north can attract dozens or hundreds of Gray Whales at a time.

FOOD: Unlike other baleen whales, the Gray Whale is primarily a bottom-feeder. Its food consists of bottom-dwelling amphipods and other invertebrates. A feeding whale dives down to the bottom and rolls onto one side, sticking out its lower lip and sucking in great volumes of food, water and

dive sequence

muck. Once its mouth is full, it uses its powerful tongue to push the silty water out through the baleen, trapping the crustaceans inside to be swallowed whole. Most Gray Whales are "right-lipped," the way humans are mainly right-handed, meaning they prefer to feed using the right side of the mouth. A close-up look at a Gray's face will determine its preference—the side it uses will have numerous white scars and no barnacles. Inside the whale's mouth, the same uneven wear is evident; on right-lipped whales the baleen plates on the right side are shorter and more worn than the plates on the left.

YOUNG: Male Gray Whales are sexually mature when they are just over 36 ft. long, and females when they are nearly 38 ft. long (from 5 to 11 years of age for both sexes). Mating occurs in December or January, and a single calf is born $13^1/_2$ months later—in the following January or February. The young start their journey northward with their mothers when they are only two months old, and they continue nursing until they are six to nine months old.

blow

SIMILAR SPECIES: The **Humpback Whale** (p. 72) is usually darker in color, with "knuckles" and bumps on its head and unmistakably long flippers that bear unique dark and light markings on their undersides.

Humpback Whale

Humpback Whale

Megaptera novaeangliae

Humpback Whales are renowned for their extensive migrations and haunting songs. These whales are commonly spotted by whale-watchers, and they seem to enjoy performing for their boat-bound admirers.

Some of the most famous places for viewing humpbacks are in the Pacific Northwest, where many whales spend their summers. There are three migrating populations of Humpbacks off the West Coast of North America. The first population summers in the Aleutian region and winters in Hawaii; the second summers in Alaska, British Columbia and probably Washington and also winters in Hawaii; and the third summers in Oregon and California and winters in Baja and Costa Rica. These populations are not absolutely distinct; small numbers of Humpbacks may alternate destinations in different years. The best time to view Humpback Whales in Washington and Oregon is between late March and early May and again from late September to November.

A Humpback's impressive song can last from a few minutes to half an hour, and the entire performance can go on for several days with only short breaks between each song. These complex underwater vocalizations are composed of trills, whines, snores, wheezes and sighs, and they are some of the loudest and most mysterious sounds produced by any animal. While the true meaning of their song eludes us, we do know that only males sing and that they perform mainly during the breeding season, implying that the main purpose is courtship.

Humpbacks breed in tropical waters in winter. Here, the males become very aggressive toward each other and battle to determine dominance. A dominant male becomes the escort to a female with a calf. Presumably, a female with a calf is one who is, or will soon be, receptive to mating.

Other than the brief bouts of fighting between males during the breeding season, Humpback Whales have gentle and docile natures. They feed primarily on schooling fish or krill, using "lunge-feeding" or "bubble nets" to concentrate their prey. When lunge-feeding, a whale approaches a school of fish and

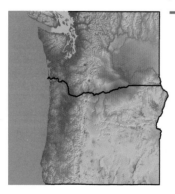

RANGE: Humpback Whales are found in all of the world's oceans, migrating seasonally from polar to tropical waters.

Total Length: up to 62 ft.; average 45 ft.

Total Weight: up to 53 tons; average 30 tons

Birth Length: 13–16 ft.

Birth Weight: 1–2 tons

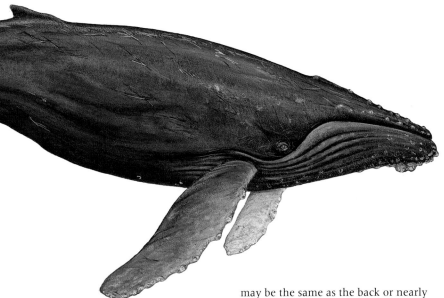

surges forward, gulping into its greatly stretched throat a large volume of both fish and water. The thick baleen permits water to be squeezed out of the whale's mouth, but the fish remain to be swallowed. When bubble-netting, one or more whales circle a school of fish or krill from below while releasing a constant stream of bubbles. The bubbles rise and momentarily trap the confused fish, and the whales surge up inside the cylindrical "net" and gulp the fish into their mouths.

DESCRIPTION: This species is slightly more robust in the body than other rorquals. Body color is either dark gray or dark slate blue, and the undersides may be the same as the back or nearly white. A Humpback's head is slender, with numerous knobs and projections around the snout. The mouth line arches downward to the eye, and 12 to 36 grooves are visible on the pale throat. The flippers are distinctively long and knobby, with a varying pattern of white markings. The tail flukes are strongly swept back and have irregular trailing edges. Like the flippers, the flukes have unique white markings that can be used to identify individuals. The

DID YOU KNOW?

As much as 5000 mi. can lie between the Humpback Whale's high-latitude feeding waters in summer and its tropical mating and calving waters in winter.

dorsal fin can be small and stubby or high and falcate, and several small knuckles are visible on the dorsal ridge between the fin and tail. Humpbacks often carry barnacles and whale lice. A female Humpback is longer than a male.

BLOW: The Humpback Whale makes a thick, orb-shaped blow that can reach up to 10 ft. high and is visible at a great distance. From directly in front or behind, the blow may appear slightly heart-shaped.

OTHER DISPLAYS: An acrobatic whale, the Humpback dazzles whale-watchers with high breaches that finish in a tremendous splash. Other behaviors that it may repeat several times include lob-tailing, flipper-slapping and spy-hopping. Humpbacks are often inquisitive, and they may approach boats if boaters are non-harassing. When they

dive sequence

breathe and dive, they roll through the water and show a strongly arched back. The tail flukes are lifted high only on deep dives.

GROUP SIZE: Humpbacks commonly live in small groups of 2 or 3 members, but some groups may have 15 members, and occasionally 1 whale is seen on its own. Good feeding and breeding waters usually draw large groups.

FOOD: Humpbacks feed only in summer, and after their winter in the tropics they are slim and hungry. A whale may feed by either lunging or bubble-netting, with much individual variation enhancing each technique. Major foods include krill, anchovies, sardines and capelin.

YOUNG: Courtship between Humpbacks is elaborate and involves lengthy bouts of singing by the males. Mating usually occurs in warm waters, and single calves are born following a gestation of about $11\frac{1}{2}$ months. The calves stay close to their mothers and nurse for about one year. Females reach sexual maturity when they are about 40 ft. long and males when they are at least 38 ft. long (about five years of age for both).

blow

SIMILAR SPECIES: The **Gray Whale** (p. 68) is slimmer and has mottled gray skin with excessive numbers of barnacles and whale lice. As well, the Gray Whale has shorter flippers that lack distinctive markings.

Gray Whale

Orca
Orcinus orca

The Orca, with its striking colors and intelligent eyes, has fascinated humankind for centuries. Once revered by indigenous peoples of the Pacific Northwest, this black-and-white giant now symbolizes everything from biodiversity protection to non-human intelligence.

Orcas are one of the most widely distributed mammals on earth, and they live in every ocean of the world, from cold polar seas to warm equatorial waters. Uncontested as the top marine predator, Orcas feed on a wider variety of creatures than any other cetaceans. They are regarded as intelligent yet fearsome creatures—they are the lions that rule the seas.

Studies done on the North Pacific Coast indicate that there are three distinct forms of Orcas. The two common groups are the "transients" and the "residents," distinguishable by appearance and behavior. Transient Orcas tend to be larger, and they have taller, straighter dorsal fins than residents. They live in smaller pods—from one to seven individuals—and they have larger home ranges. Transients also make erratic direction changes while traveling. Residents travel predictable routes. The feeding and socializing behaviors of the two groups also differ:

transients are more likely to feed on other sea mammals, they dive for up to 15 minutes, and they do not vocalize as much as residents. By contrast, resident Orcas feed mainly on fish, rarely dive longer than three or four minutes and are highly vocal. Recently, researchers have identified a new class of Orca: the "offshore" Orca resembles the resident in appearance, but this new class usually lives farther out at sea. Much more research is needed to accurately describe this group.

Unlike the rorqual whales, Orcas have never been hunted heavily by humans. Some hunting has taken place in the past several decades, but it has not threatened the total population. Unfortunately, live hunting for the aquarium trade has taken many Orcas and their close cousins, Bottlenose Dolphins (*Tursiops truncatus*), from the wild.

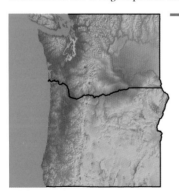

RANGE: Orcas are found in all oceans and seas.

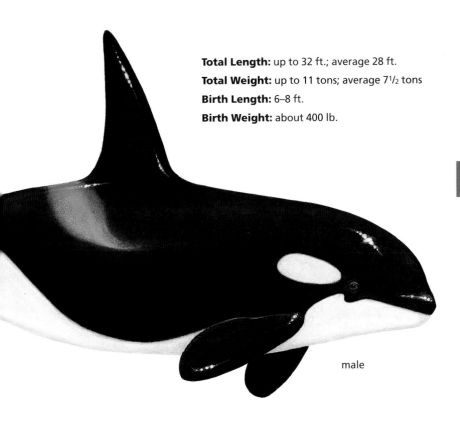

Total Length: up to 32 ft.; average 28 ft.
Total Weight: up to 11 tons; average 7½ tons
Birth Length: 6–8 ft.
Birth Weight: about 400 lb.

male

These activities cause much controversy, because whales are intelligent animals and many people feel that to keep them confined in an aquarium is unjust. Others argue that much of what we have learned about cetacean intelligence and biology comes from aquarium studies, and this knowledge helps us to better understand and protect whales in the wild.

ALSO CALLED: Killer Whale, Grampus.

DESCRIPTION: The Orca is unmistakable: its body is jet black, with white undersides and a lower jaw, as well as white patches behind the eyes and on

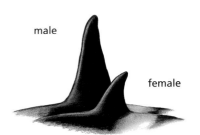

male

female

> **DID YOU KNOW?**
> Orcas have been known to eat land animals—there are records of Orca pods killing and eating Moose and Caribou, which swim across narrow channels and river mouths in northern Canada and Alaska.

its sides. Its large flippers are paddle-shaped, and its dorsal fin is tall and triangular. An old male may have a fin as tall as 6 ft., and the fins of some old individuals may be wavy when seen straight on. The female's dorsal fin is smaller and more curved than the male's. Behind the dorsal fin is often a gray or purplish "saddle." Each whale's dorsal fin and saddle patch has a unique shape, and the fin often bears scars; scientists and whale-watchers can identify individual Orcas by these characteristics. The eye is below and in front of the white facial spot, and the snout tapers to a rounded point. The flukes are dark on top and whitish below, with pointed tips, concave trailing edges and a distinct notch in the middle. The male Orca is longer than the female.

BLOW: In cool air, the blow of the Orca is low and bushy.

OTHER DISPLAYS: Orcas are extremely acrobatic for their size. They are inquisitive and often approach boats, apparently to get a better look at the humans

dive sequence

on board. They are often seen breaching clear out of the water, lob-tailing, flipper-slapping, logging and spy-hopping. They may speed-swim, or "porpoise," with their entire body leaving the water at each breath. Sub-surface beaches of rounded pebbles attract many Orcas—they seem to enjoy rubbing their bodies on the smooth stones.

GROUP SIZE: Orcas travel in pods of 3 to 25 individuals. Certain social gatherings may attract several pods at one time.

FOOD: Orcas feed on a wider variety of animals than any other whale, partly because of their global distribution. Several hundred species are potential prey to these top predators of the sea, including, but not limited to, fish of all kinds, seals, other cetaceans, sea turtles and birds.

YOUNG: Mating takes place between individuals of a pod and rarely outside the social group. Males reach maturity when they are about 19 ft. long and females when they are about 16 ft. long; females first give birth at about the age of 15. Winter appears to be the peak calving season, and gestation is believed to be 12 to 16 months.

blow hole

Dall's Porpoise

SIMILAR SPECIES: Along the Pacific Coast, the **Dall's Porpoise** (p. 84) may be mistaken for a baby Orca. The **False Killer Whale** (*Pseudorca crassidens*) is entirely black and lacks the large dorsal fin.

Pacific White-sided Dolphin
Lagenorhynchus obliquidens

The acrobatic Pacific White-sided Dolphins are favorites of whale-watchers in the Pacific Northwest. These boisterous dolphins are so inquisitive and entertaining that they frequently "steal the show" from larger, less engaging cetaceans.

Do these dolphins enjoy entertaining? It would seem so, because they often step up their antics when boats full of eager spectators are around. To the astonishment of the viewers on one occasion, an overly zealous individual leaped more than 10 ft. out of the water and accidentally landed on the deck of a large research boat. Of course, the researchers quickly returned the exhibitionist to the water, but the event remains a testament to the impressive antics of these dolphins.

As a group, white-sided dolphins are both acrobatic and sociable. Together they surf ocean waves, catch waves, ride bow waves and "porpoise" in unison. Sometimes groups of one or two thousand white-sided dolphins gather in offshore waters. They also socialize with other dolphin and marine mammal species, most notably the Northern Right-whale Dolphins (*Lissodelphis borealis*), seals and sea-lions. Despite their gentle-looking faces and intensely social behavior, they can sometimes

pester larger whales, much like crows and magpies can bother a pet dog. White-sided dolphins have been seen clustering around the heads of Orcas (p. 76) and Humpbacks (p. 72) until the large whales get fed up and dive deep to get away. Sometimes they can even be aggressive, both with other species of marine mammals and with each other.

Recently, the numbers of these dolphins have been increasing in coastal and sheltered waters, especially on inside straits between islands and the mainland. No one can adequately

explain this supposed change; the species was previously thought to prefer open ocean. One possible reason could be food availability.

Like most dolphins, Pacific White-sided Dolphins have acute senses that

RANGE: Pacific White-sided Dolphins are found only in the northern portion of the Pacific Ocean.

Total Length: up to 8 ft.; average 7 ft.
Total Weight: up to 400 lb.; average 210 lb.
Birth Length: about 3 ft.
Birth Weight: about 30 lb.

enable them to perceive their marine environment in an extremely sophisticated manner. Their sense of touch is many times greater than our own, and they feel subtle changes in the pressure of the water around them. If another dolphin or creature approaches an individual outside its field of vision, it can feel the pressure wave displacement and detect the animal's presence before it is seen or touched. Being able to detect another animal's presence is undoubtedly advantageous at night or in deep water where light cannot penetrate.

A common misconception is that dolphins have poor eyesight. Their sense of touch and their echolocation are so highly developed, people think that they can't see well. In fact, dolphins have exceptionally good eyesight both in and out of the water. They can focus the lens of the eye rapidly closer to or farther away from the retina where the image is received. Humans can't focus this way, which is why everything looks blurry to us when we take our goggles off in water—a medium about 800 times denser than air. When a dolphin leaps into the air, it can clearly visualize its surroundings.

DID YOU KNOW?

Pacific White-sided Dolphins, and other members of the same genus, are often referred to as "Lags," a diminutive of their Latin name.

ALSO CALLED: Lag, Pacific Striped Dolphin, White-striped Dolphin, Hook-finned Dolphin.

DESCRIPTION: The Pacific White-sided Dolphin has a distinct and beautiful color pattern of white, gray and nearly black. Its back is mainly dark, and beginning in front of the eye is a large, grayish patch that extends down the sides to below the dorsal fin. Along the sides of the tail stock, another similarly colored patch may narrow into a streak running forward of the dorsal fin. A distinct dark lateral line borders the pure white undersides. The eyes are dark, as is the tip of the barely discernible beak. The closely spaced conical teeth are numerous. This dolphin's most distinguishing feature is the rearward-pointing, bicolored dorsal fin, which is dark on the leading edge and pale gray on the trailing edge. The flippers may be similarly colored, but they are often

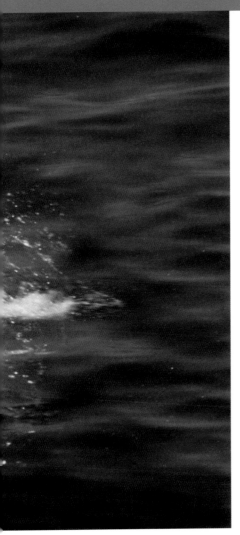

dark all over. The flukes are pointed, slightly notched in the middle and dark above and below.

BLOW: Pacific White-sided Dolphins do not make a distinct blow, but they often splash about and produce sprays that resemble a blow.

OTHER DISPLAYS: These acrobats perform dazzling breaches, somersaults and virtually any other kind of above-water display. They often swim just under the surface with their dorsal fins slicing through the water.

GROUP SIZE: These dolphins are commonly seen in groups of 10 to 50, but sometimes larger groups may form temporarily.

FOOD: White-sided dolphins eat a variety of creatures, such as squid, anchovies, hake and other small fish. They feed in groups to better herd the fish, and each adult consumes about 20 lb. per day.

YOUNG: Calving and mating occur from late spring to fall, and gestation is estimated to be 9 to 12 months (average 10 months). A mother nurses her calf up to 18 months, and soon after weaning gives birth again. Females and males reach sexual maturity when they are about 6 ft. long; social maturity influences age at first mating.

Dall's Porpoise

SIMILAR SPECIES: The less common **Striped Dolphin** (*Stenella coeruleoalba*) has one or two prominent eye stripes; the **Saddleback Dolphin** (*Delphinus* spp.) has tawny or yellowish sides; the **Harbor Porpoise** (*Phocoena phocoena*) is smaller and much grayer overall; and the **Dall's Porpoise** (p. 84) has distinct black-and-white markings.

Dall's Porpoise
Phocoenoides dalli

The second-smallest cetaceans in the Pacific Northwest—Harbor Porpoises (*Phocoena phocoena*) are smaller—Dall's Porpoises are a welcome sight for boaters and whale-watchers. They are high-speed swimmers that frequently provide hours of delight for human spectators. Fortunately, they are very tolerant of human company, so the approach of boats rarely startles them.

Despite their name, these animals do not actually "porpoise" through the water the way dolphins and other small cetaceans do. Instead, they surface only long enough for a quick breath and by doing so create the distinctive conical splashes of water that are typical of the species.

Dall's Porpoises appear to undergo short migrations along the West Coast. In summer they tend to move northward, and in winter they move farther south. Some inshore and offshore migration may occur, perhaps in response to food availability. In some years, for unexplained reasons, mass assemblies of a few thousand individuals have been monitored moving through passages near Alaska and northern British Columbia.

Like all dolphins and porpoises, Dall's Porpoises can sleep with half of the brain at a time, allowing them to be continuously vigilant for danger. The major natural enemies of Dall's Porpoises are Orcas (p. 76) and sharks.

Worldwide efforts to protect whales have had many successes. Unfortunately, Dall's Porpoises are still being

hunted on a massive scale—some countries have taken as many as 45,000 in a year. Several thousand more of these mammals are accidentally killed in fishing nets they cannot detect. It is not known how long the species may be able to sustain such losses; the Dall's Porpoise is not currently classed as endangered, but few reliable population estimates are available.

ALSO CALLED: Spray Porpoise, True's Porpoise, White-flanked Porpoise.

DESCRIPTION: Often mistaken for a baby Orca, the Dall's Porpoise is distinctly colored black and white. Its head

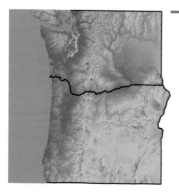

RANGE: Dall's Porpoises are found in the North Pacific between 30° N and 62° N, in the open ocean or close to land.

Total Length: up to 8 ft.; average 6 ft.

Total Weight: up to 490 lb.; average 300 lb.

Birth Length: 2½–3 ft.

Birth Weight: unknown.

is black and tapers to a narrow mouth. The "lips" of its small mouth are usually black, but on some individuals they are white. The closely spaced, spade-shaped teeth are numerous. The black body is extremely robust for its length, and a large, white patch is on the belly and sides. Two forms of this porpoise occur: the *truei*-type, which has a white patch that stretches from in front of the flippers to the tail stock, and the *dalli*-type, which has a smaller white patch on its sides, beginning about one-third down its body. The black, triangular dorsal fin has a hooked tip, and it is usually light gray or white on the trailing half. The small flippers lie close to the head, and

they are dark black above and below. When viewed from above, the flukes are shaped like a wide ginkgo leaf and have a white or gray trailing edge.

BLOW: This porpoise does not make a visible blow. As it swims and breaks the surface, a V-shaped cone of water comes off its head. This cone of water is referred to as a "rooster-tail." Many boaters look for this rooster-tail because

DID YOU KNOW?

Dall's Porpoises are among the fastest cetaceans, often clocked at speeds up to 35 m.p.h.

it can be seen from a much greater distance than the porpoise itself.

OTHER DISPLAYS: The Dall's Porpoise is not acrobatic and does not leap out of the water. Nevertheless, it is exceptionally fast and even seems hyperactive as it darts and zig-zags about. It appears to love bow riding, and it zooms toward a fast-moving boat like a black-and-white torpedo. If a Dall's Porpoise comes to the bow of your boat, don't slow down for a better look because it will quickly lose interest in a boat going slower than 12 m.p.h.

GROUP SIZE: Dall's Porpoises are commonly found in groups of 10 to 20 individuals, though aggregations of hundreds may occur in some waters.

FOOD: Dall's Porpoises feed at the surface or in deep water, and their primary foods include squid, lanternfish, hake,

mackerel, capelin and other schooling fish. Maximum feeding depth has been estimated at about 1600 ft. These porpoises have high metabolic rates and require large amounts of food at frequent intervals.

YOUNG: Two peaks in calving seem to occur, one in February to March and again in July to August. Peak mating must have a similar split, because gestation is about $11^1/_2$ months. Males reach sexual maturity when they are about 6 ft. long (four to five years), and females when they are $5^1/_2$ ft. long (three to four years).

Pacific White-sided Dolphin

SIMILAR SPECIES: The **Pacific White-sided Dolphin** (p. 80) is much grayer overall and is slimmer relative to its length. A baby **Orca** (p. 76) looks similar, but it would never be seen unattended by its mother.

CARNIVORES

This group of mammals is aptly named, because, while some members of the order Carnivora are actually omnivorous (and eat a great deal of plant material), most of them prey on other vertebrates. These "meat-eaters" vary greatly in size in Washington and Oregon, from the small Short-tailed Weasel to the large and muscular Grizzly Bear.

Cat Family (Felidae)

Excellent and usually solitary hunters, all cats have long, curved, sharp, retractile claws. Like dogs, cats walk on their toes—they have five toes on each forefoot and four toes on each hindfoot—and their feet have naked pads and furry soles. As anyone who has a housecat knows, the top of a cat's tongue is rough with spiny, hard, backward-pointing papillae, which are useful to the cat for grooming its fur.

Mountain Lion

Skunk Family (Mephitidae)

Biologists previously placed skunks in the weasel family, but recent DNA research has led taxonomists to group the North American skunks (together with the stink badgers of Asia) in a separate family. Unlike most weasels, skunks are usually boldly marked, and when threatened they can spray a foul-smelling musk from their anal glands.

Striped Skunk

Weasel Family (Mustelidae)

Most weasels are lithe predators with short legs and elongated bodies. They have anal scent glands that produce an unpleasant-smelling musk, but, unlike skunks, they use it to mark territories rather than for defense. Most species have been trapped for their valuable, long-lasting fur.

Long-tailed Weasel

Raccoon Family (Procyonidae)

Raccoons and Ringtails are small to medium-sized omnivores that, like bears (and humans), walk by using their entire foot, from heel to toe (plantigrade). They are good climbers. The Northern Raccoon is best known for its long, banded, bushy tail and distinctive black facial mask. The Ringtail, also a member of this family, is more slender than a Northern Raccoon; it has semi-retractile claws; and when it walks the heel does not touch the ground (subdigitigrade).

Northern Raccoon

Hair Seal Family (Phocidae)

The hair seals are also known as the "true seals," and they are believed to share a common ancestor with the mustelids. These seals have hindflippers that permanently face backwards; they cannot rotate their hips and hindlegs to support the weight of their bodies. Their flippers are covered with hair, and all five digits have claws. There are no external ears flaps (pinna).

Northern Elephant Seal

Eared Seal Family (Otariidae)

Eared seals include the fur seals and sea-lions, and all are believed to share a common ancestor with bears. These seals can rotate their hindlegs forward to help support their weight when they are on land. Their flippers are hairless, and only the hindflippers have nails on the middle three digits. As their name suggests, these seals have external ear flaps (pinna). Hair seals (Phocidae) and eared seals (Otariidae) are collectively referred to as pinnipeds.

Northern Sea-Lion

Bear Family (Ursidae)

The three North American members of this family—two of which occur in this region—include the world's largest terrestrial carnivores. All bears are plantigrade, and they have powerfully built forelegs and a short tail. Although most bears sleep through the harshest part of winter, they do not truly hibernate—their sleep is not deep and their temperature drops only a couple of degrees. Contrary to popular belief, bears may rouse during the winter and even come out of their dens on milder days.

Grizzly Bear

Dog Family (Canidae)

This family of dogs, wolves, Coyotes and foxes is one of the most widespread terrestrial, non-flying mammalian families. The typically long snout houses a complex series of bones associated with the sense of smell, which plays a major role in finding prey and in communication. Members of this family walk on their toes, and their claws are blunt and non-retractile.

Kit Fox

Mountain Lion
Puma concolor

A pug-mark in the snow or a heavily clawed tree trunk are two powerful reminders that some places in Washington and Oregon are still wild enough for the Mountain Lion. This large cat was once found throughout much of North America, but conflicts with settlers and their stock animals resulted in humans initiating the widespread removal of this great feline. Still, it is one of the most widespread, if not abundant, carnivores in both North and South America. Its alternate common names reflect this distribution: "puma" is derived from the name used by the Incas of Peru; "cougar" comes from Brazil.

The Mountain Lion is generally a solitary hunter, except when a mother is accompanied by her young. When the young are old enough, they follow their mother and sometimes even help her kill—a process that teaches the young how to hunt for themselves. Although Mountain Lions are capable of great bursts of speed and giant bounds, they often opt for a less energy-intensive hunting strategy. Silent and nearly motionless, a cat will wait in ambush in a tree or on a ledge until prey approaches. By leaping onto the shoulders of its prey and biting deep into the back of the neck while attempting to knock the prey off balance, the Mountain Lion can take down an adult Elk or a small Moose.

These big cats need the equivalent of about one deer a week to survive, and their densities in the wild tend to correlate with deer densities. Mountain Lions are adaptable creatures that may hunt by day or night. Hunting by day is quite common in the wilderness, but in areas close to human development the cats are active only at night.

One of the most charismatic animals of North America, the Mountain Lion is a creature everyone hopes to see … from a safe distance. This elusive cat is a master of living in the shadows, but if you spend enough time in the wilderness of Washington or Oregon, you may one day see a streak of burnished brown flash in your peripheral vision. If this streak was actually a Mountain Lion, you can count yourself among the extremely lucky. Few people—even biologists—get a glimpse of these graceful felines.

If you startle one, which is quite improbable—it usually knows of your presence long before you know of its—it will quickly disappear from sight. Only the young may come for a closer look at you. Young Mountain Lions, like most young carnivores, are extremely curious and don't yet realize that humans are best avoided.

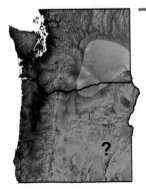

RANGE: The Mountain Lion formerly ranged from northern British Columbia east to the Atlantic and south to Patagonia. In North America, it has been extirpated by humans from most areas except the western mountains and adjacent foothills. A tiny population remains in the Everglades, and occasional reports from Maine and New Brunswick point to its presence in these locations.

Total Length: 6–9 ft.
Shoulder Height: 26–32 in.
Tail Length: 25–38 in.
Weight: 70–190 lb.

ALSO CALLED: Puma, Cougar.

DESCRIPTION: This handsome feline is the only large, long-tailed native cat in Washington and Oregon. Its body is mainly buffy gray to tawny or cinnamon in color, with pale buff or nearly white undersides. Its body is long and lithe, and its tail is almost one third of its total length. The head, ears and muzzle are all rounded. The tip of the tail, sides of the muzzle and backs of the ears are black. Some individuals have prominent facial patterns of black, brown, cinnamon and white.

HABITAT: Mountain Lions are found most frequently in remote, wooded, rocky places, usually near an abundant supply of deer. In Washington and Oregon, they inhabit mainly the montane regions, though they may venture into the brushlands or subalpine regions, depending on food availability.

FOOD: In Washington and Oregon, Mountains Lions rely mainly on deer. Other prey species include the Bighorn Sheep, Mountain Goat, Elk, Moose, American Beaver and North American Porcupine. Even mice, rabbits, birds, adult Bobcats and domestic dogs and

DID YOU KNOW?

During an extremely cold winter, a Mountain Lion can starve if the carcasses of its prey freeze solid before it can get more than one meal. This cat's jaws are designed for slicing, and it has trouble chewing frozen meat.

91

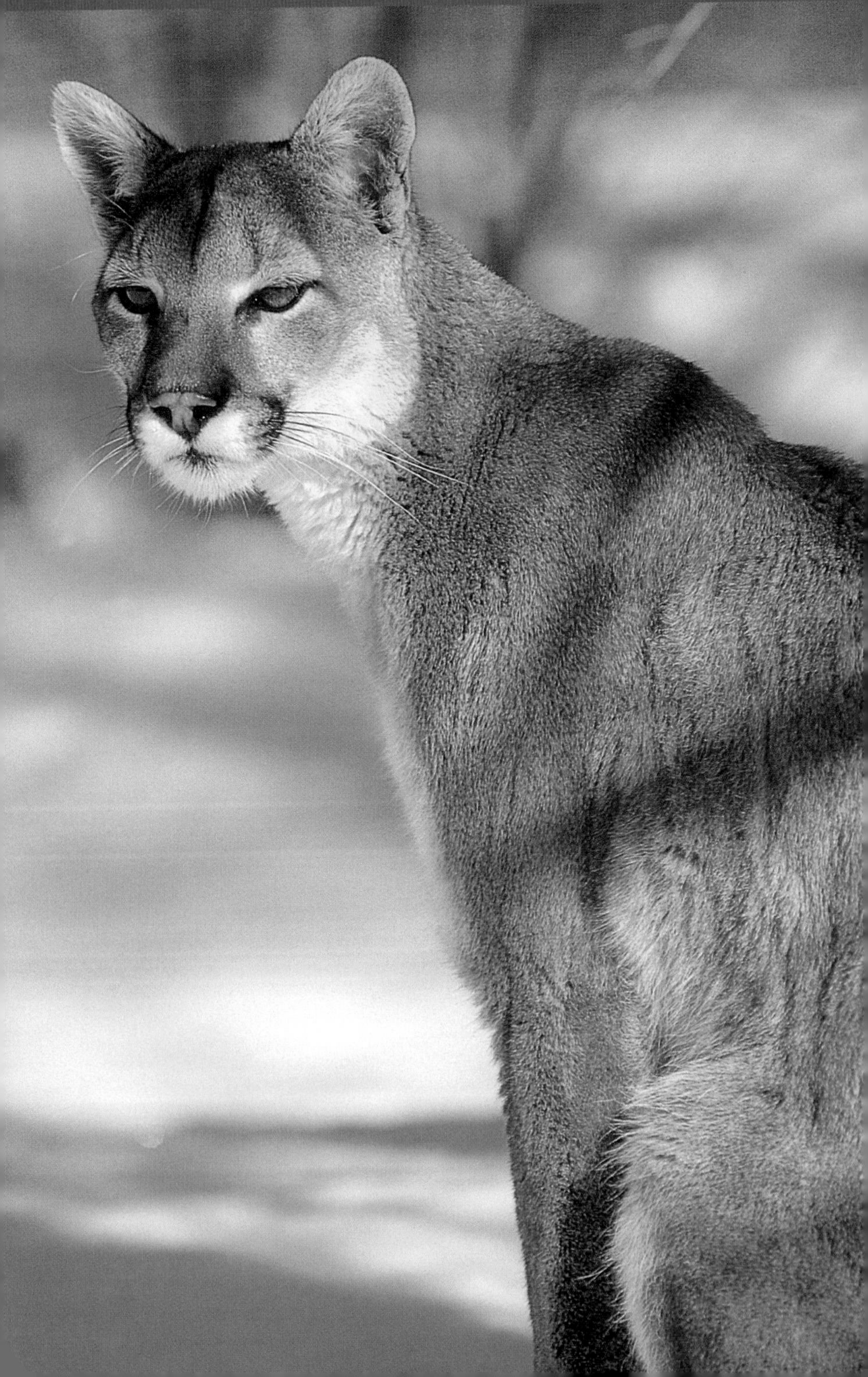

foreprint

walking trail

cats may be consumed. In harsh winters, Mountain Lions feed easily on animals weakened by starvation.

DEN: A cave or crevice between rocks usually serves as a den, but a Mountain Lion may also den under an overhanging bank, beneath the roots of a windthrown tree or even inside a hollow tree.

YOUNG: A female Mountain Lion may give birth to a litter of one to six (usually two or three) kittens at any time of the year after a gestation of just over three months. The tan, black-spotted kittens are blind and helpless at birth, but their eyes open at two weeks. Their mottled coats help camouflage them when their mother leaves to find food. As the kittens mature, they lose their spots and their blue eyes turn brown or hazel. They are weaned at about six weeks, by which time they weigh about 6½ lb. Young Mountain Lions may stay with their mother for up to two years.

SIMILAR SPECIES: The two other native cats in the region, the **Canada Lynx** (p. 94) and the **Bobcat** (p. 98), are smaller (the Bobcat more so) and have mottled coats and bobbed tails.

Canada Lynx

Canada Lynx
Lynx canadensis

Meat is on the nightly menu for the Canada Lynx, and the meal of choice is Snowshoe Hare (p. 290). The classic predator-prey relationship of these two species is now well known to all students of zoology, but it took extensive field studies to determine how and why these species interact to such a great extent. Periodic fluctuations in lynx numbers in local areas have been observed for decades: when hares are abundant, lynx kittens are more likely to survive and reproduce; when hares are scarce, many kittens starve and the lynx population declines, sometimes rapidly and usually one to two years after the decline in hares.

The reason why the Canada Lynx is so focused on the Snowshoe Hare as its primary prey may never be understood completely, but the forest community in which this cat lives certainly affects its lifestyle. Many other carnivores compete with the lynx for the same forest prey. Wolves, Coyotes, Red Foxes, Mountain Lions, Bobcats, Fishers, American Martens, Wolverines, American Minks, skunks, owls, eagles and hawks are all present in the same forests, and they all require animal prey for sustenance. Although these other predators may take a hare on occasion, none is as skilled at catching hares as the Canada Lynx.

This resolute carnivore copes well with the difficult conditions of its wilderness home. Its well-furred feet impart nearly silent movement and serve as snowshoes where snow is deep. Like other cats, the lynx is not built for fast, long-distance running—it generally ambushes or silently stalks its prey. The ultimate capture of an animal relies on sheer surprise and a sudden overwhelming rush. With its long legs, a lynx can travel rapidly while trailing evasive prey in the tight confines of a forest. It can also climb trees quickly to escape enemies or to find a suitable ambush site.

The Canada Lynx is primarily a solitary hunter of remote forests. During population peaks, however, young cats may disperse into less hospitable environs. In recent memory, the Canada Lynx has been reported within the limits of many major cities. These incidents are unusual because the Canada Lynx typically avoids contact with humans. In Washington and Oregon, the only likely place to see these agile felines is in the Rocky Mountain cordillera and the northern Cascades. The lynx, however, is elusive, so even if you are in prime lynx territory you are unlikely to see one. Your best chance to see a lynx is probably in the Selkirk Mountains.

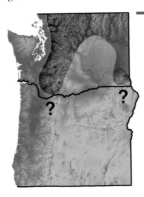

RANGE: Primarily an inhabitant of the boreal forest, the Canada Lynx occurs across much of Canada and Alaska. Its range extends south into the western U.S. mountains and into the northern parts of Wisconsin, Michigan, New York and New England.

Total Length: 31–40 in.
Shoulder Height: 18–23 in.
Tail Length: 3½–4¾ in.
Weight: 15–40 lb.

People who see a rare lynx for the first time are undoubtedly surprised—compared to the average housecat, the stilt-legged lynx is more than twice its size and gangly in appearance.

DESCRIPTION: This medium-sized, short-tailed, long-legged cat has huge feet and protruding ears tipped with 2-in. black hairs. The long, lax, silvery-gray to buffy fur bears faint, darker stripes on the sides and chest and dark spots on the belly and insides of the forelegs. There are black stripes on the forehead and a long facial ruff. The entire tip of the stubby tail is black. The long, buffy fur of the hindlegs makes a lynx look like it is wearing baggy trousers. Its large feet spread widely when it is walking, especially in deep snow. The footprint of this cat is wider than an adult human's hand.

HABITAT: The Canada Lynx is closely linked to the northern coniferous forests. Desired habitat components include numerous fallen trees and occasional dense thickets that serve as effective cover and ambush sites. The lynx depends on its prey. Its prey depends on the twigs, grasses, leaves, bark and vegetation of the dense forest.

FOOD: Snowshoe Hare typically make up the bulk of the diet, but a lynx will sustain itself on squirrels, grouse, rodents or even domestic animals.

DID YOU KNOW?

Some taxonomists consider the Canada Lynx to be the same species as the European Lynx (*L. lynx*), which occupies the northern forests of Europe and Asia.

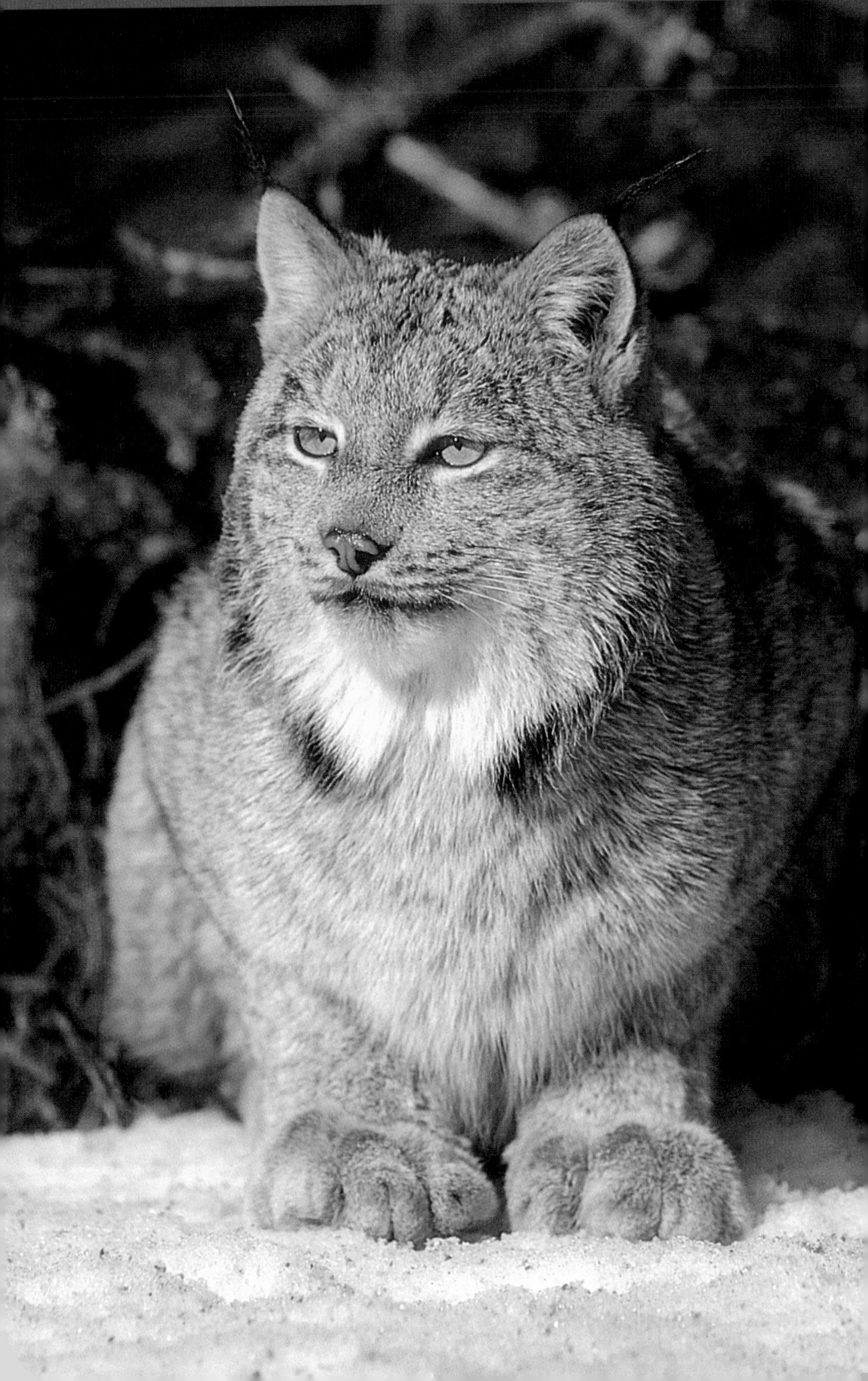

foreprint

walking trail

When lynx do not eat all of their kills, they cache the meat by covering it with snow or leafy debris.

DEN: The den is typically an unimproved space beneath a fallen log, among rocks or in a cave. Lynx do not share dens, and adult contact is restricted to mating. A mother lynx shares a den with her young until they are mature enough to leave.

YOUNG: Canada Lynx breed in March or April, and the female gives birth to one to five (usually two or three) kittens in May or June. Gestation is a little over two months. The kittens are generally gray, with indistinct longitudinal stripes and dark gray barring on the limbs. Their eyes open in about 12 days, and they are weaned at two months. They stay with their mother through the first winter and acquire their adult coats at 8 to 10 months. A female usually bears her first litter near her first birthday.

Bobcat

SIMILAR SPECIES: The only other native cat that resembles the Canada Lynx is the smaller, shorter-legged **Bobcat** (p. 98). The Bobcat has shorter ear tufts, smaller feet and the upperside of the tail has two or three black bands and a white tip. The **Mountain Lion** (p. 90) is much larger and has a long tail.

Bobcat
Lynx rufus

For those of us who are naturalists as well as feline enthusiasts, our chances of seeing a Bobcat in the wild are much greater than seeing a Mountain Lion (p. 90) or Canada Lynx (p. 94). The Bobcat seems to be more tolerant of human presence; its territories may even border on developed land. Night drives through Washington and Oregon offer some of the best opportunities for seeing Bobcats, though, at best, the experience is a mere glimpse of the cat in the headlights. Bobcats are occasionally seen in mountain parks and wildlife areas.

The Bobcat looks like a large version of a housecat, but it has little of the housecat's domestication. A wildcat in every sense of the word, it impresses observers with its light-footedness, agility and stealth, usually leaving the momentary experience forever etched in the viewer's mind.

Over the past two centuries, Bobcat populations have fluctuated greatly because of their adaptability to human-wrought change and their vulnerability to our resentment. Less restricted in diet than the Canada Lynx, the Bobcat may vary its diet of hares with any number of small animals, including an occasional turkey or chicken. Its farmyard raids did not go over well with early set-tlers, and for more than 200 years the Bobcat was considered vermin. Even today, this striking native feline remains on the out-dated "varmint" lists in some areas.

Despite its small size, the Bobcat is a ferocious hunter that can take down animals much larger than itself. Tales from long ago that told of Bobcats killing deer were considered by the uninformed to be either tall tales or cases of mistaken identity. This remarkable feat, however, is indeed possible for a surreptitious Bobcat that waits motionless on a rock or ledge for a deer to approach. The Bobcat leaps onto the neck of the unsuspecting animal and then maneuvers to the lower side of the neck to deliver a suffocating bite to the deer's throat. A Bobcat may resort to such rough tactics in late winter when food is scarce, but it usually dines on simpler prey, such as rabbits, birds and rodents. Most of its prey, big or small, is caught at night in ambush. During the day, the Bobcat rests in any handy shelter.

Finding Bobcat tracks in soft ground may be the easiest way to determine the presence of this small cat in the region. Unlike Coyote or Red Fox prints, Bobcat (and lynx) prints rarely show any claw marks, but look for one cleft on the

RANGE: The Bobcat has the widest distribution of any native cat in North America. It occurs in the Rocky Mountains and southern interior of British Columbia, across southern Canada and south through much of the U.S. to Mexico.

Total Length: 30–49 in.
Shoulder Height: 17–21 in.
Tail Length: 5–6¾ in.
Weight: 15–29 lb.

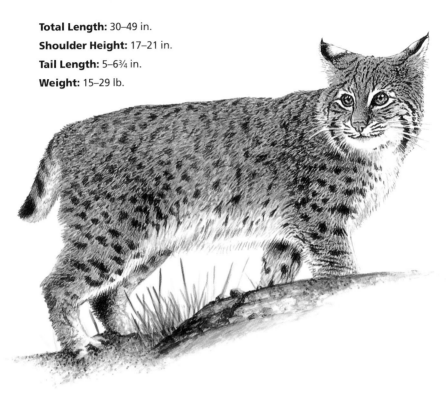

front part of the main foot pad and two on the rear. A Bobcat's print is like a large version of a housecat's, except that it tends to be found much farther from human habitation. Like all cats, the Bobcat buries its scat, and its scratches can help confirm its presence.

DESCRIPTION: The coat is generally tawny or yellowish brown, though it varies slightly with the seasons. The winter coat is usually dull gray with faint patterns. In summer, the coat often has a reddish tinge to it (the source of the scientific name, *rufus*). A Bobcat's sides are spotted with dark brown, and dark, horizontal stripes are on the breast and outsides of the legs. Two black bars run across each cheek, and there is a brown forehead stripe. The ear tufts are less than 1 in. long. The chin and throat are whitish, as is

the underside of the bobbed tail. The upper surface of the tail is barred, and the tip of the tail is black on top.

HABITAT: The Bobcat occupies open coniferous and deciduous forests and brushy areas. It especially favors willow stands, which offer excellent cover for its clandestine hunting. Where the Canada Lynx is absent, the Bobcat may range well up into mountain forests.

DID YOU KNOW?

Most cats have long tails, which they lash out to the side to help them corner more rapidly in pursuit of prey. The Bobcat and the Canada Lynx (p. 94), however, which typically hunt in brushy areas, have short, or "bobbed," tails that won't get caught in branches.

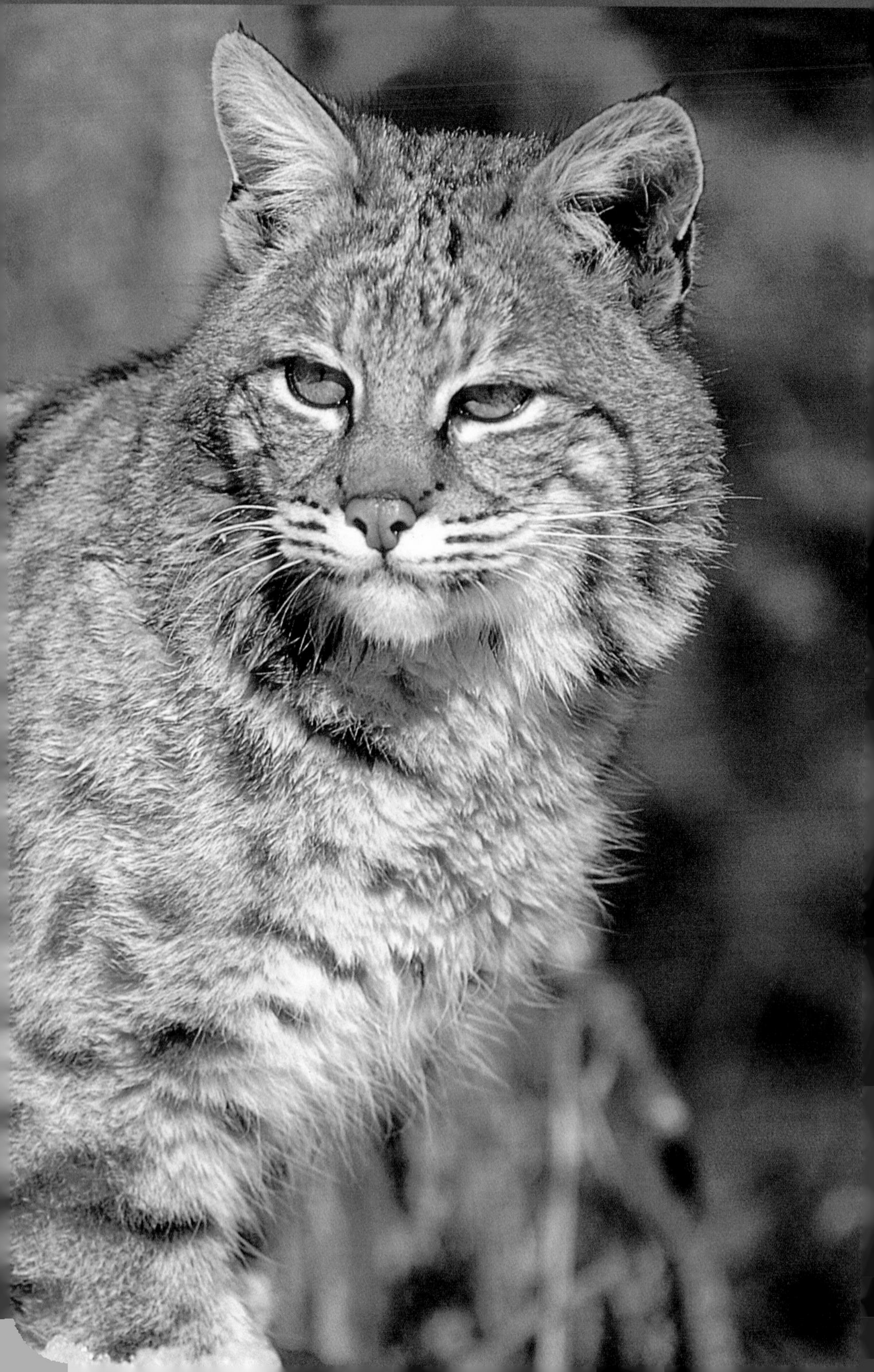

foreprint

walking trail

FOOD: The preferred food seems to be rabbit, but a Bobcat will catch and eat squirrels, rats, mice, voles, beavers, skunks, wild turkeys and other ground-nesting birds. It may even take down larger prey, such as a deer. When necessary, the Bobcat scavenges the kills of other animals.

DEN: Bobcats do not keep a permanent den. During the day, they use any available shelter. Female Bobcats prefer rocky crevices for the natal den, but they may also use hollow logs or the cavity under a fallen tree. The mothers do not provide a soft lining in the den for the kittens.

YOUNG: Bobcats typically breed in February or March, giving birth to one to seven (usually three) hairy, gray kittens in April or May, but they sometimes breed at other times of the year. The kittens' eyes open after nine days. They are weaned at two months, but they remain with the mother for three to five months. Female Bobcats become sexually mature at one year old, and males at two.

Canada Lynx

SIMILAR SPECIES: The **Canada Lynx** (p. 94) is nearly the same size, but the length of the hindlegs is very different, which makes the lynx appear taller. The lynx also has much longer ear tufts, and the tip of its tail is entirely black, without any black bars. The **Mountain Lion** (p. 90) is much larger and has a longer tail.

Western Spotted Skunk
Spilogale gracilis

To watch the antics of a Western Spotted Skunk as it prepares to spray is almost worth the putrid penalty. Almost. When agitated and fearing for its safety, the Western Spotted Skunk resorts to the practice that has made the skunk family infamous. If the skunk's foot stamping and tail raising do not convey sufficient warning, the spraying certainly will.

Unlike the more familiar Striped Skunk (p. 104), which sprays in a *U* position with its feet planted, the Western Spotted Skunk literally goes over the top when it sprays. Like a contortionist in a sideshow circus, this little skunk faces the threat and performs a handstand, letting its tail fall toward its head. The skunk can maintain this balancing act for more than five seconds, which is usually sufficient time to take aim and expel a well-placed stream of fluid into the face of the intruder. Many animals may attempt to kill and eat this skunk before it sprays, but few are successful.

Throughout diverse habitats, including wilderness and urban areas, a common occurrence is the odor of skunk in the air. While this lingering odor may be from a skunk spraying in defense, it is all too often from a road-killed skunk. Road fatalities are a major cause of death among skunks, despite the weasel-like agility and dexterity of these animals. The Western Spotted Skunk is especially nimble; with surprising ease, it can climb up to holes in hollow trees or to bird nests, where it finds shelter or food.

DESCRIPTION: This small skunk is mainly black with a white forehead spot and a series of four or more white stripes broken into dashes on the back. The pattern of white spots is different on each individual. The tail is covered with long, sparse hairs, and the tip of the tail is white with a black underside. The ears are small, rounded and black, and the face strongly resembles a weasel's. This skunk may walk, trot, gallop or make a series of weasel-like bounds. At night, its eyeshine is amber.

HABITAT: Western Spotted Skunks are found in woodlands, rocky areas, open grasslands or scrublands. They do not occupy marshlands or wet areas, but farmlands make an excellent home. They are mainly nocturnal, and even in prime habitat they are seldom seen.

FOOD: This omnivorous mammal feeds on great numbers of insects, berries, eggs, nestling birds, small rodents, lizards and frogs. Animal matter usually accounts for

RANGE: The Western Spotted Skunk ranges from southwestern British Columbia to the southern tip of Texas and south well into Mexico.

Total Length: 13–23 in.
Tail Length: 4–8¼ in.
Weight: 1–2 lb.

a larger part of its diet than vegetation does. The Western Spotted Skunk is an opportunistic forager, and it will eat nearly anything that it finds or can catch. Insects, especially grasshoppers and crickets, are the most important food in summer, and small mammals are significant in fall and spring.

DEN: The Western Spotted Skunk is nomadic by comparison to the Striped Skunk. It rarely makes a permanent den, preferring to hole up temporarily in almost any safe spot: rock crevices, fallen logs, buildings, woodpiles, abandoned burrows of other mammals and even tree cavities. The natal den is used for a longer period than other den spaces, and it differs primarily in the grass and leaves the female uses to line the inside for comfort. In harsh winters, several skunks may den together to conserve energy and wait out inclement weather.

YOUNG: Two to six (usually four) young are born in May or June. The eyes and ears are closed at birth. The young skunks are covered with fine fur that betrays their future pattern. The eyes open after one month, and the young begin playing together at 36 days. By two months they are weaned. The family frequently stays together through fall, and it may overwinter in the same den, not dispersing until the following spring.

SIMILAR SPECIES: The **Striped Skunk** (p. 104) is the only other animal in Washington and Oregon with a black-and-white coat. As its name suggests, however, its white markings are in broad stripes.

DID YOU KNOW?

Spotted skunks become sexually mature at a very young age. A male may be able to mate when he is just five months old, and a female usually mates in September or October of her first year.

Striped Skunk
Mephitis mephitis

In nature, many of the best-dressed creatures are poisonous or unsafe for other creatures in some way. Poisonous snakes, frogs and insects often bear striking colors and patterns that warn intruders of their dangerous character. The same is true for skunks; their bold black-and-white patterns convey a clear warning to stay away. Anyone not heeding this warning will likely receive a face full of foul, repugnant fluid.

A substance called "butylmercaptan" is responsible for the stink. Seven different sulfide-containing "active ingredients" have been identified in the musk, which not only smells bad, but also irritates the skin and eyes. A distressed Striped Skunk will turn its body into a *U* prior to spraying, with all four feet on the ground and its tail and head both facing the threat. If a skunk successfully targets the eyes, an intense burning, copious tearing and sometimes a short period of blindness occur. From a distance, a whiff of a skunk's musk may be tolerable, but at point blank range it is strong enough to induce nausea.

Despite all these good reasons to avoid close contact with the Striped Skunk, the species is surprisingly tolerant of observation from a discreet distance, and watching a skunk can be very rewarding—its gentle movements contrast with the hyperactive behavior of its weasel cousins. The Striped Skunk's activity begins at sundown, when it emerges from its daytime hiding place. It usually forages among shrubs, but it often enters open areas, where it can be seen with relative ease. The Striped Skunk is an opportunistic predator that feeds on whatever animal matter is available. During winter, its activity is much reduced, and skunks spend the coldest periods in communal dens.

The only regular predator of the Striped Skunk is the Great Horned Owl. Lacking a highly developed sense of smell, this owl does not seem to mind the skunk's odor—nor do the few other birds that commonly scavenge road-killed skunks.

DESCRIPTION: This cat-sized, black-and-white skunk is familiar to most people. Its basic color is glossy black. A narrow, white stripe extends up the snout to above the eyes, and two white stripes begin at the nape of the neck, run back on either side of the midline and meet again at the base of the tail. The white bands often continue on the tail, ending in a white tip, but much variation is in the amount and distribution of the white markings. The foreclaws are long and are used for digging.

RANGE: The Striped Skunk is found across most of North America, from Nova Scotia to Florida in the East and from the southwestern Northwest Territories to northern Baja California in the West. It is absent from parts of the deserts of southern Nevada, Utah and eastern California.

Total Length: 22–32 in.
Tail Length: 8–14 in.
Weight: 4¼–9¼ lb.

A pair of musk glands, one on each side of the anus, discharges the foul-smelling yellowish liquid for which skunks are famous.

HABITAT: In the wild, the Striped Skunk seems to prefer streamside woodlands, groves of hardwood trees, semi-open areas, brushy grasslands and valleys. It also regularly occurs in cultivated areas, around farmsteads and even in the hearts of cities, where it can be an urban nuisance that eats garbage and raids gardens.

FOOD: All skunks are omnivorous. Insects, including bees, grasshoppers, beetles and various larvae, make up the largest portion, about 40 percent, of the spring and summer diet. To get at bees, skunks will scratch at a hive entrance until the bees emerge and then chew up great gobs of mashed bees, thus incurring the bee-keeper's wrath. The rest of the diet is composed of bird eggs and nestlings, amphibians, reptiles, grains and green vegetation, and particularly in fall, small mammals, fruits and berries. Carrion, especially roadkill, can make up a sizable portion of a skunk's diet.

DEN: In most instances, the Striped Skunk builds a bulky nests of dried leaves and grasses in an underground burrow or beneath a building. Winter and maternal dens are underground.

YOUNG: A female Striped Skunk gives birth to 2 to 10 (usually 5 or 6) blind, helpless young in April or May, after a gestation of 62 to 64 days. The typical black-and-white pattern of a skunk is present on the skin at birth. The eyes and ears open at three to four weeks. At five to six weeks, the musk glands are functional. Weaning follows at six to seven weeks. The mother and her young will forage together into fall, and they often share a winter den.

SIMILAR SPECIES: Only the small **Western Spotted Skunk** (p. 102) also bears a black-and-white pattern, but its white areas are a series of spots or thin stripes. The **American Badger** (p. 122) has a white stripe running up its snout, but it is larger and squatter and has a grizzled, yellowish-gray body.

DID YOU KNOW?

Fully armed, the Striped Skunk's scent glands contain about 1 oz. of noxious, smelly stink. The spray has a maximum range of about 20 ft., and a skunk is accurate for half that distance.

American Marten
Martes americana

Ferocity and playfulness are perfectly blended in the American Marten. This quick, active, agile weasel is equally at home on the forest floor or among branches and tree trunks. Its fluid motions and attractive appearance contrast with its swift and deadly hunting tactics. A keen predator, the American Marten sniffs out voles, takes bird eggs, nabs fledglings and acrobatically pursues Red Squirrels (p. 278).

Unfortunately, because the marten tends to inhabit wilder areas, its playfulness, agility and insatiable curiosity are not easily observed. The American Marten has been known to occupy human structures for short periods of time—should a food source be near—but more typical marten sightings are restricted to flashes across roadways or trails. Human pursuit of a marten rarely leads to a satisfying encounter—this weasel's mastery of the forest is ably demonstrated in its elusiveness.

A close relative of the Eurasian Sable (*M. zibellina*), the American Marten is widely known for its soft, lustrous fur, and it is still targeted on traplines in remote wilderness areas. As with so many species of forest mammals, populations seem to fluctuate markedly every few years—a cyclical pattern revealed by trappers' records. Some scientists attribute these cycles to changes in prey abundance, whereas some trappers suggest that marten populations simply migrate from one area to another.

The American Marten is often used as an indicator of environmental conditions, because it depends on food found in mature coniferous forests. The loss of such forests has led to declining populations and even extirpation from some areas of the United States. Hopefully, modern methods of forest management will maintain adequate habitat for the American Marten and prevent its further decline.

ALSO CALLED: Pine Marten.

DESCRIPTION: This slender-bodied, fox-faced weasel has a beautiful pale yellow to dark brown coat and a long, bushy tail. The feet are well furred and equipped with strong, non-retractile claws. The conspicuous ears are $1^3/8$–$1^3/4$ in. long. The eyes are dark and almond-shaped. The breast spot, when present, is usually orange but sometimes whitish or cream, and it varies in size from a small dot to a large patch that occupies the entire region from the chin to the belly. A male is about 15 percent larger than a female. A well-defined scent gland,

RANGE: The range of the American Marten coincides almost exactly with the distribution of boreal and montane coniferous forests across North America. It may repopulate where mature forests have developed in areas that were formerly cut or burned.

Total Length: 20–27 in.
Tail Length: 7–9 in.
Weight: 1–2¾ lb.

about 3 in. long and 1 in. wide, is on the center of the abdomen.

HABITAT: The marten prefers mature, particularly coniferous, forests that contain numerous dead trunks, branches and leaves to provide cover for its rodent prey. It does not occupy recently burned or fully cut-over areas. In central Oregon, slash piles that harbor Golden-mantled Ground Squirrels (p. 272) can attract numerous martens.

FOOD: Although voles make up most of the diet, the American Marten is an opportunistic feeder that will eat squirrels, hares, bird eggs and chicks, insects, carrion and occasionally berries and other vegetation. In summer, it may enter the alpine zones to hunt pikas and marmots. This active predator hunts both day and night. Martens have been known to raid garbage cans and dumpsters of mountain cabins and ski lodges.

DEN: The preferred den site is a hollow tree or log that the female lines with dry grass and leaves.

YOUNG: Breeding occurs in July or August, but with delayed implantation of the embryo, so the litter of one to six (usually three or four) young is not born until March or April. The young are blind and almost naked at birth and weigh just 1 oz. The eyes open at six to seven weeks, at which time the young are weaned from a diet of milk to one of mostly meat. The mother must quickly teach her young to hunt, because when they are only about three months old she will re-enter estrus, and, with mating activity, the family group disbands. Young female martens have their first litter at about the time of their second or third birthdays.

SIMILAR SPECIES: The **Fisher** (p. 108) is more than twice as large, with a long, black tail and often frosted or grizzled-grey to black fur. It seldom has an orange chest patch. The **American Mink** (p. 116) has a white chin and irregular white spots on the chest, but it has shorter ears, shorter legs (it does not climb well) and a much less bushy, cylindrical tail.

DID YOU KNOW?

Although the American Marten, like most weasels, is keenly carnivorous, it has been known to consume an entire apple pie left cooling outside a window and to steal doughnuts off a picnic table.

Fisher
Martes pennanti

For the lucky naturalist, meeting a wild Fisher is a once-in-a-lifetime opportunity. The rest of us must content ourselves with the knowledge that this reclusive animal remains a top predator in coniferous wildlands. Historically, the Fisher was more numerous, and it once ranged throughout the northern boreal forest, the northeastern hardwood forests and the forests of the Rocky Mountains and the Pacific ranges.

The Fisher is an animal of deep, untouched wilderness, and it often disappears from an area shortly after development begins within its range. Forest clearing, habitat destruction, fires and over-trapping resulted in this animal's decline or extirpation over much of its range. A few reintroductions and a gradual recovery in some areas over the past two decades is a tiny but hopeful indicator that this animal isn't lost.

The Fisher is among the most formidable of predators here, and it could probably be considered the most athletic of this region's carnivores. Fishers are particularly nimble in trees, and the anatomy of their ankles allows the feet to rotate sufficiently so that they can descend trees headfirst. Making full use of its athleticism during foraging, the Fisher incorporates any type of ecological community into its extensive home range, which can reach 75 mi. across. According to Ernest Thompson Seton, a legendary naturalist of the 19th century, as fast as a squirrel can run through the treetops, a marten can catch and kill it, and as fast as the marten can run, a Fisher can catch and kill it.

The Fisher is a good swimmer, but, despite its name, it rarely eats fish. Perhaps this misnomer arose because of confusion with the similar-looking, though much smaller, American Mink (p. 116), which does regularly feed on fish. These two weasels are quickly distinguished by their preferred habitats: the American Mink inhabits riparian areas; the Fisher prefers deep forests.

Few of the animals on which the Fisher preys can be considered easy picking; the most notable example is the Fisher's famed ability to hunt porcupine (p. 186). What the porcupine lacks in mobility, it more than makes up for in defensive armory, and a successful attack requires all the Fisher's speed, strength and agility. This hunting skill is far less common than wilderness tales suggest, however, and Fishers do not exclusively track porcupines; rather, they opportunistically hunt whatever crosses their trails. Most of their diet consists of rodents, rabbits, grouse and other small animals.

RANGE: Fishers occur across the southern half of Canada (except the Prairies) and into the northeastern U.S. In the West, they are found through the Cascades and Sierra Nevada and in the Rocky Mountains to Wyoming.

Total Length: 31–47 in.
Tail Length: 12–16 in.
Weight: 4½–12 lb.

DESCRIPTION: The Fisher has a face that is fox-like, with rounded ears that are more noticeable than those on other large weasels. In profile, its snout appears distinctly pointed. The tail is dark and more than half as long as the body. The coloration over its back is variable, ranging from frosted gray or gold to black. The undersides, tail and legs are dark brown. There may be a white chest spot. A male has a longer, coarser coat than a female, and he is typically 20 percent larger.

HABITAT: The preferred habitat is dense coniferous forests. Fishers are not found in young forests or where logging or fire has thinned the trees. They are most active at night and thus are seldom seen. Fishers have extensive home ranges, and they may only visit a particular part of their range once every two to three weeks.

FOOD: Like other members of the weasel family, the Fisher is an opportunistic hunter, killing squirrels, hares, mice, muskrats, grouse and other birds. Unlike almost any other carnivore, however, the Fisher may hunt porcupines, which it kills by repeatedly attacking the head. It also eats berries and nuts, and carrion can be an important part of its diet.

DEN: Hollow trees and logs, rock crevices, brush piles and cavities beneath boulders all serve as den sites.

DID YOU KNOW?

The scientific name *pennanti* honors Englishman Thomas Pennant. In the late 1700s, he predicted the decline of the American Bison and postulated that Native Americans entered North America via a Bering land bridge.

Most dens are only temporary lodging, because the Fisher is always on the move throughout its territory. The natal den is more permanent, and it is usually located in a safe place, such as a hollow tree. A Fisher may excavate its winter den in the snow.

YOUNG: A litter of one to four (usually two or three) young is born in March or April. The mother will breed again about a week after the litter is born, but implantation of the embryo is delayed until January of the following year. During mating, the male and female may remain coupled for up to four hours. The helpless young nurse and remain in the den for at least seven weeks, after which time their eyes open. When they are three months old, they begin to hunt with their mother, and by fall they are independent. The female is usually sexually mature when she is two years old.

walking trail

foreprint

American Marten

SIMILAR SPECIES: The **American Marten** (p. 106) is smaller, lighter in color and usually has a buff or orange chest spot. The **American Mink** (p. 116) is smaller and has shorter ears, shorter legs and a cylindrical, much less bushy tail. The Fisher typically has a more grizzled appearance than either the marten or mink.

111

Short-tailed Weasel
Mustela erminea

In English, the name "weasel" is often used to describe pointy-nosed villains or to characterize dishonest cheats. Unfortunately, these connotations give weasels a bad reputation. Although weasels have pointed noses, they are neither villainous nor deceitful, but they are efficient predators with an exceptional talent for hunting.

The Short-tailed Weasel is common in Washington and Oregon, and, because of its relatively small territory requirement, it may even be the most abundant land carnivore. Despite its abundance, the Short-tailed Weasel is not commonly seen because, like all weasels, it tends to be most active at night and inhabits areas with heavy cover.

When Short-tailed Weasels roam about their ranges, they explore every hole, burrow, hollow log and brush pile for potential prey. In winter, they travel both above and below the snow in their search for prey. Once a likely meal is located, it is seized with a rush, and then the weasel wraps its body around the animal and drives its needle-sharp canines into the back of the skull or neck. If the weasel catches an animal larger than itself, it seizes the prey by the neck and strangles it.

The Short-tailed Weasel's dramatic change between its winter and summer coats led Europeans to give it two different names: an animal wearing the dark summer coat is called a "stoat"; in the white winter pelage it is known as an "ermine." In Washington and Oregon, the Short-tailed Weasel is just one of two weasel species that alternate between white in winter and brown in summer, so the "stoat" and "ermine" labels are best avoided to prevent confusion. Moreover, in areas lacking winter snow the weasels do not change color.

ALSO CALLED: Ermine.

DESCRIPTION: This weasel's short summer coat has brown upperparts and creamy white underparts, often suffused with lemon yellow. The feet are snowy white, even in summer, and the last third of the tail is black. The short, oval ears extend noticeably above the

winter coat

RANGE: A holarctic species, this weasel occurs in North America throughout most of Alaska and Canada and south to northern California and northern New Mexico in the West and northern Iowa and Pennsylvania in the East.

elongated head. The eyes are black and beady. The long neck and narrow thorax make it appear as if the forelegs are positioned farther back than on most mammals, giving the weasel a snake-like appearance. Starting in October and November, this animal becomes completely white, except for the black tail tip. The lower belly and inner hindlegs often retain the lemon yellow wash. In late March or April, the weasel molts back to its summer coat.

HABITAT: The Short-tailed Weasel is most abundant in coniferous or mixed forests and streamside woodlands. In summer, it may often be found in the alpine tundra, where it hunts on rockslides and talus slopes.

FOOD: The diet appears to consist almost entirely of animal prey, including mice, voles, shrews, chipmunks, pocket gophers, pikas, rabbits, bird eggs and nestlings, insects and even amphibians. These weasels are quick, lithe and unrelenting in their pursuit of anything they can overpower. They often eat every part of a mouse except the filled stomach, which may be excised with surgical precision and left on a rock.

DEN: Short-tailed Weasels commonly take over the burrows and nests of mice, ground squirrels, chipmunks, pocket gophers or lemmings and modify them for weasel occupancy. They line the nest with dried grasses, shredded leaves and the fur and feathers of prey. Sometimes a weasel accumulates the furs of so many animals that the nest grows to a diameter of 8 in. Some nests are located in hollow logs, under buildings or in an abandoned cabin that once supported a sizable mouse population.

YOUNG: In April or May, the female gives birth to 4 to 12 (usually 6 to 9) blind, helpless young that weigh just $1/16$ oz. each. Their eyes open at five weeks, and soon thereafter they accompany the adults on hunts. At about this

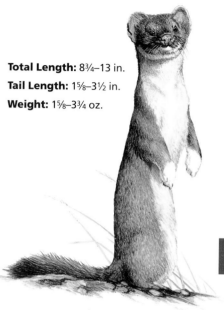

Total Length: 8¾–13 in.
Tail Length: 1⅝–3½ in.
Weight: 1⅝–3¾ oz.

summer coat

time, a male has typically joined the family. In addition to training the young to hunt, he impregnates the mother and all her young females, which are sexually mature at two to three months. Young males do not mature until the next February or March—a reproductive strategy that reduces interbreeding among littermates.

SIMILAR SPECIES: The **Long-tailed Weasel** (p. 114) is generally larger and has orangish underparts, generally lighter upperparts and yellowish to brownish feet in summer.

DID YOU KNOW?

These weasels typically mate in late summer, but after little more than a week the embryos stop developing. In early spring, up to eight months later, the embryos implant in the uterus and the young are born about one month later.

Long-tailed Weasel
Mustela frenata

On a sunny winter day, there may be no better wildlife experience than to follow the tracks of a Long-tailed Weasel. This curious animal zig-zags as though it can never make up its mind which way to go, and every little thing it crosses seems to offer a momentary distraction. The Long-tailed Weasel acts like it is continuously excited, and this bountiful energy is easily read in its tracks as it leaps, bounds, walks and circles through its range.

Long-tailed Weasels hunt wherever they can find prey: on and beneath the snow, along wetland edges, in burrows and even occasionally in trees. They can overpower smaller prey, such as mice, large insects and snakes, and kill them instantly. With a larger prey species, up to the size of a rabbit, the weasel grabs it by the throat and neck and wrestles it to the ground. As the weasel wraps its snake-like body around its prey in an attempt to throw it off balance, it tries to kill the animal with bites to the back of the neck and head.

Unlike the Short-tailed Weasel (p. 112) and the more northerly Least Weasel (*M. nivalis*), the Long-tailed Weasel only occurs in North and Central America. With the conversion of native grasslands to farmland, the Long-tailed Weasel has declined to a point where it is now regarded as a species of concern in much of its range. Still, in some native pastures that teem with ground squirrels, the Long-tailed Weasel can be found bounding about during the daytime, continually hunting throughout its waking hours.

DESCRIPTION: The summer coat is a rich cinnamon brown on the upperparts and usually orangish or buffy on the underparts. The feet are brown in summer. The tail is half as long as the body, and the terminal quarter is black. The winter coat is entirely white, except for the black tail tip and sometimes an orangish wash on the belly. As in all weasels, the body is long and slender—the forelegs appear to be positioned well back on the body—and the head is hardly wider than the neck.

HABITAT: The Long-tailed Weasel is an animal of open country. It may be found in agricultural areas, on grassy slopes and in the alpine tundra. Sometimes, in places where the Short-tailed Weasel is rare or absent, it forages in aspen parklands, intermontane valleys and open forests.

FOOD: Although the Long-tailed Weasel can successfully subdue larger

RANGE: From a northern limit in central British Columbia and Alberta, this weasel ranges south through most of the U.S. (except the southwestern deserts) and Mexico into northern South America.

Total Length: 11–17 in.
Tail Length: 4¾–11 in.
Weight: 3–14 oz.

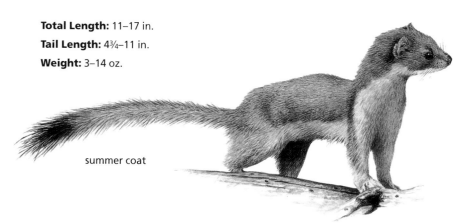

summer coat

prey than can its smaller relatives, voles and mice still make up most of its diet. It also preys on ground squirrels, woodrats, Red Squirrels, rabbits and shrews, and it takes the eggs and young of ground-nesting birds when it encounters them.

DEN: These weasels usually make their nests in the burrow of a small mammal they have eaten. Nest cavities are lined with soft materials such as hair from prey. The female makes a maternal den in the same manner, either in a burrow, in a hollow log or under an old tree stump.

YOUNG: Long-tailed Weasels typically mate in mid-summer, but, through delayed implantation of the embryos, the young aren't born until April or May. The litter contains four to nine (usually six to eight) blind, helpless young. They are born with sparse, white hair, which becomes a fuzzy coat by one week and a sleek coat in two weeks. At 3½ weeks the young begin to supplement their milk diet with meat; just after seven weeks, they are weaned when their eyes open. By six weeks, there is a pronounced difference in size, with young males weighing about 3½ oz. and females 2¾ oz. At about this time, a mature male weasel typically joins the group to breed with the mother and the

young females as they become sexually mature. The group travels together, and the male and female teach the young to hunt. The group disperses when the young are 2½ to 3 months old.

SIMILAR SPECIES: The **Short-tailed Weasel** (p. 112) is typically smaller, has a relatively shorter tail and has a white to lemon yellow (not orangish) belly and white feet in summer.

winter coat

DID YOU KNOW?

Signs of weasels are not uncommon if you know what to look for: the tracks typically follow a paired pattern, and the twisted, hair-filled droppings, which are about the size of your pinkie finger, are often left atop a rock pile.

American Mink
Mustela vison

To many people, the fluid undulations of a bounding mink are more valuable than its much-prized fur. The American Mink is a lithe weasel that was described by naturalist Andy Russell as "moving ... like a brown silk ribbon." Indeed, like most weasels, the mink seems to move with the unpredictable flexibility of a toy Slinky in a child's hands.

Minks are tenacious hunters, following scent trails left by potential prey over all kinds of obstacles and terrain. Almost as aquatic as otters, these opportunistic feeders routinely dive to depths of 10 ft. or more in pursuit of fish. Their fishing activity tends to coincide with breeding aggregations of fish in spring and fall or during winter, when low oxygen levels force fish to congregate in oxygenated areas. It is along watercourses, therefore, that minks are most frequently observed, and their home ranges often stretch out in linear fashion, following rivers for up to 3 mi.

The American Mink is active throughout the year, and it is often easiest to follow by trailing its winter tracks in snow. The paired prints left by its bounding gait trace the inquisitive animal's adventures as it comes within sniffing distance of every burrow, hollow log and bush pile. This active forager always seems to be on the hunt; scarcely any feeding opportunities are passed up. Minks may kill more than they can eat, and surplus kills are stored for later use. A mink's food caches are often tucked away in its overnight dens, which are typically dug into riverbanks, beneath rock piles or in the home of a permanently evicted muskrat.

DESCRIPTION: The sleek coat is generally dark brown to black, usually with white spots on the chin, chest and sometimes the belly. The legs are short. The tail is cylindrical and only somewhat bushy. A male is nearly twice as large as a female. The anal scent glands produce a rank, skunk-like odor.

HABITAT: The American Mink is almost never found far from water. It frequents wet zones in coniferous or hardwood forests, brushlands and streamside vegetation in the foothills and in grasslands.

FOOD: Minks are fierce predators of muskrats, but in their desire for nearly any meat they also take frogs, fish, waterfowl and their eggs, mice, voles, rabbits, snakes and even crayfish and other aquatic invertebrates.

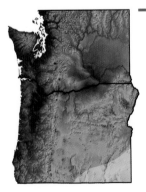

RANGE: This wide-ranging weasel occurs across most of Canada and the U.S., except for the high Arctic tundra and the dry southwestern regions.

Total Length: 19–28 in.
Tail Length: 5–8¼ in.
Weight: 1¼–3 lb.

2 x 2 loping trail

the period of delayed implantation varies in length (from one week to 1½ months), the female almost always gives birth in late April or early May. The actual gestation is about one month. There are 2 to 10 (usually 4 or 5) helpless, blind, pink, wrinkled young in a litter. Their eyes open at 24 to 31 days, and weaning begins at five weeks. The mother teaches the young to hunt for two to three weeks, after which they fend for themselves.

SIMILAR SPECIES: The **American Marten** (p. 106) has a bushier tail, longer legs and an orange or buff throat patch, and it is not as sleek looking. The **Fisher** (p. 108) is much larger and inhabits forests. The **Northern River Otter** (p. 126) is much larger and has a tapered tail and webbed feet.

DEN: The mink's den is usually in a burrow close to water. A mink may dig its own burrow, but more frequently it takes over a muskrat or beaver burrow and lines the nest with grass, feathers and other soft materials.

YOUNG: Minks breed any time between late January and early April, but because

DID YOU KNOW?

"Mink" is from a Swedish word that means "stinky animal." Although not as aromatic as skunks, minks are the smelliest of the weasels. The anal musk glands can release the stinky liquid, but not aim the spray, when a mink is threatened.

Wolverine

Gulo gulo

The Wolverine is one of the most poorly understood mammals in North America. It is an elusive animal of deep wilderness, as well as a creature of many myths and tall tales. More recently, the Wolverine has become a symbol of deep, pristine wilderness. Although most of us will never see a Wolverine, the knowledge that it maintains a hold in remote forests may reassure us that expanses of wilderness still exist.

Tales of the Wolverine's gluttony—its reputation rivals that of hyenas in Africa—have lingered in forest lore for centuries. Pioneers warned their children against the dangers of the forests, and often they meant the Wolverine. The Wolverine is an efficient and agile predator: it can crush through bone in a single bite; it has long, semi-retractile foreclaws that allow it to climb trees; and it is ferocious enough to challenge a lone bear or wolf. What we rarely hear about is this animal's intelligence, its uniqueness among its weasel relatives and its sheer vigor and beauty.

From the few behavioral studies of the Wolverine, its character emerges as being less vicious and more clever. Even simple observations of a Wolverine standing on its hindlegs and scanning the surroundings with a paw at its forehead to shield its eyes from the sun are indicative of intelligent behavior we are only now starting to understand. Nevertheless, some of the Wolverine's reputation is well deserved. True to its nickname "skunk bear," the Wolverine produces a stink that rivals skunks in foulness. The abundant, stinky scent is produced in glands beside the anus and is primarily used to mark territory.

The Wolverine's habitat preferences seem to vary as its diet shifts with seasons. In summer, it eats mostly ground squirrels and other small mammals, birds and berries; in winter it lives on carrion, mainly hoofed mammals, most of which it scavenges from wolves or roadkills. Like a vulture, the Wolverine can detect carcasses from far away.

The largest weasel of all, the Wolverine has one of the mammal world's most powerful set of jaws, which it uses to tear meat off frozen carcasses or to crunch through bone to get at the rich, nourishing marrow inside. Few other large animals are able to extract as much nourishment from a single carcass.

DESCRIPTION: Although the head is small and weasel-like, the long legs and long fur look like they belong on a small bear. Unlike a bear, however, the Wolverine has an arched back and a

RANGE: In North America, the Wolverine is a species of the coniferous forests and tundra of Alaska and northern Canada. It follows the montane coniferous forests from Alaska to as far south as California and Colorado.

Total Length: 28–43 in.
Tail Length: 6¾–10 in.
Weight: 15–35 lb.

long, bushy tail. The coat is mostly shiny, dark cinnamon brown to nearly black. Yellowish-white spots may be on the throat and chest. A buffy or pale brownish stripe runs down each side from the shoulder to the flank, where it becomes wider. These stripes meet just before the base of the tail, leaving a dark saddle.

HABITAT: The Wolverine prefers large areas of remote wilderness, where it frequently occupies wooded foothills and mountains. In summer, it forages into the alpine tundra and hunts along slopes. In winter, it drops to lower elevations and may move far away from the mountains. The Wolverine's enormous territory encompasses a great variety of habitats; this agile, determined predator is likely able to conquer almost any wild terrain.

FOOD: Wolverines prey on mice, ground squirrels, birds, beavers and fish. Deer, Caribou, Mountain Goats and even Moose have been attacked, often successfully. In winter, Wolverines often scavenge malnourished animals or the remains left by other predators. To a limited extent, they eat berries, fungi and nuts. Although Wolverines are generally thought to avoid human habitations, they are known to break

DID YOU KNOW?

The Wolverine's lower jaw is more tightly bound to its skull than most other mammals' jaws. The articulating hinge that connects the upper and lower jaws is wrapped by bone in adult Wolverines, and for the jaws to dislocate, this bone would have to break.

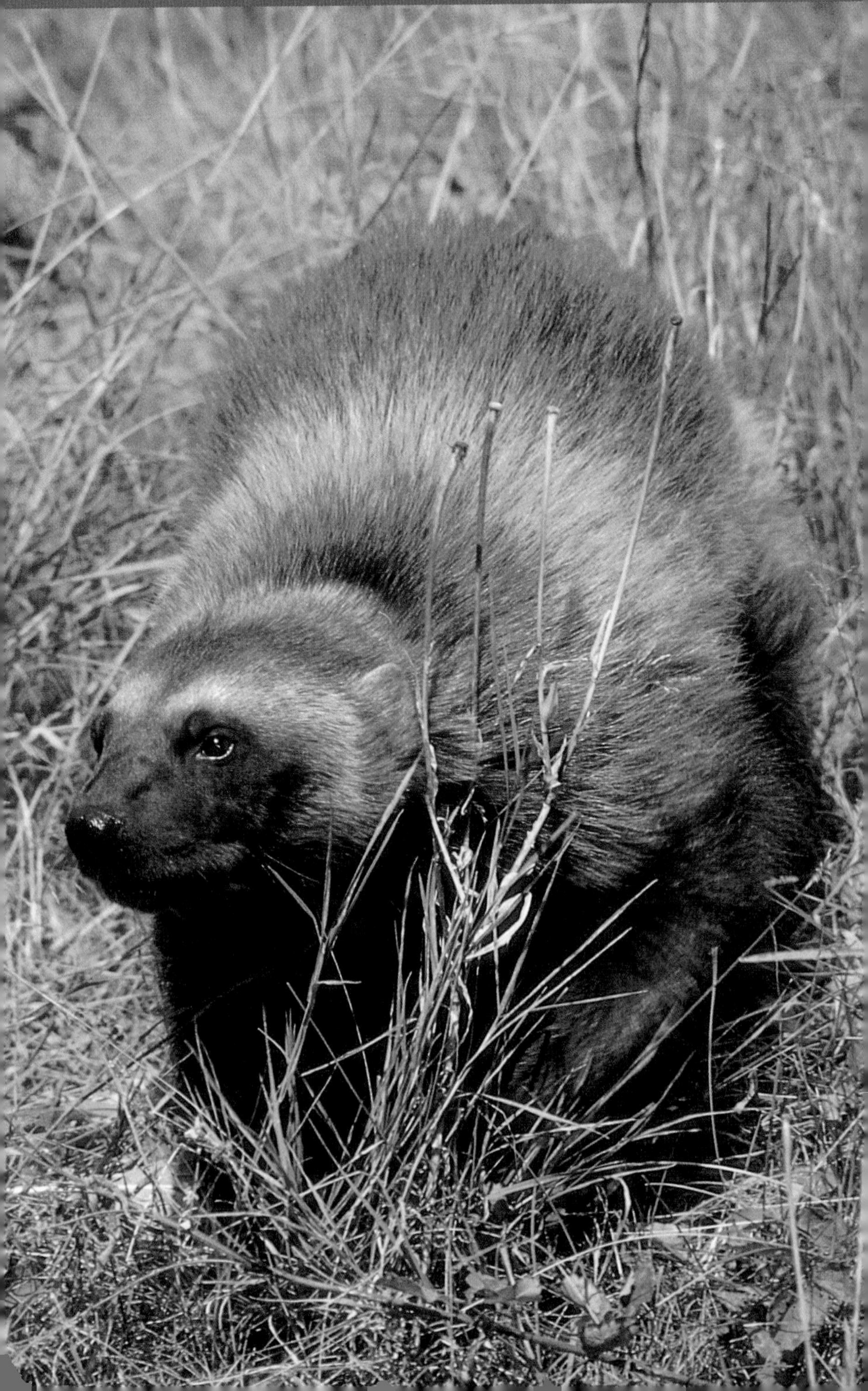

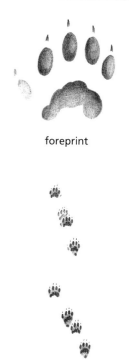

foreprint

walking trail

into wilderness cabins and meat caches to eat or destroy everything within.

DEN: The den may be among the roots of a fallen tree, in a hollow tree butt, in a rocky crevice or even in a semi-permanent snowbank. The natal den is often underground, and it is lined with leaves by the mother. A Wolverine may maintain several dens throughout its territory, ranging in quality from makeshift cover under tree branches to a permanent underground dugout.

YOUNG: Wolverines breed between late April and early September, but the embryos do not implant in the uterine wall until January. Between late February and mid-April, the female gives birth to a litter of one to five (generally two or three) cubs. The stubby-tailed cubs are born with their eyes and ears closed and with a fuzzy, white coat that sets off the darker paws and face mask. They nurse for eight to nine weeks, and then they leave the den and their mother teaches them to hunt. The mother and her young typically stay together through the first winter. The young disperse when they become sexually mature in spring.

American Badger

SIMILAR SPECIES: The **American Badger** (p. 122) is squatter, with a distinctive vertical stripe on its forehead and without the lighter side stripes of a Wolverine. The **American Black Bear** (p. 154) and the **Grizzly Bear** (p. 158) are much larger, have inconspicuous tails and lack the light buffy stripe along each side.

American Badger

Taxidea taxus

In low-elevation meadows and pastures, a lucky observer may encounter an American Badger. Badgers, with their flair for remodeling, are nature's rototillers and backhoes. The large holes left by badgers are of critical importance as den sites, shelters and hibernacula for dozens of species, from Coyotes to Black-widow Spiders. When badgers are eliminated from an area, the populations of many of these burrow-dependent animals eventually decline.

The badger enjoys a reputation for fierceness and boldness that was acquired in part from a distantly related weasel bearing the same name in Europe. While it is true that a cornered American Badger will put up an impressive show of attitude, like most animals it prefers to avoid a fight. When it is severely threatened or in competition, the badger's claws, strong limbs and powerful jaws make this animal a dangerous opponent. In spite of its impressive arsenal, the badger routinely kills only ground squirrels and other small rodents. However, rare occasions are known where badgers have taken Coyote pups. Likewise, a group of Coyotes (p. 162) may defeat a badger.

Pigeon-toed and short-legged, the American Badger is not much of a sprinter, but its heavy front claws enable it to move large quantities of earth in short order. Although a badger's predatory nature is of benefit to landowners, its natural digging skills have led many badgers to be killed by farmers, because cattle and horses have on occasion broken their legs by stepping into badger excavations.

Badgers tend to spend a great part of winter sleeping in their burrows, but they do not enter a full state of hibernation like their European relatives or like the ground squirrels upon which they feed. Instead, badgers emerge from their slumber to hunt whenever winter temperatures are more moderate.

In spite of low population densities, almost all sexually mature female badgers are impregnated sometimes during the nearly three months that they are sexually receptive. As with most members of the weasel family, once the egg is fertilized further embryonic development is put off until the embryos implant, usually in January, which will result in a spring birth.

DESCRIPTION: Long, grizzled, yellowish-gray hair covers these short-legged, muscular members of the weasel family. The hair is longer on the sides than on the back or belly, which adds to the flattened appearance of the body. A white

RANGE: From north-central Alberta and Saskatchewan, the American Badger ranges to the southeast throughout the Great Plains and Prairies and southwest to Baja California and the central Mexican highlands.

Total Length: 31–33 in.
Tail Length: 5–6¼ in.
Weight: 11–24 lb.

stripe originates on the nose and runs back onto the shoulders or sometimes slightly beyond. The top of the head is otherwise dark. A dark, vertical crescent, like a badge, runs between the short, rounded, furred ears and the eyes. The sides of the face are whitish or very pale buff. The short, bottlebrush tail is more yellowish than the body, and the lower legs and feet are very dark brown, becoming blackish at the extremities. The three central claws on each forefoot are greatly elongated for digging. Older American Badgers often have the "wrap-around" jaw articulation seen in older Wolverines.

HABITAT: Essentially an animal of open places, the badger shuns forests. It is usually found in association with ground squirrels, typically in grasslands and open parkland. In the mountains, it forages on treeless alpine slopes or in riparian meadows. It visits the alpine tundra in summer in search of marmots, pocket gophers and other burrowing prey.

FOOD: Burrowing mammals fill most of the badger's dietary needs, but it also eats eggs, young ground-nesting birds, mice and sometimes carrion, insects and snails.

DEN: An American Badger may dig its own den or take over a ground squirrel's burrow. The den may approach

DID YOU KNOW?

Badgers make an incredible variety of sounds: adults hiss, bark, scream and snarl; in play, young badgers grunt, squeal, bark, meow, chirr and snuffle; and the front claws clatter when a badger runs on a hard surface.

foreprint

walking trail

30 ft. in length and have a diameter of about 1 ft. The badger builds a bulky grass nest in an expanded chamber near or at the end of the burrow. A large pile of excavated earth is generally found to one side of the burrow entrance.

YOUNG: One to five (usually four) naked, helpless young are born between late April and mid-June. Their eyes open after a month, and at two months their mother teaches them to hunt. In early evening they leave the burrow, trailing their mother. The babies investigate every grasshopper or beetle they encounter, but the mother directs the expedition to ground squirrel burrows. She often cripples a ground squirrel and then leaves it for her young to kill. The young disperse in fall, when they are three-quarters grown. Some of the young females may mate in their first summer, but most badgers are not sexually mature until they are a year old. Delayed implantation of the embryo is characteristic.

Wolverine

SIMILAR SPECIES: The **Wolverine** (p. 118) is the primary species you might confuse with an American Badger, but the badger's body is much more flattened, and the thin, white stripe on its nose is unique. Also, Wolverines lope, whereas badgers trot. The **Striped Skunk** (p. 104) is smaller and has distinct black-and-white markings. The **Northern Raccoon** (p. 136) has a black "mask" and ringed tail.

Northern River Otter
Lontra canadensis

It may seem too good to be true, but all those playful characterizations of the Northern River Otter are founded on truth. Otters often amuse themselves by rolling, sliding, diving or "body surfing," and they may also push and balance floating sticks with their noses or drop and retrieve pebbles for minutes at a time. They seem particularly interested in playing on slippery surfaces—they leap onto snow or mud with their forelegs folded close to their bodies for a streamlined toboggan ride. Unlike most members of the weasel family, river otters are social animals, and they will frolic together in the water and take turns sliding down banks.

With their streamlined bodies, rudder-like tails, webbed toes and valved ears and nostrils, river otters are well adapted for aquatic habitats. Even when they emerge from water to clamber over rocks, there is a serpentine appearance to their progression. The large amounts of playtime they seem to have results from their efficiency at catching prey when it is plentiful. Although otters generally cruise along slowly in the water by paddling with all four feet, they can sprint after prey with the ease of a seal whenever hunger strikes. When an otter swims quickly, it propels itself mainly with vertical undulations of its body, hindlegs and tail. Otters can hold their breath for as long as five minutes, and, if so inclined, they could swim the breadth of a small lake without surfacing.

Because of all its activity, the Northern River Otter leaves many signs of its presence when it occupies an area. Its slides are the most obvious and best-known evidence—but be careful not to mistake the slippery beaver trails that are common around beaver ponds for otter slides. Despite its other aquatic tendencies, the otter always defecates on land. Its scat is simple to identify—it is almost always full of fish bones and scales.

A river otter may make extensive journeys across land, even through deep snow. Although a river otter looks clumsy on land, it can easily outrun a human with its humped, loping gait. On slippery surfaces, such as wet grass, snow and ice, the otter glides along, usually on its belly with its legs tucked either back or forward to help steer and push. On flat ground, snowslides are sometimes pitted with blurred footprints where the otter has given itself a push for momentum.

In the past, the Northern River Otter's thick, beautiful, durable fur led to excessive trapping that greatly diminished its continental population. Trapping has

RANGE: The Northern River Otter occurs from near treeline across Alaska and Canada south through forested regions to northern California and northern Utah in the West and Florida and the Gulf Coast in the East. It is rare in the Midwest and Great Plains.

Total Length: 3½–4½ ft.
Tail Length: 12–20 in.
Weight: 10–24 lb.

since been reduced, and the otter seems to be slowly recolonizing parts of North America from which it has been absent for decades. Even in areas where it is known to occur, however, it is infrequently seen, but its marks of playfulness remind us that we are not alone in our capacity for having fun.

DESCRIPTION: This large, weasel-like carnivore has dark brown upperparts that look black when wet. It is paler below, and the throat is often silver gray. The head is broad and flattened, and it has small eyes and ears and prominent, whitish whiskers. The feet are webbed. The long tail is thick at the base and gradually tapers to the tip. The male is the larger gender. This otter does not hibernate, and in winter it still chases fish under the ice.

HABITAT: Year-round, river otters live primarily in or along wooded rivers, ponds and lakes, but they sometimes roam far from water. They are common on the coast, where they eat crabs and saltwater fish and are often mistaken for Sea Otters. They may be active day or night, but they tend to be more nocturnal close to human activity. In winter in the interior of the Pacific Northwest, Northern River Otters almost invariably seek lakes with beaver lodges or bog ponds with steep banks that contain old beaver burrows, through which an otter can enter the water.

DID YOU KNOW?

When a troupe of agile river otters travel single file through the water, their undulating, lithe bodies combine to form a very serpent-like image—perhaps with enough similarity to give rise to the rumors of lake-dwelling sea-monsters.

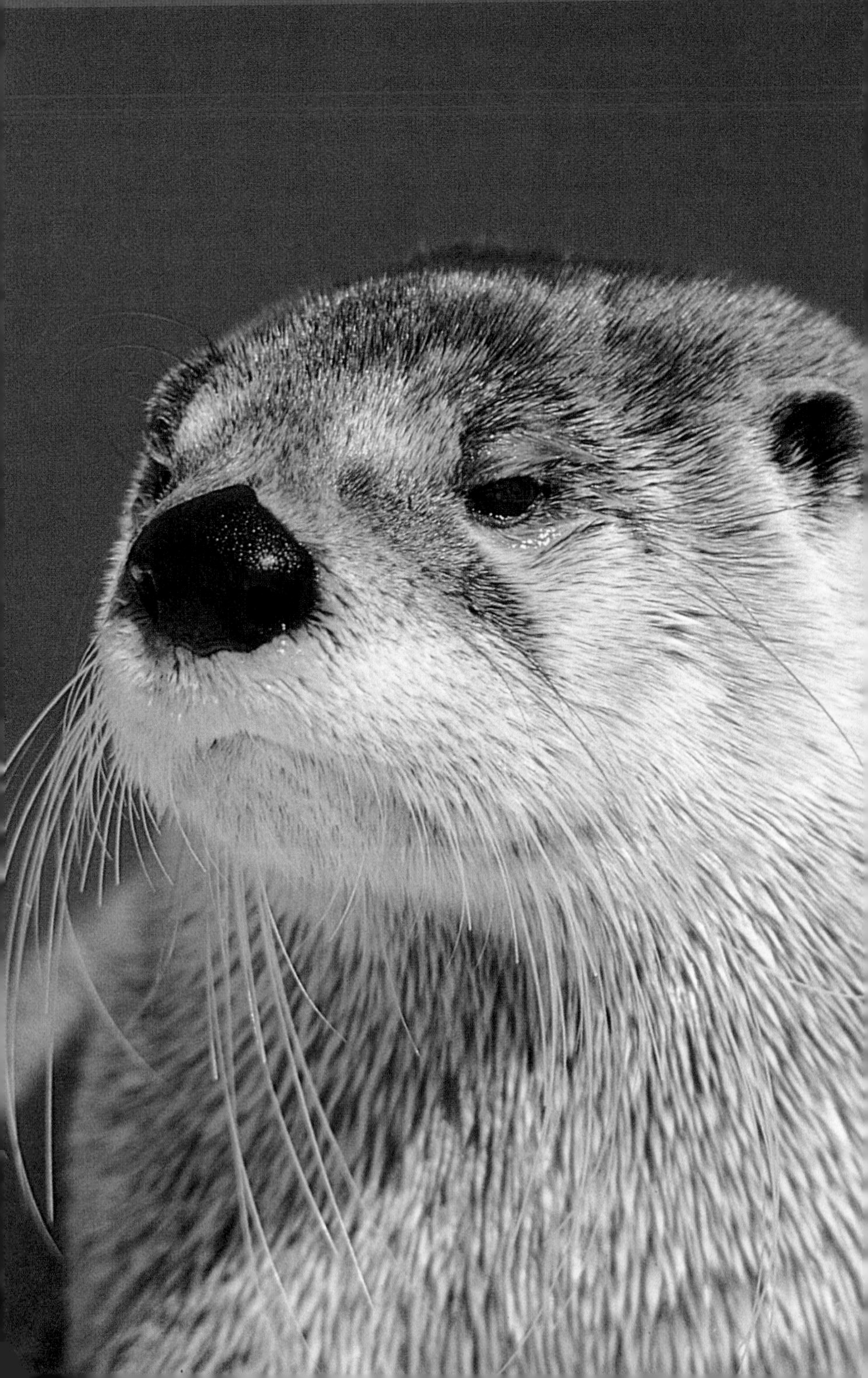

foreprint

loping trail

FOOD: Crayfish, turtles, frogs and fish form the bulk of the diet, but otters occasionally depredate bird nests and eat small mammals such as mice, young muskrats, young beavers, and sometimes even insects and earthworms.

DEN: The permanent den is often in a bank, with both underwater and above-water entrances. During its roamings, an otter rests under roots or overhangs, in hollow logs, in the abandoned burrows of other mammals or in abandoned beaver or muskrat lodges. Natal dens are usually abandoned muskrat, beaver or Woodchuck dens.

YOUNG: The female bears a litter of one to six blind, fully furred young in March or April. The young are 5 oz. at birth. They first leave the den at three to four months and leave their parents at six to seven months. Otters become sexually mature at two years. The mother breeds again soon after her litter is born, but delayed implantation of the embryos puts off the birth until the following spring.

SIMILAR SPECIES: The **Sea Otter** (p. 130) is found only in saltwater, and it rarely comes to shore. The **American Beaver** (p. 226) is stouter and has a wide, flat, hairless, scaly tail. The **American Mink** (p. 116) is smaller, its feet are not webbed, and its tail is cylindrical, not tapered.

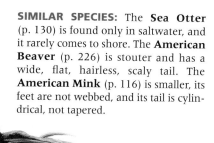

Sea Otter

Sea Otter
Enhydra lutris

For many people, the playful and intelligent Sea Otter is among the most desired animals to see while visiting the coast of northern Washington. This fully aquatic carnivore has such a buoyant body and curious demeanor that watching one is not only comical but mesmerizing. When two Sea Otters are playing, they turn somersaults at the surface and wrestle together as if trying to dunk each other under. When the Sea Otter is resting, it lounges on its back at the surface and rubs its face with curled-up paws, much like cats do when grooming. The Sea Otter is even neighborly, and it regularly hobnobs with the local sea-lions and seals.

To tell the difference between Sea Otters and Northern River Otters (p. 126) on the coast is easy—with the right information. Sea Otters do not venture more than 1 1/4 mi. from shore or into water more than 100 ft. deep. Typically, they stay close to rocky shores with abundant kelp beds. They also prefer open coastline and are therefore rarely seen along inside passages or sheltered waters. River otters, on the other hand, are frequently seen in sheltered waters. Also, river otters are well known for their travels, and an otter seen several miles from shore or one that is swimming long distances from island to island is a Northern River Otter. Any otter seen moving or eating on land is, again, a river otter. Sea Otters are very clumsy on land, and their locomotion is limited to an ungainly, heavy lope, an awkward, slow walk or an even slower, body-dragging slide. Being so limited on land, Sea Otters rarely come out of the water; they may haul out onto rocks to rest during rough or stormy weather.

At night, or for daytime rest, Sea Otters wrap themselves in kelp at the surface. The kelp is attached underwater and prevents the otter from drifting while it sleeps.

The Sea Otter does not have a layer of insulating blubber like other marine mammals; it relies on its high metabolism and thick coat to keep warm. Its full coat is both a blessing and a curse, because in the past the species was hunted for its pelt almost to extinction. Although some populations are slowly increasing, others are in decline and this otter is still listed as threatened. The current decline of some Sea Otter populations is probably attributable to habitat disturbance and Orca predation (see p. 76).

DESCRIPTION: The stout-bodied Sea Otter has a short tail and rounded head. Its slightly flattened tail is no more than

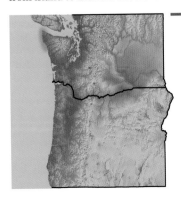

RANGE: Sea Otters are found in scattered populations on the West Coast from southern California to the Aleutian Islands. In Washington, these otters can be found on the northern and western coast of the Olympic Peninsula.

Total Length: 30–65 in.
Tail Length: 10–16 in.
Total Weight: 50–100 lb.

one-third the length of its body. Its fur may be a variety of colors, including light brown, reddish brown, yellowish gray or nearly black, and it is very thick, especially on the throat and chest. It has two "pockets," each formed from a fold of skin between its chest and each underarm. Often its head is lighter than the body; in old males the head may be nearly white. Its tiny ears may appear pinched, but they are otherwise inconspicuous. All four feet are webbed, and the hindfeet resemble flippers. Male Sea Otters are larger than females.

HABITAT: This species lives almost its entire life in shallow coastal waters, favoring areas of kelp beds or reefs with nearby or underlying rocks.

FOOD: The Sea Otter feeds primarily on sea urchins, crustaceans, shellfish and fish. An otter dives underwater for up to five minutes and returns to the surface with its prey and a stone, using the pockets of skin that run from its chest to its underarms to carry its load. One otter was seen unloading six urchins and three oysters from its "cargo holds." To unload its pockets and eat, the otter rests on its back. It places the stone on its chest and uses it as an anvil on which to bash the shell of the urchin, shellfish or crustacean repeatedly until it breaks, exposing the flesh inside. Unlike the Northern River Otter, the Sea Otter does not come onto shore to eat its meal.

DID YOU KNOW?

Sea Otters caught in oil spills have extremely low chances of survival. The oil slicks their coat and destroys the insulating and waterproofing qualities of the fur.

YOUNG: Mating occurs in the water, usually in late summer. The female gives birth to one pup 6½ to 9 months later, a gestation that probably includes a period of delayed implantation. On rare occasions, a female has two pups. She gives birth in the water, and to nurse her young she floats on her back and allows the pup to sit on her chest. The pup also plays and naps on its mother's chest. It is weaned at one year, but it may stay with its mother for several more months, even if she gives birth again. If the mother senses danger, such as an approaching shark or Orca, she will hold her pup under her forelegs and dive into a kelp bed until the danger passes.

walking trail   foreprint

SIMILAR SPECIES: The **Northern River Otter** (p. 126) has a longer tail and hindlegs that are not flipper-like; it is, almost invariably, any otter seen on land. **Seals** and **sea-lions** (pp. 140–53) have different body shapes, and their forelegs are flippers instead of paws.

Northern River Otter

Ringtail

Bassariscus astutus

With the face of a fox, the body of a weasel, the tail of a lemur, the claws of a cat and the eyes of an owl, the striking Ringtail is one of the most unique animals in the region. Such mythical descriptions are perhaps the best way to describe the Ringtail, because it seems to have many of the best qualities of other animals. Less obvious, it also has extraordinary dexterity, keen hearing and acute eyesight, all of which contribute to it being a superb nighttime hunter. Although seeing the Ringtail in the wild is a memorable experience, it is not common in our region and can only be seen in extreme southwestern Oregon.

The Ringtail is seldom seen by people because it forages almost exclusively at night. It hunts with a style similar to that of cats. It waits in ambush, and as unsuspecting prey approaches it readies itself and pounces onto the animal. The Ringtail tries to knock its prey off balance and pin it down to deliver a fatal bite to the neck. This hunting style and the Ringtail's impressive mousing skill are responsible for its alternate common name, Cacomistle. This name is derived from the language of the Mexican Nahuatl people; it means "half mountain lion." Unlike the Mountain Lion, however, the Ringtail is quite small and hunts mainly rodents, reptiles and amphibians.

Occasionally, a Ringtail is seen in the headlights of a car, particularly where roads pass over streams and rivers in southwestern Oregon. It is also well known for sneaking into camps and backyards and carrying off food items. The Ringtail is remarkably surreptitious, because it seems to equally excel in secrecy as it does in light-footed nimbleness. A Ringtail uses its semi-retractile, cat-like claws to cling onto almost sheer surfaces, and it can scale trees or nearly vertical cliffs to get at bird nests, reptiles and rodents.

ALSO CALLED: Cacomistle, Miner's Cat, Ring-tailed Cat, Civet Cat.

DESCRIPTION: Looking like a slender, big-eared, fox-faced cat, the Ringtail is gray or yellowish gray above and buff beneath. Its most noticeable characteristic is the long, bushy tail that is alternately banded black and white. This extremely agile animal almost appears to flow through the rocky terrain it inhabits.

HABITAT: The Ringtail generally occupies rocky slopes, cliffs and canyons in the southern Rockies, usually near

RANGE: Ringtails occur from southern Oregon east to southern Wyoming and south into southern Mexico.

Total Length: 24–32 in.
Tail Length: 12–17 in.
Weight: 1¾–2½ lb.

water. It has been found as high as 9000 ft.

FOOD: The omnivorous Ringtail eats insects and other invertebrates, small mammals, reptiles, amphibians, bird eggs and nestlings, carrion and fruit.

DEN: The den, which has a tiny entrance, is generally found in rocky debris or in natural caves, but sometimes a hollow tree or the space beneath an abandoned building is used.

YOUNG: After mating in late February or March, one to five (usually three to four) blind, helpless, 1-oz. babies are born, usually in May, but sometimes as late as July. Their eyes and ears open and the teeth erupt when they are one month old. At this time, they also switch from a milk diet to animal food brought in by both parents. The mother trains her offspring to hunt, and they disperse when they reach adult size by early winter. Ringtails are sexually mature before their first birthdays.

SIMILAR SPECIES: Only the **Northern Raccoon** (p. 136) has a banded tail like that of the Ringtail, but the raccoon is much stockier and sports a humped back.

DID YOU KNOW?

In remote mining operations, miners found the Ringtail's superb mousing ability so necessary that they put out food to encourage these nocturnal predators. Although cats are famous mousers, the Ringtail is better still.

Northern Raccoon
Procyon lotor

The Northern Raccoon is famous for its black bandit mask and ringed tail. The mask suits the raccoon, because it is well known as a looter of people's gardens, cabins, campsites and, yes, even garbage cans. A raccoon is likely to investigate tasty bits of food and any shiny object it finds. For all its roguish behavior, however, the Northern Raccoon has never been associated with ferociousness or savagery—it is mainly a playful and docile animal unless it is cornered or threatened. Testing a raccoon's ferocity is an unnecessary and simple-minded act, and raccoons have been known to wound and even kill attacking dogs.

Raccoons are among the most frequently encountered wild carnivores in many parts of the region. When raccoons are seen, which is usually at night, they quickly bound away, effectively evading flashlight beams and slipping into burrows or climbing to tree retreats. Should their sanctuary be found, raccoons remain still at a safe distance, waiting for the invasive experience to end.

Northern Raccoons tend to frequent muddy environments, a characteristic that allows people to find their diagnostic tracks along the edges of wetlands and waterbodies. Like bears (see pp. 154–61) and humans, raccoons walk on their heels, so they leave unusually large tracks for their body size. They will methodically circumnavigate wetlands in the hopes of finding duck nests or unwary amphibians upon which to dine.

The way that raccoons typically feel their way through the world has long been recognized. In fact, our word "raccoon" is derived from the Algonquian name for this animal, *aroughcoune,* which means "he scratches with his hands." One of the best-known characteristics of the Northern Raccoon is its habit of dunking its food in water before eating it. It had long been thought that the raccoon was washing its food—the scientific name *lotor* is Latin for "washer"—but biologists now believe that a raccoon's sense of touch is enhanced by water, and that it is actually feeling for inedible bits to discard.

Long, cold winters are an ecological barrier to the dispersal of this animal because it does not hibernate and so requires year-round food availability. Over the past century, however, raccoons have been moving into colder climes, perhaps because of increasing human habitation in these areas. When raccoons first appeared in Winnipeg, Manitoba, in the 1950s, many people

RANGE: The Northern Raccoon occurs from southern Canada south through most of the U.S. and Mexico. It is absent from parts of the Rocky Mountains, central Nevada, Utah and Arizona.

Total Length: 26–38 in.
Tail Length: 7½–16 in.
Weight: 12–31 lb.

were quite surprised and took them to the local zoo, thinking they were escapees rather than a new species of urban "wildlife."

DESCRIPTION: The coat is blackish to brownish gray overall, with lighter, grayish-brown underparts. The bushy tail, with its four to six alternating blackish rings on a yellowish-white background, makes the raccoon one of the most recognizable North American carnivores. A black "mask" is across the eyes, bordered by white "eyebrows" and a mostly white snout, and a strip of white fur separates the upper lip from the nose. The ears are relatively small. Northern Raccoons are capable of producing a wide variety of vocalizations: they can purr, growl, snarl, scream, hiss, trill, whinny and whimper.

HABITAT: Raccoons are most often found near streams, lakes and ponds.

They are not typically found high in the mountains because they favor montane woodlands.

FOOD: The Northern Raccoon fills the role of medium-sized omnivore in the food web. Besides eating fruits, nuts, berries and insects, it avidly seeks out and eats clams, frogs, fish, eggs, young birds and rodents. Just as a bear does, the raccoon consumes vast amounts of food in fall to build a large fat reserve that will help sustain it over winter.

DEN: The den is often located in a hollow tree, but raccoons are increasingly

DID YOU KNOW?

Raccoons have thousands of nerve endings in their "hands" and "fingers." It is an asset they constantly put to use, probing under rocks and in crevices for food.

using sites beneath abandoned buildings or under discarded construction materials. In the foothills, a den can sometimes be found in rock crevices, where grasses or leaves carried in by the female may cover the floor.

YOUNG: After about a two-month gestation, the female bears two to seven (typically four) young in late spring. The young weigh just 2 oz. at birth. Their eyes open at about three weeks, and when they are six to seven weeks old they begin to feed outside the den. At first, the mother carries her young about by the nape of the neck, as a cat carries kittens. About a month later, she starts taking them on extended nightly feeding forays. Some young disperse in the fall, but others remain until their mother forces them out when she needs room for her next litter.

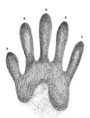

walking trail

foreprint

Ringtail

SIMILAR SPECIES: The **Ringtail** (p. 134) lacks the black mask, has a longer and bushier tail, and is slimmer and more weasel-like. The **American Badger** (p. 122) could possibly be confused with a Raccoon, but a badger is much squatter; its facial markings are vertically oriented, unlike the horizontal "mask" of a raccoon; and its shorter, thinner tail doesn't have the raccoon's distinctive rings.

Harbor Seal
Phoca vitulina

Inquisitive Harbor Seals are well-known residents of the western coast. These seals bespeckle the rocky coastline at almost any time of day throughout the year. They bask on rocks either alone or in large groups, and beach-goers often see them on rocky islets close to shore. Most Harbor Seals are timid and will dive if approached, but others are accustomed to the presence of humans and may frequent waters near marinas and large piers.

Harbor Seals are frequently referred to as sociable or gregarious, but this perception is not entirely true. Although many seals may bask on rocks together, they pay very little attention to their neighbors and seldom interact. Only during the pupping season is there interaction, and it is primarily between females. Mothers with newborn pups may congregate in a "nursery" in shallow water where the pups can sleep. These nursery groups are not truly social; they are formed solely as a protective measure against possible predation. While most of the females and pups sleep, some are likely to be awake and watchful for danger.

The same is true for hauled-out seals. Where several seals are together, chances are good that there is always at least one individual awake and wary of an approaching Orca (p. 76) or other threat.

Harbor Seals cannot sleep at the surface like sea-lions (pp. 149–53) and Sea Otters (p. 130). During the day, they can sleep underwater in shallow coastal water by resting vertically just above the bottom. Young pups commonly rest in this manner. They can go without breathing for nearly 30 minutes, and

RANGE: Harbor Seals are found along the northern coasts of North America, Europe and Asia. They inhabit the entire coast from Alaska to California.

Total Length: 4–6 ft.
Tail Length: 3½–4⅜ in.
Total Weight: 110–310 lb.

though they sometimes wake up to breathe, they frequently rise to the surface and take a breath without awakening, and then sink back to the bottom. At night when the tide is out, they sleep high and dry in their preferred haul-out site. They frequently rest with their heads and rear flippers lifted above the rock. Along the Oregon coast, Harbor Seals can usually be seen sleeping on offshore rocks during the day.

Harbor Seals tend to be wary of humans, and if you approach them they are likely to dive immediately into the water. On the other hand, many kayakers and boaters have enjoyed watching inquisitive individuals that approach their boats for a better look. This kind of experience is controlled by the seal; if it wants to see you, it will come closer. If the seal is afraid of you, it will leave. Do not approach a seal that has tried to flee you, because it can cause unnecessary stress to the animal.

DESCRIPTION: A Harbor Seal is typically dark gray or brownish gray with light, blotchy spots or rings. The reverse color pattern is also common— light gray or nearly white with dark spots. The undersides are generally lighter than the back. The outer coat is composed of stiff guard hairs about ³/₈ in. long, and this characteristic is what gives seals in this family the name "hair seals." The guard hairs cover an insulating undercoat of sparse curly hair about ¼ in. long. Pups bear a spotted silvery or gray-brown coat at birth. The head is large and round, and there are no visible ears. Each of the short

DID YOU KNOW?

Sometimes these seals follow fish several hundred miles up major rivers; there are even permanent populations in some inland lakes.

front flippers bears long, narrow claws. The male is the larger gender.

HABITAT: This nearshore species is frequently found in bays and estuaries. Common haul-out sites include intertidal sandbars, rocks and rocky shores, and favored spots are used by Harbor Seals generation after generation.

FOOD: Harbor Seals feed primarily on fish, such as rockfish, cod, herring, flounder and salmon. To a lesser extent, they also feed on mollusks, such as clams, squid and octopus, and crustaceans, such as crabs, shrimp and crayfish. Newly weaned pups seem to consume more shrimp and mollusks than do adults. Adult Harbor Seals have been seen taking fish from nets, and some

have even entered fish traps to feed, making a clean getaway afterwards.

YOUNG: The breeding season for Harbor Seals varies geographically. The farther north a population, the later the breeding and pupping. Gestation lasts 10 months, and a single pup is born between April and August. The pups are weaned at four to six weeks—after they have tripled their birth weight on their mothers' milk, which is more than 50 percent fat. Within a few days of weaning their pups, females mate again. Harbor Seals become sexually mature at three to seven years. Captive seals have lived more than 35 years, though the typical life span for males is 20 years and for females 30 years.

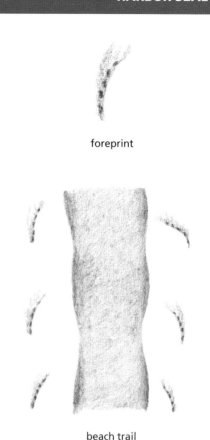

foreprint

beach trail

SIMILAR SPECIES: The **Northern Fur Seal** (p. 146) and the **sea-lions** (pp. 148–53) are usually larger and have long, hairless hindflippers that can rotate under the body to support their weight. As well, they have longer muzzles, small pinnae and more dog-like faces than the Harbor Seal. The **Northern Elephant Seal** (p. 144) is much larger and has a distinctively large snout.

Northern Fur Seal

Northern Elephant Seal
Mirounga angustirostris

The enormous Northern Elephant Seal is one of the largest of all seals. Only its southern hemisphere counterpart, the Southern Elephant Seal (*M. leonina*), is slightly larger.

Elephant seals are famous for their incredible diving capabilities. When they dive for food, they can remain underwater for a maximum of two hours and reach depths below 4800 ft. Of mammals, only the Sperm Whale (*Physeter macrocephalus*) and some of the beaked whales can dive deeper or longer than this.

Northern Elephant Seals are also known for their long migrations—two per year. Each year, a male Northern Elephant Seal may cover 13,000 mi. and spend more than 250 days at sea. Sometime between December and March the adults arrive at sandy beaches in California or Mexico, where females give birth and mate. Afterwards, the adults and the young of the year depart for good feeding waters. Adult males and some juveniles may venture as far north as the Gulf of Alaska and the Aleutian Islands, where they feast on the abundant sea life. Most females and young of the year do not travel quite as far; they prefer feeding in waters between 40° N and 45° N.

After feeding for two to five months, Northern Elephant Seals return to the sandy shores of Mexico and California to molt, sometime between April and August. When elephant seals molt, they shed the short, dense, yellowish-gray pelage along with large patches of old skin. During both the mating and molting seasons, elephant seals fast and lose up to 36 percent of their body weight. After the molting season, they once again venture out to food-rich waters to replenish their bodies before mating.

Commercial harvest for oil during the heavy whaling years reduced the number of Northern Elephant Seals to somewhere between 100 and 1000 individuals, with local populations completely extirpated. These seals are now fully protected under the Marine Mammal Protection Act, and their numbers have increased dramatically. More sightings off the coast of Washington and Oregon are now being reported.

DESCRIPTION: The sheer size of the Northern Elephant Seal gives away its identity. If you have any doubt, however, a closer look at its nose will confirm it. Both sexes of this large seal have a nose that extends past the mouth, but an adult male has a pendulous, inflatable, foot-long snout that resembles a trunk. This seal is mainly gray or light brown in color, with similarly colored

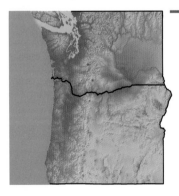

RANGE: These enormous seals are found from coastal Baja California to the Gulf of Alaska. They probably disperse within a few hundred miles from the coast during the non-breeding season.

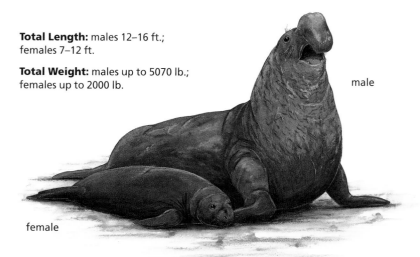

Total Length: males 12–16 ft.; females 7–12 ft.

Total Weight: males up to 5070 lb.; females up to 2000 lb.

male

female

sparse hair. Its hindflippers appear to be lobed on either side and have reduced claws. The tough skin of the male's neck and chest is covered with creases, scars and wrinkles, a feature absent in females. Pups are born black but molt to silver at one month.

HABITAT: The Northern Elephant Seal lives in the temperate waters off the West Coast. It migrates between northern feeding waters and southern breeding and molting beaches twice a year. During the breeding and molting seasons, the Northern Elephant Seal hauls out onto sandy beaches. It does not haul out onto rocks, but it may cross over rocks if necessary to reach a sandy beach. This seal rarely hauls out during the feeding season; instead, it rests at the surface of the water and can stay offshore for weeks at a time.

FOOD: Northern Elephant Seals feed on a variety of sea creatures, including squid, octopus, small sharks, rays, pelagic red crabs and large fish. Adult males feed on larger prey than do females and pups.

YOUNG: The breeding range for this species includes only the southernmost parts of the Oregon coast, California and Baja. These seals are polygamous, but they are not strongly territorial. During the breeding season from December to March, males arrive on shore first and battle fiercely for status in the social hierarchy; a high status means they can have a large harem. The females come to shore a couple of weeks after the males, and within a few days each gives birth to a pup conceived in the previous breeding season. Gestation is 11 months, and nursing takes place for no more than one month, during which time the mothers fast. Just a few days before their pups are to be weaned, the females mate, and then, after weaning, they leave. Females are sexually mature at 2 to 5 years, but males cannot win a harem until they are 9 or 10 years old.

SIMILAR SPECIES: The **Harbor Seal** (p. 140) and **sea-lions** (pp. 148–53) in the region are much smaller, and none have the distinctive snout of the Northern Elephant Seal.

DID YOU KNOW?

When on land, Northern Elephant Seals are very noisy—the males produce a series of loud, rattling snorts, and the females make sounds resembling monstrous belches.

Northern Fur Seal
Callorhinus ursinus

Completely at home in the ocean, the Northern Fur Seal almost never comes to shore, except during its breeding season. The rest of the year, this seal is pelagic off the coast of Washington and Oregon and neighboring regions.

In general, these seals are not gregarious; they are either alone or in a group of no more than three individuals. Even during the breeding season, when large numbers come together on rocky islands, interaction is limited to courtship and mating behavior. The bulls savagely defend their territories, and though the females are less aggressive, they still keep to themselves. When the females have finished nursing their young, they depart the rocky shores and leave the pups to fend for themselves. Many pups die of disease within the first month or two after birth, but many of those that make it to weaning will survive even though they never see their mothers again.

The Northern Fur Seal travels more at sea than almost any other seal or sealion; only the Northern Elephant Seal (p. 144) covers more miles each year. A Northern Fur Seal tallies about 6000 mi. of travel each year, which includes the distance it covers feeding at sea and its migrations to and from breeding islands.

DESCRIPTION: The Northern Fur Seal has a small head with long whiskers, small external ears, large eyes and a short, pointed nose. Its tail is very short, but the flippers are extremely large in relation to the size of the body. When the seal is wet, it is sleek and black. When it is dry, the male is mostly dark grayish black, and the female shows a brownish or reddish throat and often some silvery-gray underparts. Adult males have a thickened neck and are more than twice the weight of females. Newborn pups are black, and male pups are larger than female pups.

HABITAT: Northern Fur Seals are pelagic for 7 to 10 months of the year. They come ashore only to breed, mainly on rocky beaches of the Pribilof and Commander islands.

FOOD: Northern Fur Seals feed mainly on squid, along with herring, capelin and pollack, up to 10 in. long. Almost all feeding takes place at night, when fish are closer to the surface. These seals may dive in search of food; the maximum recorded dive depth is 755 ft., but most seals forage at depths of 230 ft. or less.

YOUNG: Males come to shore in late May and June and battle to establish

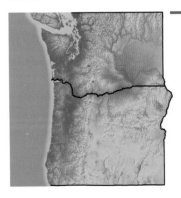

RANGE: This wide-ranging species is found from California up the Pacific Coast and across the North Pacific to Japan.

Total Length: males 6–7½ ft.;
females 3½–5 ft.

Tail Length: 2 in.

Total Weight: males 330–620 lb.;
females 84–120 lb.

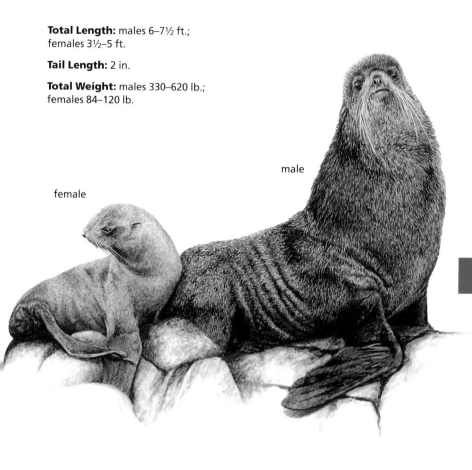

male

female

their territories. Females come to shore in mid-June or July, and within two days they give birth to a pup conceived the previous summer. Mating occurs 8 to 10 days later. The pup nurses for four or five months.

SIMILAR SPECIES: The **Harbor Seal** (p. 140) is a true seal that does not rotate its hindflippers under its body, and it usually has spots. The **Northern Sea-Lion** (p. 148) is larger, and the **California Sea-Lion** (p. 152), which is usually larger, has relatively shorter hindflippers.

DID YOU KNOW?

When this seal is resting in the water, it often keeps one hindflipper straight up and waving in the wind. No one knows why, but it does make the animal easy to spot from a boat.

Northern Sea-Lion
Eumetopias jubatus

The large Northern Sea-Lion is a familiar sight to many people who frequent coastal areas. This gregarious creature is usually seen in groups of hundreds or thousands. Its social system is more advanced than that of the Harbor Seal (p. 140), the other common pinniped on the coast. For example, when a group of sea-lions is feeding, all individuals dive at the same time and surface together as well. This behavior means that no one sea-lion dives first and scares the fish away, ruining the feeding opportunities for the others.

During the breeding and pupping season, thousands of sea-lions congregate at rookery sites used generation after generation. Several rookeries can be found in Oregon, but there are no known rookeries in Washington. In a rookery, mature bulls make a roaring sound, and when this roaring is combined with the grumbles and growls of the others, the resulting cacophony can be heard almost a mile away. Outside the pupping season, the "bachelors," the young of the year, some barren cows and the odd mature bull form loose colonies, feeding together and otherwise interacting.

Adult male Northern Sea-Lions are the largest of the eared seals. There is great sexual dimorphism, with adult males three to four times as heavy as the females. A large difference in weight is characteristic of pinnipeds with territorial males that hold a harem. The females form loose aggregations with their pups within a male's territory, and they are far faster and more agile than the males.

Northern Sea-Lions are well known for their curiosity and playfulness. They are very active, sometimes leaping clear out of the water and occasionally throwing rocks back and forth. They have even been seen jumping across surfaced whales. Their smaller cousins, the California Sea-Lions (p. 152), share this playfulness and are commonly seen performing tricks in marine park shows.

For many years, sea-lions were killed because it was believed that they fed on commercially valuable fish. Research indicates, however, that they feed opportunistically on any readily available fish—commonly octopus, squid and "scrap" fish, such as herring and greenling. Although intentional killing has decreased, sea-lion populations have declined by as much as 80 percent of historic numbers. The causes of this decline are unknown.

A unique characteristic of sea-lions is that they frequently swallow rocks as large as 5 in. across. Although no one

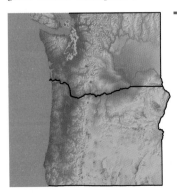

RANGE: Northern Sea-Lions are found near shore from southern California up to Alaska and the Aleutian Islands and across to Siberia and Japan.

Total Length: males 8½–11 ft.;
females 6–6½ ft.

Total Weight: males up to 2200 lb.;
females 600–790 lb.

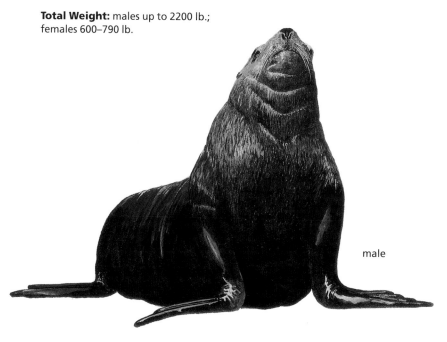

male

knows for sure, the most likely explanation is that, as in birds, the stones help pulverize food inside their stomachs. Sea-lions' teeth are ill suited for chewing, and these mammals regularly swallow large chunks of meat and whole fish.

ALSO CALLED: Steller Sea-Lion.

DESCRIPTION: Adults are light buff to reddish brown when dry and brown to nearly black when wet. Their fur is underlaid by a thick blubber layer. Adult males develop a huge neck that supports a mane of long, coarse hair. Females are sleek, without the massive neck. During the breeding season, adult males evicted from the colony often bear huge cuts and tears on the neck

and chest, reminders of the vicious battles waged over a territory. The hind-flippers are drawn forward under the body and—like all eared seals—Northern Sea-Lions can jump and clamber up steep rocky slopes at an amazing rate.

HABITAT: Northern Sea-Lions live mainly in coastal waters near rocky shores, and they are seldom found more than 160 ft. from the water. During the breeding season, they occupy

DID YOU KNOW?

Although Northern Sea-Lions are saltwater mammals, they have been known to swim up major rivers in search of lamprey and salmon.

rocky, boulder-strewn beaches or rock ledges. Sea-lions may rest in the water in a vertical position with their heads above the surface. They prefer to stay in the water during inclement weather, but when the sun shines they usually haul out and bask on the rocks.

FOOD: These sea-lions feed primarily on blackfish, greenling, rockfish and herring. Others foods include squid, octopus, shrimp, clams, salmon and bottom fish. Males do not eat for one to two months while defending a territory.

YOUNG: Males come to shore in early May and battle to establish their territories. Females come to shore in mid-May or June, and within three days give birth to a pup conceived during the previous summer. Females form loose aggregations with their pups in a male's territory, and mating occurs within two weeks after the pups are born. Pups nurse for about one year, but some have been known to nurse as long as three years. Females may live to be 30 years old and are sexually mature at three to seven years. Males probably do not breed before age 10.

Northern Fur Seal

SIMILAR SPECIES: The **Northern Fur Seal** (p. 146) and the more common **California Sea-Lion** (p. 152) are both smaller. The **Northern Elephant Seal** (p. 144) is much larger and has a distinctively long snout. The **Harbor Seal** (p. 140) is much smaller and lacks the ability to rotate its hindflippers under its body.

California Sea-Lion
Zalophus californianus

The famous California Sea-Lion has received our admiration, but it has also suffered our persecution. Each year, thousands of children and adults watch in awe as these sea-lions flip in the air and perform stunts with hoops and big red beach balls. Sea-lions are major attractions at marine aquariums around the world, and, at best, these performances leave lasting impressions of the talent and special intrigue of our fellow mammals. Unfortunately, these good feelings are not always shared by the animal, and many sea-lions in captivity die of health problems or accidents.

In the wild, females and young pups frequently play and cavort, and they are even known to play with other species. Flinging a piece of kelp around in the water and hitting the wild waves for some good body surfing are just part of the daily routine. A sea-lion's true grace is apparent underwater, where it turns sinuous loops and spirals in an aquatic ballet that belies its terrestrial ancestry.

Many visitors to coastal areas are rewarded with sightings of this sea-lion, and lucky individuals have even had personal encounters. Kayakers and even swimmers have been approached by juveniles and females that want to play.

Despite being much adored by children and tourists, California Sea-Lions in the wild often receive harsh treatment. Because these sea-lions potentially feed on many fish valuable to fisheries, there is widespread interaction between them and the fishermen. California Sea-Lions, like all other marine mammals, are protected by law, and killing them is punishable. In the 19th and early 20th centuries, California Sea-Lions were killed in great numbers for oil (from their blubber) and hides. Later in the 20th century, they were also killed for the pet food industry. This kind of killing is now unlawful, but each year thousands of sea-lions still die. Most of these deaths are attributable to fishing nets, discarded net material and fibrous garbage, all of which entrap and drown sea-lions. Because of intentional and accidental deaths, the California Sea-Lion population is much reduced from historic numbers, and the species may never fully recover.

On the coast of Washington and Oregon, wintering California Sea-Lions may be encountered from August to April. The breeding season lasts from May to July, but the breeding grounds are much further south. Some females may stay near their breeding grounds all year-round, while younger males are more likely to be found at the northern limits of their range during winter.

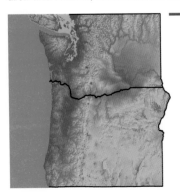

RANGE: This sea-lion inhabits coastal waters of the North Pacific from Mexico to Vancouver Island. There are also good numbers in the Galapagos Islands and three small, isolated populations in the Sea of Japan.

Total Length: males 6½–8 ft.;
females 4½–6½ ft.

Total Weight: males 440–860 lb.;
females 100–250 lb.

feed on commercially valuable and even endangered species of fish.

DESCRIPTION: This sea-lion has a slender, elongated body, a blunt snout and a short but distinct tail. The adult male is brown, and the female is tan with the chest and abdomen slightly darker. An adult male develops a noticeably raised forehead that helps distinguish it from the Northern Sea-Lion. The front flippers are long and bear distinct claws. California Sea-Lions have coarse guard hair that covers only a small amount of underfur. They are a noisy bunch—the males produce a honking bark, the cows wail and the pups bleat.

HABITAT: California Sea-Lions are normally seen in coastal waters around islands with rocky or sandy beaches. Preferred haul-out sites include sandy or boulder-strewn beaches below rocky cliffs. In some places they occupy sea caverns. They tend to avoid the rocky islets preferred by Northern Sea-Lions.

FOOD: These sea-lions eat a wide variety of foods, including at least 50 species of fish and many types of squid, octopus and other mollusks. In some regions, such as Seattle, sea-lions are known to

YOUNG: Males establish their territories on rocky or sandy beaches in May, June or July in warmer regions south of Oregon. Females arrive on the breeding grounds in May or June. If a female conceived the previous year, she will give birth to a pup, and within one month she mates again. Most pups are weaned by eight months, but a few may nurse for a year or more. Pups begin eating fish before they are weaned.

SIMILAR SPECIES: The **Northern Sea-Lion** (p. 148) is larger and paler. The **Northern Fur Seal** (p. 146) is smaller and often more reddish on its undersides. The **Northern Elephant Seal** (p. 144) is much larger and has a distinctive snout. The **Harbor Seal** (p. 140) is smaller and, like the Northern Elephant Seal, lacks the ability to rotate its hind-flippers under its body.

DID YOU KNOW?

The name "pinniped," which refers to all seals and sea-lions, literally means "feather-footed"—an apt description of their fan-shaped flippers.

American Black Bear
Ursus americanus

The black bear, an inhabitant of forests throughout Washington and Oregon, is often feared by city dwellers who come to state and national parks to appreciate the scenery and wilderness. People who are more experienced with the wild forest and with animal behavior tend to regard the black bear with a healthy respect, but perhaps less apprehension.

Contrary to popular belief and its classification as a carnivore, the black bear does not readily hunt larger animals. It is primarily an opportunistic forager and feeds on what is easy and abundant—usually berries, horsetails, other vegetation and insects, though it won't turn up its nose at fish, young fawns or another carnivore's kill. A black bear sow with young cubs is the most likely to attack young Moose (p. 52), deer (pp. 44–51) and Elk (p. 40).

In the past few decades, the ubiquitous dandelion has become increasingly abundant in the mountains along roadsides and swaths cut into the forests, especially in central interior regions. As a result, black bears are now more frequently seen along roadsides, and if a bear glances up at your passing car, it will betray its new favorite food. With dandelion leaves sticking out of its mouth and the puffy seeds stuck over its face and muzzle, the bear looks like a little kid covered in its favorite ice cream. Unfortunately, together with an increase in bear sightings along roadsides, vehicle collisions that can claim bears' lives are also increasing.

Within its territory, a bear has favorite feeding places and follows well-traveled paths to these sites. Keep in mind that the trails you hike in the mountains may be used not only by humans, but also by bears en route to lush meadows or rich berry patches.

Normally, black bears are reclusive animals that will flee to avoid contact with humans if they hear them coming. If you surprise a bear, however, back away slowly. In particular, heed its warning of a foot stamp, a throaty "huff" or the champing sound of its teeth. The bear is agitated and probably does not like you, and it is giving you a clear warning to retreat from its territory in respect of its dominance. Many cases of bear attacks occur when these warning signals are not understood by a person who instead remains frozen in place. The bear likely interprets such behavior as a challenge.

One grim threat to bears throughout the world is the illegal trade in body parts. Bear paws and gall bladders have high black-market values, and poaching

RANGE: Across North America, the black bear occurs nearly everywhere there are forests, swamps or shrub thickets. It avoids grasslands and deserts.

Total Length: 4½–6 ft.
Shoulder Height: 3–3¾ ft.
Tail Length: 3–7 in.
Weight: 88–595 lb.

occurs in both Canada and the United States, but fortunately to a lesser extent than elsewhere. As populations of many bears around the world shrink, however, North American bears face an increasing threat. With bear numbers dwindling and black-market values increasing, it is feared that the generally well-protected animals in the mountains may become prime targets of the trade.

DESCRIPTION: The coat is long and shaggy and ranges from black to brown to honey colored. The body is relatively short and stout, and the legs are short and powerful. The large, wide feet have sharp, curved, black claws. The head is large and has a straight profile. The eyes are small, and the ears are short, rounded and erect. The tail is very short. An adult male is about 20 percent larger than a female.

HABITAT: Black bears are primarily forest animals, and their sharp, curved foreclaws enable them to easily climb trees, even as adults. In spring, they often forage in natural or roadside clearings.

FOOD: Away from human influences, up to 95 percent of the black bear's diet is plant material: leaves, buds, flowers, berries, fruits and roots are all consumed. This omnivore also eats animal matter, including bees (and honey) and other insects; even young hoofed mammals may be killed and eaten. Carrion and human garbage are eagerly sought out.

DEN: The den, which is only used during winter, may be in a cave or hollow tree, beneath a fallen log or the roots of a wind-thrown tree, or even in a

DID YOU KNOW?

During its winter slumber, a black bear loses 20 to 40 percent of its body weight. To prepare for winter, the bear must eat thousands of calories a day during late summer and fall.

foreprint

walking trail

haystack. The bear usually carries in a few mouthfuls of grass to lie on during its sleep. It will not eat, drink, urinate or defecate during its time in the den. The hibernation is not deep; instead, it is as if the bear is very groggy or heavily drugged. Rarely, a bear may rouse from this torpor and leave its den on mild winter days.

YOUNG: Black bears mate in June or July, but the embryos do not implant and begin to develop until the sow enters her den in November. The number of eggs that implant seems to be correlated with the female's weight and condition—fat mothers have more cubs. One to five (usually two or three) young are born in January, and they nurse while the sow sleeps. Their eyes open and they become active when they are five to six weeks old. They leave the den with their mother when they weigh $4^1/_2$–$6^3/_4$ lb., usually in April. The sow and her cubs generally spend the next winter together in the den, dispersing the following spring. Black bears typically bear young in alternate years.

Grizzly Bear

SIMILAR SPECIES: The **Grizzly Bear** (p. 158) is generally larger and has a dished-in face, a noticeable shoulder hump and long, brown to ivory-colored, blunt claws. The **Wolverine** (p. 118) looks a little like a very small black bear, but it has a long tail, an arched back and pale side stripes.

Grizzly Bear
Ursus arctos

The mighty Grizzly Bear, more than any other animal, makes camping and traveling in wild areas of northeastern Washington an adventure, not just another picnic. Since before the time of European settlement, Grizzlies have had an almost mythical presence—a kind of fearsome power that can be sensed whenever you venture into Grizzly country. Fueled by a mix of fear and curiosity, visitors to Washington's northern wilderness scan the roadsides and open meadows in hopes of catching a glimpse of this wilderness icon. Most people leave without a personal grizzly experience, but when a bear is sighted, the ensuing excitement is likely greater than that which surrounds any other mountain animal.

Grizzly Bears are indisputably strong: their massive shoulders and skull anchor muscles that are capable of rolling 200-lb. rocks, dragging elk carcasses and crushing some of the most massive ungulate bones. Ironically, Grizzlies do not commonly feed in a manner that requires such brute strength. Instead, their routine and docile foraging is concentrated on roots, berries and grasses.

An adaptable diner, the Grizzly changes its diet from spring through fall to match the availability of foods. For instance, it eats huge quantities of berries when they are available in late summer. A bear swallows many of the berries whole, and its scat often ends up looking like blueberry pie filling or raspberry jam. During this time of feasting, a Grizzly's weight may increase by a pound or more each day, preparing it for the long winter ahead. It will remain active through fall, until the bitter cold of November limits foods and favors sleep.

Although mountain parks and coastal salmon streams boast the highest numbers of bears, the status of Grizzly Bears throughout their range is uncertain. No one can predict their future, but we can increase their chances of survival. Some of the seminal work on Grizzlies dates back to the foundation of conservation biology. In working with these large carnivores, pioneering biologists invented tagging, radio-tracking and other research techniques that have benefited not only the Grizzly, but many other carnivores as well, including the Bengal Tiger (*Panthera tigris*) and the Polar Bear (*U. maritimus*).

ALSO CALLED: Brown Bear.

DESCRIPTION: The usually brownish to yellowish coat typically has

RANGE: In North America, this holarctic species is largely confined to Alaska and northwestern Canada, with montane populations extending south into extreme northern Washington, Idaho, Montana and Wyoming. It formerly ranged much more widely, but Euroamerican settlers extirpated the open-area populations.

Total Length: 6–8½ ft.
Shoulder Height: 3–4 ft.
Tail Length: 3–7 in.
Weight: 240–1160 lb.

white-tipped guard hairs that give it a grizzled appearance (from which the name "grizzly" is derived). Some individuals are completely black; others can be nearly white. The face has a concave (dished) profile. The eyes are relatively small, and the ears are short and rounded. A large hump at the shoulder makes the forequarters higher than the rump in profile. The large, flat paws have long, curved claws; several of the front claws can be nearly 4 in. long.

HABITAT: Originally, most Grizzly Bears were animals of open rangelands, where they used their long claws to dig up roots, bulbs and the occasional burrowing mammal. Although their current range is largely forested, mountain bears often forage on open slopes and in the alpine tundra.

FOOD: Although 70 to 80 percent of a Grizzly's diet is plants, including leaves, stems, flowers, roots and fruits, it eats more animals, including other mammals, fish and insects, than its black cousin does. A Grizzly may dig insects, ground squirrels, marmots and even mice out of the ground. Young hoofed mammals are eagerly sought by sows with cubs, and even large adult cervids and Bighorn Sheep may be attacked and killed. Particularly after it emerges from its winter sleep, a bear is attracted to carrion, which it can smell from 10 mi. away. The Grizzly Bear can eat huge meals of meat: one adult consumed an entire road-killed Elk in four days.

DEN: Most mountain dens are on north- or northeast-facing slopes, in

DID YOU KNOW?

Because an adult Grizzly's long, curved foreclaws are typically blunt from digging, it cannot easily climb trees. If you think you can escape a bear by climbing a tree, however, you better climb high, because some Grizzlies can reach almost 12 ft. up a tree trunk.

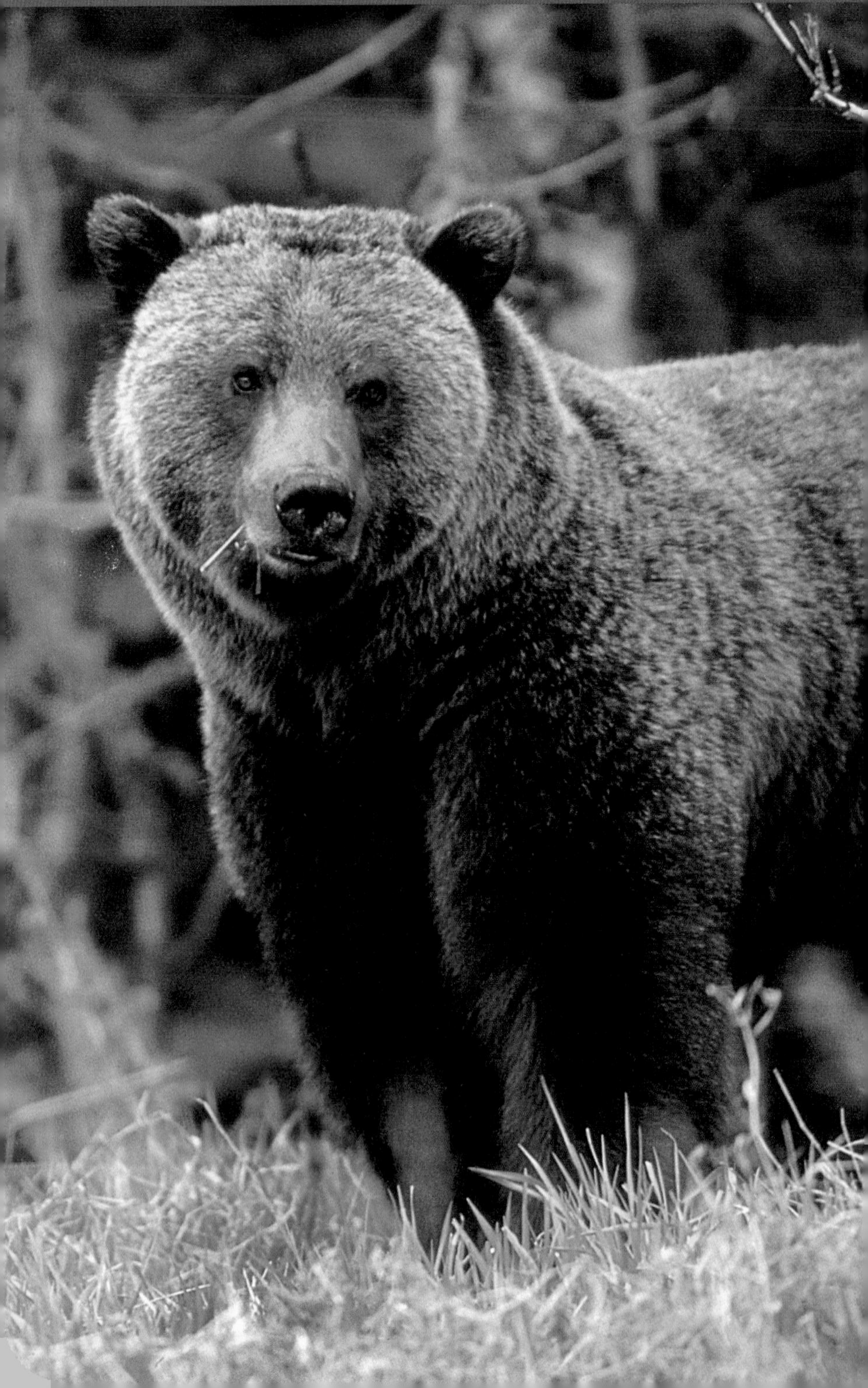

areas where snowmelt does not begin until late spring. The den is usually in a cave, or it is dug into tree roots. The bear enters its den in late October or November, during a heavy snowfall that will cover its tracks. It soon falls asleep and will not eat, drink, urinate or defecate for six months.

YOUNG: A sow has litters in alternate years, typically having her first after her seventh birthday. Grizzlies mate in June or July, but with delayed implantation of the embryo the cubs are not born until some time between January and early March, when the mother is asleep in her den. The one to four (generally two) cubs are born naked, blind and helpless. They nurse and grow while their mother continues to sleep, and they are ready to follow her when she leaves the den in April or May. A sow and her cubs typically den together the following winter.

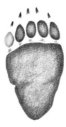

walking trail   foreprint

SIMILAR SPECIES: The **American Black Bear** (p. 154) is generally smaller, is tallest at the rump (it doesn't have a humped shoulder) and has a straight profile and shorter, black, curved claws. The **Wolverine** (p. 118) looks a little like a young bear, but it has a long tail, an arched back and pale side stripes.

American Black Bear

Coyote
Canis latrans

A chorus of yaps, whines, barks and howls complements the darkening skies in wild areas of Washington and Oregon. Although Coyote calls are most intense during late winter and spring, corresponding to courtship, these excited sounds can be heard during suitable weather at any time of the day or year. Often initiated by one animal, many family groups soon join in and the calls pour from the valleys, making it obvious to all that these animals relish joining together and making noise.

Two centuries ago, the early explorers of this continent made frequent references in their journals to foxes and wolves, but they seldom mentioned Coyotes. Coyotes have increased their numbers across North America in the past century in response to the expansion of agriculture and forestry and the reduction of wolf populations. Despite widespread human efforts to exterminate them, they have thrived.

One of the few natural checks on Coyote abundance seems to be the Gray Wolf (p. 166). As the much larger and more powerful canids of the wilderness neighborhood, wolves typically exclude Coyotes from their territories. Prior to the 19th century, the natural condition favored wolves, but changes in Washington and Oregon since then have greatly benefited Coyotes. They are now so widely distributed and comfortable with human development that almost every valley, and even many cities, holds a healthy population.

Because of its relatively small size, the Coyote typically preys on small animals, such as mice, voles, ground squirrels, birds and hares, but it has also been known to kill Bighorn Sheep (p. 32) and deer (pp. 44–51), particularly their young. Although it usually hunts alone, the Coyote occasionally forms packs, especially when it hunts hoofed mammals during winter. The Coyotes may split up, with some waiting in ambush while the others chase the prey toward them, or they may run in relays to tire their quarry; Coyotes, the best runners among the North American canids, typically cruise at 25 to 30 m.p.h.

Coyotes owe their modern-day success to their varied diet, early age of first breeding, high reproductive output and flexible living requirements. They consume carrion throughout the year, but they also feed on such diverse offerings as eggs, mammals, birds and berries. Their variable diet and nonspecific habitat choices allow them to adapt to just about any region of North America.

RANGE: Coyotes are not found in the western third of Alaska, the tundra regions of northern Canada and the extreme southeastern U.S.; their range covers essentially the remainder of North America.

Total Length: 3½–4½ ft.
Shoulder Height: 23–26 in.
Tail Length: 12–16 in.
Weight: 18–44 lb.

DESCRIPTION: Coyotes look like gray, buffy or reddish-gray, medium-sized dogs. The nose is pointed, and there is usually a gray patch between the eyes that contrasts with the rufous top of the snout. The long, bushy tail has a black tip. The underparts are light to whitish. When frightened, a Coyote runs with its tail tucked between its hindlegs. Coyotes in the northern part of the region tend to be considerably larger than those in the south.

HABITAT: Coyotes are found in all terrestrial habitats in North America, except the barren tundra of the far north and the humid southeastern forests. They have greatly expanded their range, in part because of Gray Wolf extirpations, and in part because forest clearing has brought about favorable changes in habitat for Coyotes.

FOOD: Although primarily carnivorous, feeding on squirrels, mice, hares, birds, amphibians and reptiles, Coyotes will sometimes eat cactus fruits, melons, berries and vegetation. Most ranchers

DID YOU KNOW?

Coyotes can, and do, interbreed with domestic dogs. The "coydog" offspring often become nuisance animals, killing domestic livestock and poultry.

foreprint

walking trail

dislike Coyotes because they have been known to take sheep, calves and pigs that are left exposed. They may even attack and consume dogs and cats.

DEN: The den is usually a burrow in a slope, frequently an American Badger or Woodchuck hole that has been expanded to 1 ft. in diameter and about 10 ft. deep. Rarely, Coyotes have been known to den in an abandoned car, a hollow tree trunk or a dense brush pile.

YOUNG: A litter of 3 to 10 (usually 5 to 7) pups is born between late March and late May, after a gestation of about two months. The furry pups are blind at birth. Their eyes open after about 10 days, and they leave the den for the first time when they are three weeks old. Young Coyotes fight with each other and establish dominance and social position at just three to four weeks of age.

Gray Wolf

SIMILAR SPECIES: The **Gray Wolf** (p. 166) is generally larger, with a broader snout, larger ears, much bigger feet and longer legs, and it carries its tail straight back when it runs. The **Red Fox** (p. 170) is generally smaller, much redder, and has a white tail tip and black forelegs. The smaller **Common Gray Fox** (p. 178) has a crest of black hairs on the top of its tail as well as a black spot on each side of the muzzle. Coyote-like **Domestic Dog breeds** generally have more bulging foreheads and usually carry their tails straight back when they run.

Gray Wolf
Canis lupus

For many North Americans, the Gray Wolf represents the apex of wilderness, symbolizing the pure, yet hostile, qualities of all that remains wild. Other people disparage this representation, characterizing wolves as blood-lusting enemies of domestic animals and the ranchers who care for them. Objective opinions about the Gray Wolf are few; caricatures, whether positive or negative, abound.

Perhaps the persecution of wolves over the last few hundred years was not really against *Canis lupus,* but against the salivating wolf-beast that lives only in the wild human imagination. The fear of wolves, without an understanding of their basic nature, resulted in tens of thousands of wolves killed in vengeance of crimes they did not commit. By studying and observing wolves, we demystify the beast and learn acceptance and even admiration for these remarkable creatures.

Observations and behavioral studies of wolves indicate that the social structure of a wolf pack is extremely sophisticated. A pack behaves like a "super organism," cooperatively making it possible for more animals to survive. By hunting together, pack members can catch and subdue much larger prey than if they were acting alone. Members of the pack adhere to a strict social hierarchy, and moments of tension rarely break the orderly communal environment.

A wolf pack can be described in terms of the alpha pair (the top male and female), the subordinate adults, one or more "outcasts" and the pups and immature individuals. Usually, only the alpha animals reproduce, while the other pack members help with bringing food to the pups and defending the group's territory. In most packs, the subordinate adults are non-breeding, though they might mate in spite of the rules, especially if the dominant pair is not paying attention or is otherwise occupied. If there is an outcast in the group, it is often picked on and usually gets just a shred of the good meals. The energetic pups of a wolf pack demand constant attention; they are always ready to pounce on their mother's head or tackle an unsuspecting sibling.

As the pups grow, they develop important skills that will aid them as adults. At the entrance to the den, they make their first attempts at hunting when they swat and bite at beetles and the occasional mouse or vole. These animals, however, do not react in quite the same way as larger prey does, and so the next step in the pups' apprenticeship as

RANGE: Much reduced from historic times, the Gray Wolf is a holarctic species and its North American range currently covers most of Canada and Alaska, except the Canadian Prairies and southern parts of eastern Canada. It extends south into Minnesota and Wisconsin and along the Rocky Mountains into Idaho, Montana and Wyoming.

Total Length: 4½–6½ ft.
Shoulder Height: 26–38 in.
Tail Length: 14–20 in.
Weight: 57–170 lb.

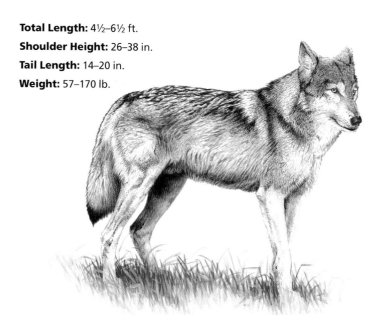

hunters is to watch their parents take down a big meal item such as an Elk.

A wolf pack generally occupies a large territory—usually 100–300 sq. mi.—so individual densities are extremely low. Moreover, because of widespread extermination efforts in the last century, wolves are absent over much of their historic range. Today, in this region, you have a chance of seeing them only in the wilderness of north-eastern Washington. Lone wolves that wander and explore new territory may be encountered further south into Washington and maybe into Oregon, but such individuals do not represent a population.

ALSO CALLED: Timber Wolf.

DESCRIPTION: A Gray Wolf resembles an over-sized, long-legged German Shepherd with extra-large paws. Although typically thought of as being a grizzled-gray color, a wolf's coat can range from coal black to creamy white. Black wolves are most common in dense forests; whitish wolves are char-acteristic of the high Arctic. The bushy tail is carried straight behind the wolf when the wolf runs. In social situations, the height of the tail generally relates to the social status of that individual.

HABITAT: Although wolves formerly occupied grasslands, forests, deserts and tundra, they are now mostly restricted to forests, streamside woodlands and Arctic tundra.

FOOD: Gray Wolves hunt primarily cervids and Bighorn Sheep. Although large mammals typically make up about

---

DID YOU KNOW?

Wolves are capable of many facial expressions, such as pursed lips, smile-like, submissive grins, upturned muzzles, wrinkled foreheads and angry, squinting eyes. Wolves even stick their tongues out at each other, which is a gesture of appeasement or submission.

foreprint

walking trail

80 percent of the diet, wolves also prey on rabbits, mice, nesting birds and carrion when available.

DEN: Wolf dens are usually located on a rise of land near water. Most dens are bank burrows, and they are often made by enlarging the den of a fox or burrowing mammal. Sometimes a rock slide, hollow log or natural cave is used. Sand or soil scratched out of the entrance by the female is usually evident as a large mound. The burrow opening is generally about 23 in. across, and the burrow extends back 6–33 ft. to a dry natal chamber with a floor of packed soil. The beds from which adults can keep watch are generally found above the entrance.

YOUNG: A litter generally contains 5 to 7 pups (with extremes of 3 to 13), which may be of different colors. The newborn pups resemble Domestic Dogs in their development: their eyes open at 9 to 10 days, and they are weaned at 6 to 8 weeks. The pups are fed regurgitated food until they begin to accompany the pack on hunts. A wolf becomes sexually mature a couple of months before its third birthday, but the pack hierarchy largely determines the first incidence of mating.

Coyote

SIMILAR SPECIES: The **Coyote** (p. 162) is smaller, has more pointed ears and has a much more slender snout. A Coyote's bushier tail is always tipped with black, and it holds its tail pointing downward, whereas a wolf holds its tail horizontally. The **Red Fox** (p. 170) is much less than half the size and has a white-tipped tail.

Red Fox
Vulpes vulpes

More than other native canids, the Red Fox has received some favorable representations in literature and modern culture. From *Aesop's Fables* to sexy epithets, the fox is often symbolized as a diabolically cunning, intelligent, attractive and noble animal. Many people favor having foxes nearby because of this species' skill at catching mice. Foxes have a well-deserved nickname, "reynard," from the French word *renard,* which refers to someone who is unconquerable owing to their cleverness. The fox's intelligence, undeniable comeliness and positive impact upon most farmlands have endeared it to many people.

Foxes at work in their natural habitat embody playfulness, roguishness, stealth and drama. Young fox kits at their den wrestle and squabble in determined sibling rivalry. If its siblings are busy elsewhere, a young kit may amuse itself by challenging a plaything, such as a stick or piece of old bone, to a bout of aggressive mock combat. An adult out mousing will sneak up on its rustling prey in the grass and jump stiff-legged into the air, hoping to come down directly atop the unsuspecting rodent. If the fox misses, it stomps and flattens the grass with its forepaws, biting in the air to try to catch the mouse.

Usually, the fox wins, but, if not, it will slip away with stately composure as though the display of undignified abandon never occurred.

Oddly enough, Red Foxes exhibit both feline dexterity and a feline hunting style. Foxes hunt using an ambush style, or they creep along in a crouched position, ready to pounce on unsuspecting prey. Another un-dog-like characteristic is the large gland above the base of the tail, which gives off a strong musk somewhat resembling the smell of a skunk. This scent is what allows foxhounds to easily track their quarry. Foxes are territorial, and the males, like other members of the dog family, mark their territorial boundaries with urine.

Despite its vast range, the Red Fox is rarely seen. Its primarily nocturnal activity is probably the main reason, but a fox's keen senses of sight, hearing and smell enhance its elusive nature. Winter may be the best time to see a fox: it is more likely to be active during the day, and its color stands out when it is mousing in a snow-covered field. The Red Fox has adapted to human activity, and many of them live in agricultural areas and even in cities. In the northern and mountain wilderness, this diminutive carnivore lives on mice and carcasses in the shadow of the Gray Wolf (p. 166).

RANGE: In North America, this holarctic species occurs throughout most of Canada and the U.S., except for the high Arctic, northwestern B.C. and much of the western U.S. The most widely distributed carnivore in the world, it also occurs in Europe, Asia, north Africa and as an introduced species in Australia.

Total Length: 35–44 in.
Shoulder Height: 15–16 in.
Tail Length: 14–17 in.
Weight: 8–15 lb.

DESCRIPTION: This small, slender, dog-like fox has an exceptionally bushy, long tail. Its upperparts are usually a vivid reddish orange, with a white chest and belly, but there are many color variations: a Coyote-colored phase; the "cross fox," which has darker hairs along the back and across the shoulder blades; and the "silver fox," which is mostly black with silver-tipped hairs. In all color phases, the tail has a white tip and the backs of the ears and fronts of the forelegs are black.

HABITAT: The Red Fox prefers open habitats mixed with brushy shelter year-round. It avoids extensive areas of dense coniferous forest with heavy snowfall.

FOOD: This opportunistic feeder usually stalks its prey and then pounces on it or captures it after a short rush. In winter, small rodents, rabbits and birds make

---

DID YOU KNOW?

The Red Fox's signature feature—its white-tipped, bushy tail—provides balance when the fox is running or jumping, and during cold weather a fox wraps its tail over its face.

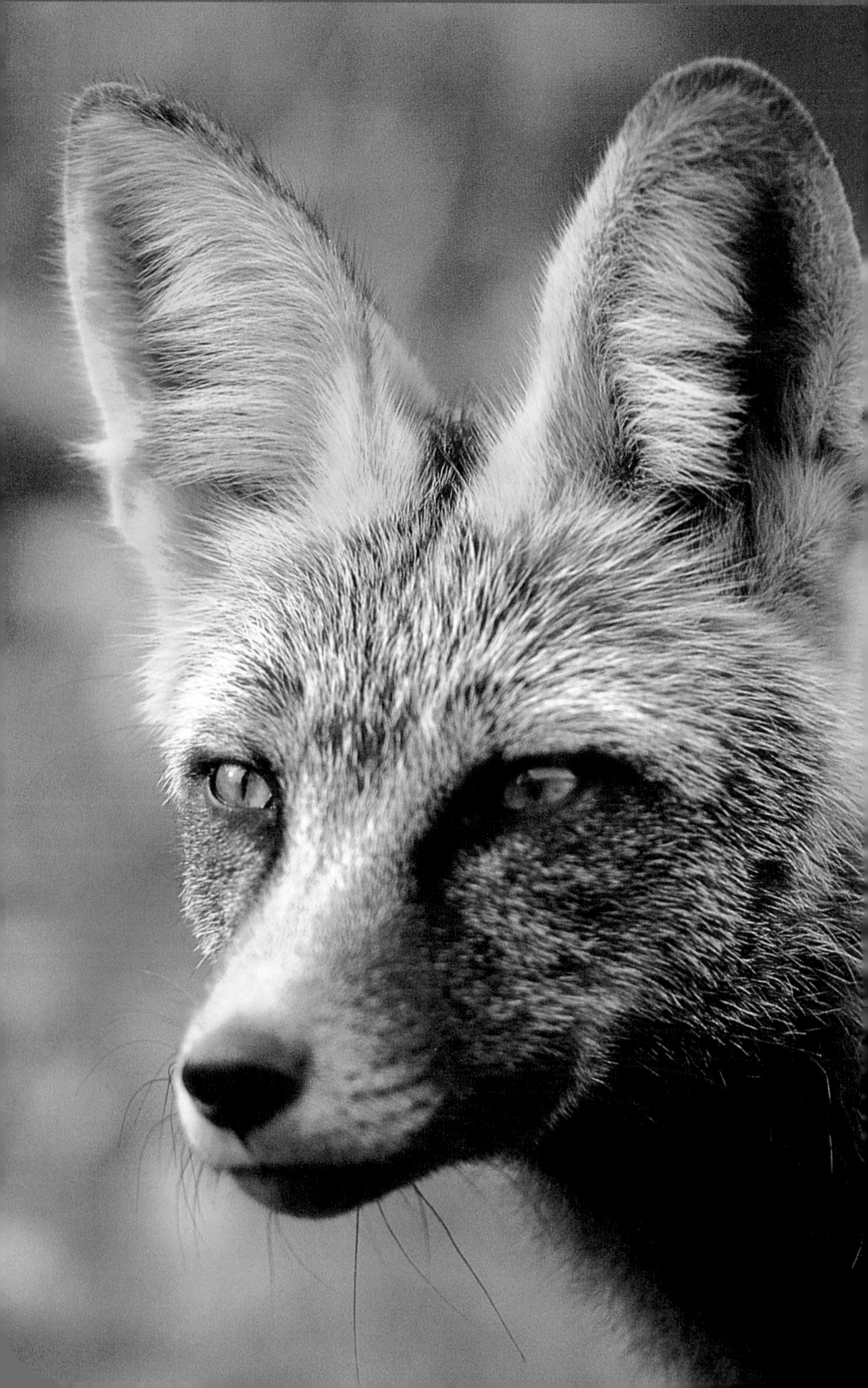

foreprint

walking trail

up most of the diet, but dried berries are also eaten. In more moderate seasons, invertebrates, birds, eggs, fruits and berries supplement the basic small-mammal diet.

DEN: The Red Fox generally dens in a burrow, which the vixen either digs herself or, more usually, makes by expanding a marmot or badger hole. The den is sometimes located in a hollow log, in a brush pile or beneath an unoccupied building.

YOUNG: A litter of 1 to 10 kits is born in April or May after a gestation of about $7^1/_2$ weeks. The kits weigh about $3^1/_2$ oz. at birth. Their eyes open after nine days, and they are weaned when they are one month old. The parents first bring the kits dead food and later crippled animals. The father may bring back to the den several voles, or perhaps a hare and some mice, at the end of a single hunting trip. After the kits learn to kill, the parents start taking them on hunts. The young disperse when they are three to four months old; they become sexually mature well before their first birthdays.

SIMILAR SPECIES: The larger **Coyote** (p. 162) has a dark-tipped tail and does not have black forelegs, and the distinctive **Gray Wolf** (p. 166) can be more than twice the size. The smaller **Common Gray Fox** (p. 178) usually has less red overall and has a crest of black along the top of the black-tipped tail.

Coyote

Kit Fox
Vulpes macrotis

The cat-sized Kit Fox has a history of misnomers, persecution and unfortunate decline. It has long been debated whether the Swift Fox (*V. velox*) and the Kit Fox are the same species or two different ones. Much evidence supports their distinct status, but research has shown that there is some interbreeding in eastern New Mexico and western Texas. Nevertheless, many mammalogists agree to treat them separately—as they are in this book. The Latin name of the Kit Fox aptly describes the animal. *Vulpes* is Latin for "fox," and *macrotis* is Greek, derived from the words *makros* for "long" and *ōtos* for "ear." Translated, the name means "the fox with long ears." Not surprisingly, their ears are proportionately the longest of any canid in North America.

For many years, Kit Foxes were exterminated as "vermin," along with Gray Wolves, Coyotes, other foxes and birds of prey. "Vermin" were considered to be any animal that could potentially kill a domestic animal, or that preyed upon a wild animal that humans wanted to hunt, such as deer. The result of this massive extermination effort is that very few canids exist now in the United States. Kit Foxes are now known to be extremely valuable in the ecosystem, because they feed primarily on small rodents and insects. In areas where Kit Foxes have been extirpated, rodents such as kangaroo rats, pocket mice and others, increase in numbers to such an extent that they may pose serious threats to agriculture, grazing and health.

Although we now understand the important of Kit Foxes in the ecosystem, they are still unfortunate victims of poaching, hunting and poisoning. Some are killed because of out-dated ideas of "vermin," some are hunted for their fur, and others are killed accidentally either by poisoned meat intended for other animals, or by consuming rodents that have been poisoned.

The behavior of Kit Foxes is unlike the behavior of Swift Foxes. Swift Fox populations that have been recently studied indicate the animals are very sociable and often live in groups. Kit Foxes are primarily solitary, except during times of breeding. In the mating season, males may return to their previous mate, and some have been known to have the same mate throughout their life (the same is true for Swift Foxes). During the remainder of the year, the males prefer a solitary lifestyle. Once the young disperse from the female, she also hunts alone. Calls of the Kit Fox are quite variable. Their repertoire includes a shrill yap, whines, growls and a rumbling purr.

RANGE: The Kit Fox is found in southeastern Oregon, much of Nevada, central and southern California, western Utah, much of Arizona and New Mexico, southwestern Colorado and eastern Texas.

Total Length: 24–33 in.
Tail Length: 9–13 in.
Weight: 3–6 lb.

DESCRIPTION: This small fox is mainly grayish yellow above, sometimes with flecks of rusty or black-colored hairs. They are whitish or buff below, their feet are similarly light-colored, and their tails are black-tipped. On some individuals a black spot is also at the upper base of the tail. The tail makes up almost 40 percent of their total length. The soles of their feet are well-haired, perhaps an adaptation that gives greater traction on desert sand. Their large, triangular ears are dark behind and whitish inside. In between their eyes and nose, on either side of the muzzle, are nearly black patches of fur.

HABITAT: Inhabitants of deserts and arid regions, Kit Foxes are associated with sagebrush flats and creosote/grass communities. They may hunt in sand dunes, but they are generally found in areas of some groundcover on light, sandy desert soils.

FOOD: In many parts of the southwestern states, the Kit Fox is an important predator of small rodents. Normal

DID YOU KNOW?

Although they are wary of intruders and human disturbance, Kit Foxes can be unusually indifferent to us. On many occasions, campers have been surprised by a Kit Fox walking into their campfire circle and helping itself to a choice cut of meat.

Kit Fox populations keep in check the numbers of rodents on pasture and cultivated land. Their primary prey species include kangaroo rats, pocket mice and rabbits. Other species that are consumed to a lesser extent include reptiles, ground-nesting birds and insects.

DEN: The Kit Fox digs burrows similar to those of the Red Fox, only somewhat smaller. As a rule, the Kit Fox spends the heat of the day in its cool den and comes out in the evenings and at night. Kit Fox burrows could be mistaken for those of a badger, but the badger's burrow is elliptical or flattened, much like the overall shape of the badger itself. A pregnant vixen cleans and arranges several possible den sites before she chooses the one that suits her needs best.

YOUNG: Males join company with a female in October or November, and mating occurs in December. Like Swift Foxes, Kit Foxes are monogamous and may mate for life. Gestation ranges from 49 to 56 days, whereupon a litter of four or five altricial pups are born. The pups nurse for the first few weeks, and as they are weaned the males bring in fresh food for them. The pups emerge when they are one month old, and begin hunting when they are three or four months old. In October, the young of the year disperse.

foreprint

walking trail

SIMILAR SPECIES: The **Swift Fox** (*V. velox*) is very similar and is often considered as the same species. Studies have shown they interbreed in some areas where their ranges meet. The **Common Gray Fox** (p. 178) is larger and has more red in its coat, as well as a distinctive black crest on the tail.

Common Gray Fox

Common Gray Fox
Urocyon cinereoargenteus

Truly a crafty fox, the Common Gray Fox is known to elude predators by taking the most unexpected of turns—running up a tree. Unlike other canids, this fox seems comfortable in a tree, and it may climb into the branches to rest and sleep. There are even rare records of these foxes denning in natural tree cavities and raising their litters as high as 20 ft. off the ground. It is the only North America member of the dog family that can climb.

The Common Gray Fox's tendency to live in areas of tree cover means it is less frequently seen than other foxes. Furthermore, the majority of its activity occurs during the dark or twilight hours, enhancing its clandestine nature. This fox is not likely to be found in Washington, but your chances of seeing one in Oregon are very good. Remember, you may have to turn your eyes skyward and scan the trees, especially those with thick, heavily forked trunks or leaning branches.

After the mating season, the male stays with the female and helps with raising the young. His primary role after the female gives birth is to bring her food, because she must remain with the young constantly for several days. Gray foxes often cache their food, especially large kills that cannot be consumed at once. Small kills may be buried right near the den during the whelping season, partly to provide the female with ready food, but also to stimulate the interest of the pups. Large cache sites are made either in heaped up vegetation or in holes dug into loose dirt.

Many of the fox populations in North America suffered great losses during the peak of the fur trade. To most foxes, Coyotes and wolves, humans are the worst enemy. Fortunately for the Common Gray Fox, its pelt is of lower quality (to humans, that is—the fox certainly appreciates it). The beautifully patterned, grizzled fur is very stiff, rather than soft and long like the winter coat of a Red Fox (p. 170), so it was trapped less. The Common Gray Fox has also suffered less persecution from farmers, because it is quite shy and rarely hunts domestic animals. Unlike the Red Fox, the Common Gray Fox is not inclined toward chickens. It prefers to hunt the mice that abound around a henhouse, and its mousing ability is so good that it is even considered a welcome visitor to a barnyard.

DESCRIPTION: This handsome fox has an overall grizzled appearance because of the long, grayish fur over its back. Its undersides are reddish in color, as are

RANGE: Common Gray Foxes have an extensive distribution in the U.S. They range through most of the eastern states and from Texas west to California and up the West Coast through most of Oregon. Some populations can be found in Colorado and Utah.

Total Length: 31–44 in.
Shoulder Height: 14–15 in.
Tail Length: 11–17 in.
Weight: 7½–13 lb.

the back of the head, throat, legs and feet. Sometimes the belly may be mostly white with only reddish highlights. The tail, which always has a black crest and a black tip, is otherwise grayish with reddish undersides. The ears are pointed and mainly gray in color, with patches of red on the back side. A distinct black spot is present on either side of the muzzle.

HABITAT: The Common Gray Fox inhabits a variety of different environments, always near trees or groundcover. This fox prefers foraging in wooded areas rather than open environments.

DEN: This fox's den can be found in a variety of places. Most commonly, it is on a ridge or rocky slope or under brush cover in a woodland, but it may also be underground. If necessary, a fox digs a burrow itself, but more often it refurbishes the abandoned burrow of another animal, such as a Woodchuck or American Badger.

DID YOU KNOW?

Although this fox is quite small, it can run very quickly over short distances. In one record, a Common Gray Fox topped 28 m.p.h.

FOOD: Gray foxes are more omnivorous than other foxes. They consume a variety of small mammals, such as rabbits, rodents and birds, as well as large amounts of insects and other invertebrates. Late in summer, grasshoppers, crickets and other agricultural pests constitute much of the diet. A significant part of the diet is vegetable matter, such as fruits and grasses. Favorite items include apples, grapes, persimmons and nuts.

YOUNG: Mating occurs in January or February, and after a gestation of about 53 days, one to seven young are born. They are born blind and almost hairless, and for the first several days they require constant care by the mother. After 12 days their eyes open. They venture out of the den when they are 1½ or 2 months old. When they are four months old, they learn how to hunt and accompany their parents while foraging. By the fifth month, they have dispersed to start their own dens.

walking trail

foreprint

SIMILAR SPECIES: The **Kit Fox** (p. 174) is smaller, less reddish overall and lacks the black crest and tip on the tail. The **Red Fox** (p. 170) is much redder overall and has a white-tipped tail. The **Coyote** (p. 162) is larger and lacks the black spots on either side of the muzzle.

Kit Fox

RODENTS

In terms of sheer numbers, rodents are the most successful group of mammals in Washington and Oregon. Because we usually associate rodents with rats and mice, the group's most notorious members, many people look on all rodents as filthy vermin. You must remember, however, that the much more endearing chipmunks, marmots, beavers and squirrels are also rodents. Most small rodents are important prey species for a wide variety of reptiles, birds and other mammals.

A rodent's best-known features are its upper and lower pairs of protruding incisor teeth, which continue to grow throughout the animal's life. These four teeth have pale yellow to burnt orange enamel only on their front surfaces. The teeth retain their knife-sharp cutting edges because the soft dentin at the rear of each tooth is continually worn away by the action of gnawing. Most rodents are relatively small mammals, but beavers and porcupines can grow quite large. Of the rodents, only porcupines, beavers and Nutrias give birth to precocial young that from birth can feed themselves and otherwise look after themselves to a high degree. Their litter sizes are on average smaller than those of other rodents, which all have altricial young that require more parental care.

Nutria Family (Myocastoridae)

The Nutria was introduced into North America from South America. It is the sole species in its family, and though it looks similar to a muskrat, the two are not closely related. The Nutria has a long, rounded tail, and the webbing on each hindfoot joins only four of the five hindtoes.

Nutria

Porcupine Family (Erethizontidae)

The stocky-bodied North American Porcupine has some of its hairs modified into sharp-pointed quills that it uses in defense. Its sharp, curved claws and the rough soles of its feet are adapted for climbing.

North American
Porcupine

Jumping Mouse Family (Dipodidae)

Jumping mice are named for the long leaps they take when they are startled. The hindlegs are much longer than the forelegs, and the tail, which is longer than the combined length of the head and body, serves as a counterbalance during jumps. Jumping mice are almost completely nocturnal.

Western Jumping Mouse

Mouse Family (Muridae)

This diverse group of rodents is the largest and most successful mammal family in the world. Its members include the familiar rats and mice as well as voles and lemmings. The representatives of this family in Washington and Oregon vary in size from the tiny Western Harvest Mouse to the Common Muskrat.

Deer Mouse

Beaver Family (Castoridae)

The American Beaver is one of only two species world-wide in its family, and it is the only representative on our continent. North America's largest rodent, it is one of the most visible mammals in the region. After humans, it is probably the animal with the biggest impact on the wilderness landscape of Washington and Oregon.

American Beaver

Pocket Mouse Family (Heteromyidae)

Pocket mice, kangaroo mice and kangaroo rats make up a group of small- to medium-sized rodents that are somewhat adapted to a subterranean existence. They feed mainly on seeds, and they use their external, fur-lined cheek pouches to transport food to caches in their burrows. Typically inhabitants of dry environments, many of them can live for a long time without drinking water. Most members of this family, and all of those in Washington and Oregon, use bipedal leaps when moving quickly, in what is known as "ricochetal locomotion."

Great Basin Pocket Mouse

Pocket Gopher Family (Geomyidae)

Almost exclusively subterranean, all pocket gophers have small eyes, tiny ears, heavy claws, short, strong forelegs and a short, sparsely haired tail. Their fur-lined cheek pouches, or "pockets," are primarily used to transport food. The lower jaw is massive, and the incisor teeth are used in excavating tunnels.

Northern Pocket Gopher

Squirrel Family (Sciuridae)

This family, which includes chipmunks, tree squirrels, flying squirrels, marmots and ground squirrels, is considered the second most structurally primitive group of rodents. All its members, except the flying squirrels, are active during the day, so they are seen more frequently than other rodents.

Least Chipmunk

Mountain Beaver Family (Aplodontidae)

The Mountain Beaver is the sole living member of its family, and it is usually considered the most primitive rodent. A Mountain Beaver resembles a small, stout marmot with a tiny tail. The name "Mountain Beaver" is misleading; other than being a fellow rodent, it is not related to the American Beaver.

Mountain Beaver

Nutria

Myocastor coypus

The Nutria was introduced into North America to be farmed for its thick fur. Most of the farmers who raised these South American rodents found the business unprofitable, and many animals were deliberately or accidentally released. Where moderate winters prevail, such as in western parts of Washington and Oregon, these escapees established populations. In some areas, native animals may suffer food shortages because of Nutria activity.

Interestingly, some American Beavers that were imported into Argentina for fur production also escaped and are expanding their range. There appears to be no predator to control the beavers, which are responsible for widespread cutting of Argentina's riparian forests.

These two examples show the potential dangers of introducing a species into a similar habitat in a distant geographical area. Such a newcomer is exempt from the intricate system of checks and balances that has evolved among native species over long periods of time.

ALSO CALLED: Coypu.

DESCRIPTION: The Nutria is a grayish to brownish aquatic rodent with a long, dark brown, sparsely haired, scaly, cylindrical tail. Numerous whitish or yellowish hairs occur throughout the coat, and a distinct white patch can usually be seen on the tip of the muzzle. The Nutria has webbed hindfeet, with only four of the five hindtoes on each foot included in the web. The Nutria is very similar in appearance to the Common Muskrat.

HABITAT: Nutrias require rivers, lakes and marshes with abundant emergent or submerged vegetation. They cannot live where the entire water surface freezes in winter.

FOOD: These rodents eat large amounts of wetland vegetation. Like lagomorphs (pp. 284–97), Nutrias reingest their fecal pellets to maximize nutrient absorption.

DEN: The den is dug in a bank; one or two entrances are located above the water and continue about a yard into the bank. The nest of reeds, cattails and sedges is found inside a small chamber.

YOUNG: Breeding takes place throughout the year, and most females produce two litters a year, starting when they are one year old. Following a 100- to 135-day gestation period, three to eight precocious young, each weighing 7–9 oz.,

RANGE: In addition to its natural range in South America, the Nutria is found in the southeastern U.S., isolated locations in the central states, western Washington and Oregon and southern Ontario.

Total Length: 26–55 in.
Tail Length: 12–18 in.
Weight: 5–25 lb.

walking trail

are born. They may swim and eat some vegetation their first day.

SIMILAR SPECIES: The **Common Muskrat** (p. 224) is slightly smaller, lacks the light hairs in the coat and the white patch on the muzzle, and has a laterally compressed tail. The larger **American Beaver** (p. 226) has a wide, flat tail and makes unmistakable lodges and dams.

DID YOU KNOW?

In the evenings, Nutrias make loud, grunting calls and can be heard from quite a distance around their wetland homes.

North American Porcupine
Erethizon dorsatum

Although it lacks the charisma of large carnivores and ungulates, the North American Porcupine's claim to fame is its unsurpassed defensive mechanism. A porcupine's formidable quills, numbering about 30,000, are actually stiff, modified hairs with overlapping, shingle-like barbs at their tips. Contrary to popular belief, a porcupine cannot throw its quills, but if it is attacked it will lower its head in a defensive posture and lash out with its tail. The loosely rooted quills detach easily, and they may be driven deep into the attacker's flesh. The barbs swell and expand with blood, making the quills even harder to extract. Quill wounds may fester, or, depending on where the quills strike, they can blind an animal, preventing it from hunting and eating, or even puncture a vital organ.

Porcupines are strictly vegetarian, and they are frequently found feeding in agricultural fields, willow-edged wetlands and forests. The tender bark of young branches seems to be a porcupine delicacy, and though you wouldn't think it from their size, with their deliberate climbing porcupines can move far out on very thin branches. Accomplished, albeit slow, climbers, porcupines use their sharp, curved claws, the thick, bumpy soles of their feet and the quills on the underside of their tail in climbing. These large, stocky rodents often remain in individual trees and bushes for several days at a time, and when they leave a foraging site, the naked, cream-colored branches are clear evidence of their activity.

The North American Porcupine is mostly nocturnal, and it often rests by day in a hollow tree or log, in a burrow or in a treetop. It is not unusual to see a porcupine active by day, however, either in an open field or in a forest. It often chews bones or fallen antlers for calcium, and the sound of a porcupine's gnawing can sometimes be heard at a considerable distance.

Unfortunately for the North American Porcupine, its armament is no defense against vehicles—highway collisions are a major cause of porcupine mortality—and most people see porcupines only in the form of roadkill.

DESCRIPTION: This large, stout-bodied rodent has long, light-tipped guard hairs surrounding the center of the back, where abundant, long, thick quills crisscross one another in all directions. The young are mostly black, but adults are also variously tinged with yellow. The upper surface of the powerful, thick tail is amply supplied with dark-tipped, white

RANGE: The porcupine is widely distributed from Alaska across Canada, south to Pennsylvania and New England and through most of the West into Mexico.

Total Length: 21–37 in.
Tail Length: 5½–9 in.
Weight: 7¾–40 lb.

to yellowish quills. The foreclaws are curved and sharp. The skin on the soles of the feet is strongly dimpled, like the soles of deck shoes. Gray patches may be on the cheeks and between the eyes.

HABITAT: Porcupines occupy a variety of habitats, ranging from montane forests to open tundra and even rangelands.

FOOD: Completely herbivorous, the North American Porcupine is like an arboreal counterpart of the American Beaver. It eats leaves, buds, twigs and especially young bark or the cambium layer of both broad-leaved and coniferous trees and shrubs. During spring and summer, it eats considerable amounts of herbaceous vegetation. The porcupine typically puts on weight during spring and summer and loses it during fall and winter. It seems to have a profound fondness for salt, and it will chew wooden handles, boots or other material that is salty from sweat or urine.

DEN: Porcupines prefer to den in caves or shelters along watercourses or beneath rocks, but they sometimes move into abandoned buildings, especially in winter. They are typically solitary animals, denning alone, but they may share a den during particularly cold weather. Sometimes a porcupine will sleep in a treetop for weeks, not bothering to den, while it completely strips the tree of bark.

DID YOU KNOW?

The name "porcupine" comes from the Latin *porcospinus* (spiny pig) and underwent many variations— Shakespeare used the word "porpentine"—before its current spelling was established in the 17th century.

foreprint

YOUNG: The porcupine's impressive armament inspires many questions about how it manages to mate. Although males may fight with one another, the female does most of the courtship, and she is apparently stimulated by having the male urinate on her. When she is sufficiently aroused, she relaxes her quills and raises her tail over her back so that mating can proceed. Following mating in November or December and a gestation period of 6½ to 7 months—unusually long for a rodent—a single precocious "porcupette" is born in May or June. The young porcupine is born with quills, but they are not dangerous to the mother—the baby is born head-first in a placental sac with its soft quills lying flat against its body. The quills harden within about an hour of birth. Porcupines have erupted incisor teeth at birth, and though they may continue to nurse for up to four months, they begin eating green vegetation before they are one month old. Porcupines become sexually mature when they are 1½ to 2½ years old.

walking trail

SIMILAR SPECIES: No other animal in Washington or Oregon closely resembles the porcupine, but a **Northern Raccoon** (p. 136) seen in poor light might possibly be mistaken for a porcupine.

Northern Raccoon

Western Jumping Mouse
Zapus princeps

Total Length: 8½–10 in.

Tail Length: 5–6⅜ in.

Weight: ½–1¼ oz.

True to its name, a jumping mouse is capable of exceptional leaps, powered by large hindfeet and balanced by a long tail. The two species of jumping mice in Washington and Oregon are virtually indistinguishable from each other in the field, which may create some confusion in areas where their ranges overlap. Their hopping escape maneuvers and supremely long tails, however, are sufficiently distinctive for even novice naturalists to distinguish them from most other rodents.

DESCRIPTION: A broad, dark, longitudinal band extends from the nose to the rump. This dorsal stripe is primarily dull brown, with some blackish hairs. The sides of the body are yellowish olive, often with some orangish hairs. The belly is a clear, creamy white. The flanks and cheeks are golden yellow. The nearly naked tail is olive brown above and whitish below. The hindfeet are greatly elongated.

RANGE: This western species is found from the southern Yukon southeast to North Dakota and south to central California and northern New Mexico.

HABITAT: This jumping mouse prefers areas of tall grass, often near streams, that may have brush or trees. In the mountains, it ranges from valley floors up to treeline and even into tundra sedge meadows. It frequently enters the water and appears to swim well, diving as deep as 3½ ft.

FOOD: In spring and summer, it eats berries, tender vegetation, insects and a few other invertebrates. As fall approaches, grass seeds and the fruits of forbs are taken more frequently. Subterranean fungi are also favored.

DEN: The hibernation nest, made of finely shredded vegetation, is 1–2 ft. underground in a burrow that is 3½–10 ft. long. The breeding nest is typically built among interwoven broad-leaved grasses or in sphagnum moss in a depression.

YOUNG: Breeding takes place within a week after the female emerges from hibernation. Following 18 days of gestation, four to eight young are born in late June or early July. The eyes open after two to five days. The young nurse for one month. Some females have two or even three litters a year.

SIMILAR SPECIES: The **Pacific Jumping Mouse** (p. 191) is difficult to distinguish by appearance alone; it generally occurs to the west of the range of the western species. *Peromyscus* **mice** (pp. 193–97) have much shorter tails.

Pacific Jumping Mouse
Zapus trinotatus

Total Length: 8¼–9⅞ in.

Tail Length: 4¼–6 in.

Weight: ¾–1 oz.

Like other jumping mice, Pacific Jumping Mice are long-term hibernators—adults sleep from October until April. All the Pacific Jumping Mice in an area will emerge from hibernation at the same time; the stimulus is the rise in soil temperatures around their winter nests. Before entering hibernation, fat is accumulated in their bodies, and this fat sustains them during their long dormancy.

Jumping mice jump by pushing off with the hindfeet and landing on their forefeet. They can leap well over a yard almost straight up when trying to escape a threat. The long tails are critical for balance when jumping, and they are sometimes drummed against the ground when the mouse is alarmed.

DESCRIPTION: Down the back from the nose to the rump runs a dark brown dorsal stripe flecked heavily with black. The sides are ochreous to golden in color, and the undersides are creamy white. The dorsal hair is short and rough. The forelegs are short, and the hindlegs and feet are extremely long. The thin, scaly, bicolored tail is as long as, or longer than, the body; sparsely haired, it does not have a white tip. The ears are dark with light edges, and the whiskers are abundant.

HABITAT: These mice favor areas where plant cover is dense, such as streamsides, thickets, moist fields and some woodlands. They appear to be especially common where skunk cabbage grows. In mountains, they range from valley floors to above treeline in wet alpine sedge meadows.

FOOD: Underground fungi, grass seeds, berries and tender vegetation are staples. In spring, many insects and other invertebrates are eaten.

DEN: The hibernation nest, which is made of finely shredded vegetation, is 1–2 ft. underground in a burrow; the burrow is 3½–10 ft. long. The burrow entrance is plugged solidly before hibernation. The breeding nest is typically built among interwoven broad-leaved grasses or in sphagnum moss in a depression.

YOUNG: These mice emerge from hibernation between mid-May and mid-June. Breeding takes place within a week after the female emerges. Following a gestation period of 18–23 days, four to eight naked, hairless, blind young are born. The young nurse for a month and grow slowly; nevertheless, they must reach a critical weight and size if they are to survive hibernation. Females have one or two litters a year.

SIMILAR SPECIES: The **Western Jumping Mouse** (p. 190) is usually less distinctly tricolored and is found in areas to the east of this species. *Peromyscus mice* (pp. 193–97) have much shorter tails.

RANGE: This jumping mouse is found from extreme southwestern mainland British Columbia through Washington and Oregon to north-coastal California.

Western Harvest Mouse
Reithrodontomys megalotis

Total Length: 4¼–6 in.
Tail Length: 2⅜–3⅛ in.
Weight: ⁵⁄₁₆–⅞ oz.

Probably the smallest mouse in Washington and Oregon, the Western Harvest Mouse is most active during the two hours after sunset, but its activity may continue almost until dawn, particularly on dark, moonless nights. It often uses vole runways through thick grass to reach foraging areas. The Western Harvest Mouse is named for its habit of collecting grass cuttings in mounds along trail networks. It does not store food in any great quantities, however, which is understandable for an animal that usually lives for less than a year.

DESCRIPTION: This native mouse closely resembles the House Mouse: it is small and slim, with a small head and pointed nose, and it has a conspicuous, long, sparsely haired tail and large, naked ears. The bicolored tail is grayish above and lighter below. The upperparts are brownish, and the underparts are grayish white or sometimes pale cinnamon. This mouse is the only one in this region to have a longitudinal groove on each incisor.

RANGE: This mouse ranges from extreme southern Alberta and British Columbia south nearly to the Yucatan Peninsula. It does not inhabit rough mountain regions.

HABITAT: Harvest mice occur in both arid and moist places—grasslands, sagebrush, weedy waste areas, fencelines and even cattail-choked marsh edges—as long as overhead cover is abundant.

FOOD: The Western Harvest Mouse eats lots of green vegetation in spring and early summer, and at those times of year its runways may sport piles of grass cuttings. During most of the year, however, seeds and insects dominate the diet.

DEN: This mouse builds its ball-shaped nest, which is about 3 in. wide, either on the ground or low in shrubs or weeds. The nest is made of dry grasses and is lined with soft material, such as cattail fluff. One nest may house several mice and have multiple entrances.

YOUNG: Reproduction occurs in the warmer months, or all year if conditions are favorable. The average litter of four is born after a 23- to 24-day gestation period. Hair is visible by 5 days; the eyes open after 10 to 12 days; and at 19 days the young are weaned. A female becomes sexually mature at four to five months.

SIMILAR SPECIES: The **House Mouse** (p. 206) is generally larger and has a hairless tail. The **Deer Mouse** (p. 194) has much whiter undersides.

Northwestern Deer Mouse

Peromyscus keeni

Total Length: 7–9¼ in.
Tail Length: 3½–4½ in.
Weight: ⅜–1 oz.

One of the major features distinguishing the Northwestern Deer Mouse from the somewhat less arboreal Deer Mouse (p. 194) is its long tail. Long tails appear to benefit animals that climb into shrubs and bushes. The Northwestern Deer Mouse harvests berries from shrubs, and its lengthy tail aids in balance as the mouse scampers along thin branches. In the Pacific Northwest from west-central Washington northward, this mouse is a predominant member of its genus and may even be more common than the Deer Mouse.

ALSO CALLED: Keen's Mouse.

DESCRIPTION: The Northwestern Deer Mouse is gray above and bright white below. The large ears extend well above the fur on the head, and the beady black eyes protrude. The tail is distinctly bicolored: slate gray above and white below. The feet and heels are white.

HABITAT: The Northwestern Deer Mouse inhabits coastal rainforest dominated by western hemlock, Sitka spruce and red alder. The usually heavy underbrush includes blueberries, salmonberry and devil's club.

FOOD: These mice have a diverse, omnivorous diet that changes seasonally and that includes seeds, assorted vegetation and insects. The primary food is seeds and berries, with an emphasis on spruce and hemlock seeds. Northwestern Deer Mice appear to eat fewer invertebrates than Deer Mice.

DEN: Nests are located in burrows, among rocks and in logs, buildings or other sheltered areas. The nest is a sphere of grass and fine, dry, vegetation, about 4 in. wide.

YOUNG: The breeding season extends from May to September. Following a gestation period of 21 to 27 days, one to seven young are born. The pink, naked, blind young weigh about ¹⁄₁₆ oz. at birth and are weaned about three to four weeks later. During summer, the female breeds immediately after giving birth, so the weanlings are soon evicted from the nest to make room for the new litter.

SIMILAR SPECIES: The **Deer Mouse** (p. 194), which is the only *Peromyscus* species whose range overlaps that of the Northwestern Deer Mouse in Washington, has a shorter tail.

RANGE: The Northwestern Deer Mouse is found in Washington's Olympic Peninsula

and northwestern Cascades. Its range extends north through coastal British Columbia and adjacent islands to extreme southern Alaska.

Deer Mouse

Peromyscus maniculatus

Upon first seeing a Deer Mouse, many people are struck with how cute this little animal is. The large, protruding, coal black eyes give it a justifiably inquisitive look; in addition, its dainty nose and long whiskers continually twitch as it senses the changing odors in the wind.

Wherever they can find groundcover, anything from thick grass to deadfall, Deer Mice scurry about with great liveliness. These small mice are omnipresent over much of their range, and they may well be the most numerous mammal in Washington and Oregon. When you walk through forested wilderness areas, they are in your company, even if their presence remains hidden.

Deer Mice most frequently forage along the ground, but they are known to climb trees and shrubs to reach food. During winter, Deer Mice are the most common of the small rodents to travel above the snow. In doing so, however, they are vulnerable to nighttime predators. The tiny skulls of these rodents are among the most common remains in the regurgitated pellets of owls, a testament to their importance in the food web.

The Deer Mouse, which is named for the similarity of its coloring to that of the White-tailed Deer (see p. 48), commonly occupies farm buildings, garages and storage sheds, often alongside the House Mouse (p. 206). In a few high-profile cases, people have died from exposure to hantavirus, which is associated with the feces and urine of many of the Deer Mice in our region. The virus can become airborne, so if you find Deer Mouse droppings, it is best to wear a HEPA-rated mask and spray the area with water and bleach before attempting to remove the animal's waste.

DESCRIPTION: Every Deer Mouse has protruding black, lustrous eyes, large ears, a pointed nose, long whiskers and a sharply bicolored tail with a dark top and light underside. In contrast to these constant characteristics, the color of the adult's upperparts is quite variable: they can be yellowish buff, tawny brown, grayish brown or blackish brown. However, the upperparts are always set off sharply from the bright white undersides and feet. A juvenile has uniformly gray upperparts.

HABITAT: These ubiquitous mice occupy a variety of habitats, including grasslands, mossy depressions, brushy areas, tundra and heavily wooded regions. Another habitat these little mice greatly favor is the human building—our

RANGE: The Deer Mouse is the most widespread mouse in North America. Its range extends from Labrador west almost to Alaska and south through most of North America to south-central Mexico.

Total Length: 5½–8¼ in.
Tail Length: 2⅛–4 in.
Weight: ⅝–1¼ oz.

warm, food-laden homes are palatial residences to Deer Mice.

FOOD: Deer Mice horde food, and their caches can be almost anywhere, such as hollow logs, tree cavities, burrows or abandoned bird nests. Their main foods include seeds or fruits from grasses, chokecherries, buckwheat and other plants. They also eat insects, nestling birds and eggs.

DEN: As the habitat of this mouse changes, so does its den type: in meadows it nests in a small burrow or makes a grassy nest on raised ground; in wooded areas it makes a nest in a hollow log or under debris. Nests can also be made in rock crevices, and certainly in human structures.

YOUNG: Breeding takes place between March and October, and gestation lasts for three to four weeks. The helpless young number one to nine (usually four or five) and weigh about ¹⁄₁₆ oz. at birth. They open their eyes between days 12 and 17, and about four days after that they venture out of the nest. At three to five weeks the young are completely weaned and are soon on their own. A female is sexually mature in about 35 days; a male matures in about 45 days.

SIMILAR SPECIES: The **House Mouse** (p. 206) and the **Western Harvest Mouse** (p. 192) lack the distinct bright white belly and sharply bicolored tail. **The Northwestern Deer Mouse** (p. 193), **Canyon Mouse** (p. 196) and **jumping mice** (pp. 190–91) have relatively longer tails. The **Northern Grasshopper Mouse** (p. 198) is larger and more robust.

DID YOU KNOW?

Adult Deer Mice displaced a mile from where they were trapped were generally able to return to their home burrows within a day. Perhaps they range so widely in their travels that they recognized where they were and simply scampered home.

Canyon Mouse
Peromyscus crinitus

Total Length: 6⅜–7½ in.
Tail Length: 3⅛–4⅝ in.
Weight: ⅜–¾ oz.

This interesting mouse is named for the dry, rocky habitats in which it lives. The Canyon Mouse often lives on buttes and mesas devoid of vegetation, and it therefore needs to have a particularly effective metabolism for life in arid regions. It rarely drinks—it can survive on the water metabolized from its food—and in situations of extreme aridity and heat it rests in torpor until conditions improve. As a result of this tie to dry conditions, ancient remains of this animal can hint at past climatic conditions. For example, Canyon Mouse bones dating to the 13th century were found to the east and southeast of its present range, which may indicate that conditions there were drier at that time.

DESCRIPTION: The Canyon Mouse has very large, sparsely furred ears. Its thinly haired tail is longer than the head and body, and it is distinctively bicolored. The underparts and feet are white. The upperparts are brown.

HABITAT: Bare rock seems to be a habitat requirement of the Canyon Mouse. It is found on desert pavement or rocky canyon walls where stands of black-brush, saltbush, bunchgrass and sagebrush grow. Canyon Mice are often found at higher elevations than other *Peromyscus* mice.

FOOD: These mice have a diverse, omnivorous diet that changes seasonally between seeds and other vegetation and insects.

DEN: Nests are located in protected areas, such as burrows, among rocks, in logs or in old buildings.

YOUNG: Typically, the Canyon Mouse has two litters a year. Breeding occurs in early spring and early fall, and the average litter size is one to five young.

RANGE: The Canyon Mouse is found west of the Continental Divide, from eastern Oregon and Idaho through Nevada, Utah and Colorado

SIMILAR SPECIES: Habitat and range are often the best indicators of a mouse's identity. The **Pinyon Mouse** (p. 197) is larger, and it has longer ears and hindfeet. The **Deer Mouse** (p. 194) tends to have a shorter tail.

Pinyon Mouse
Peromyscus truei

Total Length: 6¾–9⅛ in.
Tail Length: 3–4⅞ in.
Weight: ⅝–1⅛ oz.

In scattered areas of central and southern Oregon, Pinyon Mice can be found living in arid and semi-arid environments. As their name suggests, these mice are associated with pinyon pines—and with junipers—and they nearly always live among rocky outcroppings where these plants are abundant. Pinyon Mice are well adapted to heat and aridity, and during the hottest part of the day they rest inside their cool, sheltered nests. These mice do not hibernate, but they may enter a torpid state in response to severe aridity. Even when these mice are not active, they can be detected by their most significant sign: pinyon and juniper seed husks tossed in loose piles tell the story of their food preferences.

DESCRIPTION: The dorsal area, which is variable in color and can be lead-colored, brownish, cinnamon or rich tawny, contrasts sharply with the white to creamy white underparts. The thin tail is distinctly hairy and bicolored, with dark above and white below. The ears are longer than the hindfeet and sparsely haired, the eyes are large and protruding, the nose is pointed and the whiskers are long. The feet are white.

HABITAT: The Pinyon Mouse is an inhabitant of arid foothill lowlands, and it is seldom found above 7000 ft. It seems restricted to areas of pinyon and juniper, particularly those where rocky slopes dominate.

FOOD: During summer, most of the diet consists of insects and spiders. From late summer to spring, seeds and nuts, particularly from junipers, are important.

DEN: Nests are located among rocks, in logs and hollow trunks, in buildings or in other protected areas.

YOUNG: The Pinyon Mouse has several litters between April and September, each consisting of three to six altricial young.

SIMILAR SPECIES: The **Canyon Mouse** (p. 196), which also inhabits rocky areas, has smaller ears.

RANGE: The Pinyon Mouse ranges from central Oregon to Colorado and south through Mexico.

Northern Grasshopper Mouse
Onychomys leucogaster

Although it superficially resembles the Deer Mouse (p. 194), the Northern Grasshopper Mouse is the "bulldog" of the mice in this region. It is a chunky resident of sandy environments that often lives in close association with kangaroo rats. The stocky form of the Northern Grasshopper Mouse befits its predatory nature—up to 90 percent of its diet consists of animal matter, primarily grasshoppers and other insects, but also including prey as large as other mice and voles. Studies of Northern Grasshopper Mice indicate that they have characteristics normally associated with carnivores: they exhibit social bonds and elaborate courtship, and they have long claws, enhanced jaw muscles and teeth suitable for shearing animal matter. Unlike other mice, they even "howl." Their howl is within human hearing and can carry far in dry air.

This mouse is reputed to have a fierce disposition (even toward non-prey species), and it frequently usurps the homes of other small mammals, eats them and modifies their burrows for its own needs. Its nest burrow, located only a short distance below the surface, is built in loose, dry, sandy soil. On the surface, this sandy soil is ideal for dust-bathing.

In contrast to its attitude toward strangers, the Northern Grasshopper Mouse seems to make a devoted parent. Both the male and female care for the young, bringing food to the nest until they become self-sufficient.

DESCRIPTION: The back is gray (in the north) to yellowish buff (in the south), and the entire belly is white. The nose is pointed, the dark, lustrous eyes protrude noticeably, and the ears are large. The short tail—it is less than twice the length of the hindfoot—is thick, sharply bicolored (darker above, lighter below) and has a white tip. The thick legs, broad feet and broad shoulders of this mouse give an impression of burliness. Animals seen in the wild may appear rumpled. The rumpled appearance and stink that grasshopper mice tend to develop is reduced by sand bathing.

HABITAT: This mouse occurs in a wide variety of open habitats with sandy or gravelly soils, from grasslands to sandy brushlands, but it avoids alkali flats, marshy areas and rocky sites. Although it does not occur in the high mountains, it occupies the foothills in a few places.

FOOD: Only a little more than 10 percent of the summer diet consists of

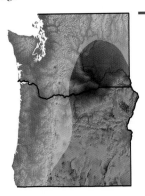

RANGE: This mouse is found in much of western North America, on both sides of the Rocky Mountains and from the prairie provinces in Canada to northern Mexico.

Total Length: 5–6 in.
Tail Length: 1⅛–1⅝ in.
Weight: 1¹⁄₁₆–1⅞ oz.

vegetation, mostly the seeds of grasses and forbs. Grasshoppers, crickets and beetles make up about 60 percent. In winter, up to 40 percent of the diet is composed of seeds and vegetation. This fierce little predator may also eat scorpions, spiders, moths and butterflies. It typically bites off a scorpion's sting and then eats the animal, tail first. It can even overpower and kill mice and birds up to three times its own weight. Northern Grasshopper Mice do not appear to store food, and many them that are fat in fall lose weight over winter.

DEN: Nest burrows are U-shaped and about 1½ in. across. The nest is located about 6 in. below the surface. The entrance is plugged by day, which helps retain moisture. Nests may also be found under vegetation or debris, or in holes dug by other animals.

YOUNG: Breeding occurs between March and August. A female's first pregnancy lasts about one month, but subsequent litters are typically born 32 to 38 days after mating. A litter usually contains three or four young, which weigh ¹⁄₁₆–⅛ oz. and are naked and blind at birth. The incisors begin to erupt at nine days, the eyes open at two to three weeks, and weaning follows by day 24. Most females breed during the spring following their birth, as do males, and they may bear two or three litters each summer.

SIMILAR SPECIES: The **Deer Mouse** (p. 194) has a similar coloration but lacks the burly proportions and has a thinner, longer tail.

DID YOU KNOW?

The Northern Grasshopper Mouse can produce complex vocalizations. Mated pairs hunt together, and they keep in contact with frequent, variable calls. Their "howls," at a frequency of 12 kHz, can be heard for nearly 200 yd.

Desert Woodrat
Neotoma lepida

Total Length: 8⅞–16 in.
Tail Length: 3¾–7⅞ in.
Weight: 3⅞–4¾ oz.

Small and forceful, the Desert Woodrat is famous for its dominating presence in the deserts and other arid regions of the Southwest. Among the great variety of nocturnal desert rodents, this woodrat is the dominant species. In such arid regions, Desert Woodrats build their homes underneath prickly pear cacti, in burrows, or even inside the plants. When the dry season begins and drought negatively affects most animals, each woodrat staunchly defends its own cactus, permitting no other rodent to share in this valuable water source. The Desert Woodrat is quite at home in the cactus, running freely and uninjured over the dangerous spines that fend off most other animals.

DESCRIPTION: Desert Woodrats are mainly buff, gray or sooty colored above and light gray to white underneath. Their tails are sparsely furred and sharply bicolored, with sooty gray above

and buff below. Their hindfeet are white, but all the hairs, even the white ones, are gray at the base.

HABITAT: These woodrats are found in arid regions of many types: deserts, juniper and pinyon areas and sagebrush flats.

FOOD: This woodrat's diet is composed of cactus pulp and fruits as well as the nuts, seeds, fruits and bark of other plants.

DEN: Primarily associated with *Opuntia* cacti, these woodrats live in burrows under or, less frequently, inside a cactus. Their nests look like ramshackle arrangements of twigs, cactus spines, vegetation and other odds and ends.

YOUNG: Mating occurs in early spring. After a gestation period of roughly one month, a litter of three or four altricial young is born. The young mature quickly, and by day 15 their eyes are open.

SIMILAR SPECIES: The **Dusky-footed Woodrat** (p. 201) is larger, and its feet and ankles are dusky colored. The **Bushy-tailed Woodrat** (p. 202) has a well-furred, bushy tail.

RANGE: This woodrat is found in southeastern Oregon, southwestern Idaho, Nevada, southern and coastal California, much of Utah and extreme northwestern Arizona.

Dusky-footed Woodrat
Neotoma fuscipes

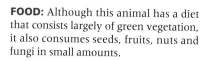

Total Length: 13–19 in.
Tail Length: 6¼–8⅞ in.
Weight: 8¼–9⅜ oz.

These semi-arboreal rodents are accomplished home-makers and gatherers. They build nests either on the ground or in a tree, sometimes as high as 50 ft. off the ground. Nest building is very time-consuming, and the home is never finished. Woodrats are famed for their preoccupation with caching things. Usually it is food that is carried away to special chambers in their twiggy nest, but sometimes such things as shiny bits of metal, an old fork, a piece of plastic or anything of "value" according to the sensibilities of the woodrat are also cached away. The nests are often occupied by more than one woodrat and usually several other animal species as well. Small mammals, frogs, beetles and other invertebrates are commonly found inside the home of a Dusky-footed Woodrat.

DESCRIPTION: This woodrat is grayish or buff brown on its back and pale gray or white underneath. Its gray fur extends over its ankles and the tops of its feet. The head is usually grayer than the body, sometimes a sooty color. This woodrat has a sparsely furred tail that is longer than those of several other *Neotoma* species.

HABITAT: Favoring areas with lots of sticks and twigs, these woodrats are found in dense chaparral, woodlands and shrubby areas.

FOOD: Although this animal has a diet that consists largely of green vegetation, it also consumes seeds, fruits, nuts and fungi in small amounts.

DEN: These woodrats make large piles of sticks, barks, plants and miscellaneous objects on the ground or in a well-supported fork of a tree. Inside is a maze of passageways and chambers for caching or sleeping. Multiple individuals occupy the nests, and though the individuals change, a nest may be used for many generations.

YOUNG: Mating can occur from early spring to late fall, with females having only one litter a year. Gestation lasts about 33 days, and the litter size is two to four altricial young.

SIMILAR SPECIES: The larger **Bushy-tailed Woodrat** (p. 202) has a flattened and bushy tail. The smaller **Desert Woodrat** (p. 200) has white hindfeet.

RANGE: These woodrats are found along the West Coast from Oregon through California.

Bushy-tailed Woodrat
Neotoma cinerea

Although most people have heard of "packrats," few people know that it was for woodrats that this nickname was originally coined. The Bushy-tailed Woodrat is a fine example of a packrat—it is widely known for its habit of collecting all manner of objects into a heap. This animal is also sometimes called a "trade rat," because it is nearly always carrying something in its teeth, only to drop that item to pick up something else instead. Thus, camping gear, false teeth, tools or jewelry may disappear from a campsite, with a stick, bone or pinecone kindly left in its place.

Bushy-tailed Woodrats tend to nest in rocky areas, and because their nests are large and messy, woodrat homes are easier to find than the residents. The places in which woodrats can build their nests are limited, and rival males fight fiercely over their houses. Female woodrats are likely attracted to males who have secure nests, and several females may be found nesting with a single male.

The Bushy-tailed Woodrat may have proportionally the longest whiskers of any rodent in the region. Extending well over the width of the animal's body on either side, a woodrat's whiskers serve it well as it feels its way around in the darkness of caves, mines and the night. Woodrats are most active after dark, so a late-night prowl with flashlight in hand may catch the reflective glare of a woodrat's eyes as the animal investigates its territory.

DESCRIPTION: The back is gray, pale pinkish or a grizzled brown. The belly is white. The long, soft, dense, buffy fur is underlain by a short, soft underfur. The long, bushy, almost squirrel-like tail is gray above and white below. Juveniles and sub-adults have distinct pelages: a juvenile's back is gray, and it has short tail hairs; a sub-adult has brown hues in its back, and its tail has long guard hairs. A tawny adult pelage is developed in fall. All woodrats have large, protruding black eyes, big, fur-covered ears and long, abundant whiskers.

HABITAT: This woodrat's domain usually includes rocks and shrubs or abandoned buildings, mine shafts or caves. It has a greater elevational range than other woodrats, extending from grasslands to the alpine.

FOOD: Leaves of shrubs are probably the most important component of the diet, but conifer needles and seeds, juniper berries, mushrooms, fruits,

RANGE: The Bushy-tailed Woodrat is the most northerly woodrat; its range extends from the southern Yukon southeast to western North Dakota and south to central California and northern New Mexico.

Total Length: 11–18 in.
Tail Length: 4¾–8¾ in.
Weight: 2¾–18 oz.

grasses, rootstocks and bulbs are all eaten or stored for later consumption. To provide adequate winter supplies, a woodrat gathers and stores about 2 gal. of food. One woodrat may make several caches.

DEN: Large numbers of sticks, plus a large variety of bark, dung and other materials, are piled in a rock cleft or talus near the nest site. This accumulation often has no inner passages or chambers. Instead, the den is a lined, ball- or cup-shaped nest built of fibrous material and situated nearby, usually more than 11 ft. above the ground, either in a narrow crevice, in the fork of a tree, on a shelf or sometimes even in a stove in an abandoned cabin.

YOUNG: Mating usually takes place between March and June. Following a 27- to 32-day gestation period, three or four helpless young are born. They are ⁷/₁₆–⁵/₈ oz. at birth and their growth is rapid. Special teeth help them hold onto

their mother's nipples almost continuously. Their incisors erupt at 12 to 15 days, and their eyes open on day 14 or 15. They first leave the nest at about 22 days, and they are weaned at 26 to 30 days. The young reach sexual maturity the spring following their birth. Some females bear two litters in a season.

SIMILAR SPECIES: The **Desert Woodrat** (p. 200) and the **Dusky-footed Woodrat** (p. 201) lack bushy tails. The similar-sized **Norway Rat** (p. 204) also does not have a bushy tail and tends to live near human activity. The **American Pika** (p. 296) has no visible tail, and its muzzle is shorter.

DID YOU KNOW?

When a very old woodrat nest in an old cabin near a hotel was torn apart some years ago, a collection of silverware dating back to the earliest days of the hotel was found.

Norway Rat
Rattus norvegicus

Total Length: 13–18 in.
Tail Length: 4¾–8¾ in.
Weight: 7–17 oz.

Despite its evolutionary success and excellent adaptability, the Norway Rat is mainly reviled by people around the world. The montane and northern regions of Washington and Oregon are largely inhospitable to Norway Rats, but these rodents may be found in developed areas and ranching country. Everywhere Norway Rats occur, they are the objects of loathing and intensive pest control measures.

The geography and climate of interior Washington and Oregon help limit the spread of rats through the region. A rat is capable of dispersing 3–5 mi. from its starting point in a summer, but mountains are a barrier, largely because winter temperatures below 0° F will prove fatal if it is unable to find adequate shelter, such as in a building or garbage dump. The greatest influx of rats in the region comes courtesy of modern transportation. Rats hitchhiking on trucks and trains are of concern, because they often disembark into warm buildings in mountain cities and towns.

Norway Rats were introduced to North America in about 1775, and they have established colonies in most cities and towns south of the boreal forest. These great pests feed on a wide variety of stored grain, garbage and carrion, they gnaw holes in walls, and they contaminate stored hay with urine and feces. They have also been implicated in the transfer of diseases to both livestock and humans.

More than any other animal, Norway Rats are viewed with disgust by most people. As one of the world's most studied and manipulated animals, however, much of our biomedical and psychological knowledge can be directly attributed to experiments involving these animals—a rather significant contribution for a hated pest.

DESCRIPTION: The back is a grizzled brown, reddish brown or black. The paler belly is grayish to yellowish white. The long, round, tapered tail is darker above and lighter below, and it is sparsely haired and scaly. The prominent ears are covered with short, fine hairs. Occasionally, someone releases an albino, white or piebald Norway Rat that had been kept in captivity.

HABITAT: Norway Rats nearly always live in proximity to human habitation. Where they are found away from

RANGE: The Norway Rat is concentrated in cities, towns and farms throughout coastal North America, southern Canada and most of the U.S.

humans, they prefer thickly vegetated regions with abundant cover. Abandoned buildings in the wilderness are more frequently occupied by Bushy-tailed Woodrats than by Norway Rats.

FOOD: This rat eats a wide variety of grains, insects, garbage and carrion. It may even kill young chickens, ducks, piglets and lambs. Seeds from birdfeeders and green legume pods are also popular items, and some shoots and grasses are consumed.

DEN: A cavity scratched beneath a fallen board or a space beneath an abandoned building may hold a bulky nest of grasses, leaves and often paper or chewed rags. Although Norway Rats are able to, they seldom dig long burrows.

YOUNG: After a gestation period of 21 to 22 days, 6 to 22 pink, blind babies are born. The eyes open after 10 days. The

young are sexually mature in about three months. In Washington and Oregon, Norway Rats seem to breed mainly in the warmer months of the year, but in some cities they may can breed year-round.

SIMILAR SPECIES: The **Bushy-tailed Woodrat** (p. 202) has a white belly and its tail is covered with long, bushy hair. The **Common Muskrat** (p. 224) is larger and has a laterally compressed tail.

DID YOU KNOW?

Some historians attribute the end of the Black Death epidemics in Europe to the southward invasion of the Norway Rat and its displacement of the less aggressive Black Rat, which was much more apt to inhabit human homes, carrying with it the bacteria-infected fleas that spread the plague.

Black Rat
Rattus rattus

Total Length: 13–18 in.
Tail Length: 6¼–10 in.
Weight: 4½–12 oz.

The Black Rat is generally restricted to the southern and coastal United States, but the numbers in western Washington and Oregon appear to be increasing. Widescale food transportation between cities greatly aids dispersal for this species.

This rat is slimmer and darker than the Norway Rat, and it has a tail that is longer than its head and body combined.

House Mouse
Mus musculus

Thanks to its habit of catching rides with humans, first aboard ships and now in train cars, trucks and containers, the House Mouse is now found in most countries of the world. In fact, the House Mouse's dispersal closely mirrors the agricultural development of our species. As humans began growing crops on the great, sweeping plains of middle Asia, this mouse, native to that region, began profiting from our storage of surplus grains and our concurrent switch from a nomadic to a relatively sedentary lifestyle.

Within the small span of a few hundred human generations, farmed grains began to find their way into Europe and Africa for trade. Along with these and subsequent grain shipments, stowaway House Mice were spread to every corner of the globe. Even in harsh parts of the mountains of Washington and Oregon, where most non-native mice and rats are unable to survive, the House Mouse is found wherever humans provide it free room and board. Unlike many of the introduced animals in the region, however, this species seems to have had a minimal negative impact on native animal populations.

House Mice are known to most people who have spent some time on farms or in warehouses, university labs and disorderly places. The white mice commonly used as laboratory animals are an albino strain of this species.

DESCRIPTION: The back is yellowish brown, gray or nearly black, the sides may have a slightly yellow wash, and the underparts are light gray. The head is small, and the pointed nose is surrounded by abundant whiskers. The large ears are almost hairless, and the protruding eyes are black. The long, tapered, hairless, gray tail is slightly lighter below than above. The brownish feet tend to be whitish at the tips.

HABITAT: This introduced mouse inhabits homes, outbuildings, barns, granaries, haystacks and trash piles. It cannot tolerate temperatures below 14° F around its nest, and it seems to be unable to survive winters in the harsh ecozones without access to heated buildings or haystacks. In summer, it may disperse slightly more than 2 mi. from its winter refuge into fields and grasslands, only to succumb the following winter. Wilderness cabins occupied only in summer are far more apt to be invaded by Deer Mice than by House Mice.

FOOD: Seeds, stems and leaves constitute the bulk of the diet, but insects,

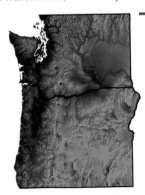

RANGE: The House Mouse is widespread in North America, inhabiting nearly every city, hamlet or farm from the Atlantic to the Pacific and north to the tundra.

Total Length: 5–7¾ in.

Tail Length: 2½–4 in.

Weight: ½–⅞ oz.

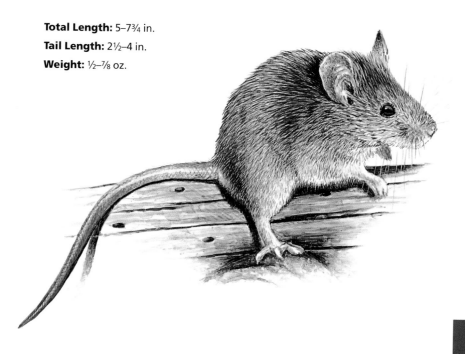

carrion and human food, including meat and milk, are eagerly consumed.

DEN: The nest is constructed of shredded paper and rags, vegetation and sometimes fur combined into a 4-in. ball beneath a board, inside a wall, in a pile of rags or in a haystack. It may occur at any level in a building. House Mice sometimes dig short tunnels, but they generally do not use them as nest sites.

YOUNG: If abundant resources are available, as in a haystack, breeding may occur throughout the year, but populations away from human habitations seem to breed only during the warmer months. Gestation usually takes three weeks, but it may be extended to one month if the female is lactating when she conceives. The litter usually contains four to eight helpless,

pink, jellybean-shaped young. Their fur begins to grow in two to three days, the eyes open at 12 to 15 days, and they are weaned at 16 to 17 days. At six to eight weeks, the young become sexually mature.

SIMILAR SPECIES: The **Western Harvest Mouse** (p. 192) looks very similar, but it has a clearly bicolored tail (lighter below) and a distinct longitudinal groove on the front of each upper incisor tooth. The **Deer Mouse** (p. 194) has a bright white belly and distinctively bicolored tail.

DID YOU KNOW?

The word "mouse" probably derives from the Sanskrit *mus*—also the source, via Latin, of the genus name—which itself came from *musha*, meaning "thief."

Southern Red-backed Vole
Clethrionomys gapperi

Total Length: 4¾–6¼ in.

Tail Length: 1⅛–2¼ in.

Weight: ⁷⁄₁₆–1½ oz.

This attractive little vole, which is active both day and night, can be heard rustling in the leaf litter of forests in most of Washington and eastern Oregon. It is almost never seen, however, as it scurries along almost invisible runways on the forest floor on its short legs.

The Southern Red-backed Vole is a classic example of a "subnivean" wanderer, a small mammal that lives out cold winters between the snowpack and the frozen ground. The snow's insulating qualities create a layer at ground level within which the temperature is nearly constant. This vole does not cache food; instead, it forages widely under the snow for vegetation or any other digestible foods.

DESCRIPTION: The reddish dorsal stripe makes this animal one of the easiest voles to recognize. On rare occasions, the dorsal stripe is a rich brownish black or even slate brown. The sides are grayish buff, and the undersides and feet are

grayish white. Compared with most voles, the black eyes seem small and the nose looks slightly more pointed. The short tail, which is slender and scantily haired, is gray below and brown above. The ears are rounded and project somewhat above the thick fur.

HABITAT: This vole is found in a variety of habitats, including damp coniferous forests, bogs, swampy land and sometimes drier aspen forests.

FOOD: Green vegetation, grasses, berries, lichens, seeds and fungi form the bulk of the diet.

DEN: Summer nests, made in shallow burrows, rotten logs or rock crevices, are lined with fine materials, such as dry grass, moss and lichens. Winter nests are subnivean; that is, above the ground but below the snow.

YOUNG: Mating occurs between April and October. Following a gestation period of about 20 days, two to eight (usually four to seven) helpless, pink young are born. They nurse almost continuously, and their growth is rapid. By two weeks they are well-furred and have opened their eyes. Once the young are weaned, they are no longer permitted in the vicinity of the nest. This vole reaches sexual maturity at two to three months.

RANGE: This vole is widespread across most of the southern half of Canada and

south through the Cascades and Rocky Mountains as far as northern New Mexico and through the Appalachians to North Carolina.

SIMILAR SPECIES: The **Western Red-backed Vole** (p. 209) is found to the west and south of this species. The **Red Tree Vole** (p. 211) has a visibly longer tail.

Western Red-backed Vole
Clethrionomys californicus

Total Length: 5½–6⅝ in.
Tail Length: 1¾–2¼ in.
Weight: ⅝–1³/₁₆ oz.

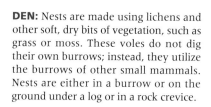

Although many voles leave runways on the forest floor as a result of routine foraging expeditions, the Western Red-backed Vole follows no set foraging route and is thus unlikely to leave such telltale runways. To further disguise its whereabouts, this vole rarely runs out in the open. Using the cover of leaf litter, logs, rocks and thick vegetation, this vole remains safely out of sight from all but the most perceptive of predators. Forest-dwelling hawks, Coyotes, weasels and owls are among the species that prey upon Western Red-backed Voles.

Like other voles, this one does not hibernate. Instead, it remains active, and in areas of snow it makes burrows below the snow but above the ground.

DESCRIPTION: This vole is a dark chestnut brown with reddish highlights, often mixed with black above. The sides lighten considerably, and the undersides are buffy gray in color. The tail is slightly bicolored and is about half the length of the head and body.

HABITAT: A vole of deep forests, the Western Red-backed Vole favors dense coniferous woodland with abundant fallen logs and debris.

FOOD: These voles primarily eat green vegetation, but some seeds or fruit may also be consumed.

DEN: Nests are made using lichens and other soft, dry bits of vegetation, such as grass or moss. These voles do not dig their own burrows; instead, they utilize the burrows of other small mammals. Nests are either in a burrow or on the ground under a log or in a rock crevice.

YOUNG: Mating normally occurs from February to November, though in some parts of its range this vole mates throughout the year. Gestation takes about 18 days, and litter size is two to seven altricial young.

SIMILAR SPECIES: The **Southern Red-backed Vole** (p. 208) is a close relative, but its range is to the north and east of this vole's, and it is much redder in color. The **Red Tree Vole** (p. 211) has a visibly longer tail. The **White-footed Vole** (p. 210) does not have any reddish coloration.

RANGE: This vole is found from the south shore of the Columbia River southward into northern California.

White-footed Vole
Arborimus albipes

Total Length: 6⅜–7½ in.

Tail Length: 2¼–3 in.

Weight: ⅝–1 oz.

This secretive and rare vole was once considered a member of the genus *Phenacomys*, like the Western Heather Vole (p. 212). It lives only along the coastal region of Oregon and northern California. Although its range hugs the coastline, this vole favors alder and dense forests along freshwater streams. In both California and Oregon, this vole is considered a sensitive species that may become an endangered species. No reliable population estimates exist for this rodent, but it is rarely seen or caught. Its major predators include weasels, owls, minks, spotted skunks and Domestic Cats. Our household cats are efficient hunters that can very seriously threaten populations of indigenous animals.

DESCRIPTION: This fairly large vole is a rich brownish gray in color, with lighter gray or brown undersides. The sparsely haired tail is sharply bicolored, with a dusky stripe on top and a wider, whitish stripe below. This vole has small eyes and large, nearly naked ears.

HABITAT: These voles prefer moist, dense deciduous forests close to freshwater streams. Old logs and other debris make suitable cover for these elusive rodents.

FOOD: These voles consume large quantities of leaves and smaller amounts of roots and moss. They are not known to feed on fungi, seeds, fruits or animal matter.

DEN: In a well-covered area, such as underneath a log or a dense shrub, this vole builds a small ground nest using dry grasses and other soft plant material.

YOUNG: Mating appears to occur year-round in this species, but only in ideal conditions will a female mate more than once a year. Litter size is two to four young, but little else is known about the reproduction of this vole.

RANGE: White-footed Voles occur along the coast of Oregon and into northern California.

SIMILAR SPECIES: The outwardly similar **Long-tailed Vole** (p. 220) is usually larger. The otherwise similar **Western Red-backed Vole** (p. 209) often has red highlights or a red streak over its back.

Red Tree Vole
Arborimus longicaudus

Total Length: 6¼–8⅛ in.
Tail Length: 2³⁄₈–3¾ in.
Weight: ⅞–1⅝ oz.

High up in old-growth conifers on the Pacific Coast runs the agile Red Tree Vole. In its arboreal world, the twigs and branches mesh together to form a complex system of shortcuts and highways. These transportation routes are so efficient that this vole rarely descends to the ground. In mature coniferous forests, the Spotted Owl is the main predator of this vole. The greatest threat to this rare vole, however, is the logging of old-growth forests. Extensive logging fragments its habitat to such a great extent that populations become irrevocably isolated or disappear entirely.

DESCRIPTION: True to its name, the Red Tree Vole is cinnamon or bright reddish in color. The undersides are nearly white and the long, well-haired tail is blackish. Juveniles are more brown than red, but they still have black tails.

HABITAT: These tree voles prefer extensive forests of old-growth Douglas-fir. If Douglas-fir habitat is not available, they may also inhabit redwood and Sitka spruce areas within their range.

FOOD: These voles feed entirely on the coniferous trees they live in, primarily Douglas-fir. Tender young needles are eaten whole, but with mature needles the vole first bites off the resin ducts so that they can be used as building materials inside the nest.

DEN: The Red Tree Vole builds a tree nest up to 150 ft. above the ground in a Douglas-fir. The bulky nest is made of twigs and leftover plant parts. The nest is molded inside and secured to the tree using fecal pellets. Nests can become quite complex and may be used by generations of voles. Sometimes this vole will use an old squirrel, woodrat or bird nest instead of building its own.

YOUNG: The reproduction of Red Tree Voles is not well studied. It is known that they are able to mate throughout the year and that after a gestation period of about 28 days, a litter of one to four young is born.

SIMILAR SPECIES: The **red-backed voles** (pp. 208–09) are not as red as this vole, and they live on the ground; all other vole species in the region lack red coloration entirely.

RANGE: Red Tree Voles are found in coastal Oregon and into northern California.

Western Heather Vole
Phenacomys intermedius

Total Length: 4¼–6¼ in.

Tail Length: 1–1⅝ in.

Weight: ⅞–1¾ oz.

colors are seen, but the most common is a grizzled buffy brown. The roundish ears scarcely extend above the fur and have tawny or orangish hair inside.

The Western Heather Vole generally occupies the alpine tundra, but it is also found in the same woodlands as its red-backed kin, and skulls of each species are frequently found in the same owl pellets.

This vole's common name refers to its preference for high-elevation environments where heathers are common. As well, this vole may feed on the inner bark of heathers. It consumes a high percentage of bark seasonally, and (like other voles) it has intestines especially suited to digesting this fibrous, lignin-rich food.

DESCRIPTION: This gentle vole has a short, thin, bicolored tail that is slate gray above, sometimes with a few white hairs, and white below. The tops of the feet are silvery gray, and the belly hairs have light tips, giving the entire undersurface a light gray hue. Various dorsal

HABITAT: This vole seems to prefer open areas in a variety of habitats in the mountains, including alpine tundra and coniferous forest.

FOOD: The Western Heather Vole feeds primarily on green vegetation, grasses, lichens, berries, seeds and fungi. It also often eats the inner bark of various shrubs of the heather family.

DEN: The summer nest is made in a burrow up to 8 in. deep, and it is lined with fine dry grass and lichens. In winter, the nest is built on the ground in a snow-covered runway.

YOUNG: Mating occurs between April and October. Following a gestation period of about three weeks, one to eight (usually four or five) helpless, pink young are born. They nurse almost continuously, and their growth is rapid. By two weeks, they are well furred and have opened their eyes. This vole becomes sexually mature after two to three months, but a young male does not breed in his first year.

SIMILAR SPECIES: The **Long-tailed Vole** (p. 220) has a longer tail, and both it and the **Meadow Vole** (p. 213) have slate gray hindfeet.

RANGE: The Western Heather Vole occurs from northwestern British Columbia south to central California and northern New Mexico.

Meadow Vole
Microtus pennsylvanicus

Total Length: 5–7½
Tail Length: 1¼–1¾ in.
Weight: ⅝–2¼ oz.

This primarily northern vole is well adapted to the winters of north-eastern Washington. When the snows recede from the land in spring, an elaborate network of Meadow Vole activity is exposed to the world. Highways, chambers and nests, previously insulated from winter's cold by deep snows, await the growth of spring vegetation to conceal them once again. These tunnels often lead to logs, boards or shrubs, where the voles can find additional shelter.

Many Meadow Voles die in their first months, and very few voles seem to live longer than a year.

DESCRIPTION: The body varies from brown to blackish above and gray below. The protruding eyes are small and black. The rounded ears are mostly hidden in the long fur of the rounded head. The tops of the feet are blackish brown. The tail is about twice as long as the hindfoot.

HABITAT: The Meadow Vole can be found in a variety of habitats, provided grasses are present. Grasslands, pastures, marshy areas, open woodlands, taiga and mountain meadows are all potential homes for this vole.

FOOD: The green parts of sedges, grasses and some forbs make up the bulk of the spring and summer diet. In winter, large amounts of seeds, some bark and insects are eaten. Other foods include grains, roots and bulbs.

DEN: The summer nest is made in a shallow burrow and lined with fine materials, such as dry grass, moss and lichens. The winter nest is subnivean—above the ground but below the snow.

YOUNG: Spring mating occurs between late March and the end of April. Gestation takes about 20 days, and the average litter size is four to eight. From birth, the helpless young nurse almost constantly to support their rapid growth. Their eyes open in 9 to 12 days, and they are weaned at 12 to 13 days. At least one more litter is born, usually in fall.

SIMILAR SPECIES: The **Montane Vole** (p. 216), which is difficult to distinguish from this one, has a more extensive range in Washington and Oregon. The **Western Heather Vole** (p. 212) has silvery-gray fur on the tops of its feet.

RANGE: This widespread vole ranges from central Alaska to Labrador and south to northern Arizona and New Mexico in the West and Georgia in the East.

Water Vole

Microtus richardsoni

If you linger next to streams when hiking high-elevation trails in the mountains, you may have an opportunity to become familiar with the Water Vole. This large vole is like a small alpine muskrat in many ways as it dives and forages with ease along the icy snowmelt creeks. It is almost exclusively nocturnal, so you are more likely to experience examples of its distinctive sign than the animal itself.

The Water Vole's diagnostic well-worn runways criss-cross the margins of alpine streams, connecting the burrows and foraging areas of small colonies. These damp pathways are often under the mat of roots and plant debris on the ground surface. Vegetation cuttings often line the paths. This semi-aquatic vole's burrows may be in such close proximity to the water that you would expect them to flood with each rainfall. Water Voles appear to abandon these tunnel networks through the winter months, remaining adequately protected from the winter's chill by the snows that deeply coat and insulate their habitat. Few Water Voles survive more than one winter.

DESCRIPTION: This large vole is brownish black above, with paler gray sides. The belly is gray, with a grayish-white wash. The fur is thick, with a dense water-repelling undercoat. The very long hindfeet aid in swimming. The tail is indistinctly bicolored: blackish above and dark gray below. The ears are rounded and scarcely extend above the thick fur. The protruding eyes are small and black.

HABITAT: True to its name, the Water Vole lives primarily along the water, specifically alpine and subalpine streams and lakes. It favors clear, swift, gravel-bottomed streams that are lined with mixed stands of low willows and dense herbage.

FOOD: In summer, Water Voles feed on the stems of various sedges and grasses, plus the leaves, stems, roots and flowers of forbs. Winter foods include the bark of willows and bog birch, various roots and rhizomes and the fruits and seeds of available green vegetation.

DEN: This vole digs extensive burrow systems, with tunnels up to 4 in. wide, through moist soil at the edges of streams or waterbodies. The nest chamber, which is about 4 in. high and 6 in. long, is lined with moss and dry grass or leaves. It is often situated under a rise, log or stump. A Water Vole will excavate

RANGE: The Water Vole has two disjunct populations in the region: the western population extends along the Cascade Mountains from central British Columbia to southern Oregon; the eastern population occurs in the Rocky Mountains from central Alberta to south-central Utah.

Total Length: 7½–11 in.
Tail Length: 2⅛–3⅞ in.
Weight: 1⅛–4¼ oz.

and re-excavate its burrow system throughout summer. The winter nest will be in a snow-covered runway located farther from the water.

YOUNG: Water Voles probably breed periodically from May through September, with usually two or more litters of 2 to 10 young born each year. Gestation takes at least 22 days. The young are helpless at birth, but they grow rapidly, reaching maturity quickly. They may even breed during their birth year.

SIMILAR SPECIES: The Water Vole's large hindfoot, which is more than 1 in. long, and its generally large size distinguish it from most other voles in the region. The **Townsend's Vole** (p. 219) is smaller.

DID YOU KNOW?

The Water Vole is an excellent swimmer, and it will often seek refuge from martens, weasels and other predators in the water.

Montane Vole
Microtus montanus

Total Length: 5¼–7¼ in.
Tail Length: 1¼–2¼ in.
Weight: ½–1¾ oz

In many parts of Washington and Oregon, the Montane Vole is one of the most abundant small mammals. This great abundance means that if you see a vole in Montane Vole habitat, chances are good that it is indeed a Montane Vole. More importantly, the high numbers of this vole indicate its ecological importance. These numerous voles are a steady food supply for larger carnivores, such as owls and other raptors, weasels, Coyotes and more. At their highest densities, these voles are reported to reach numbers of more than 2500 an acre, though their populations cycle and numbers usually peak well below 500 an acre.

DESCRIPTION: The small, thickset Montane Vole has short ears that are largely hidden in the fur and dark, protruding eyes. The back is brown to black. The belly is a lighter gray. The head is rounded, and the snout is blunt. Most of each limb is hidden in the body's skin, giving the animal a short-legged appearance. The comparatively long, bicolored tail is sparsely covered with hair.

HABITAT: This vole is found in mountain meadows, valleys and some arid sagebrush communities.

FOOD: Green shoots form the majority of the diet when they are available. At other times of the year, seeds or even bark may be eaten.

DEN: The winter nests are often located aboveground along well-used runways. The Montane Vole's runways and nests are easiest to observe soon after the snow melts in spring. Its summer nests are in short burrows, under logs or at the bases of shrubs.

YOUNG: Montane Voles may have several litters in a year, but reproduction usually takes place between spring and fall. Gestation takes about 21 days, after which six to eight young are born.

SIMILAR SPECIES: Other voles may not be readily distinguishable. The **Townsend's Vole** (p. 219) is larger. The **Meadow Vole** (p. 213), though darker, looks extremely similar, but it is found only in northeastern Washington. The **Long-tailed Vole** (p. 220) has a longer tail. The **Sagebrush Vole** (p. 222) has a shorter tail.

RANGE: The Montane Vole occurs from southern British Columbia to Montana and south to New Mexico and California.

Gray-tailed Vole
Microtus canicaudus

Total Length: 5½–6⅝ in.

Tail Length: ¾–1¾ in.

Weight: about 1¾ oz.

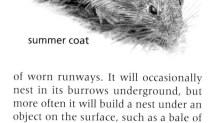

summer coat

This robust vole has the unfortunate luck of living in areas prone to heavy rains. In times of flooding, Gray-tailed Voles may remain in their burrows, utilizing pockets of trapped air for breathing. To get to the ground surface or to search for food, these voles swim through their flooded tunnels while holding their breath. When the fields are heavily flooded and their burrows and nest chambers fill with water, large numbers of Gray-tailed Voles can be seen clinging to fence posts or trees surrounding their water-logged homes. If a predator or even an observer approaches these voles, they quickly leap into the water and swim away.

DESCRIPTION: This robust vole has mostly yellowish brown or yellowish gray fur, with undersides of light gray. The mildly two-toned tail is brown to grayish, with a distinct darker dorsal stripe. This animal's overall coloration is darker in winter.

HABITAT: These voles live almost exclusively in grasslands, amidst grain crops and in legume or grassy pastures.

FOOD: Gray-tailed Voles probably feed on a variety of vegetation, but they are well known to feed on grasses, clover, wild onion and false dandelion.

DEN: This vole excavates a complex system of burrows and forms a network of worn runways. It will occasionally nest in its burrows underground, but more often it will build a nest under an object on the surface, such as a bale of hay or a piece of wood.

YOUNG: Little is known about the mating behavior of Gray-tailed Voles in the wild, but presumably mating occurs in spring. Gestation takes 21 to 23 days, and litter size ranges from two to eight, with an average of five. The female of this highly fecund species can breed successfully when she is as young as 18 days old.

SIMILAR SPECIES: In Washington, the **Townsend's Vole** (p. 219) has a much longer tail, and the **Creeping Vole** (p. 221) is not as robust in body shape. The **Long-tailed Vole** (p. 220) has an obviously longer tail. The **Montane Vole** (p. 216) lacks the distinct dark stripe on the tail and has a different range.

RANGE: This vole has a very small range that encompasses only extreme south-central Washington and north-central Oregon.

California Vole
Microtus californicus

Total Length: 6¼–8⅜ in.
Tail Length: 1½–2⅝ in.
Weight: 1½–3½ oz.

While walking through the forest in southwestern Oregon, stop to look at the ground around you. If you find numerous runways in the surface debris that resemble miniature bobsled runs, a lot of cut grass or vegetation and small holes in the soil, you may be in California Vole territory. The ability of this little creature to so significantly alter the appearance of its home ground is quite prodigious. If you're lucky, following one of the runways may lead you to a food source or a nest.

These voles can be extremely common—up to 200 individuals an acre. In non-cultivated areas this density is sustainable, but in orchards, vineyards and cropland, these rodents may reach pest proportions.

DESCRIPTION: This vole is a grizzled brown color, often flecked with black, above and lighter gray below. The tail is long and distinctly bicolored, being brownish above and paler below. This animal has pale brown or grayish feet and inconspicuous furred ears.

HABITAT: These voles are comfortable over a large range of elevations in a variety of habitats that include dry, grassy slopes, salt or freshwater marshes and moist meadows.

FOOD: This vole eats a variety of vegetation: in winter it feeds mainly on roots and tubers, and in summer it dines on grasses, seeds and leaves.

DEN: Like the majority of voles, the California Vole digs burrows. Nests are made of grass and moss and are found either in a small burrow chamber or directly under surface cover, such as a log or rock.

YOUNG: Breeding occurs throughout the year, but it ceases in periods of drought. Gestation takes 21 days, and females may have multiple litters of one to nine young in a year. The young are blind and nearly hairless at birth. Their growth is fast, and at two weeks their eyes are open and weaning follows.

SIMILAR SPECIES: This vole differs from most other voles by having a visibly shorter tail and pale feet.

RANGE: Common throughout its range, this vole occurs in southwestern Oregon and throughout most of California.

Townsend's Vole
Microtus townsendii

Total Length: 6⅝–9 in.
Tail Length: 2–2¾ in.
Weight: 1⅝–4 oz.

The Townsend's Vole is one of the largest voles in North America. As with many vole species, populations periodically erupt and then abruptly crash, but the mechanism that triggers these fluctuations is unknown.

Runways are used by generations of voles and may be up to 2 in. deep. In these well-used networks, the intersections often serve as latrines. In extreme cases, the pile of droppings can be 7 in. long by 3 in. wide, creating a ramp 5 in. high—an obstacle the voles simply scurry over as they travel the runways.

DESCRIPTION: The large, dark brown Townsend's Vole has broad ears that extend noticeably above the fur. It has a long, blackish-brown tail and similarly colored feet with brown claws. The protruding black eyes measure more than ³⁄₁₆ in. wide.

HABITAT: These voles occur in moist fields, sedge meadows and sometimes boggy areas. Occasionally, they can be found even in subalpine and alpine meadows.

FOOD: Townsend's Voles prefer tender marsh and grassland vegetation. They may also consume the bark of shrubs, some stems and roots of conifers and starchy roots.

DEN: During rainy seasons, nests are placed on or above the soil surface, often on hummocks. During dry periods, subterranean burrow systems and nests are used. The nests are made of dry grasses.

YOUNG: Breeding occurs from early February until October. Following a gestation period of 21 to 24 days, one to nine young are born in the grassy nest. They are weaned and leave the nest by 15 to 17 days. Young females born early will mate and bear litters their first summer. Males mature later.

SIMILAR SPECIES: The **Montane Vole** (p. 216) and **Creeping Vole** (p. 221) are smaller. The **Water Vole** (p. 214) is larger. The **Gray-tailed Vole** (p. 217) has a shorter tail with a distinct dark dorsal stripe. The **Long-tailed Vole** (p. 220) has a longer tail that is not uniformly dark. The **Sagebrush Vole** (p. 222) has a much shorter tail and a different habitat and range.

RANGE: The Townsend's Vole occurs from southern British Columbia south through western Washington and Oregon into northern California.

Long-tailed Vole
Microtus longicaudus

Total Length: 6¾–9 in.
Tail Length: 2¼–2⅞ in.
Weight: 1¼–2 oz.

are paler than the back, and the undersides are paler still. The indistinctly bicolored tail of this vole accounts for more than one-third of the animal's total length). The uppersides of the feet are gray.

The Long-tailed Vole is widespread in Washington and Oregon, but with an unusual distribution pattern. During the cooler climatic conditions of the Pleistocene, this vole was able to spread throughout the region. As the climate changed, it could no longer thrive everywhere it used to. Poorly adapted to hot and dry conditions, it is rarely found outside of suitable moist habitats. In northern parts of its range it may be found at lower elevations in moist areas, but southern populations are confined to mountains and equally cool, moist places.

This vole, which does not follow well-defined trails like other voles do, ranges widely at night.

DESCRIPTION: The upperparts are variously colored, ranging from a grizzled grayish to dark gray-brown, but the black tips on the guard hairs may give this vole a dark appearance. The sides

HABITAT: This vole lives in a variety of habitats, including grassy areas, mountain slopes, coniferous forests and alpine tundra, and also among alders or willows in the vicinity of water.

FOOD: Summer food consists of green leaves, grasses and berries. In winter, the Long-tailed Vole consumes the bark of heathers, willows and trees.

DEN: The simple burrows made by this vole under logs or rocks are often poorly developed. The nest chamber is lined with fine, dry grass, moss or leaves. Winter nests are subnivean.

YOUNG: Mating is presumed to occur from May to October, with the females often having two litters of two to eight (usually four to six) young a year. Gestation takes about three weeks. The young are helpless at birth, but at about the same time their eyes open, at two weeks of age, they are weaned and leave the nest. Some young females have their first litter when they are only six weeks old.

RANGE: The Long-tailed Vole ranges south from eastern Alaska and the Yukon along the Rocky Mountains to New Mexico and Arizona. From this eastern limit, its range extends west to the Pacific as far south as central California.

SIMILAR SPECIES: The **Townsend's Vole** (p. 219) has a mildly bicolored blackish tail. The **White-footed Vole** (p. 210) is smaller. **All other voles** in the region have shorter tails.

Creeping Vole
Microtus oregoni

Total Length: 4¾–6 in.
Tail Length: 1³⁄₁₆–1⅝ in.
Weight: ½–⅞ oz.

Decades of walking through prime Creeping Vole habitat will, on very rare occasions, produce encounters with this secretive animal. "Creeping" probably refers to this vole's preference for underground burrows and runways. This kind of concealment means seeing one in the wild is very unlikely. The Creeping Vole is also the smallest vole in its range, making it that much more difficult to spot.

DESCRIPTION: This small, slender vole appears to have very plush fur, because the guard hairs are about as long as the underfur. A Creeping Vole is dull or sooty brown above and gray below. Its feet and tail are dark gray. The eyes and ears are small.

HABITAT: Openings in moist coniferous forests from sea level to the mountains are preferred habitat for this species. Its burrows are found in easily crumbled woodland soils and mossy bogs. This vole has also been found in brushland beside cultivated fields.

FOOD: The Creeping Vole eats a wide variety of plant stems and roots. Potatoes and fallen apples are favorite foods when available. When this vole uses mole tunnels to feed in people's gardens, the guiltless mole gets blamed for the pilfering.

DEN: The nest is a mass of grasses or fine vegetation located just beneath a log or rotten stump. Numerous tunnels just below the soil surface extend out from the nest. Most of the time this vole lives a subterranean existence, and it often uses the burrows of the Coast Mole (p. 323).

YOUNG: Mating begins in March, and after a gestation period of 23 to 24 days, one to five naked, blind, pink young are born. A female may have up to five litters in a summer, but three is more common. The young are weaned at 13 days, and they then disperse. The females are sexually mature at 22 days; males at 42 days. Very few of these animals live for a full year.

SIMILAR SPECIES: Other voles in the region are larger. The **Long-tailed Vole** (p. 220) and the **Townsend's Vole** (p. 219) have longer tails. The **Gray-tailed Vole** (p. 217) is more robust and has a distinct dark dorsal stripe on the tail.

RANGE: The Creeping Vole is a species of the Pacific Northwest, ranging from southwestern British Columbia to northern California.

Sagebrush Vole
Lemmiscus curtatus

Total Length: 4¼–5½ in.
Tail Length: 1¹⁄₁₆–1⅛ in.
Weight: ¾–1⅜ oz.

The unusual Sagebrush Vole is unlike other voles in the region. Whereas most voles live in moist or wet areas, this vole prefers arid or semi-arid canyon and brushland habitat. Rodents that live in such dry habitats usually adapt to a diet heavy in insects, but the Sagebrush Vole remains a strict vegetarian, feeding solely on green vegetation and seeds.

This vole is colonial, and up to 30 burrow entrances can be found in a cluster. Colony numbers vary greatly because of yearly population fluctuations.

DESCRIPTION: This small, stout vole has short ears and legs and long, lax hair. It is a very pale ashy gray in color, with buffy tinges around the ears and nose. The undersides are silvery. The tail is shorter than the hindfoot, and it is dark above and light below.

RANGE: The U-shaped range of this vole, which skirts much of western Montana

and northern Idaho, extends from southern Alberta east to North Dakota, south to northern Colorado, southwest to southern Nevada and north to central Washington.

HABITAT: In keeping with its name, the Sagebrush Vole thrives in sagebrush flats, and also in arid grassland regions and dry canyons.

FOOD: The spring and summer diets include a variety of plant material, especially the new green shoots of grasses and leaves of forbs. In fall and winter, this vole may switch from its preferred diet of green material and feed on seeds, roots and the inner bark of shrubs.

DEN: A shallow but extensive system of burrows leads to a grass-lined nest chamber. Colonies vary greatly in size and density, but burrow entrances in a colony typically number from 8 to 30. Colonies are often located under debris, such as dead sagebrush or wood.

YOUNG: Mating occurs mainly between April and September. After a gestation period of about 25 days, a litter of 1 to 13 helpless young is born. The young grow rapidly, and they are weaned and out of the nest within three weeks.

SIMILAR SPECIES: The **Long-tailed** (p. 220), **Townsend's** (p. 219) and **Montane** (p. 216) **voles** all have tails that are both longer than 1 in. and longer than the hindfoot.

Northern Bog Lemming
Synaptomys borealis

Total Length: 4⅜–5½ in.
Tail Length: ⅝–1¹/₁₆ in.
Weight: ¾–1¼ oz.

Limited in this region to the northern border of Washington, the Northern Bog Lemming favors cool sphagnum bogs, but black spruce forests, subalpine meadows and tundra sedge meadows can also host populations. Although this animal is rarely seen, its workings are easy enough to identify. The mossy runways are frequently marked by evenly clipped grasses in neat piles, like cut trees awaiting logging trucks along haulroads.

DESCRIPTION: The whole body of this stout lemming is covered in thick fur. Although various color phases exist, the sides and back are usually chestnut or dark brown, and the underparts are usually grayish. The ears scarcely project above the fur of the head, and a little patch of tawny hair lies just behind them. The claws are strong and curved, and those on the middle two toes of each forefoot become greatly enlarged in winter, which aids in digging in frozen soils.

HABITAT: This lemming thrives in wet tundra conditions, such as tundra bogs, alpine meadows and even spruce woods.

FOOD: The diet is primarily composed of grasses, sedges and similar plants. If this vegetation is scarce, other emergent plants are eaten.

DEN: In summer, nests are located in tunnels about 6 in. underground. The nests are made of dry grass and fur. Nearby chambers are used for wastes. In winter, the nests are located aboveground, but under the snow.

YOUNG: Little is known about the Northern Bog Lemming, but it is thought to breed between spring and fall, with a gestation period of about three weeks. The litter contains two to six helpless young. Growth is rapid: the young are furred by one week, are weaned by three weeks and leave to start their own families soon thereafter.

SIMILAR SPECIES: Voles (pp. 208–22) are very similar, but they usually have longer tails and a less robust appearance.

RANGE: The Northern Bog Lemming ranges across most of Alaska and Canada south of the Arctic tundra. It occurs as far south as the northern parts of Washington, Idaho and western Montana.

Common Muskrat
Ondatra zibethicus

Although some muskrats live where winters are ice-free, those in the interior of Washington and Oregon are restricted to living beneath the ice of their pond and in their burrows for the duration of winter. When the snow and ice melt, muskrats might be seen out on dry land. In early spring, many first-year animals, now sexually mature, venture from their birth ponds to establish their own territories. These dispersing muskrats are commonly seen traveling over land, a tragic requirement for many—their numbers can be tallied all too easily in May roadkill surveys.

The Common Muskrat is not a "mini-beaver," nor is it a close relative of that large rodent; rather, it is a highly specialized aquatic vole that shares many features with the American Beaver as a result of their similar adaptations to similar environments. Like a beaver, a muskrat can close its lips behind its large, orange incisors so it can chew underwater without getting water or mud in its mouth. Its eyes are placed high on its head, and a muskrat can often be seen swimming with its head and sometimes its tail above water. The Common Muskrat dives with ease: it can remain submerged for over 15 minutes and can swim the length of a football field before surfacing.

Muskrats lead busy lives. They are continually gnawing cattails and bulrushes, whether eating the tender shoots or gathering the coarse vegetation for home building. Muskrat homes rise above shallow waters throughout the region; these structures are of tremendous importance not only to these aquatic rodents, but also to geese and ducks, which make use of muskrat homes as nesting platforms.

Both sexes have perianal scent glands that enlarge and produce a distinctly musk-like discharge during the breeding season. Although this scent is by no means unique to the Common Muskrat, its potency is sufficiently notable to have influenced this animal's common name. An earlier name for this species was "musquash," from the eastern Native American Abnaki name *moskwas*, but through the association with musk, the name changed to "muskrat."

DESCRIPTION: The coat generally consists of long, shiny, tawny to nearly black guard hairs overlying a brownish-gray undercoat. The flanks and sides are lighter than the back. The underparts are gray, with some tawny guard hairs. The long tail is black, nearly hairless, scaly and laterally compressed, and it has both a dorsal and a ventral keel. The

RANGE: This wide-ranging rodent occurs from the southern limit of the Arctic tundra across nearly all of Canada and the lower 48 states, with the exception of most of Florida, Texas and California.

Total Length: 1½–2 ft.
Tail Length: 7¾–11 in.
Weight: 1¾–3½ lb.

legs are short. The large, partially webbed hindfeet have an outer fringe of stiff hairs. The tops of the feet are covered with short, dark gray hair. The claws are long and strong.

HABITAT: Muskrats occupy sloughs, lakes, marshes and streams that have cattails, rushes and open water. They are not present in the high mountains.

FOOD: The summer diet includes a variety of emergent herbaceous plants. Cattails, rushes, sedges, irises, water lilies and pondweeds are staples, but a few frogs, turtles, mussels, snails, crayfish and an occasional fish may be eaten. In winter, muskrats feed on submerged vegetation.

DEN: Muskrat houses are built entirely of herbaceous vegetation, without the branches or mud of beaver lodges. The dome-shaped piles of cattails and rushes have underwater entrances. Muskrats can also dig bank burrows, which are 15–50 ft. long and have entrances that are below the usual water level.

YOUNG: Breeding takes place between March and September. Each female produces two or sometimes three litters a year. Gestation lasts 25 to 30 days, after which six to seven young are born. The eyes open at 14 to 16 days, the young are weaned at three to four weeks, and they are independent at one month. Both males and females are sexually mature the spring after their birth.

SIMILAR SPECIES: The **American Beaver** (p. 226) is larger and has a broad, flat tail, and typically only its head is visible above water when it swims. The **Nutria** (p. 184) is larger, has a white patch on its muzzle and has a round tail. The **Norway Rat** (p. 204) is smaller and has a round tail. The **Mountain Beaver** (p. 282) has a very short tail.

DID YOU KNOW?

Muskrats are highly regarded by native peoples. In one story, it was Muskrat who brought some mud from the bottom of the flooded world to the water's surface. This mud was spread over a turtle's back, thus creating all the dry land we now know.

American Beaver
Castor canadensis

The American Beaver is truly a great North American mammal. Its much-valued pelt motivated the earliest explorers to discover the riches of the wilderness, and even today, the beaver serves as an international symbol for wild places. Quite surprisingly to many Americans, foreign tourists often hold out great hopes of seeing these aquatic specialists during their visits. Fortunately, the American Beaver can be regularly encountered in wet areas throughout Washington and Oregon—except in winter in the interior—where its engineering marvels can be studied in awe-inspiring detail.

One of the few mammals that significantly alters its habitat to suit its needs, the beaver often sets back ecological succession and brings about changes in vegetation and animal life. Nothing seems to bother a beaver like the sound of running water, and this busy rodent builds dams of branches, mud and vegetation to slow the flow of water. The deep pools that the beaver's dams create allow it to remain active beneath the ice in winter, at a cost of vast amounts of labor—a single beaver may cut down hundreds of trees each year to ensure its survival.

Beavers live in colonies that generally consist of a pair of mated adults, their yearlings and a set of young kits. This family group generally occupies a tightly monitored habitat that consists of several dams, terrestrial runways and a lodge. In most cases, the lodge is ingeniously built of branches and mud. Some beavers, especially adult male beavers, tunnel into the banks of rivers, lakes or ponds for their den sites. In areas where trees do not commonly grow or currents are swift, females may also occupy bank dens.

Although the American Beaver is not a fast mover, it more than compensates with its immense strength. It is not unusual for this solidly built rodent to handle and drag—with its jaws—a 20-lb piece of wood. The beaver's flat, scaly tail, for which it is so well known, increases the animal's stability when it is cutting a tree, and it is slapped on the water or ground to communicate alarm.

Beavers are well adapted to their aquatic lifestyles. They have valves that allow them to close their ears and nostrils when they are submerged, and they have clear membranes that slide over the eyes to protect them. Because the lips form a seal behind the incisors, beavers can chew while they are submerged without having water and mud enter the mouth. In addition to their waterproof fur, into which they contin-

RANGE: Beavers can be found from the northern limit of deciduous trees south to northern Mexico. They are absent only from the Great Basin, the deserts of the Southwest and extensive grassland areas devoid of trees.

Total Length: 3–4 ft.
Tail Length: 11–21 in.
Weight: 35–66 lb.

ually groom an oily secretion to keep their skin dry, beavers have a thin layer of fat to help protect them from cold waters.

The American Beaver is an impressive and industrious animal that shapes the physical settings of many wilderness areas. Although most tree cutting and dam building occur at dusk or at night, you may see beavers during the day—sometimes working, but usually sunning themselves.

DESCRIPTION: The chunky, dark brown American Beaver is the second-largest rodent in the world, taking a backseat only to the South American Capybara. It has a broad, flat, scaly tail, short legs, a short neck and a broad head with short ears and massive, protruding, orange-faced incisors. The underparts are paler than the back and lack the reddish-brown hue. The nail on the second toe (and sometimes also the first) of each webbed hindfoot is split, allowing it to be used as a comb in grooming the fur. The forefeet are not webbed.

HABITAT: Beavers occupy freshwater environments wherever suitable woody vegetation grows nearby. They are sometimes even found feeding on dwarf willows above treeline.

FOOD: Bark and cambium, particularly that of aspen, willow, alder and birch, is favored, but aquatic pond vegetation is eaten in summer. Beavers sometimes come ashore to eat grains or grasses.

DEN: Beaver lodges are cone-shaped piles of mud and sticks. Beavers construct a great mound of material first and then chew an underwater access tunnel into the center and hollow out a den. The lodge is typically located away from shore in still water; in flowing water it is generally attached to a bank. Access to the lodge is from about 3½ ft.

DID YOU KNOW?

Beavers are not bothered by lice or ticks, but a tiny, flat beetle has evolved to live in beaver fur and nowhere else. This beetle feeds on beaver dandruff, and its meanderings probably tickle sometimes, because beavers often scratch themselves when they are out of water.

foreprint

walking trail

below the water's surface. A low shelf near the two or three plunge holes in the den allows much of the water to drain from the beavers before they enter the den chamber. Beavers often pile more sticks and mud on the outside of the lodge each year, and shreds of bark accumulate on the den floor. Adult males generally do not live in the lodge but dig bank burrows across the water from the lodge entrance. These burrows, the entrances to which are underwater, may be as long as 160 ft., but most are much shorter.

YOUNG: Most mating takes place in January or February, but occasionally it occurs as much as two months later. After a gestation period of four months, a litter of usually four kits is born. A second litter may be born in some years. At birth, the 12–23-oz. kits are fully furred, their incisors are erupted, and their eyes are nearly open. The kits begin to gnaw before they are one month old, and weaning takes place at two to three months. Beavers become sexually mature when they are about two years old, at which time they often disperse from the colony.

Common Muskrat

SIMILAR SPECIES: The **Common Muskrat** (p. 224) is much smaller, and its long tail is laterally compressed rather than paddle-shaped. The **Northern River Otter** (p. 126) has a tapered, long, round, fur-covered tail, a streamlined body and a small head. The **Nutria** (p. 184) is smaller and has a grizzled coat, a white patch on the muzzle and a round tail.

Great Basin Pocket Mouse
Perognathus parvus

Whereas some wild mammals literally come to your back door, to see others requires a visit to their special place of residence. The Great Basin Pocket Mouse is among the latter—it is a specialized rodent that lives only in arid, sparsely vegetated flatlands east of the Cascades in Washington and Oregon. Pocket mice are fond of dust-baths: they roll and dig in sandy areas and then brush their fur with both their forefeet and hindlimbs. They even invert their cheek pouches to clean them against the sand.

Pocket mice have large hindfeet and small forelegs. They tend to sit on their hindlegs outside the burrow, but the body remains horizontal. They move either in a slow walk or an unusual hop that involves all four limbs. The Great Basin Pocket Mouse typically relies on speed, agility and quick escapes into its burrow to evade such predators as hawks, owls, snakes, foxes and weasels. Individuals have been known to jump 2 ft. straight up in response to a sudden alarm.

Unlike hibernating rodents, pocket mice do not build up a store of fat for winter; instead, they pack their burrows with massive quantities of seeds. The number of seeds stored by each individual is phenomenal when you consider that each seed is handled individually and that many of them are smaller than the head of a pin. Equally amazing is the considerable competition for seeds that occurs between pocket mice and ants in some areas.

When outside food supplies dwindle, during the winter or extreme summer heat, these pocket mice retreat to their burrows and enter torpor, a state of dormancy that is not as deep as hibernation. They arouse periodically to feed on their stored seeds and to urinate, but they consume less than half the amount of food eaten on active days.

DESCRIPTION: The back is a glossy, yellowish buff; the many black-tipped hairs overlying the fur give it a peppered appearance. A narrow buffy line separates the back color from the uniform white or buffy-white underparts and feet. The tail is generally more than half the animal's total length, and it is darker above and lighter below. The hindfoot is ⅞–1 in. long.

HABITAT: These pocket mice live in sandy soils in semi-arid and arid areas.

FOOD: Cheatgrass seeds form the bulk of the diet, but this mouse also eats grain and seedlings of winter wheat, as well as

RANGE: The Great Basin Pocket Mouse is found in semi-desert areas of the interior of British Columbia, south to California, Nevada and northern Arizona and east as far as southwestern Wyoming.

Total Length: 6–8 in.
Tail Length: 3⅜–4½ in.
Weight: ½–1 oz.

the seeds of Russian thistle, wild mustards, antelope bitterbrush and pigweed. Caterpillars and adult insects also supplement its diet; in spring in particular, considerable numbers of insects are eaten.

DEN: Summer tunnels are shallow and form a network of storage and refuge burrows. The tunnel entrances are often plugged with soil by day. Winter burrows are much deeper, extending as far as 6½ ft. below the surface. Inside the winter burrow is a chamber with a grass nest. Prior to entering torpor, the pocket mouse may plug up to 3 ft. of the burrow entrance with soil.

YOUNG: A female mates soon after she emerges from hibernation in April. About four to six helpless young are born after a gestation period of 21 to 28

days. The young are weaned at 25 days, when they weigh about ¼ oz. Some females born early enough in the season may reach maturity and have their own litters in late summer. Mid- and late-season young become sexually mature the spring after their birth.

SIMILAR SPECIES: This pocket mouse is easily distinguished from other mice by its long, bicolored tail that is slightly crested near the tip. The **Little Pocket Mouse** (p. 232) has a pale brown tail.

DID YOU KNOW?

Pocket mice never need to drink—small amounts of water are already present in most of what they eat, and they obtain even more through the metabolism of their food.

Little Pocket Mouse

Perognathus longimembris

Total Length: 4¼–6 in.
Tail Length: 2⅛–3⅜ in.
Weight: about ¼ oz.

Small and abundant, these pocket mice are nocturnal inhabitants of arid areas in the western states. At their peak population density, these mice can number up to 400 individuals an acre. High densities like this can quickly diminish the available food sources, but these little mice have mechanisms to cope with food scarcity. If hunger persists for more than 24 hours, the mouse slips into dormancy for a few days, thus conserving energy. Throughout their range in southeastern Oregon, these mice experience either a dry or cold season during which food is unavailable. To outlast such seasons, they remain dormant in their burrows.

DESCRIPTION: This pocket mouse has soft fur that is usually grayish yellow in color, though color varies regionally as soil color changes. The fur may be flecked with black hairs above, and the undersides may be brownish to nearly white. This rodent has two external cheek pouches for carrying food or nesting material. At the base of the ears are two conspicuous patches of white fur. The tail, which is longer than the length of the head and body, is pale brown.

HABITAT: This pocket mouse lives in sandy or gravelly soils of deserts, brushy areas, rocky outcroppings and rolling terrain.

FOOD: When foraging, the pocket mouse eats fresh green vegetation, such as forbs and grass. The food that it carries back to the burrow for storage consists mainly of non-perishable seeds.

DEN: Pocket mice excavate burrows with chambers for sleeping, nesting and food storage. The burrow openings are marked with piles of dirt, but usually the entrance is plugged.

YOUNG: Breeding varies in response to the environment, but good conditions favor multiple litters from spring to late summer. Gestation lasts 22 or 23 days, and litter size is one to six young.

RANGE: This pocket mouse is found from southeastern Oregon southward through most of Nevada, the western edge of Utah and central and southern California.

SIMILAR SPECIES: The more widespread **Great Basin Pocket Mouse** (p. 230) is larger and has a slightly two-toned tail.

Dark Kangaroo Mouse

Microdipodops megacephalus

Total Length: 5⅞–7 in.

Tail Length: 2⅝–4 in.

Weight: ⅜–⅝ oz.

Walking primarily on its hind-feet rather than on all four, the Dark Kangaroo Mouse shares characteristics of both kangaroo rats and pocket mice. Its tail is not tufted like a kangaroo rat's tail, but it is nearly as long. This rodent's large hindfeet are specialized for hopping, like those of a kangaroo rat, but its body is small, like a pocket mouse. Because the Dark Kangaroo Mouse is the only member of its genus in this region, recognizing it in the field should not be too difficult. Keep in mind, however, that if you surprise this mouse close to its nest, you will antagonize it, and it will likely stand on its hindlegs to staunchly defend its territory.

DESCRIPTION: The Dark Kangaroo Mouse is blackish or gray above. The fur below is nearly white; it is sometimes sooty in appearance, because the base of each hair is gray. The black-tipped tail is not tufted. Research indicates that fat is stored in the tail, which is widest in the middle and tapers at either end. The incisors are not grooved.

HABITAT: These mice are common in sagebrush flats and scrubby areas, and in places with loose sands and gravel.

FOOD: The main foods of these mice are arthropods, seeds and some green vegetation, such as forbs and grasses. Other plant seeds are consumed to a smaller extent, as are insects. Seeds and non-perishable foods are stored in the burrow.

DEN: The Dark Kangaroo Mouse excavates a burrow for sleeping and storage of food. The burrow will be quite simple and 2–4 ft. in length.

YOUNG: These kangaroo mice mate throughout spring and summer, but most females bear their litter between May to June. Litter size varies from two to seven young.

SIMILAR SPECIES: This is the only kangaroo mouse in the region, and the following rodents have tails that are not wider in the middle than at the ends. **Kangaroo rats** (pp. 234–37) are similar but larger, often with white patches on their faces and necks and bicolored, tufted tails. **Pocket mice** (pp. 230–32) are usually smaller and more uniformly colored.

RANGE: These mice range from southeastern Oregon southward through most of Nevada, as well as into western Utah and extreme eastern parts of California.

Ord's Kangaroo Rat
Dipodomys ordii

Finding sand dunes within this gentle rodent's range is challenging in itself; locating an individual kangaroo rat requires luck and knowledge. This nocturnal hopper is best seen on dark, moonless and overcast nights. If you shine a flashlight across the dunes or drive slowly along sandy roadcuts, this sand-dweller might be revealed. A kangaroo rat's motion is distinctive—like a kangaroo, it does not use its forelimbs for locomotion. By daybreak, kangaroo rats retire to their plugged burrows in the sand.

Much of a kangaroo rat's food is taken from the sand; it forages slowly, sifting out seeds with its sharp foreclaws. Seeds that are to be eaten immediately are first husked, but those to be stored are left intact. The kangaroo rat transports the food to its burrow in spacious external cheek pouches that can be turned inside-out for cleaning and combing with the foreclaws. Sand is critical to this mammal's cleanliness: dust-bathing is an important part of the kangaroo rat's grooming routine.

The Ord's Kangaroo Rat can live its entire life without drinking any water. It can survive just on the water produced through the metabolic breakdown of the oils and fats in the seeds it eats. This water is used in all body functions, including digestion, excretion, reproduction and milk production. Despite this ability, kangaroo rats will nonetheless lap available droplets of dew, and they will sometimes eat a bit of green vegetation.

DESCRIPTION: The back is yellowish buff, with a few black hairs down the center, the sides are clear buff, and the belly is white. The eyes are large, luminous and protruding. The eye has a white spot above it, and the brownish-black ear has one behind it. A black patch on the side of the nose, above the white lip, marks the base of the whiskers. A diagonal white line crosses the hip. The extremely long hindfeet have five toes and are white on top and brownish black on their hairy soles. The greatly reduced forelegs are held up off the ground and are often not visible in profile as the animal sits hunched over, supporting itself on its hindfeet. The tail, which is longer than the body, is tufted at the tip. It has white sides and brownish-black upper and lower surfaces.

HABITAT: This kangaroo rat occupies sandy, semi-desert grassland and sagebrush sites. Disturbed areas, whether produced by drifting sand, road building or traffic, and having scattered shrubs,

RANGE: This widely distributed kangaroo rat occurs from southeastern Alberta and southwestern Saskatchewan south through the Great Plains and western Texas into Mexico, and from eastern Oregon south through the Great Basin into Arizona.

Total Length: 9–11 in.
Tail Length: 5½–6¼ in.
Weight: 1½–3⅜ oz.

grasses and herbaceous plants, seem particularly attractive.

FOOD: Seeds make up more than three-quarters of the year-round diet. Insects, such as ants, butterfly pupae, adult beetles and larval ant-lions, account for one-fifth of the diet in spring, and grasshoppers and roots are eaten in summer.

DEN: Burrows, which are usually located in the sides of sand dunes, dry eroded channels or road slopes, are about 3 in. in diameter. The entrances are plugged during the day. The tunnels branch frequently, with some branches used for food storage and at least one as a nest chamber. Most of the burrow system is often within 1 ft. of the surface. The burrow system is actively defended against invasion by other kangaroo rats.

YOUNG: Breeding occurs in early to mid-spring, and sometimes again in mid-summer. After a 29- to 30-day gestation period, a litter of usually three to five young is born in a nest built just beforehand. The helpless newborns,

weighing about ³⁄₁₆ oz., are groomed by the mother. At two weeks their eyes open, and at three weeks they have functioning cheek pouches. After the young reach adult size, at five to six weeks, they disperse to develop their own burrows. The mortality rate in the first year may be as high as 80 percent.

SIMILAR SPECIES: The lower incisors of the **Chisel-toothed Kangaroo Rat** (p. 236) are broad and have flat edges, like chisels. The **California Kangaroo Rat** (p. 237) is larger and darker, has only four toes on its hindfeet and has a prominent white tuft on the tip of its tail.

DID YOU KNOW?

All kangaroo rats have comparatively huge auditory bullae—bony capsules enclosing the middle and inner ear—that make up a major portion of the rear of the skull. Able to hear very low-frequency sounds, kangaroo rats can avoid a rattlesnake's bite, presumably because they are able to hear the snake's movement.

Chisel-toothed Kangaroo Rat

Dipodomys microps

Total Length: 9⅝–12 in.

Tail Length: 5¼–6⅞ in.

Weight: 1⅞–2⅝ oz.

This mainly nocturnal kangaroo rat is unique in the genus *Dipodomys* in having broad, flat-edged lower incisors. All the others have awl-like lower incisors. As useful as this characteristic is to mammalogists, it might not be very useful for field identification. A Chisel-toothed Kangaroo Rat in the wild is not likely going to open its mouth to you for easy viewing. When you are in kangaroo rat country during the spring mating season, listen closely in the evening. If you are lucky, you will hear the male drumming his feet on the ground in an attempt to draw the female out of her burrow.

DESCRIPTION: This kangaroo rat is tawny or dusky colored above and has whitish undersides. It has five toes on the hindfoot. Light spots are found above each eye and behind the ears. The tail has a wide dark stripe on both the dorsal surface and the ventral surface; the white stripe in between is narrower than either of the two dark stripes. The lower incisors are broad and flat across the top, unlike those of any other kangaroo rat. The fur of the cheek pouches is gray.

HABITAT: This kangaroo rat is common in open pinyon/juniper woodlands and scrubby areas, such as sagebrush or shadscale flats.

FOOD: This rodent feeds on green vegetation when it is available. It uses its chisel-like teeth to scrape off the salty epidermis of favored leaves, allowing it access to the nutrients without the difficulty of a high salt intake. At other times, seeds are the main component of the diet. They are eaten fresh or stored in the burrow for later.

DEN: The Chisel-toothed Kangaroo Rat makes burrows in soft banks or other high ground. Burrows include chambers for sleeping, nesting and storing food. The entrances may be clustered into a mound 1 ft. high and up to 13 ft. across.

YOUNG: Mating occurs in February or March, and after a gestation period of just over a month, one to four young are born. Females usually have just one litter a year.

SIMILAR SPECIES: The other kangaroo rats may be difficult to visually distinguish from this one, but no other member of the genus has flat lower incisors or gray fur on its cheek pouches. The **California Kangaroo Rat** (p. 237) has only four toes on its hindfeet, is larger and darker and has a white tuft at the tip of its tail.

RANGE: This species is found in southeastern Oregon, throughout much of Nevada, as well as in northwestern Utah, southern California and extreme northwestern Arizona.

California Kangaroo Rat
Dipodomys californicus

Total Length: 10–13 in.
Tail Length: 6–8½ in.
Weight: about 1¾ oz.

As is true for many small mammals, climate plays a significant role in regulating the population sizes of kangaroo rats. California Kangaroo Rats, for example, appear to suffer greater losses from wet weather in severe winters than by the natural predation of foxes, Coyotes and owls. Entire populations can be decimated in one bad winter. Despite this sensitivity to weather extremes, California Kangaroo Rats can cope very well with milder weather fluctuations in the summer. They are active even on nights with light rain, staying inside only during storms. After rainstorms, these hardy creatures diligently carry out the blobs of mud that have accumulated in their burrows.

DESCRIPTION: This large kangaroo rat is dark gray above and nearly white below. It has four toes on the hindfoot, and its tail has a white tip. This rodent hops on its hindlegs.

HABITAT: This species lives primarily in desert regions, but sometimes it occupies scrubby areas or chaparral. It favors well-drained soils to burrow in.

FOOD: This kangaroo rat feeds heavily on seeds and berries. In spring and summer, it feeds significantly on green vegetation.

DEN: The burrows of this rodent are typical of the genus, often having several tunnels, a nest chamber, a sleeping chamber, a food store and several escape passageways.

YOUNG: Although mating usually occurs from February to April, the breeding season extends through to September. Females may have more than one litter a year, averaging two to four young a litter. Gestation lasts about one month.

SIMILAR SPECIES: This is the largest and darkest kangaroo rat in this region and the only one with four toes on the hindfoot and a prominent white tuft on the tip of the tail. The **Chisel-toothed Kangaroo Rat** (p. 236) is smaller and lighter in color. The tuft on the tail of an **Ord's Kangaroo Rat** (p. 234) is not white.

RANGE: This species is found from south-central Oregon south into northern California.

Northern Pocket Gopher
Thomomys talpoides

The Northern Pocket Gopher is one of nature's rototillers. This ground-dwelling rodent continually tunnels through rich, dark soils, and one individual is capable of turning over 16 tons of soil a year. Evidence of pocket gopher workings is commonplace on the land, in the form of freshly churned earth neatly piled in crescent-shaped mounds, with the burrow entrance (usually plugged with soil) near the center of the crescent. In many agricultural areas, the Northern Pocket Gopher is the most controlled "nuisance" mammal because of its mounds, which can damage machinery and cover vegetation.

Pocket gopher mounds hide the access holes to a system of burrows. From the rodent's viewpoint, the surface provides a space to dump the dirt from tunnel excavation. When the ground is covered by snow, pocket gophers still bring waste soil to the surface, and they pack it into tunnels in the snow. When the snow melts, these soil cores (also known as "gopher cores" or "crotovinas") are left exposed.

The Northern Pocket Gopher is extremely well suited to an underground existence. It has small eyes, which it rarely needs in its darkened world; reduced external ears that do not interfere with tunneling; short, lax fur that does not impede either backward or forward movement in the tunnels and a short, sparsely haired tail that serves as a tactile organ when the animal is tunnel-running in reverse.

To dig its elaborate burrows, the pocket gopher has heavy, stout claws on short, strong forelegs and a massive lower jaw armed with long incisors. Once the soil is loosened with tooth and claw, it is initially pushed back under the body with the forefeet, and then further with the hindfeet. When sufficient soil has accumulated behind the animal, the gopher turns, guides the mound with its forefeet and head and pushes with its hindlegs until the soil is in a side tunnel or on the surface.

Pocket gophers are named for their large, externally opening, fur-lined cheek pouches. As in the related pocket mice and kangaroo rats, these "pockets" are used to transport food, but they have no direct opening to the animal's mouth. Many people incorrectly call pocket gophers "moles," but true moles have long, mobile snouts, tiny eyes and shovel-like forelegs.

DESCRIPTION: This squat, bullet-headed rodent has visible incisors, long foreclaws and a thick, nearly hairless tail. A row of stiff hairs surrounds the

RANGE: This species occupies most of the northern Great Plains (in Canada from Manitoba to Alberta) and most of the central Rockies as far south as northern Arizona and New Mexico. It occurs as far east as western Minnesota and as far west as western Washington and Oregon.

Total Length: 7½–10 in.

Tail Length: 1⅝–3 in.

Weight: 2⅝–7⅜ oz.

naked soles of the forefeet. The upperparts, which are slightly darker than the underparts, often match the soil color—individuals may be black, dark gray, brown or even light gray.

HABITAT: This adaptable animal avoids only dense forests, wet or waterlogged, fine-textured soils, very shallow rocky soils or areas exposed to strong winter freezing of the soil.

FOOD: Succulent underground plant parts are the staple diet, but in summer pocket gophers emerge from their burrows at night to collect green vegetation.

DEN: The burrow system may spread 150–500 ft. laterally and extend anywhere from 2 in. to 10 ft. deep. A tunnel's diameter is about 2 in. Often the burrow system is two-tiered, with the upper level used for foraging and as a latrine and the lower (more permanent) level used for food storage and nesting. Spoil from tunneling is spread fan-wise to one side of the burrow entrance, and then the burrow is plugged from below. Only a single gopher occupies a burrow system, except during the breeding season,

when a male may share a female's burrow for a time.

YOUNG: Breeding occurs once a year, in April or May. Following a 19- to 20-day gestation period, three to six young are born in a grass-lined nest. Weaning takes place at about 40 days. When the young weigh about 1½ oz., they leave to either occupy a vacant burrow system or begin digging their own. They are sexually mature the following spring.

SIMILAR SPECIES: Other **pocket gophers** (pp. 238–43) can be difficult to distinguish from this one, but range can be a good indicator. **Voles** (pp. 208–22) are smaller and do not have the large, external cheek pouches, nearly hairless tail or long foreclaws of pocket gophers, though their color patterns are similar.

DID YOU KNOW?

A pocket gopher's incisor teeth can grow at a spectacular rate: lower incisors are reported to grow as much as 0.04 in. a day; for upper incisors, it's 0.02 in. a day. If that rate were continuous for all seasons, the lower incisors could grow 14 in. in a single year.

Western Pocket Gopher
Thomomys mazama

Total Length: 7¼–9⅜ in.
Tail Length: 2⅛–3⅛ in.
Weight: 1⅞–3⅜ oz.

Despite being perfectly adapted to subterranean existence, the Western Pocket Gopher is one of the only members of this genus to regularly come aboveground. Usually emerging in nighttime hours or on warm, overcast days, this pocket gopher may be seen feeding on grasses or forbs. When aboveground, it will reach up and bend the vegetation down to get at the tender buds or seeds. Like most other rodents, pocket gophers have enamel only on the front parts of their constantly growing incisors. As the rodent gnaws, the back of the tooth is worn away quickly more quickly than the enameled front layer. This uneven wear produces a very sharp edge on the teeth.

DESCRIPTION: This richly colored pocket gopher can be reddish brown, gray, plain brown, or nearly black. The color of an individual is dependent on the color of the soil in which it lives. The distinctly pointed ears have large patches of dark fur directly behind their bases.

HABITAT: This pocket gopher is found in a variety of habitats, from flat grasslands to low mountain regions.

FOOD: Western Pocket Gophers feed on green herbaceous vegetation, but they have a preference for grasses, false dandelions and lupines. Often these gophers feed from underground, eating roots and tubers and then pulling the aboveground plant parts into their burrows from underneath.

DEN: These pocket gophers make two types of burrows: a shallow burrow that is used for feeding on surface and subsurface plants and a deeper burrow that is used for food storage and a den chamber.

YOUNG: For these pocket gophers, very little is known about reproduction. Mating probably occurs in spring or early summer, and litter size averages about five young.

SIMILAR SPECIES: The **Camas Pocket Gopher** (p. 241) is much larger. All **pocket gophers** (pp. 238–43) can be very difficult to distinguish from each other, but range is often a good indicator.

RANGE: The Western Pocket Gopher occurs in the western third of Washington, through much of western Oregon and into northern California.

Camas Pocket Gopher
Thomomys bulbivorus

Total Length: 10–13 in.
Tail Length: 2¾–3½ in.
Weight: about 18 oz.

The Camas Pocket Gopher is the largest members of this genus. Its large size, however, does not necessarily confer great strength, and it is relatively weak in the forearms. However, this gopher's large head and large incisors are significant. In many areas where it lives, the soil is hard and packed for much of the year. Digging through such soil is very difficult, so this gopher uses both its teeth and claws to scrape loose the dirt in its lateral tunnels. As dirt is loosened, it is pushed through an inclined branch of the tunnel and out onto the ground surface. The resulting fan-shaped pile of dirt is often the only visible sign that a Camas Pocket Gopher is present.

DESCRIPTION: This large pocket gopher is dark grayish brown, with a white spot on the chin. Its tail is sparsely furred and relatively short. The male is larger than the female. Its incisors protrude even when its mouth is closed, and its round ears are more conspicuous than those of other pocket gophers.

HABITAT: Camas Pocket Gophers live in areas of clay soils that are heavy when wet and very hard when dry.

FOOD: Unlike moles, which have a similar lifestyle but a different diet, Camas Pocket Gophers are herbivores and eat mainly roots, seeds and green vegetation.

DEN: This gopher spends the majority of its life underground, sleeping in a special chamber of its burrows.

YOUNG: Mating occurs anytime from April to June, and litter size is four to nine. The altricial young are about 2 in. long, including the tail.

SIMILAR SPECIES: The **Western Pocket Gopher** (p. 240) is much shorter and less massive. Other **pocket gophers** (pp. 238–43) can be difficult to distinguish from this one, but range can be a good indicator.

RANGE: This gopher lives only in the Willamette Valley of northwestern Oregon.

Botta's Pocket Gopher
Thomomys bottae

Total Length: 6⅝–11 in.
Tail Length: 1⅝–3¾ in.
Weight: 2½–8⅞ oz.

Most people have mixed feelings about pocket gophers. In natural areas, pocket gophers are an important component of the ecosystem. Annually, these animals turn up large volumes of soil, which aerates the ground, cycles the soil nutrients and aids water absorption. Studies have shown that where pocket gophers live in normal numbers, some plants grow better, and others, such as dandelions (which are a favorite pocket gopher food) are less abundant. Gopher mounds can interfere with agricultural machinery, however, and the gophers may compete with livestock for vegetation.

DESCRIPTION: Botta's Pocket Gophers are dark or grayish brown above and slightly paler below. Their sparsely furred tails are tawny or gray in color. Their ears are rounded and inconspicuous.

RANGE: The Botta's Pocket Gopher is found from southwestern Oregon through California into Baja and western Mexico and east to Colorado, western Texas and north-central Mexico.

HABITAT: These pocket gophers live in a variety of habitats and soil types, anywhere from deserts to mountain meadows and from sandy to clay soils.

FOOD: Pocket gophers feed on vegetation of all sorts, especially roots and tubers they encounter while burrowing and shoots they pull down into their burrows. They also consume some aboveground plant parts, such as leaves, seeds and fruit.

DEN: Like other pocket gophers, the Botta's spends most of its life underground. It digs nest chambers, special wastes tunnels, deep lateral tunnels for dens and food storage and shallow tunnels for foraging routes.

YOUNG: Botta's Pocket Gophers may have several litters in one season. In ideal habitats, they may breed throughout the year. Litters average six young each, and the gestation period is 18 or 19 days.

SIMILAR SPECIES: All **pocket gophers** (pp. 238–43) can be very difficult to distinguish from each other, but range is often a good indicator.

Townsend's Pocket Gopher
Thomomys townsendii

Total Length: 9–14 in.
Tail Length: 2¼–4⅜ in.
Weight: 4½–13 oz.

As exceptional burrowing rodents, all pocket gophers have special adaptations for life underground. The incisors of a pocket gopher remain outside the lips even when the mouth is closed. This characteristic allows the gopher to eat food underground or dig through the earth without getting soil particles in its mouth. Another unusual characteristic of these gophers is the external cheek pouches that are used to carry food and nesting material. Daily grooming involves cleaning the fur-lined cheek pouches. Oddly, the cheek pouches can be turned inside-out to make grooming easier. Special muscles in the cheek maintain the pouches and pull them back inside after the grooming is finished.

DESCRIPTION: These gophers are slaty black or sooty gray above—usually the same as the color of the soils in which they live—and slightly paler below. Their tails are sparsely furred and grayish in color. Their ears are rounded and have dark spots to the rear.

HABITAT: These pocket gophers live in areas of deep soil, such as river valleys and old lake beds.

FOOD: These gophers feed on vegetation of all sorts, especially roots, tubers and shoots protruding into their burrows. They also consume some aboveground plant parts, such as leaves, seeds and fruit.

DEN: As with others of the genus, these gophers spend most of their life underground. They sleep in special nest chambers and have special tunnels for wastes. Deep lateral tunnels are for dens and food storage, whereas shallow tunnels are foraging routes.

YOUNG: Townsend's Pocket Gophers may have two or more litters in one season. In ideal habitats, they can breed throughout the year. Litter size range from 3 to 10 young, and gestation lasts 18 or 19 days.

SIMILAR SPECIES: All **pocket gophers** (pp. 238–43) can be very difficult to distinguish from each other, but range is often a good indicator.

RANGE: The Townsend's Pocket Gopher is found scattered throughout Idaho, western Montana, southeastern Oregon, northern Nevada and northeastern California.

Yellow-pine Chipmunk
Tamias amoenus

The sound of scurrying among fallen leaves, a flash of movement and sharp, high-pitched "chips" will direct your attention to the fidgety behavior of a Yellow-pine Chipmunk. Using fallen logs as runways and the leaf litter as its pantry, this busy animal inhabits much of central and eastern Oregon and Washington. This chipmunk and the very similar Least Chipmunk are the most commonly seen chipmunks in the region.

The word "chipmunk" is thought to be derived from the Algonquian word for "head first," which is the manner in which a chipmunk descends a tree, but contrary to cartoon-inspired myths, chipmunks spend very little time in high trees. They prefer the ground, where they bury food and dig golf ball–sized entrance holes to their networks of tunnels. Chipmunk burrows are known for their well-hidden entrances, which never have piles of dirt to give away their locations.

In certain heavily visited parks and golf courses, Yellow-pine Chipmunks that have grown accustomed to human handouts can be very easy to approach. These exchanges contrast dramatically with the typically brief sightings of wild chipmunks, which scamper away at the first sight of humans. In the wild, chipmunks rely on their nervous instincts to survive in their predator-filled world.

DESCRIPTION: This chipmunk is brightly colored, from tawny to pinkish cinnamon. The face has three dark and two light stripes; the back has five dark and four light stripes. The light stripes are white or grayish. The dark stripes are nearly black, and the central three extend all the way to the rump. The sides of the body and the underside of the tail are ochreous. Females tend to be larger than males.

HABITAT: The Yellow-pine Chipmunk inhabits a wide variety of areas, including open coniferous forests, sagebrush flats, rocky outcroppings and pastures with small shrubs. It may be seen at ranches or farms well away from mountains or forests, attracted there by livestock feed.

FOOD: This chipmunk loves to dine on ripe berries, such as chokecherries, pin cherries, strawberries, raspberries or blueberries. Other staples in the diet include nuts, seeds, grasses, mushrooms and even insects and some other animals. It may be an important predator on eggs and nestling birds during the nesting season. A chipmunk may be

RANGE: This mountain chipmunk occurs in British Columbia, extreme western Alberta and the northwestern U.S.

Total Length: 7¾–9½ in.
Tail Length: 3¼–4¼ in.
Weight: 1⅝–3 oz.

attracted to domestic animal feed, and sometimes one can be seen filling its cheek pouches from a pile of oats shared by a horse.

DEN: The Yellow-pine Chipmunk usually lives in a burrow that has a concealed entrance. It can sometimes be found in a tree cavity, but it seldom builds a tree nest.

YOUNG: The young are born in May or June, after spring mating and about one month of gestation. Usually five or six young are born in a grass-lined chamber in the burrow. They are blind and hairless at birth, but their growth is rapid, and they are usually weaned in about six weeks.

SIMILAR SPECIES: It is very difficult to distinguish chipmunk species in the field, but ranges often help. The **Red-tailed Chipmunk** (p. 251) has a brick red tail underside. The **Least Chipmunk** (p. 246) tends to have duller colors. The **golden-mantled ground squirrels** (pp. 261–73) are much larger and lack stripes on their faces.

DID YOU KNOW?

During summer, a chipmunk's body temperature is 95°–108° F. During winter, when it is hibernating in its burrow, its body temperature drops to 41°–45° F.

Least Chipmunk
Tamias minimus

Total Length: 7–9½ in.

Tail Length: 3–4¼ in.

Weight: 1¼–2½ oz.

Like the Yellow-pine Chipmunk, the Least Chipmunk is very common and can be seen by anyone willing to invest the time and effort in a search. In Washington and Oregon, this chipmunk is a shrub-steppe species, and it is especially common near campgrounds. In some areas it can be the most commonly seen chipmunk species.

The coat of this chipmunk changes seasonally: in summer its coat is new and bright, and in winter its coat is duller, as if it rolled in the dust to mute its colors.

DESCRIPTION: Like all chipmunks, this tiny chipmunk has three dark and two light stripes on its face, and five dark and four light stripes on its body. The central dark stripe runs from the head to the base of the tail, but the other dark stripes end at the hips. Overall, it is grayer and paler than other chipmunks, and the underside of the tail is yellower. The tail is quite long—more than 40 percent of the animal's total length, and it is usually held erect when the chipmunk runs.

HABITAT: This chipmunk is common in brushy or rocky areas of coniferous mountain forests and northern forests in Washington and Oregon.

FOOD: The bulk of the diet consists of conifer seeds, nuts, berries and insects. It is common for chipmunks, including this one, to eat eggs, fledgling birds, young mice or even carrion. Chipmunks have internal cheek pouches in which they carry food to their caches.

DEN: Least Chipmunks generally den in underground burrows with concealed entrances, but some individuals live in tree cavities or even make spherical nests among the branches.

YOUNG: Breeding occurs about two weeks after chipmunks emerge from hibernation in spring. After about a one-month gestation period, a litter of two to seven (usually four to six) helpless young is born in a grass-lined nest chamber. The young develop rapidly, and the mother may later transfer them to a tree cavity or tree nest.

SIMILAR SPECIES: Range and habitat help identify chipmunk species. The slightly larger **Yellow-pine Chipmunk** (p. 244) has brighter colors. The **Red-tailed Chipmunk** (p. 251) is larger and may be grayer, but it is most easily distinguished by the rufous underside of its tail.

RANGE: The range of this species includes much of the western U.S., as well as a broad band running southeast from the central and southern Yukon to western Quebec and Wisconsin.

Allen's Chipmunk
Tamias senex

Total Length: 9–10 in.
Tail Length: 3¾–4⅜ in.
Weight: 2⅜–3⅞ oz.

Among the chipmunks, Allen's Chipmunks have an inordinate fondness for fungi. Little craters where a mushroom or truffle was dug up can be found throughout areas inhabited by these chipmunks. Humid forests and lush brushy areas are the favored habitats of Allen's Chipmunks. A good clue to confirm the identity of these chipmunks in such areas is their call; unlike any other chipmunk species, Allen's Chipmunks call out three to five metallic barks followed by a single chirped note. Habitat, vocalizations and the holes they make in the ground are the best ways to identify Allen's Chipmunks. Their pelage, however, is highly variable, changing both seasonally and regionally.

DESCRIPTION: This large, grayish chipmunk has indistinct stripes. Only its dark dorsal stripe is conspicuous. It has a white spot behind each ear, and its tail is a pale tawny color with light edges.

HABITAT: Allen's Chipmunks prefer humid white fir and red fir forests and lush, brushy areas. In Oregon they are associated with rocky outcrops near moist areas of ponderosa pine, manzanita and antelope bitterbrush ecozones.

FOOD: These chipmunks feed primarily on mushrooms and other fungi and some insects, but little vegetation.

DEN: Like other chipmunks, the Allen's Chipmunk usually excavates simple burrows. The design includes a nest chamber, possibly a separate food chamber and an escape entrance. This animal may also build its nest in a log crevice.

YOUNG: The mating season lasts for one month, starting in April. A litter of three to five young is born sometime in late spring. The young are pink and blind at birth, but within four to five weeks they resemble little adults.

SIMILAR SPECIES: The closely related **Townsend's Chipmunk** (p. 248)— which is hard to distinguish visually— does not sound a chirped note after a series of metallic barks, and it has a different range.

RANGE: This chipmunk has a thin range in central Oregon that extends south and east into California and slightly into northwestern and north-central Nevada.

Townsend's Chipmunk

Tamias townsendii

The tell-tale sign of a Townsend's Chipmunk is its upright tail. Whether it's darting across hot stretches of beach sand or jumping through fern-shaded coastal forests, this chipmunk's tail advertises its whereabouts. In thick foliage, all that may be visible is the vertical tail, and only close inspection will reveal the chipmunk preceding it.

This chipmunk is very dark in color, and it is among the largest of western chipmunks. Females are the largest—they top the scales at 4 oz.—and newborn Townsend's Chipmunks are the largest chipmunk babies. This robust chipmunk is an excellent climber and avid explorer. It may travel more than half a mile in search of its diverse food, and with internal cheek pouches that can hold more than a hundred oats, it is able to transport large quantities of food to its larder.

In the northern or high-altitude parts of their range, Townsend's Chipmunks hibernate throughout winter; in mild southern climates or coastal areas, they tend to remain active all year. As adults, these chipmunks are usually solitary, but they can be locally abundant and give the appearance of a colony in some areas. Each chipmunk is far too concerned with gathering food for itself, however, to worry about home territories or trespassers.

DESCRIPTION: This is the largest of the western chipmunks. The dark stripes over its face and back are indistinct and low in contrast: dark stripes are dark brown, never black; light stripes are ochreous or tawny, never white. The undersides range from tawny to nearly white, and the tail is grayish above and reddish below. This chipmunk usually runs with its tail at a 45° angle.

HABITAT: Townsend's Chipmunks occupy areas of dense cover, such as driftwood beaches, dense hardwood and mixed forests and fern-filled moist coniferous forests. They may be found at elevations up to 6500 ft.

FOOD: This chipmunk consumes a wide variety of foods, including roots, bulbs, grass seeds, conifer seeds, hazelnuts, berries, dandelion flowers, fungi, large insects, eggs, fledgling birds and sometimes carrion.

DEN: The entrance to this chipmunk's hole lacks a dirt pile. When it digs, this animal uses a "work hole" to excavate and dump the dirt, and when the burrow is finished, it seals the work hole

RANGE: The Townsend's Chipmunk is found in extreme southwestern British Columbia and south through western Washington and most of western Oregon.

Total Length: 8½–14 in.
Tail Length: 3½–6 in.
Weight: 1¾–4 oz.

and opens a new, debris-free entrance in a concealed location. This entrance is usually located at the base of a tree or stump or in a crevice among rocks. The burrow descends about 1 ft., then levels off for 3–4 ft. before terminating in a 4–5-in wide chamber filled with a nest of shredded vegetation. Sometimes a store of seeds is found in this nest chamber.

YOUNG: These chipmunks become active in late April to early May, when they emerge from hibernation. They mate within a week, and following a 30-day gestation period, two to seven blind, hairless babies weighing almost ⅛ oz. are born. The babies are weaned five weeks later, and by the end of August they disperse. Females have a single litter each year, and young are sexually mature after their first winter.

SIMILAR SPECIES: Most other chipmunks are smaller and have brighter colors than the Townsend's Chipmunk. The **Allen's Chipmunk** (p. 247) and the **Siskiyou Chipmunk** (p. 250) both have more distinct dorsal stripes. The **golden-mantled ground squirrels** (pp. 271–73) are larger and lack stripes on their faces.

DID YOU KNOW?

This chipmunk was named for John K. Townsend, an ornithologist on Thomas Nuttall's 1834 expedition to Oregon.

Siskiyou Chipmunk
Tamias siskiyou

Total Length: 8⅝–11 in.

Tail Length: 3⅝–5 in.

Weight: 1¾–4 oz.

getting walloped and tossed out by the slightly larger female.

DESCRIPTION: This is a large chipmunk with wide, nearly black dorsal stripes. The ears are slightly bicolored: tawny in front, gray in back. The bushy tail is dark on top, red below and fringed with white-tipped hairs.

HABITAT: These chipmunks live in brushy areas and open forests of coastal regions.

FOOD: These chipmunks eat a variety of foods including seeds, nuts, fruits, some vegetation and adult and larval insects.

DEN: Siskiyou Chipmunks usually live in simple burrows, but they may take up residence in a tree cavity or hollow log.

YOUNG: After mating in early spring, gestation lasts for 30 or 31 days. The female has a litter of three to five pups. The young are pink and blind at birth. After just five weeks, the young are almost full grown and have full-color coats.

SIMILAR SPECIES: Chipmunks can be difficult to distinguish visually, but the distinct dark stripes of the Siskiyou Chipmunk help distinguish it from the **Townsend's Chipmunk** (p. 248), which also has a different range.

This chipmunk species is a member of a closely related group of four chipmunk species. The Siskiyou, Townsend's, Yellow-cheeked and Allen's chipmunks were at one time considered the same species. All four have similar outward appearances, and they are the largest of the western chipmunks.

Like most chipmunks, Siskiyou Chipmunks prefer solitary lifestyles. Social interactions between these chipmunks are rare and short-lived. In spring, males are energetic and on the lookout for receptive females. Courtship involves playful games of tag where two or even three chipmunks dart through the underbrush. As is true in the courtship of many mammal species, a certain level of propriety is necessary if mating between the chipmunks is to occur. Ill-mannered males who act inappropriately once in the burrow may end up

RANGE: Siskiyou Chipmunks are found only in the western and coastal areas of southern Oregon and northern California.

Red-tailed Chipmunk
Tamias ruficaudus

Total Length: 8¼–9¾ in.
Tail Length: 3¾–4¾ in.
Weight: 1⅞–2⅝ oz.

The richly colored Red-tailed Chipmunk is difficult to find, because in this region it lives only in high mountain forests in the northeastern corner of Washington. As well, the Red-tailed Chipmunk is more arboreal than others of their kind, so seeing it usually involves scanning the treetops.

These chipmunks do not always hibernate in winter. They often remain awake in their dens, feeding lightly on their grand stores of food. If they do become dormant, it will be only a light torpid state that is easily broken.

DESCRIPTION: Like its kin, this large chipmunk has three dark and two light stripes on the face, and five dark and four light stripes on the back. The inner three dark stripes on the back are black; the dark facial stripes and the outermost dark stripes on the back are brownish. The rump is grayish. In keeping with its name, this chipmunk has a tail that is rufous above and brilliant reddish below, and it is bordered with black and pale pinkish orange.

HABITAT: This chipmunk inhabits coniferous mountain forests and boulder-covered slopes below treeline.

FOOD: Although conifer seeds, nuts, some berries and insects form most of the diet, it is not uncommon for all species of chipmunks to feed on eggs, fledgling birds, young mice or even carrion.

DEN: As do all chipmunks, the Red-tailed Chipmunk usually spends winter in a burrow. A mother often bears young in tree nests or cavities—this species makes spherical tree nests more often than do many other chipmunks.

YOUNG: Breeding occurs in spring, and after a one-month gestation period, a litter of usually four to six young is born in May or June. The young are born blind and hairless. They grow rapidly, and they are usually weaned in about six weeks.

SIMILAR SPECIES: The **Least Chipmunk** (p. 246) is smaller, and both it and the **Yellow-pine Chipmunk** (p. 244) have grayish-yellow, not brick red, on the underside of the tail.

RANGE: The small range of this chipmunk includes only southeastern British

Columbia, the extreme southwestern corner of Alberta, northeastern Washington, northern Idaho and western Montana.

Woodchuck
Marmota monax

For most of the year, Woodchucks are tucked quietly away more than 6½ ft. underground, relying on a lethargic metabolism to keep them alive during hibernation. They lie motionless, breathing an average of once every six minutes and sustained by a metabolic furnace fed with a trickle of fatty reserves. Once May returns (never as early as February's Groundhog Day), Woodchucks awake from their catatonic slumbering to breed and to forage on the palatable new green shoots emerging with the warmer weather.

Woodchucks range across much of Canada and the eastern United States, but in our area they are found only in the extreme northeastern part of Washington. They mainly inhabit low-elevation areas, finding shelter for their burrows in rock piles, under outbuildings and along riversides.

In general, Woodchucks are more solitary in nature than other kinds of marmots, and they are rarely seen far from their protective burrows, valuing security over the temptations of foraging. When Woodchucks do venture out to feed, it is often during the early twilight hours or shortly after dawn. Even then, they are wary and usually outrun predators in an all-out sprint back to the burrow. A shrill whistle of alarm typically accompanies a Woodchuck's disappearance into its burrow.

Historically, the Woodchuck lived in forested areas, and it can still be found in woodlands, though it now appears to favor cultivated land—the Woodchuck is among the few mammals to have prospered from human activity. Unhesitant about pilfering, Woodchucks living near humans often graze in sweet alfalfa crops to help fatten their waistlines. The luckiest Woodchucks find their way into people's backyards, where they stuff themselves on tasty apples, carrots, strawberries, corn, peas and other garden delights.

ALSO CALLED: Groundhog.

DESCRIPTION: This short-legged, stout-bodied, ground-dwelling marmot is brownish and has an overall grizzled appearance. It has a prominent, slightly flattened bushy tail and small ears.

HABITAT: Woodchucks favor pastures, meadows and old fields close to wooded areas.

FOOD: In wild areas, this ground dweller follows the standard marmot diet of grasses, leaves, seeds and berries,

RANGE: The Woodchuck occurs from central Alaska east to Labrador, as far south as northeastern Washington and northern Idaho in the West and eastern Kansas, northern Alabama and Virginia in the East.

Total Length: 18–26 in.
Tail Length: 4¼–6¼ in.
Weight: 4–12 lb.

which it supplements with bark and sometimes a bit of carrion.

DEN: The Woodchuck's powerful digging claws are used to excavate burrows in areas of good drainage. The dirt at the main burrow entrances is often populated by an assortment of plant species that is unique to these spoil piles. The main burrow is 10–50 ft long, and it ends in a comfortable grass-lined nest chamber. One or two plunge holes, without spoil piles, often lead directly to the nest chamber. A separate, smaller chamber is used for wastes.

YOUNG: Mating occurs in spring, within a week after the female emerges from hibernation. After a gestation period of about a month, one to eight (usually three to five) young are born. The helpless newborns weigh only about 9 oz. In four weeks their eyes open, and they look like proper, though small, Woodchucks after five weeks.

The young are weaned at about 1½ months. Their growth accelerates once they begin eating plants, and they continue growing throughout summer to put on enough fat for winter hibernation and early spring activity.

SIMILAR SPECIES: The **Hoary Marmot** (p. 256) is generally gray and white with contrasting black markings, and it is typically found at higher elevations. The **Yellow-bellied Marmot** (p. 254) has, appropriately enough, a yellow or ochreous belly.

DID YOU KNOW?

Woodchucks are superb diggers that are responsible for turning over massive amounts of earth each year. As they burrow, they periodically turn themselves around and bulldoze loose dirt out of the tunnel with their suitably stubby heads.

Yellow-bellied Marmot
Marmota flaviventris

True to its name, the Yellow-bellied Marmot has a distinct yellowish or burnt-orange belly. When this marmot is curious about or watchful of something, it often sits back on its hindlegs in an upright position that displays its delightfully bright tummy.

Yellow-bellied Marmots have a fairly lackadaisical routine: they sleep late in the morning, eat heartily for breakfast and then snooze dreamily in the shade for the afternoon. Counting hibernation and nighttime sleep, Yellow-bellied Marmots spend about 80 percent of their lives in their burrows. They like their dens to be kept clean, and when they emerge from hibernation they throw out their used bedding and replace it with fresh grass and leaves. Throughout summer, they continue to keep their bedding clean and their burrows free of debris.

Colonies of Yellow-bellied Marmots have a strict social order, and whenever members of a colony are eating or wrestling with their family members, at least one marmot plays watchdog. This sentinel is responsible for warning the others if danger approaches. The alarm call is a loud chirp, which may vary in duration and intensity depending on the nature of the threat: short, steady notes probably translate as "Heads up, pay attention"; loud, shrill notes convey the message "Into your burrows, now!" Different urgent warnings are reserved for immediate dangers, such as a circling eagle or an approaching fox.

In Washington and Oregon, marmot population sizes seem to be regulated by the availability of suitable hibernation sites. The dominant male of a colony evicts younger males as they become sexually mature, and these banished marmots appear to suffer especially high overwinter mortalities.

ALSO CALLED: Rockchuck.

DESCRIPTION: The back is tawny or yellow-brown, made to appear grizzled by the light tips of the guard hairs. The feet and legs are blackish brown. The head has whitish-gray patches across the top of the nose, from below the ear to the shoulder and from the nose and chin toward the throat, which leaves a darker brown patch surrounding the ear, eye and upper cheek on each side of the face. The ears are short and rounded. The whiskers are dark and prominent. This marmot often arches its dark, grizzled, bushy tail behind it and flags it from side to side. The bright buffy yellow color of the belly, sides of

RANGE: Yellow-bellied Marmots are found from central British Columbia and extreme southern Alberta southward as far as central California and northern New Mexico.

Length: 19–26 in.

Tail Length: 5–7½ in.

Weight: 3½–11 lb.

the neck, upper jaw and hips is responsible for the common name.

HABITAT: Large rocks, either in the form of talus or outcrops, are a necessity, which accounts for this animal's alternate name, "Rockchuck." The Yellow-bellied Marmot may be found in valley bottoms, high deserts or alpine tundra, but never in dense forests. In Washington and Oregon it occurs mainly in subalpine, semi-open areas and arid grasslands with abundant broken rock or stone piles.

FOOD: Abundant herbaceous or grassy vegetation must be available within a short distance of the den. This marmot occasionally feeds on roadkill carrion, and there have been reports of cannibalization of young.

DEN: Each adult maintains its own burrow, with individuals of the highest social status nearest the colony center. A burrow is typically 8–14 in. across. It slants down for 20–39 in. and then extends another 10–15 ft. to end beneath or among large rocks in a bulky nest lined with grass.

YOUNG: The litter of three to eight young is born in June after a 30-day gestation period. Naked and blind at birth, they first emerge from the burrow at three to four weeks old. Well-fed females become sexually mature before their first birthday. Males and females born at higher elevations usually do not get a chance to breed until they are at least two years old.

SIMILAR SPECIES: The **Hoary Marmot** (p. 256) has gray cheeks and a gray belly, and it occupies higher elevations and rougher terrain. The **Woodchuck** (p. 254) is uniformly brownish, without the yellowish belly. The **Columbian Ground Squirrel** (p. 262) is much smaller and lacks the black coloration on its face.

DID YOU KNOW?

Yellow-bellied Marmots frequently bask in the morning sun, probably to warm up. At about midday they retire to their cool burrows, but in late afternoon they re-emerge to feed. They seem to have poor control of their body temperature: in summer it may range from 93° F to 104° F.

Hoary Marmot
Marmota caligata

These stocky sentinels of alpine vistas pose graciously on boulders, gazing for untold hours at the surrounding mountain scenery. They customarily emerge from their burrows soon after sunrise, but they remain hidden on windy days and during snow, rain or hailstorms.

Hoary Marmots occupy exclusively high-elevation environs, where long summer days allow rapid plant growth during an annual growing season that often lasts only 60 days. Despite the shortened summer season, these marmots seldom seem hurried; rather, most of their time seems to be spent staring off into the distance, perhaps on the lookout for predators.

Where they are frequently exposed to humans, Hoary Marmots become surprisingly tolerant of our activities. These photo-friendly individuals contrast sharply with the wary animals that live in more isolated areas. In the backcountry, the presence of an intruder in an alpine cirque or talus slope is greeted by a shrill and resounding whistle, from which this marmot's nickname "Whistler," *siffleur* in French, is derived. When alarmed, marmots travel with surprising grace over the rocky terrain, quickly finding one of their many escape tunnels.

Being chunky is most fashionable in Hoary Marmot circles. Although at first glance their alpine surroundings may appear to hold few dietary possibilities, these areas are in fact rich in marmot foods. Marmots consume great quantities of green vegetation throughout summer, putting on thick layers of fat as their metabolism slows. They will rely on this fat during their eight- to nine-month hibernation period. A considerable portion of stored fat remains when the marmots emerge from hibernation, but they need it for mating and other activities until the green vegetation reappears.

ALSO CALLED: Whistler.

DESCRIPTION: The head is gray and white with contrasting black markings. The cheeks are gray. A black band across the bridge of the nose separates the white nose patches from the white patches below the eyes. The ears are short and black. The underparts and feet are gray. A black stripe extends from behind each ear toward the shoulder. The shoulders and upper back are a grizzled gray, changing to buffy brown on the lower back and rump, where black-tipped guard hairs top the underfur. The bushy, brown tail is so dark it often

RANGE: The Hoary Marmot occurs from northern Alaska south through the northern Cascades and Rocky Mountains to southern Montana and central Idaho.

Total Length: 27–32 in.
Tail Length: 7–9½ in.
Weight: 11–15 lb.

appears black. This marmot often fails to groom its lower back, tail and hindquarters, so the fur there appears matted and rumpled.

HABITAT: Hoary Marmots require large talus boulders or rocky outcroppings near abundant vegetation in moist surroundings. They most commonly occur in alpine tundra and high subalpine areas.

FOOD: Copious quantities of many tundra plants are consumed so avidly that the vegetation near the burrows is often lawn-like because of frequent clipping. Grasses, sedges and broad-leaved herbs are all eaten.

DEN: A burrow will typically run about 6½ ft. into a slope, where it may end with a cave up to 3½ ft. in diameter beneath a large rock. The nest chamber is often filled with soft grasses.

YOUNG: A litter of four to five young is born in mid- to late May, about 30 days after mating. The fully furred young first emerge from the burrows in about the third week of July, when they weigh 7–11 oz. They are weaned soon after emerging and grow rapidly until they enter hibernation in September. Sexual maturity is achieved during their third spring.

SIMILAR SPECIES: The **Yellow-bellied Marmot** (p. 254) has a bright buffy-yellow belly and a grizzled brown back. In areas where their range overlaps that of the Hoary Marmot, Yellow-bellied Marmots and **Woodchucks** (p. 252) will be at lower elevations. The **Olympic Marmot** (p. 258) is brown to nearly gold and is the only marmot inhabiting the Olympic Peninsula.

DID YOU KNOW?

Hoary Marmots often use nose-to-cheek "kisses" when greeting other colony members. Late morning, following avid feeding, is a peak period of socializing. The kisses are shared among members of both sexes.

Olympic Marmot
Marmota olympus

With the smallest range of any North American marmot, the Olympic Marmot occurs only in the mountains of Clallam County in Washington's Olympic Peninsula. This highly sociable marmot lives in well-established colonies. Usually each colony consists of one male, two females and an assortment of yearlings and young of the season.

Olympic Marmots live in burrows under rocks of talus slopes in alpine and subalpine meadows. In the meadows, these marmots can be seen feeding each day in the morning and in late afternoon. Their feeding habits greatly influence the vegetation in the meadows. Plants they like to eat greatly decrease in abundance, whereas plants that are unpalatable tend to increase in the area. They have two main eating periods a day, and they spend many hours lying on warm rocks in the sun. When they get too warm, they retire to their shady burrows. By the end of summer, they have spent so much time in the sun that their coats have bleached from brown to golden in color. On cloudy or cold days, the marmots must spend more time eating to make up for the lack of thermal energy from the sun. After foraging on a cold day, they slip inside their burrows and rest.

During hibernation, Olympic Marmots lose one third of their body weight or more. Upon emergence, they begin feeding right away. Some individuals have a small store of food in a special chamber of their burrow. If the snow cover is still great when they emerge, they will thus have at least one guaranteed meal from their larder.

DESCRIPTION: This marmot resembles its close cousin, the Hoary Marmot. A pale band of fur over the bridge of the nose, light patches in front of the eyes and indistinct color patterns on the head help to distinguish this species from the Hoary Marmot. The Olympic Marmot has a light-colored bushy tail, a brown or golden coat, small, dark ears and brown feet. The fronts of the forelegs and the chest may appear grizzled or silvery.

HABITAT: Olympic Marmots are high-mountain mammals, favoring subalpine and alpine meadows and talus slopes.

FOOD: These marmots feed mainly on hardy subalpine plants, such as heathers, sedges, lilies, grasses and mosses. Marmots can be quite choosy, and where forbs are abundant they ignore the sedges and grasses. In preparation for hibernation, they double their

RANGE: As their name suggests, these marmots are found only in the Olympic Mountains of Washington.

Total Length: 18–31 in.
Tail Length: 7⅝–8⅞ in.
Weight: 8–18 lb.

weight during the brief mountain summers to survive the winter without food. The general assumption is that marmots must eat large amounts of food in order to gain this much weight. Oddly, this conclusion is not always true, and some marmots have even been known to eat less in summer than they did in spring. Marmots put on weight mostly by a great reduction in their metabolism, allowing much of the food that is eaten to be stored as fat rather than used for active energy.

DEN: Olympic Marmots make their burrows underneath the rocks of their subalpine homes. Burrow entrances may be quite large, up to 12 in. across. The burrow is simple, often just one passage that ends in a nest chamber. During the winter, they hibernate in their burrows. In years of heavy snowfall, they often have to burrow through snow to reach the surface when they emerge in the spring. The first thing they do once they are out is dig right back into the snow to open all of the previous year's burrow entrances. Whether they do this by memory of the outside terrain or by a

"map" of their own burrow in their head is unknown.

YOUNG: Mating occurs in spring immediately after hibernation, though any particular female usually mates and has a litter only every other year. Gestation takes 30 to 32 days, and the average litter size is four young. Females prepare a special natal burrow and line it with grasses before they bear their litter. The young are altricial, but they grow rapidly. The young disperse in their second year.

SIMILAR SPECIES: Range alone is sufficient to distinguish this marmot from other marmots.

DID YOU KNOW?

When marmots hide from a predator in their burrow, they stay hidden for different lengths of time depending on the predator. If the danger is an eagle, the marmot will stay underground only for a short time, because the eagle will leave quickly to search for food elsewhere. If the predator is a cunning fox, the marmot will stay hidden for a long time.

White-tailed Antelope Squirrel
Ammospermophilus leucurus

Total Length: 7⅝–9⅜ in.
Tail Length: 2⅛–3⅜ in.
Weight: 3–5½ oz.

White-tailed Antelope Squirrels live in large aggregations in which each adult maintains at least one burrow, and a strict social order is established among the males. In the northern parts of their range, White-tailed Antelope Squirrels may hibernate for about two months, though as a whole the genus does not hibernate. White-tailed Antelope Squirrels have special adaptations for surviving hot desert environments rather than cold winter conditions. To survive the heat of the desert, antelope squirrels press their bellies to the dirt in shaded areas to quickly draw heat out of their bodies. They can also deal with being too hot by climbing into shady shrubs to catch a cooling breeze or retiring to their burrows.

DESCRIPTION: These antelope squirrels have a distinct pale band down each side. In summer they have tawny coats, and in winter their coats are cast with gray. The undersides are pale, and the tail is white underneath.

HABITAT: The most widespread *Ammospermophilus* species, the White-tailed Antelope Squirrel inhabits deserts, valley bottoms, gravelly washes, sagebrush plateaus, creosote flats and foothills.

FOOD: These squirrels eat green vegetation, seeds, insects and other invertebrates and some vertebrates.

DEN: White-tailed Antelope Squirrels make simple burrows without a mound of dirt at the entrance. Inside the burrow is a chamber used for sleeping and raising young.

YOUNG: Mating occurs anytime from February to June, and the litter size is 5 to 14 young. As the young mature, they spar and wrestle to determine dominance.

RANGE: This squirrel is found southward from southeastern Oregon and southwestern Idaho to southern California and in a patchy distribution eastward to western Colorado and northwestern New Mexico.

SIMILAR SPECIES: Chipmunks (pp. 244–51) are smaller and have more stripes, including facial stripes. The **Golden-mantled Ground Squirrel** (p. 272) is larger and has dark stripes bordering its pale side stripe. In the Oregon part of this antelope squirrel's range, no other animals are likely to be confused with it.

Townsend's Ground Squirrel
Spermophilus townsendii

Total Length: 6⅝–11 in.
Tail Length: 1¼–2⅞ in.
Weight: 4½–12 oz.

The Townsend's Ground Squirrel spends most of its life hibernating underground. Its dormant period starts as estivation in July and continues into hibernation, which lasts until the end of January. Between February and July, the squirrel requires 120 to 135 days of eating to sufficiently fatten itself for dormancy. Females and juveniles usually take a bit longer to do this than males. If, by late July, an individual has not put on enough weight to survive until February, it may wake up to feed again in fall after only a short period of estivation. Ideally, the squirrel remains dormant for the entire seven months, and on some occasions as long as nine months.

ALSO CALLED: Sage Squirrel.

DESCRIPTION: This small ground squirrel is typically pale smoky gray above, sometimes with a pinkish tinge. The undersides are nearly white or buff, and the face, hindlegs and underside of the tail are reddish or tawny in color. The short tail is usually edged with white. This ground squirrel does not have spots.

HABITAT: These ground dwellers prefer open, dry areas, such as sagebrush flats or deserts, but the densest populations are found near the water sources within such areas.

FOOD: These squirrels feed on leafy vegetation, grasses, seeds, insects and carrion.

DEN: These squirrels may form large colonies with complex burrows. Each burrow is about 50 ft. long and up to 6 ft. below the surface. Most adults also dig a second, auxiliary burrow for safety.

YOUNG: Mating occurs immediately after emergence from hibernation. Gestation lasts roughly one month, and litter size is 4 to 10 young. The young open their eyes between 18 and 22 days, and they stop suckling after about 32 days.

SIMILAR SPECIES: The **Piute Ground Squirrel** (p. 265)—once considered the same species as the Townsend's—is found north of the Yakima River in Washington, whereas the Townsend's is found to the south. The **Washington Ground Squirrel** (p. 266) has light-colored dappling over its back. The **Wyoming Ground Squirrel** (p. 267) and the **California Ground Squirrel** (p. 268) are both larger.

RANGE: The Townsend's Ground Squirrel is found only in a small part of south-central Washington that lies between the Yakima River and the Columbia River.

Columbian Ground Squirrel
Spermophilus columbianus

From montane valleys to alpine meadows, the Columbian Ground Squirrel is a common resident of northern Washington and northeastern Oregon. Within its range, it seems that virtually every meadow has a population of this large rodent thriving among the grasses. At heavily visited day-use areas and campgrounds, colonies of this ground squirrel attract a great deal of tourist attention.

Columbian Ground Squirrels are robust, sleek and colorful animals that chirp loudly, often at the first sight of anything unusual. The chirps coincide with a flick of the tail and a quick dash to the edge of the burrow. When a suspected predator approaches, the chirp becomes a loud trill, and the ground squirrel disappears down the hole. Also, different alarms are used for avian versus terrestrial predators and for squirrel intruders from outside the colony. Making sense of the repertoire of different ground squirrel sounds may require more effort than most people are prepared to devote to the matter.

Colony members interact freely and non-aggressively with one another in most instances, sniffing and kissing their neighbors upon each greeting. The dominant male, however, has his burrow near the center of the colony and maintains his central location throughout the breeding season. Ground squirrels from outside the colony are typically attacked by one or several members of the colony, and they are driven far afield.

Dispersing individuals, forced to emigrate from their home colony, are exceedingly vulnerable to predation. Away from the sanctuary of communal life, these large rodents are a highly valued dietary choice for other mammals and birds. Several hawk and falcon species, for example, seasonally focus their hunting efforts on Columbian Ground Squirrels.

ALSO CALLED: Red Digger.

DESCRIPTION: The entire back is cinnamon buff, but because the dorsal guard hairs have black tips, a dappled, black-and-buffy effect results. The top of the head and the nape and sides of the neck are a rich gray with black overtones. A buffy ring circles the eye. The nose and face are a rich tawny color, sometimes fading to ocher-buff on the forefeet, but more frequently continuing tawny over the forefeet, underparts and hindfeet. The base of the tail is sometimes tawny or, more rarely, rufous. The moderately bushy tail is

RANGE: The Columbian Ground Squirrel is found from east-central British Columbia south to northeastern Oregon, Idaho and western Montana.

Total Length: 13–16 in.
Tail Length: 3¼–4¾ in.
Weight: 16–20 oz.

brown overall, but it is overlain with hairs having black subterminal bands and buffy white tips.

HABITAT: This wide-ranging ground squirrel may occupy intermontane valleys, forest edges, open woodlands, alpine tundra and even open plains. Although it is primarily an animal of meadows and grassy areas, some individuals have learned to climb trees.

FOOD: All parts of both broad-leaved and grassy plants are consumed. Carrion is eaten when it is found, and adults, especially males, have on several occasions been reported cannibalizing the young. Insects and other invertebrates are also eaten. Squirrels ordinarily store only seeds or bulbs in their burrows.

DEN: The colony develops its burrow system on well-drained soils, preferably loams, on north- or east-facing slopes in the mountains. The tunnels are 3–4¼ in. wide and descend for 3½–6½ ft. Each colony member's burrow system has 2 to 35 entrances and may spread to a diameter of more than 27 yd. A central chamber, up to 30 in. across, is filled with insulating vegetation. Several other burrows, each up to 5 ft. long and with a single entrance, serve as temporary refuges around the colony.

YOUNG: Mating occurs in the female's burrow soon after she emerges from hibernation. After a gestation period of 23 to 24 days, she delivers a litter of two to seven young. The upper incisors erupt by day 19, the eyes open at about day 20, and the young are weaned at about one month. All Columbian Ground Squirrels are sexually mature after two hibernation periods, though some females may mate after their first winter.

SIMILAR SPECIES: The **Yellow-bellied Marmot** (p. 254) is much larger and has dark facial markings. Most other **ground squirrels** are smaller and lack rich, red-colored highlights on the nose and body.

DID YOU KNOW?

Columbian Ground Squirrels have been known to hibernate for up to 220 days. During hibernation, the squirrels wake at least once every 2½ weeks to urinate, and sometimes defecate, and to eat some stored food.

Merriam's Ground Squirrel
Spermophilus canus

Total Length: 6⅝–11 in.
Tail Length: 1¼–2⅞ in.
Weight: 4½–12 oz.

Tis species was only recently recognized as a separate species from the Townsend's Ground Squirrel (p. 261). Like the Townsend's Ground Squirrel, the Merriam's is a colonial, yet somewhat antisocial, ground dweller. Although it lives in colonies that can be very large, friendly behavior is reserved for immediate family members only. Like other ground squirrels, this one has both a shrill squeak that is used to keep colony members in contact and a multi-note trill to warn of danger. The main predators that this ground squirrel must be constantly alert for are American Badgers, foxes, hawks and Coyotes. In late summer, this ground squirrel begins estivation to avoid summer heat and drought. Estivation continues into winter hibernation and lasts until late February.

ALSO CALLED: Columbia Plateau Ground Squirrel.

RANGE: The Merriam's Ground Squirrel is found in central and eastern Oregon, northern Nevada and southwestern Idaho.

DESCRIPTION: These small ground squirrels are an unmottled gray in color, often with pinkish highlights, and the undersides are pale. The short tail is fringed with white, and it is reddish underneath.

HABITAT: An inhabitant of open areas, this squirrel is usually found in arid flatlands, deserts and sagebrush regions, though it sometimes lives in more humid valleys.

FOOD: Like other ground squirrels, the Merriam's feeds on seeds, green vegetation, insects and carrion.

DEN: These ground squirrels dig colonial burrows with long tunnels leading to nest chambers. Multiple entrances improve safety. Each entrance hole has a pile of dirt around it.

YOUNG: Mating occurs in early spring, and a litter of 4 to 10 young is born in March. The altricial young require their mother's milk for at least three weeks. By two months of age, the young look like small adults.

SIMILAR SPECIES: The **Piute Ground Squirrel** (p. 265) is nearly identical. Most other **ground squirrels** in the same range are larger and more colorful.

Piute Ground Squirrel
Spermophilus mollis

Total Length: 6⅝–11 in.
Tail Length: 1¼–2⅞ in.
Weight: 4½–12 oz.

Prior to 1997, the Piute Ground Squirrel and Merriam's Ground Squirrel (p. 264) were both considered as subspecies of the Townsend's Ground Squirrel (p. 261) Studies have found no hybridization between these three species, which differ chromosomally from each other even though they are nearly identical in appearance.

Piute Ground Squirrels both estivate and hibernate, starting in July and lasting at least until the end of January. Before July, individuals must fatten themselves sufficiently to survive the dormant period.

ALSO CALLED: Great Basin Ground Squirrel.

DESCRIPTION: These ground squirrels resemble Townsend's Ground Squirrels—they are small and typically pale smoky gray above, sometimes with a pinkish tinge. Their undersides are pale, and the short tail is fringed with white and is reddish underneath. Often their faces have a reddish tinge as well.

HABITAT: These ground squirrels occur in desert and semi-arid communities, especially areas dominated by sagebrush or greasewood. Sometimes they live on or near agricultural land, where they may become very abundant.

FOOD: The Piute Ground Squirrel feeds on vegetation, insects and carrion.

DEN: These ground squirrels form colonies of up to 30 adults per hectare. The burrow system has multiple entrances; each one is marked by the piled-up dirt around it.

YOUNG: Females have one litter a year, after mating in early spring. In March or April, the litter of 6 to 10 young is born. The altricial young require their mother's milk for at least three weeks.

SIMILAR SPECIES: The **Merriam's Ground Squirrel** (p. 264) is nearly identical. The **Townsend's Ground Squirrel** (p. 261) is found only between the Yakima River and the Columbia River. Most other **ground squirrels** in the same range are larger and more colorful. The **Washington Ground Squirrel** (p. 266) has a dappled coat and a black-tipped tail.

RANGE: The Piute Ground Squirrel is found in two disjunct populations: one  small one in central Washington just north of the Yakima River and a larger one from southeastern Oregon and central Idaho to extreme northeastern California.

Washington Ground Squirrel
Spermophilus washingtonii

Total Length: 7¼–9⅝ in.
Tail Length: 1¼–2½ in.
Weight: 5⅜–10 oz.

S mall and timid, the Washington Ground Squirrel is an inhabitant of only two small, dry open areas in south-central Washington. Agricultural activity in the Columbia Basin has dramatically reduced the available habitat of this species, and so this animal is no longer abundant in any part of its range. Next to the effects of human activities, predation by the American Badger (p. 122) appears to be the most important threat to this ground squirrel. When a badger or other potential predator is spotted, the squirrel emits a soft, wheezy whistle that puts all nearby colony members at attention. They stand upright on their hindlegs to survey the landscape, and then, if the predator approaches, they quickly scurry for safety.

DESCRIPTION: This ground squirrel is mainly gray in color, with light-colored dapples over the back. Its undersides are a light buffy color. The hindlegs and the snout usually have a slight reddish or tawny tinge, and the short tail has a black tip.

HABITAT: Populations of these ground dwellers are strongly associated with native bunch grasses, forbs and easily crumbled soils.

FOOD: These squirrels eat a variety of foods, including seeds, stems, roots, leaves, grasses, crop plants and insects.

DEN: Washington Ground Squirrels dig simple burrows up to 23 ft. in length and about 5½ ft. below the surface. They may form loose colonies of up to 250 individuals.

YOUNG: Mating occurs after hibernation, and gestation takes about one month. The female gives birth in March to a litter of about eight young. By late April they are half grown, and by late May it is difficult to distinguish the young from the adults.

SIMILAR SPECIES: The **Townsend's Ground Squirrel** (p. 261) and the **Piute Ground Squirrel** (p. 265), which are both found in Washington, lack the light-colored dappling that occurs on this squirrel's back. The **California Ground Squirrel** (p. 268) and the **Columbian Ground Squirrel** (p. 262) are much larger and more colorful and have longer tails.

RANGE: Washington Ground Squirrels live in southeastern Washington and northeastern Oregon.

Wyoming Ground Squirrel
Spermophilus elegans

Total Length: 10–12 in.
Tail Length: 2⅜–3⅛ in.
Weight: 10–14 oz.

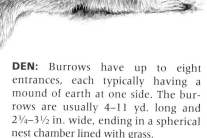

The Wyoming Ground Squirrel was long considered to be a subspecies of the Richardson's Ground Squirrel (*S. richardsonii*), which it closely resembles. A detailed study of its biology, however, revealed that although these two species do sometimes interbreed, their hybrids have reduced viability and do not survive long. Although distinguishing these two ground squirrels can be difficult, they have very little range overlap. In our region, the Wyoming Ground Squirrel is found only in extreme southeastern Oregon, whereas the Richardson's Ground Squirrel is completely absent from our region.

DESCRIPTION: The back is a grayish buffy brown, the top of the nose is pinkish or cinnamon, and the eye has a light ring around it. The rump may have indistinct brown barring. In early summer, the sides and belly are yellowish buff. Later in the season they become grayer. The tail is grayish buffy to speckled black above; below it is pale orange or buffy. The call is a weak, cricket-like alarm: *chirr*.

HABITAT: Dry slopes with sandy, gravelly or silty soils and short herbaceous vegetation are preferred.

FOOD: Green vegetation, especially sage and legumes, are important early in the season. Insects, other invertebrates and carrion are often eaten.

DEN: Burrows have up to eight entrances, each typically having a mound of earth at one side. The burrows are usually 4–11 yd. long and 2¾–3½ in. wide, ending in a spherical nest chamber lined with grass.

YOUNG: In spring, a litter of usually six to seven young is born after a 22- to 23-day gestation period. The eyes open and the upper incisors erupt when the young are about 23 days old. They then emerge from the burrow and switch to a diet of vegetation.

SIMILAR SPECIES: The **Townsend's Ground Squirrel** (p. 261) is smaller. The **Belding's Ground Squirrel** (p. 270) has a pinkish nose and body highlights.

RANGE: The Wyoming Ground Squirrel is found in three separate areas: in the

Rocky Mountains of northeastern Idaho and southwestern Montana; in northeastern Utah, southern Wyoming and central Colorado; and in southeastern Oregon and northern Nevada.

California Ground Squirrel

Spermophilus beecheyi

This impressive, sturdy ground squirrel is a daring creature that easily climbs 20 ft. up cottonwood trees to feed on the tasty catkins. This behavior, as well as its large size and long, bushy tail, may cause someone to mistakenly identify a California Ground Squirrel as a tree squirrel. This ground squirrel seems antisocial in comparison to most other ground dwellers: it either lives alone or in informal colonies. When in colonies, each member avoids the living space of the others.

These ground squirrels enter hibernation by mid November. Unlike some members of the genus, they generally do not estivate first, leaving lots of time for them to fatten their waistlines. They feed primarily on grains, seeds and green vegetation, though insects and other animal protein may be consumed. During hibernation, their heart rate, metabolism and respiration all slow, and in this state they outlast winter. When they awake in spring, they are only half the squirrel they used to be. Most of these resourceful squirrels pack a small amount of food into their winter dens so that they have an easy meal waiting for them.

Like most squirrels, California Ground Squirrels spend a fair portion of each day sunbathing on warm rocks or sand, or even in the branches of a shrub.

They cannot tolerate too much heat, however, and before long the hot squirrels retire to their cool burrows.

ALSO CALLED: Gray Digger, Douglas' Ground Squirrel.

DESCRIPTION: This large ground squirrel is mainly brown in color, with light-colored dapples over the back. A good diagnostic feature is the V-shaped pattern of light fur that begins at the nape of the neck and runs over each shoulder to the sides. This light-colored "V" encloses an area of much darker brown fur. This squirrel also has a long, conspicuously bushy tail that is edged with white.

HABITAT: These ground dwellers favor open areas such as pastures, rocky outcroppings and rolling hills. Overall, however, they are not too particular about where they live. In some parts of our region they inhabit sparsely wooded hillsides, and in Oregon they are even found in rocky areas where rivers enter the ocean—an unusual kind of place to find ground squirrels.

FOOD: This squirrel is certainly not choosy about what it eats: it consumes the seeds, stems, leaves, roots and fruits

RANGE: The California Ground Squirrel is found in south-central Washington, western Oregon, most of California and west-central Nevada.

Total Length: 14–20 in.
Tail Length: 5¾–8⅞ in.
Weight: 9⅞–26 oz.

of most plants, as well as regularly eating insects and small vertebrates. Sometimes the feeding activity of this squirrel can damage crops of grain, fruits and berries.

DEN: The burrows excavated by these ground squirrels are 5–200 ft. long and 3–6 in. across. The adults form loose colonies and may even share burrows, though each animal will have its own entrance. The prime location for a burrow is under a log, a boulder or a tree, if such surface protection is available. In the absence of these features, the ground squirrel excavates its burrow out in the open, with a mound of dirt at the main entranceway.

YOUNG: Soon after emerging from hibernation, mating occurs. Gestation lasts for almost one month, and litter size is usually five to eight young. The altricial young are completely dependent on their mother for the first few weeks, but they grow quickly. At just eight weeks of age, the young resemble

the adults and are beginning to burrow for themselves. In some parts of their range, the young of the season may not hibernate during their first winter, remaining active to feed and mature more quickly instead.

SIMILAR SPECIES: Other **ground squirrels** in the region do not have long, bushy tails. The **Townsend's Ground Squirrel** (p. 261) and the **Washington Ground Squirrel** (p. 266) are both much smaller and grayer. The **Columbian Ground Squirrel** (p. 262) has reddish fur on the nose, undersides and front part of the forelegs.

DID YOU KNOW?

When California Ground Squirrels share burrows, each adult has its own entrance. When threatened and seeking escape to the burrow, an adult runs only to its own entranceway, even if another squirrel's entrance is nearer.

Belding's Ground Squirrel
Spermophilus beldingi

Total Length: 9–12 in.

Tail Length: 1¾–3 in.

Weight: 8–12 oz.

Belding's Ground Squirrels, and their relatives who also estivate, hibernate longer than any other North American mammal. They enter estivation in August, and this state continues on to become hibernation. Waking finally in mid- to late March, these squirrels spend two-thirds of the year dormant. As with all other squirrels, the males emerge from their winter burrows first, and the females follow two weeks later. About five days after the females emerge, they are receptive to mating. The males, ready since they emerged three weeks earlier, battle fiercely for the females. The fighting is intense, because the females are receptive for a mere three to six hours.

DESCRIPTION: The Belding's Ground Squirrel is richly colored, with a slight pinkish tone. Down its back this squirrel has a broad, chestnut brown stripe. The top of the head and the underside of the tail are a cinnamon-pink color, as are the forelegs and chin.

HABITAT: These squirrels inhabit subalpine meadows and grassy areas, such as farmland, mowed areas and golf courses.

FOOD: A diet of grains, green vegetation, seeds, insects and small vertebrates allows these ground squirrels to at least double their weight before they enter dormancy.

DEN: These semi-colonial squirrels make long, simple burrows that end in nest chambers. Although many individuals share the same vicinity, the burrows are not connected.

YOUNG: Mating occurs after emergence from hibernation, and after a gestation period of about 22 days, a litter of three to eight young is born.

SIMILAR SPECIES: The **California Ground Squirrel** (p. 268) and the **Columbian Ground Squirrel** (p. 262) have dappled coats, are much larger and have much longer tails. The **Wyoming Ground Squirrel** (p. 267) also has a mottled or flecked coat but occupies a much different habitat.

RANGE: These ground squirrels are found in central and eastern Oregon, southwestern Idaho, central Nevada and northeastern California.

Cascade Golden-mantled Ground Squirrel

Spermophilus saturatus

Total Length: 10–13 in.
Tail Length: 3½–4¾ in.
Weight: 7½–10 oz.

The Cascade Golden-mantled Ground Squirrel shares its limited range and habitat with two of its cousins, the Yellow-pine Chipmunk and the Townsend's Chipmunk. These three species appear to feed on similar foods and burrow in the same areas, but they manage to avoid direct competition through slight differences in their specific niches that allow them to live together harmoniously.

The major predators of Cascade Golden-mantled Ground Squirrels are owls, hawks, eagles, foxes and weasels. The importance of these ground dwellers as a prey species contributes to a typical maximum life expectancy of four years.

DESCRIPTION: This ground squirrel is mainly dull pinkish or grayish brown with pale buff undersides. The head, neck and shoulders are tinged with russet. The eye is encircled by a white ring. A whitish stripe runs down each side of the back and is bordered on either side by a faint dark stripe. Often the inner dark stripe is paler than the outer. The upper side of the tail is grayish, the underside is yellowish brown, and it usually has a margin of dark hairs.

HABITAT: Talus slopes and rocky outcroppings are preferred, at elevations of no more than 7550 ft.

FOOD: Green vegetation, fruits, seeds and fungi make up the bulk of the diet, but insects and some vertebrates are eaten.

DEN: The burrows are short and do not have large spoil piles at their entrances. The hibernation nest is a mat of vegetation on the floor of a cavity 6 in. wide. Short tunnels off the sleeping chambers serve as either storage areas or latrines.

YOUNG: Most males emerge from hibernation in April. Mating occurs when females emerge a week later. Following a 28-day gestation period, two to eight altricial young are born. When they are a month old and weigh about 1½ oz., they are weaned.

SIMILAR SPECIES: The **Townsend's Chipmunk** (p. 243) and the **Yellow-pine Chipmunk** (p. 244) have stripes on their faces. The **Golden-mantled Ground Squirrel** (p. 272) has a different range.

RANGE: This ground squirrel is found only in the Cascade Mountains of Washington and southwestern British Columbia.

Golden-mantled Ground Squirrel
Spermophilus lateralis

Throughout much of Oregon and parts of Washington, this charming ground squirrel wins the attention of many campers and hikers in wilderness areas. This squirrel can be very bold and shows genuine curiosity toward humans. This handsome animal is frequently the victim of mistaken identity. Misled by the long white and black side stripes, onlookers often call this small ground squirrel a chipmunk. Closer inspection, however, reveals that the stripes stop at the ground squirrel's neck. In contrast, all chipmunks have stripes running through their cheeks. As well, chipmunks have a dark dorsal stripe.

The rotund Golden-mantled Ground Squirrel is an attractive beast with bold, buffy-white eye rings that frame its rich brown eyes. On talus slopes, these squirrels are found alongside pikas, and both of these small mammals continually appear and disappear among the boulders. If you can imitate the high-pitched cries of either of these two animals, the ground squirrels may approach, suddenly appearing perched on a rock surprisingly close by. At close range, you can often see their bulging cheek pouches crammed with seeds and other foods ready to be stored in their burrows.

Although Golden-mantled Ground Squirrels are common around camp-sites and picnic areas and they frequently mooch handouts from visitors, feeding them (or any other wildlife) is illegal in national parks. Human handouts often lead to extreme obesity in animals, which is unhealthy. Perhaps when visitors to natural areas become better informed, they will resist the temptation to feed these and other "friendly" animals, instead satisfying their interest with close observations and photography.

DESCRIPTION: The head and front of the shoulders are a rich chestnut. The buffy-white eye ring is broken toward the ear. Two black stripes, one on each side of a white stripe, run along each side of the animal from the top of the shoulder to near the top of the hip. The back is grizzled gray. The belly and feet are pinkish buff to creamy white. The tail has a black subterminal band, and its blackish top is bordered with a cinnamon buff fringe. The center of the lower surface of the tail is also cinnamon buff.

HABITAT: This squirrel inhabits montane and subalpine forests wherever rocky outcroppings or talus slopes provide adequate cover. In summer, if not permanently, low numbers reside in or beside the alpine tundra. In Oregon this

RANGE: This rock-dwelling squirrel's range is restricted to the Rocky Mountains, southern Cascades and Sierra Nevada.

Total Length: 11–13 in.
Tail Length: 3¾–4¾ in.
Weight: 6–12 oz.

squirrel may inhabit open coniferous zones and high deserts.

FOOD: Green vegetation forms a large part of the early summer diet. Later, more seeds, fruits, insects and carrion are eaten; still later, conifer seeds become a major component of the fall diet. Fungi are another common food.

DEN: This squirrel's burrow typically begins beneath a log or rock. The entrance is 3 in. wide and lacks an earth mound. The tunnel soon constricts to 2 in., and though most burrows are about 3½ ft. long, others may extend to 15 ft. Two or more entrances are common. The nest burrow ends in a chamber that is 6 in. wide and has a mat of vegetation on the floor. Nearby blind tunnels serve as food storage sites. Like many ground squirrels, this species closes the burrow with an earth plug upon entering hibernation, and sometimes when it retires for the night.

YOUNG: Breeding follows soon after the female emerges from hibernation in spring. After a gestation period of 27 to 28 days, four to six naked, blind pups are born between mid-May and early July. At birth, the young weigh about ⅛ oz. The eyes open and the upper incisor teeth erupt at 27 to 31 days. The young are weaned when they are 40 days old. They enter hibernation between August and October, and they are sexually mature when they emerge in spring.

SIMILAR SPECIES: The **Cascade Golden-mantled Ground Squirrel** (p. 271) is very similar, but it has muted colors and occupies a different and much smaller range. **Chipmunks** (pp. 244–51) are much smaller, and their stripes extend through the face. The **White-tailed Antelope Squirrel** (p. 260) lacks the dark stripes bordering the light side stripe.

DID YOU KNOW?

Golden-mantled Ground Squirrels are deep hibernators, and studies conducted on dormant individuals have greatly contributed to our understanding of hibernation.

Western Gray Squirrel
Sciurus griseus

This large tree squirrel is a common resident of the humid deciduous forests of the West Coast of the United States. Intermingling tree branches are like highways to these squirrels, allowing them to cover great distance without ever touching the ground. Their nests are at least 20 ft. off the ground, often near the tops of tall trees. Such heights effectively remove them from the reach of many carnivores. In winter, they ignore their leafy nests, which are now too easily visible among the leafless branches, and take up lodging in a tree cavity instead. Tree cavities tend to be warmer as well as more secret, thereby helping this non-hibernating squirrel survive winter. Like all squirrels, this one prefers mild days and will not leave its nest during stormy, windy or cold weather.

When searching for food, Western Gray Squirrels travel in trees and on the ground, and much of what they collect is stashed away for future use. They make their caches in forked tree branches, under fallen logs or buried in the ground. When they forget about a food cache, the seeds may germinate and replenish the plants on which they feed.

The Western Gray Squirrel is an extremely curious and adept problem solver. If a trap is set to catch one, the squirrel investigates the trap and fiddles with it, rather than entering and getting caught. Many gray squirrels learn to pilfer the nuts from the trigger mechanism of a trap without getting caught, and so squirrel traps are often found empty and overturned.

ALSO CALLED: California Gray Squirrel, Columbian Gray Squirrel, Silver Gray Squirrel.

DESCRIPTION: This large tree squirrel, which is mainly gray above, is speckled with many white-tipped hairs. The undersides are white or nearly white, and the backs of the ears are reddish or tawny in color. Its bushy tail is colored at the edges with bands of gray, white and black. Unlike the two introduced large tree squirrels, the Eastern Fox Squirrel and the Eastern Gray Squirrel (p. 276), this species almost completely lacks rusty or yellowish hairs in its coat, other than on its ears.

HABITAT: This squirrel is abundant in woodland areas, especially oak woods. It can be found anywhere from sea level to low elevations in the central and western parts of Washington and Oregon. The only places it avoids are dry, treeless deserts and high mountain areas.

RANGE: This squirrel is found only on the western fringe of the U.S., from northern Washington south to extreme southern California.

Total Length: 18–24 in.
Tail Length: 9 ⅜–12 in.
Weight: 15–34 oz.

FOOD: Western Gray Squirrels feed heavily on nuts, such as acorns, hazelnuts and almonds, and also on conifer cones, seeds and berries. Sometimes these squirrels consume bark, buds, sap, fungi and insects. A squirrel gnawing on bone or antler, from which it gets many essential minerals, is a common sight. The predilection of Western Gray Squirrels for eating nuts can make them serious pests in nut orchards. In some areas, these squirrels dine almost exclusively on truffles (*hypogeous* or underground fungi).

DEN: Western Gray Squirrels are adept at making large dreys (spherical leaf-and-twig nests) high up in trees. These nests can measure more than 2 ft. wide. In winter these squirrels do not hibernate, but they may move into tree cavities and wait out excessively cold days.

YOUNG: Mating can occur as early as November in the southern part of the range, but usually mating occurs in early spring. Litters of three to five young can be born anytime from February to June. The altricial young, looking like pink "gummy bears" at birth, are completely dependent on their mother for the first few weeks. Females usually have one litter a year, but in favorable conditions two litters is not uncommon.

SIMILAR SPECIES: The **Eastern Fox Squirrel** (p. 276) and the **Eastern Gray Squirrel** (p. 276) both have more red or yellow in their coats. Both the **Red Squirrel** (p. 278) and the **Douglas' Squirrel** (p. 277) are smaller and much browner in color. Most **ground squirrels** (pp. 261–73) burrow in the ground and rarely, if ever, climb trees.

DID YOU KNOW?

If you are out in the forest during the day and you hear a hoarse barking sound, it's very likely not the sound of a dog following you but the call of the Western Gray Squirrel.

Eastern Gray Squirrel
Sciurus carolinensis

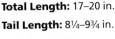

Total Length: 17–20 in.
Tail Length: 8¼–9¾ in.
Weight: 14–25 oz.

In many cities and surrounding areas of Washington and Oregon, people can watch the sinuous movements of this large, introduced tree squirrel. This species is quite similar to the native Western Gray Squirrel (p. 274). They are both called "gray" squirrels, but black and albino forms may occur.

DESCRIPTION: This squirrel is mainly gray with yellow or ochreous highlights on the sides and a nearly pure white belly. The bushy tail is flattened top to bottom. Some individuals and even certain populations may be black.

HABITAT: These squirrels prefer mature deciduous or mixed forests with lots of nut-bearing trees.

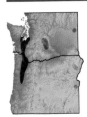

RANGE: This squirrel's native range encompasses the eastern U.S. and parts of Canada to southern Manitoba in the north and eastern Texas in the south.

FOOD: These nut-lovers feed mainly on the seeds of oaks, maples, ashes and elms. In spring and summer they also eat buds, flowers, leaves and occasionally animal matter, such as eggs or nestling birds.

DEN: Eastern Gray Squirrels den in trees year-round. They either build dreys (spherical leaf-and-twig nests) or use natural tree cavities or woodpecker holes.

YOUNG: Breeding occurs from December to February, rarely in July or August. Most females have only one litter a year. Gestation lasts 40 to 45 days, after which a litter of one to eight helpless young is born.

SIMILAR SPECIES: The **Western Gray Squirrel** (p. 274) is very similar but lacks the yellowish or ochreous highlights on its sides. The **Eastern Fox Squirrel** has rusty or yellowish highlights on the face, underside, forelegs and tail. The **Red Squirrel** (p. 278) and **Douglas' Squirrel** (p. 277) are smaller and browner.

Eastern Fox Squirrel *Sciurus niger*

This large and colorful tree squirrel is an introduced species in Washington and Oregon, and it can be seen in numerous cities and nearby nut orchards. The individuals here are gray or orangish above with yellow to rusty highlights on the face, ears, undersides, forelegs and tail.

Douglas' Squirrel
Tamiasciurus douglasii

Total Length: 11–14 in.
Tail Length: 3⅞–6⅛ in.
Weight: 5¼–11 oz.

Famous for its large repertoire of calls, the Douglas' Squirrel is a frequently heard inhabitant of West Coast forests. Living almost exclusively in coniferous forests, this squirrel leaps easily from limb to limb as it searches for food.

Douglas' Squirrels have a seemingly insatiable appetite for conifer cones. Running along conifer branches, they nip the cones free and let them fall to the ground. On a busy day, these squirrels bombard the forest floor with cones for much of the morning. When enough cones are cut, these squirrels eagerly transfer them to large cone caches beside tree stumps or under fallen logs.

ALSO CALLED: Chickaree.

DESCRIPTION: The ear tufts are black, as are the flank stripes that separate the brown back and orange underside. The bushy tail is dark reddish in color. In summer, the eye ring, feet and underparts are pumpkin orange, and the back and head are a grizzled olive brown. The winter coat is more grizzled and gray.

HABITAT: The coniferous coastal rainforest and the Cascade and Sierra Nevada forests are home to this species, though it sometimes ventures out into logged areas.

FOOD: This squirrel feeds mainly on fir, pine, spruce and hemlock seeds and green cones, but it also consumes maple samaras, alder catkins, other seeds and nuts, berries and mushrooms.

DEN: The nest is typically in a hollow tree, but the squirrel may construct a drey (leaf-and-twig nest) high in a conifer, often using an abandoned hawk's or crow's nest as a foundation.

YOUNG: Following mating in early April, two to eight (usually four) young are born after a gestation period of 35 days. The young are weaned at two months and then have to establish their own territories. Juveniles are sexually mature following their first winter.

SIMILAR SPECIES: The **Red Squirrel** (p. 278) is very similar, but its belly is white or silvery gray, and its back is redder. The **Western Gray** (p. 274), **Eastern Gray** (p. 276) and **Eastern Fox** (p. 276) **squirrels** are all much larger. The **Northern Flying Squirrel** (p. 280) is a similar size but is a sooty pewter color and has distinct glide membranes.

RANGE: The Douglas' Squirrel is found from southern British Columbia southward through Washington and Oregon to the Sierra Nevada of southern California.

Red Squirrel
Tamiasciurus hudsonicus

Few squirrels have earned such a reputation for playfulness and agility as the Red Squirrel. This squirrel is a well-known backyard and ravine inhabitant that often has a saucy regard for its human neighbors. Like a one-person band, the Red Squirrel firmly scolds all intruders with shrill chatters, clucks and sputters, falsettos, tail flicking and feet stamping. Even when it is undisturbed, this chatterbox often chirps as it goes about its daily routine. A Red Squirrel is delightful, but difficult, to watch, because it is very active, and, by comparison, we are too slow and awkward in our movement along the forest floor.

For this industrious squirrel, the daytime hours are devoted almost entirely to food gathering and storage. It urgently collects conifer cones, mushrooms, fruits and seeds in preparation for the winter months. The Red Squirrel remains active throughout winter, except in severely cold weather. At temperatures below −13° F, it stays warm, but awake, in its nest.

Because the Red Squirrel does not hibernate, it needs to store massive amounts of food in winter caches. These food caches, which in extreme cases can reach the size of a garage, are the secret to the Red Squirrel's winter success.

Much of its efforts throughout the year are concentrated on filling these larders, and biologists speculate that the Red Squirrel's characteristically antagonistic disposition is a result of having to continually protect its food stores.

By the end of winter, Red Squirrels are ready to mate. Their courtship involves daredevil leaps through the trees and high-speed chases over the forest floor. Later, the playful youngsters frequently challenge nuts or mushrooms to bouts of aggressive mortal combat.

ALSO CALLED: Pine Squirrel, Chickaree.

DESCRIPTION: The shiny, clove brown summer coat sometimes has a central reddish wash along the back. A black longitudinal line on each side separates the dorsal color from the grayish to white underparts. The eye has a white ring, and the whiskers are black. The backs of the ears and the legs are rufous to yellowish. The longest tail hairs have a black subterminal band and buffy tip, which gives the tail a light fringe. The longer, softer winter fur tends to be bright to dusky rufous on the upperparts, with fewer buffy areas, and the head and belly tend to be grayer.

RANGE: The Red Squirrel occupies coniferous forests across most of Alaska, Canada and the north-central and northeastern U.S. In the West, its range extends southward through the Rocky Mountains to southern New Mexico. Further east, this squirrel occurs as far south as Iowa and Virginia.

Total Length: 11–14 in.
Tail Length: 3⅝–6¼ in.
Weight: 5–8⅞ oz.

HABITAT: Boreal coniferous forests and mixed forests make up the primary habitat, but towns with trees more than 40 years old also support populations of Red Squirrels.

FOOD: Most of the diet consists of seeds extracted from conifer cones. A midden is formed where discarded cone scales and cores pile up below a favored feeding perch. In addition, this squirrel eats flowers, berries, mushrooms, eggs, birds, mice, insects and even baby Snowshoe Hares or chipmunks.

DEN: Tree cavities, growths of witch's broom (created in conifers in response to mistletoe or fungal infections), logs and burrows may serve as den sites. The burrows or entrances are about 6 in. wide, with an expanded cavity housing a nest ball that is 16 in. across.

YOUNG: In areas of long winters, females bear just one litter a year. The peak breeding time, in April and May, is associated with frenetic chases and multiple copulations lasting up to seven minutes each. After a 35- to 38-day gestation period, a litter of two to seven (usually four or five) pink, blind, helpless young is born. The eyes open at four to five weeks, and the young are weaned when they are seven to eight weeks old. Red Squirrels are sexually mature by the following spring.

SIMILAR SPECIES: The **Douglas' Squirrel** (p. 277) is very similar but has a browner, duller coat and ochreous undersides and is found only in the Cascade and Coast ranges. The **Northern Flying Squirrel** (p. 280) is of similar size, but is a sooty pewter color and has distinct glide membranes. The **Western Gray** (p. 274), **Eastern Gray** (p. 276) and **Eastern Fox** (p. 276) squirrels are all much larger.

DID YOU KNOW?

In a race against time, a Red Squirrel works to store conifer cones—as many as 14,000—in damp caches that prevent the cones from opening. If the cones open naturally on the tree, the valuable, fat-rich seeds are lost to the wind.

Northern Flying Squirrel
Glaucomys sabrinus

Like drifting leaves, Northern Flying Squirrels seem to float from tree to tree in forests throughout much of Washington and Oregon. These arboreal performers are one of two species of flying squirrels in North America that are capable of distance gliding.

Although flying squirrels are not capable of true flapping flight—bats are the only mammals to have mastered the ability—their aerial travels are nevertheless impressive, with extreme glides of up to 110 yd. Enabling the squirrels to "fly" are their cape-like glide membranes of furred skin that extend down the length of the body from the forelegs to the hindlegs.

Before a glide, a squirrel identifies a target and maneuvers into the launch position: a head-down, tail-up orientation in the tree. Then, using its strong hindlegs, the squirrel propels itself into the air with its legs extended. Once airborne, it resembles a flying paper towel that can make rapid side-to-side maneuvers and tight downward spirals. Such control is accomplished by making minor adjustments to the orientation of the wrists and forelegs. On the ground and in trees, flying squirrels hop or leap, but the skin folds prevent them from running. They are not able to swim, either.

The call of the Northern Flying Squirrel is a loud *chuck chuck chuck* that increases in pitch to a shrill falsetto when the animal is disturbed. Like other tree squirrels, the Northern Flying Squirrel does not hibernate. On severely cold days, however, groups of 5 to 10 individuals can be found huddled in a nest to keep warm.

DESCRIPTION: Flying squirrels have a unique web or fold of skin that extends laterally to the level of the ankles and wrists to become the abbreviated "wings" with which a squirrel glides. These animals have large, dark, shiny eyes. The back is light brown, with hints of gray from the lead-colored hair bases. The feet are gray on top. The underparts are light gray to cinnamon precisely to the edge of the gliding membrane and the edge of the tail. The tail appears flattened because of long hairs that extend only to the sides; this feather-shaped tail adds to the buoyancy of the "flight" and helps the tail function the way the rudder and elevators do on an airplane.

HABITAT: Coniferous mountain forests are prime flying squirrel habitat, but these animals are sometimes found in aspen and cottonwood forests.

RANGE: This flying squirrel occurs in eastern Alaska and across most of Canada in appropriate habitats. Its range extends southward through the western mountains to California and Utah, as well as around the Great Lakes and through the Appalachians.

Total Length: 9¾–15 in.
Tail Length: 4¼–7 in.
Weight: 2⅝–6½ oz.

FOOD: The bulk of the diet consists of lichens and fungi, but flying squirrels also eat buds, berries, some seeds, a few arthropods, bird eggs and nestlings and the protein-rich, pollen-filled male cones of conifers. They cache most of their non-perishable foods.

DEN: Nests in tree cavities are lined with lichen and grass. Leaf nests, called dreys, are located in a tree fork close to the trunk. Twigs and strips of bark are used on the outside, with progressively finer materials used inside, until the center consists of grasses and lichens. If the drey is for winter use, it usually has thicker walls for better insulation.

YOUNG: Mating takes place between late March and the end of May. After a six-week gestation period, typically two to four young are born. They weigh about ³⁄₁₆ oz. at birth. The eyes open after about 52 days. Ten days later the young first leave the nest, and they are weaned when they are about 65 days old. Young squirrels first glide at three months; it takes them about a month to become skilled. Flying squirrels are not sexually mature until after their second winter.

SIMILAR SPECIES: No other mammal in the region has the distinctive flight membranes of a flying squirrel. The **Red Squirrel** (p. 278) and the **Douglas' Squirrel** (p. 277) are browner overall and are generally active during the day.

DID YOU KNOW?

Northern Flying Squirrels are often just as common in an area as Red or Douglas' Squirrels, but they are nocturnal and therefore rarely seen. Flying squirrels routinely visit bird-feeders at night; they value the seeds as much as sparrows and finches do.

Mountain Beaver
Aplodontia rufa

The Mountain Beaver is considered the most primitive living rodent. Unlike other rodents, the Mountain Beaver depends on the availability of ferns in its environment. Although ferns are toxic to most other rodents, they are the primary food for this creature, which suggests how little this mammal has changed since it first evolved in ancient times.

The Mountain Beaver's cheek teeth are also unlike those of most other rodents: they have a single central lobe of dentin surrounded by a ridge of enamel. In contrast, other rodents have teeth that show complex folding with a proliferation of enamel. When digging a burrow, if a Mountain Beaver comes across stones or lumps of clay about 3–4 in. across, it may keep them in its burrow and occasionally gnaw upon them to sharpen its teeth. These "Mountain Beaver baseballs" are also used to block the entrances of vacated burrows.

Mountain Beavers can climb sapling trees as high as 13 ft., allowing them to eat the tender shoots. They can also swim for short distances. When foraging, they collect leafy branches and other vegetation and carry the spoils to their burrows. There these beavers sit on their short tails, and they grasp the vegetation in their forepaws using their semi-opposable thumbs.

Like a lagomorph, the Mountain Beaver reingests its soft fecal pellets, allowing better absorption of nutrients the second time, through the action of bacteria. Hard fecal pellets, the result of the reingested soft pellets, are seized with the incisors and thrown into a burrow latrine.

ALSO CALLED: Sewellel, Boomer.

DESCRIPTION: At first glance, the Mountain Beaver looks similar to a muskrat or like a giant pocket gopher, except that it has a very short, well-furred tail. Its stocky body is covered with coarse, reddish-brown or grayish-brown fur. It has light grayish-brown or tawny undersides. The short, strong limbs each have five toes, and the forelimbs are equipped with long, laterally compressed, cream-colored claws. The soles of the feet are naked to the heel. Each short, round ear has a light spot below it, and the white whiskers are abundant.

HABITAT: The Mountain Beaver occupies wooded areas from near sea level to treeline. It favors early seral vegetative stages with an abundance of shrubs,

RANGE: The Mountain Beaver is a western North American species that ranges from the Nicola Valley in British Columbia to southeast of San Francisco near the Nevada–California border in the Sierra Nevada.

Total Length: 1–1½ ft.
Tail Length: ¾–2 in.
Weight: ⅝–3 lb.

forbs and young trees. The highest densities of these animals appear to be in the deciduous forests of mountain parks; few occupy dense, old coniferous forests.

FOOD: These animals consume a wide variety of plants, but sword fern and bracken fern generally form the bulk of the diet during all seasons. Bracken fern is poisonous to most herbivores, but the Mountain Beaver is unharmed by it. In October, when the protein content of red alder leaves is highest, up to three-quarters of a male's diet may be composed of these leaves. Mountain Beavers may also feed on seedlings and the cambium of saplings.

DEN: The Mountain Beaver constructs an extensive burrow system consisting of tunnels 5–7 in. high by 6–10 in. wide radiating out from nest chambers. Numerous burrows penetrate to the surface, but only a few have dirt piles around their openings. The nest chambers, about 1 ft. in diameter, contain dried leaves and grasses trampled into a flat pad. Generally the nest is 1–5 ft. beneath the surface, but burrows may penetrate up to 10 ft. underground.

Pockets in the walls of some larger burrows may contain roots, stems and leaves. Sometimes tent-like structures of sticks, leaves and succulent vegetation are found over burrow entrances.

YOUNG: After a gestation period of 28 to 30 days, the young are born in March or April in the subterranean nest. Each of the one to four altricial young weighs about ⅞ oz. Their eyes open at 45 to 54 days, and they then begin to eat vegetation and grow exponentially. Neither sex appears to be sexually mature until the second winter.

SIMILAR SPECIES: All **marmots** (pp. 254–59) have longer, bushy tails. The **Common Muskrat** (p. 224) has a long, naked, scaly tail and is associated with water.

DID YOU KNOW?

The Mountain Beaver is rarely seen in winter, but it does not hibernate. It stays underground, awake in its warm, moist den, where it feeds on stored vegetation.

RABBITS, HARES & PIKAS

These rodent-like mammals are often called "lagomorphs" after the scientific name of the order, Lagomorpha, which means "hare-shaped." Rabbits, hares and pikas share the rodents' trademark chisel-like upper incisors, and taxonomists once grouped the two orders together. Unlike rodents, however, lagomorphs have a second pair of upper incisors. Casual observers never see these tiny, peg-like teeth, which lie immediately behind the first upper incisor pair.

Lagomorphs are strict vegetarians, but they have relatively inefficient, non-ruminant stomachs that have trouble digesting such a diet. To make the most of their meals, they defecate pellets of soft, green, partially digested material that they then reingest to obtain maximum nutrition. Bacteria that enter the food in the intestines contribute to better digestion and absorption of nutrients the second time around. The pellets excreted after the second digestive process are brown and fibrous.

Hare Family (Leporidae)

Rabbits and hares are characterized by their long, upright ears, long jumping hindlegs and short, cottony tails. These timid animals are primarily nocturnal. Rabbits build maternity nests for their altricial young, which are blind and naked at birth. Hares and some rabbits spend most of the day resting in shallow depressions called "forms." Unlike rabbits, hares are precocial—the young are born fully furred, with open eyes, and soon after birth they begin to feed on vegetation.

Brush Rabbit

Pika Family (Ochotonidae)

Pikas are the most rodent-like lagomorphs, and with their short, rounded ears and squat bodies, they look a lot like small guinea pigs. Their front and rear limbs are about the same length, so pikas do not hop like rabbits and hares. They scurry and make small bounds among the rocks and talus of their home territories. Pikas are most active during the day, and they are often seen in rocky mountain areas.

American Pika

Pygmy Rabbit
Brachylagus idahoensis

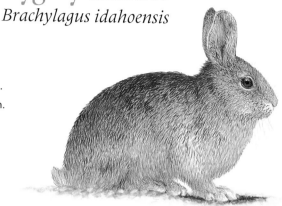

Total Length: 10–12 in.
Tail Length: 1³⁄₁₆–1¼ in.
Weight: 10–15 oz.

Unlike all other native rabbits, the Pygmy Rabbit excavates a burrow for itself, which it does in the hard soil of sagebrush flats. This rabbit is considered a keystone species for this habitat type, meaning that it is unable to thrive anywhere else and that many other species in the habitat depend on its presence. This rabbit's burrows are also home to many species of invertebrates and some vertebrates, and the rabbit itself is reliable prey for predators in the sagebrush community. When you are walking through waist-high sagebrush, you might stir up the occasional Pygmy Rabbit that will dart quickly away from you.

DESCRIPTION: This tiny rabbit is tawny or cinnamon in color. Sometimes the coat is dark gray to nearly black. Each nostril has a small, white spot on its side. The small tail is entirely gray.

HABITAT: The Pygmy Rabbit is always found in association with dense stands of sagebrush or rabbitbrush. It favors desert or semi-desert conditions, wherever it can find earth soft enough for digging.

FOOD: The bitter leaves of sagebrush make up the bulk of the diet. When available, grasses and other succulent vegetation are eaten.

DEN: This small rabbit digs burrows that are about 3 in. across. At least two entrances are usually beneath large, dense sagebrush plants. A shallow trench typically radiates out from each entrance, and the rabbit often crouches in the trench so only its ears and eyes are visible.

YOUNG: Pygmy Rabbits mate in spring or early summer. After a gestation period of 27 to 30 days, a litter of six naked, blind young is born between late May and early August.

SIMILAR SPECIES: The Pygmy Rabbit is so small that it could only be confused with a juvenile of a different species of rabbit. The **Mountain Cottontail** (p. 288) is larger and paler and has longer ears. The **Brush Rabbit** (p. 286) is larger and occupies a different range and habitat.

RANGE: The Pygmy Rabbit is primarily a Great Basin animal that ranges between the Rocky Mountains and the Cascades in Montana, Idaho, Utah, Nevada, California and Oregon.

Brush Rabbit
Sylvilagus bachmani

Total Length: 11–15 in.
Tail Length: ¾–1⅝ in.
Weight: 1–2 lb.

Brush Rabbits of the Pacific Coast are good examples of Allen's Rule, which states that animals of the same species in warmer regions tend to have longer appendages and larger external features than those in cooler places. The Brush Rabbits living in the hot areas of lower California have much longer ears than those living in Oregon. Allen's Rule suggests that this elongation is a method of cooling, because the ears are thin and contain many blood vessels. Another explanation is that sound travels poorly in hot, dry air, so larger ears may be an adaptation for better hearing.

DESCRIPTION: This small rabbit ranges in color from tawny brown to reddish brown, and it is often flecked throughout with dark gray base hairs. The undersides are lighter than the back, but they are not white. In winter the coat color is slightly lighter than in summer. The whiskers are black, and the ears are just over 2 in. long. The rounded tail is mainly white.

HABITAT: True to their name, Brush Rabbits favor areas with shrubs or open to heavy brush cover.

FOOD: Throughout summer, Brush Rabbits feed on grasses, clover and berries. In winter or in periods of drought, woody vegetation is eaten.

DEN: These rabbits sleep in forms and raise their young in fur-lined forms. When the mother leaves her nesting form, she covers it with a layer of grass.

YOUNG: These rabbits can have up to five litters a year, from February to August. Gestation lasts 22 days, and the litter size averages three or four young.

SIMILAR SPECIES: The **Pygmy Rabbit** (p. 285) is smaller and has shorter ears and a gray tail, and it inhabits areas east of the Brush Rabbit's range.

RANGE: The Brush Rabbit ranges from western Oregon down to the West Coast to Baja California.

Eastern Cottontail
Sylvilagus floridanus

Total Length: 16–18 in.
Tail Length: 1½–2¾ in.
Weight: 28–56 oz.

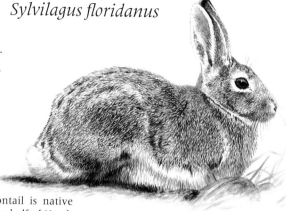

The Eastern Cottontail is native only to the eastern half of North America, but it has been widely introduced throughout many of the western states. It is now the most widespread cottontail in North America, and its success is partly because of its ability to adapt to a wide variety of habitats. The main requirement for this rabbit is tall grasses or shrubs that provide adequate protection from predators. Although accurate population figures for this highly fecund cottontail are not known for Washington and Oregon, its numbers are probably increasing.

DESCRIPTION: This rabbit is pale buffy gray above, with somewhat paler sides. The nape of the neck is orangish, and the legs are cinnamon in color. The undersides are whitish. The tail is brown above and white below, but the white shows only when the animal is running.

HABITAT: This rabbit prefers brushy riparian sites, but it is occasionally seen on lawns with nearby shrubs.

FOOD: This species favors clover, grasses, a wide variety of forbs and the bark of young trees.

DEN: Brush piles, holes and leaf litter are used for escape cover. Before giving birth, the female digs a nest about 10 in.

x 6 in. and lines it with grasses and her own fur; she then covers the depression so it is nearly impossible to see.

YOUNG: In suitable climates, these cottontails can breed at any time of the year. Following mating and a gestation period of 18 to 30 days, one to nine bunnies are delivered in the nest. At one month they are independent, and at four months the young females may breed, resulting in a litter by fall.

SIMILAR SPECIES: The **Mountain Cottontail** (p. 288) is slightly smaller and has a different range, but it is difficult to distinguish from this hare. The larger **Snowshoe Hare** (p. 290) and **White-tailed Jackrabbit** (p. 294) both change color in winter. The **European Rabbit** (p. 295) is usually larger and may have a multi-colored coat.

RANGE: This rabbit is common in the eastern U.S.; introduced populations live in

northern California, western and northeastern Oregon, western Washington and the Fraser River Delta area of British Columbia.

Mountain Cottontail
Sylvilagus nuttallii

During the early evening and twilight, Mountain Cottontails emerge from their daytime hideouts to graze on succulent vegetation. If you are a patient observer, you may see them as they daintily nip at grasses, always just a short leap from dense bushes or a rocky shelter.

The prime habitat for a Mountain Cottontail is neither fully wooded areas nor completely open flats. It requires good protective cover to hide from predators, but in areas where foliage is too dense it is handicapped in its ability to detect an approaching predator. This cottontail is preyed upon heavily by Bobcats (p. 98), Coyotes (p. 162), owls and hawks.

The Mountain Cottontail spends most of its day sitting quietly in dug-out depressions, called "forms," beneath impenetrable vegetation or under boards, rocks, abandoned machinery or buildings. This mid-sized herbivore has a small home range that rarely exceeds the size of a baseball field. Heavy rains greatly diminish cottontail activity, restricting it to its hideouts for the duration of the storm. The Mountain Cottontail does not hibernate during winter, but it limits its movements to traditional trails that it can easily locate after a snowfall.

The scientific name of the Mountain Cottontail refers to Thomas Nuttall, an explorer in the early 1800s. Although Nuttall was primarily a botanist, he made significant contributions to all fields of natural history. He was also renowned for his absent-mindedness and misadventures. During his journey across the continent to the Pacific Ocean on the Wyeth expedition in 1834, he became lost on many occasions. This misguided explorer did identify many new species of plants and animals, despite his frequent gaffes and mishaps along the way.

ALSO CALLED: Nuttall's Cottontail.

DESCRIPTION: This rabbit has dark, grizzled, yellowish-gray upperparts and whitish underparts year-round. The tail is blackish above and white below. The nape of the neck has a rusty-orange patch, and the front and back edges of the ears are white. The ears are usually held erect when the rabbit runs.

HABITAT: A major habitat requirement is cover, whether it is brush, rocky outcroppings or buildings. These rabbits like edge situations where the trees meet meadows or where the brushy areas meet agricultural land.

RANGE: The western limit of this rabbit's range parallels the eastern border of northern California, running north into the Okanagan region of British Columbia. The eastern edge of the range runs south from southern Saskatchewan along the Montana–North Dakota border and onward to northern New Mexico.

Total Length: 13–16 in.
Tail Length: 1¼–2½ in.
Weight: 1½–2¼ lb.

FOOD: Grasses and forbs are the primary foods, but in many areas these cottontails feed heavily on sagebrush and juniper berries.

DEN: Mountain Cottontails sometimes live in burrows and rock crevices, but they usually rest in forms beneath dense vegetation. The young are born in a nest that is dug out by the female and lined with grass and fur. The doe lies over the top while the young nurse. The nest is essentially invisible, and a casual observer would never suspect that the female was nursing or that a nest of babies lay beneath her.

YOUNG: Breeding begins in April, and after a 28- to 30-day gestation period, a litter of one to eight (usually four or five) young is born. The female is in estrus and breeds within hours of giving birth. There can be two litters a season. The young are born blind, hairless and with their eyes closed. They grow quickly and are weaned just before the birth of the subsequent litter.

SIMILAR SPECIES: Both the **Snowshoe Hare** (p. 290) and the **White-tailed Jackrabbit** (p. 294) are larger and become white in winter. The **Eastern Cottontail** (p. 287) is slightly larger and has a different range, but it is difficult to distinguish from the Mountain Cottontail. The **Pygmy Rabbit** (p. 285) is smaller and darker and has smaller ears. The **European Rabbit** (p. 295) is usually larger and may have a multi-colored coat.

DID YOU KNOW?

Rabbits and hares depend on intestinal bacteria to break down the cellulose in their diets. Because the bacteria in the gut are beyond the site of absorption, rabbits eat their pellets to run the material through the digestive tract a second time.

Snowshoe Hare
Lepus americanus

The Snowshoe Hare is able to withstand the most unforgiving aspects of northern and mountain wilderness, because it possesses several fascinating adaptations for winter. For example, as its name implies, the Snowshoe Hare has very large, furry hindfeet and can easily walk on areas of soft snow, whereas most other animals sink into the powder. This ability is a tremendous advantage for an animal that is preyed upon by so many different species of carnivores. Unfortunately, for this hare, it is of minimal help against the equally big-footed Canada Lynx (p. 94), a specialized hunter of the Snowshoe Hare.

It is well known that populations of lynx and hares fluctuate in close correlation with one another, but few people realize that other species are involved in the cycle. Recent studies have shown that as hares increase in number, they overgraze willow and alder in their habitat. These plants are their major source of food during the winter months. In response to overgrazing, willow and alder shoots produce a distasteful and toxic substance that is related to turpentine. This substance protects the plants and initiates starvation in the hares. As the hares decline, so do the lynx. Once the plants recover their growth after a season or two, their shoots become edible again, and the hare population increases.

In response to shortening day lengths at the onset of winter, Snowshoe Hares in most of their range start molting into their white winter camouflage, whether snow actually falls or not. The hares have no control over the timing of this transformation. If the year's first snowfall is late, these rabbbits will lose their usual concealment, becoming visible from great distances—to naturalists and predators alike—as bright white balls in a brown world. The hares seem to be aware of this predicament, and they often seek out any small patch of snow on which to squat. In parts of western Washington and Oregon, these hares do not turn white in winter, an adaptation to the lack of significant snowfall.

DESCRIPTION: The summer coat is rusty brown above, with the crown of the head darker and less reddish than the back. The nape of the neck and top of the tail are grayish brown, and the ear tips are black. The chin, belly and lower surface of the tail are white. Adults have white feet; juveniles have dark feet. In winter, in areas where the hares turn color, the terminal portion of nearly every body hair becomes white,

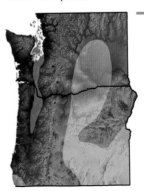

RANGE: The range of the Snowshoe Hare is associated with the boreal coniferous forests and mountain forests that extend from northern Alaska and Labrador south to California and New Mexico in the West and into the Allegheny Mountains in the East.

Total Length: 15–21 in.
Tail Length: 1⅞–2⅛ in.
Weight: 2¼–3¼ lb.

but the hair bases and underfur are lead gray to brownish. The ear tips remain black.

HABITAT: Snowshoe Hares can be found throughout most of Washington and Oregon, almost anywhere forest or dense shrubbery grows. Despite their name, these hares live even in coastal areas that lack winter snow.

FOOD: In summer, a wide variety of grasses, forbs and brush may be consumed. In winter, mostly the buds, twigs and bark of willow and alder are eaten. Hares occasionally eat carrion.

DEN: Snowshoe Hares do not keep a customary den, but they sometimes enter hollow logs or the burrows of other animals or run beneath buildings.

YOUNG: Breeding activity begins in March and continues through August. After a gestation period of 35 to 37 days, one to seven (usually three or four) young are born under cover but often not in an established form or nest. The female breeds again within hours of the birth, and she may have as many as three litters in a season. The precocial young hares can hop within a day, and they feed on grassy vegetation within 10 days. In five months they are fully grown.

SIMILAR SPECIES: The larger **White-tailed Jackrabbit** (p. 294) has longer ears and a slightly longer tail, and its winter underfur is creamy white. The larger **Black-tailed Jackrabbit** (p. 292) has longer ears and does not turn white in winter. The **cottontails** (pp. 287–89) are generally smaller and do not turn white in winter.

DID YOU KNOW?

When alarmed, this hare may drum its hindfeet on the ground, a characteristic that might have inspired "Thumper" in Disney's *Bambi*.

Black-tailed Jackrabbit
Lepus californicus

Despite this hare's common name, the Black-tailed Jackrabbit's most prominent feature is its ears. Black-tipped ears that extend far above this hare's head are a characteristic that, more than any other, identifies this large, open-country mammal. In fact, when fully opened, the ears may account for about 19 percent of the hare's total body surface.

The three hares of Washington and Oregon demonstrate a relationship between the size of their ears and the latitude at which they live: the Black-tailed Jackrabbit, the most southerly hare, has the longest ears; the White-tailed Jackrabbit (p. 294) has intermediate sized ears; and the Snowshoe Hare (p. 290), the most northerly hare, has the shortest ears. The huge ears of the Black-tailed Jackrabbit, which occupies hot, arid areas, help cool it. At the other extreme, the Snowshoe Hare's smaller ears prevent precious energy from escaping during cold winters. Ear size may also contribute to hearing ability—sound moves better through cold air than it does through warm air. Hares that live in warmer climates have evolved larger ears; perhaps they are better equipped for hearing approaching predators.

The Coyote (p. 162) is the major predator of the Black-tailed Jackrabbit, and in some areas the density of the Coyote population has been found to correlate with fluctuations in Black-tailed Jackrabbit numbers. In turn, Black-tailed Jackrabbit densities were directly proportional to summer precipitation.

During the day, a Black-tailed Jackrabbit will lie quietly in a form scraped out beneath a sagebrush bush or beside some other type of cover. This hare lies quietly and motionless, depending upon its camouflage for protection. With the approach of a predator, however, a jackrabbit will rocket from its shelter and quickly attain speeds of up to 35 mph. It will attempt to elude danger by changing direction abruptly and using Olympian leaps up to 6 ft. high and 20 ft. long.

DESCRIPTION: This gray to grayish-brown hare has extremely large, long, black-tipped ears. The belly is white to buffy white. The tail has a black mid-dorsal stripe that runs up onto the back. This hare never turns white in winter, and it molts only once a year.

HABITAT: The Black-tailed Jackrabbit occupies nearly all habitats within its range, except high mountain forests. Although it prefers valley bottoms or irrigated fields in intermontane valleys,

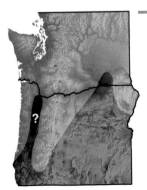

RANGE: The Black-tailed Jackrabbit currently occupies the southwestern quarter of North America, but it appears to be slowly expanding its range northward. In some places it may be displacing the White-tailed Jackrabbit (p. 294).

Total Length: 20–24 in.
Tail Length: 2¾–3¾ in.
Weight: 5–10 lb.

it can also be found on barren ridges devoid of trees.

FOOD: These jackrabbits feed on a wide variety of both herbaceous and woody vegetation, with a larger proportion of shrubby material being consumed in winter. Studies have revealed that 30 Black-tailed Jackrabbits together eat about as much as one cow. These hares have been known to display peculiar eating habits: one plant may be eaten in its entirety while neighboring plants of the same species are ignored.

DEN: This hare has no den, but it spends most of the day crouched in a form it scratches into the ground.

YOUNG: After a gestation period of 41 to 47 days, a litter of one to eight (usually two to four) young is born. The newborns are fully furred and have their eyes open. Instead of staying in a common nest, they are distributed more than 300 ft. apart, and the female nurses each one separately throughout the night. The young are weaned at six

to seven weeks. At 10 weeks they are 90 percent of their adult size. Within hours after giving birth, the female becomes attractive to males, but she flees if one approaches. A vigorous chase ensues that may cover a few miles. Ultimately, the male seizes the female by the nape of her neck and mates with her. Adult females may have up to four litters in a season, and young females from early litters may mature fast enough to have their own litters late in the season.

SIMILAR SPECIES: The **White-tailed Jackrabbit** (p. 294) has slightly shorter ears, turns white in winter and has a grayish upper surface on its tail. The **Snowshoe Hare** (p. 290) has shorter ears and turns white in winter.

DID YOU KNOW?

The name "jackrabbit" is a shortened and more refined version of "jackass rabbit." These mammals were so-named in recognition of their large, donkey-like ears.

White-tailed Jackrabbit
Lepus townsendii

Total Length: 21–25 in.
Tail Length: 2¾–4¼ in.
Weight: 6½–12 lb.

The White-tailed Jackrabbit is a lean sprinter and the largest hare in Washington and Oregon, but it can only be found in the eastern halves of the two states. A creature of open country, the White-tailed Jackrabbit may be encountered either by day as it bursts from a hiding place with ears erect and tail extended or at night in the flash of car headlights.

Like most herbivores, the White-tailed Jackrabbit is drawn to salt, which is found in great abundance on roads. Its need for salt, together with this hare's preference for traveling on solid surfaces, results in high numbers of roadway deaths each year.

ALSO CALLED: Prairie Hare.

DESCRIPTION: In summer, the upperparts of this large hare are a light grayish brown, and the belly is nearly white. By mid-November, the entire coat is white,

except for the grayish forehead and muzzle and the black ear tips. This animal has a fairly long, white tail that sometimes bears a grayish band on the upper surface.

HABITAT: This hare prefers open areas. It will enter open woodlands to seek shelter in winter, but it avoids forests.

FOOD: Grasses and forbs make up most of the diet.

DEN: This hare has no true den, but a shallow form beside a rock or beneath sagebrush serves as a daytime shelter. In winter, jackrabbits may dig depressions or short burrows as shelters in snowdrifts.

YOUNG: One to nine (usually three or four) young are born in a form after a 40-day gestation period. The fully furred newborns have open eyes and soon disperse, meeting their mother to nurse only once or twice a day. By two weeks they are eating some vegetation; at five to six weeks they are weaned, often just before the birth of the next litter.

RANGE: This jackrabbit seems to be expanding its range northward, perhaps in association with land clearing. It can be found from eastern Washington east to southern Manitoba and south to central California and eastern Kansas.

SIMILAR SPECIES: The more widespread **Snowshoe Hare** (p. 290)—also appearing white in winter—has lead gray, not creamy white, hair bases. The **Black-tailed Jackrabbit** (p. 292) has longer ears and does not turn white in winter. The **cottontails** (pp. 286–89) are much smaller and have shorter legs.

European Rabbit
Oryctolagus cuniculus

Total Length: 18–24 in.
Tail Length: 2⅝–3½ in.
Weight: 3–5 lb.

The Hudson's Bay Company, as well as individual settlers, raised European Rabbits and introduced them into the wild in the Pacific Northwest. The idea was to populate common hunting areas with a rapidly reproducing game rabbit larger than a cottontail.

As with most species introductions, the people responsible did not foresee the consequences. These prolific burrowers honeycombed so much of one of the San Juan Islands that the local lighthouse nearly fell over, and parts of the shoreline crumbled into the ocean.

The distribution and abundance of the European Rabbit in Washington and Oregon are not well documented, and there may be no self-maintaining populations in Oregon. In some coastal areas of Washington, however, the European Rabbit appears to be a common naturalized resident. It probably also occurs on many of the islands in northern Washington.

DESCRIPTION: This rabbit comes in an array of grays and browns, as well as black and white. Some individuals have multicolored coats as a result of being descended from pet rabbits that were bred for color variation. The medium-sized ears are about 2½–4 in. long, and the bicolored tail is dark above and white below.

HABITAT: This Old World rabbit generally avoids heavily wooded areas in favor of open fields, brushy areas and parkland. It does not have strict dietary requirements and can therefore quickly populate most areas where it is introduced or has escaped.

FOOD: These rabbits feed on short grasses and leafy herbaceous plants. In some areas, these rabbits seriously threaten both native plant species and other animals that depend on them.

DEN: Although these rabbits may be found singly, they often live in large colonies of dozens or hundreds of individuals and dig extensive burrows. The area around a warren is typically denuded of vegetation.

YOUNG: Each year a female can have as many as six litters, with up to 12 young in each litter. The young are altricial, but they grow rapidly.

SIMILAR SPECIES: **Cottontail rabbits** (pp. 286–89) are usually smaller, and **all hares** (pp. 290–94) have distinctly longer ears. Any rabbit with unusual coloration is a European Rabbit.

RANGE: This rabbit occurs in scattered populations in much of the U.S. and parts of Canada. Some of these populations are the result of escaped pets.

American Pika
Ochotona princeps

Inhabiting an intricate landscape of boulders high in the mountains, the American Pika is often regarded as one of the cutest animals in the alpine wilderness. This relative of the rabbit scurries among the rocks of talus slopes as it makes its way between feeding areas and shelter. When it returns from gathering food, an American Pika carries vegetation clippings crossways in its mouth—a bundle sometimes half as large as the pika itself. The large piles of clippings accumulated on or under the rocks in a pika's territory will feed the animal during winter.

Pikas are extremely vocal animals that are often heard before they are seen. The proper pronunciation of their name is *pee-ka*, which mimics their high-pitched voices: they emit bleats reminiscent of a tricycle horn whenever they see something out of the ordinary. These sounds are often the best clues of their activity, because pikas are difficult to distinguish from the background in their boulder-strewn habitat; when a pika is momentarily glimpsed from afar, one is never quite sure whether it is a genuine sighting or just a pika-sized rock. To the patient naturalist intent on pika observations, however, viewing can be intimate and rewarding because these animals often permit a close approach. When you see a pika escape into a crevice beneath the rocks, sit quietly and wait—soon it will come out again, seemingly oblivious to your unobtrusive presence.

In winter, pikas dig snow tunnels as far as 100 yd. out from their rock shelters to collect and eat plants. The talus slopes that are their homes often receive great quantities of snow, which help insulate the animals from the mountain winters. Rarely venturing into the chill of the open air, pikas tend to remain beneath the snow, feeding upon the grass they so meticulously gathered and dried during the preceding summer.

DESCRIPTION: This gray to tawny gray, chunky, soft-looking mammal has large, rounded ears and beady, black eyes. The whiskers are long. The American Pika has no external tail. The front and rear legs are nearly equal in length, so this animal scampers or make quadrupedal leaps.

HABITAT: Pikas generally occupy talus slopes in the mountains, though they have occasionally been spotted among the jumbled logs swept down by avalanches. Interestingly, the north-facing (Oregon) side of the Columbia River Gorge, roughly between Wyeth and

RANGE: The American Pika occurs from the mountains of west-central Alberta and southern British Columbia south to California, Utah and northern New Mexico.

Total Length: 6⅜–8½ in.
Tail Length: No tail is visible.
Weight: 4¼–6¼ oz.

Multnomah falls, has the lowest elevation population of pikas in the lower 48 states.

FOOD: The pika diet includes a wide variety of plants that are found in the vicinity of this animal's rocky shelter. Broad-leaved plants, grasses and sedges are all clipped and consumed.

DEN: Pikas build grass-lined nests, in which the young are born, beneath the rocks of their home.

YOUNG: Mating occurs in spring, and after a 30-day gestation period, a litter of two to five (usually three) young is born. The furry newborns have closed eyes and weigh ¼–5⁄16 oz. The eyes open after 10 days. The young are weaned when they are 30 days old and

two-thirds grown. Pikas are sexually mature after the first winter. A second breeding period may occur in summer.

SIMILAR SPECIES: The **Bushy-tailed Woodrat** (p. 202) is the only other gray mammal of comparable size that might occupy the same rocky slopes as the American Pika, but woodrats have long, bushy tails.

DID YOU KNOW?

Pikas have high-frequency calls that "bounce" readily, so though they are often heard, they can be difficult to locate. This characteristic is advantageous to a pika in allowing it to warn fellow pikas without revealing its whereabouts to a potential predator.

BATS

O nly three groups of vertebrates have achieved self-powered flight: bats, birds and the now-extinct reptilian pterosaurs. In an evolutionary sense, bats are a very successful group of mammals. Worldwide, bats make up about 20 per-cent of all mammalian species, and they are second only to rodents in both diversity of species and number of individuals. Across North America, however, populations of several bat species appear to be declining, and some have been placed on rare and endangered species lists.

Unlike the feathered wing of a bird, a bat's wing consists of double layers of skin stretched across the modified bones of the fingers and back to the legs. On the hand, only the thumb is free. A small bone, the calcar, juts backward from the foot to help support the tail membrane, which stretches between the tail and each leg. The calcar is said to be keeled if a small piece of skin projects from its side.

Bats generate lift by pushing their wings against the air's resistance, so they tend to have a large wing-surface area for their body size. This method of flight is less efficient than the airfoil lift provided by bird or airplane wings, but it allows bats to fly slower and gives them more maneuverability. Slower flight is a real advantage when trying to catch insects or hovering in front of a flower.

All bats have good vision, but their nocturnal habits have led to an increased dependence on their sense of hearing—most people are acquainted with the ability of many bat species to navigate or capture prey in the dark using echolocation. The tragus, a slender lobe that projects from the inner base of many bats' ears, is thought to help in determining an echo's direction.

No other mammals in Washington and Oregon are as misunderstood as bats. They are thought to be mysterious creatures of the night, souls of the dead or blind, rabid creatures that commonly become tangled in people's hair. In truth, bats are extremely beneficial creatures whose considerable collective hunger for night-fly-ing insects results in fewer agricultural pests.

Free-tailed Bat Family (Molossidae)

The free-tailed bats are so named because they have tails that extend beyond the edge of the membrane that stretches between their hindlegs. Most free-tailed bats occur in warm tropical parts of the world, but one species can be found in southwestern Oregon. Free-tailed bats are sometimes called "mastiff bats," because their snub noses and wrinkled faces resemble those of mastiff dogs.

Brazilian Free-tailed Bat

Evening Bat Family (Vespertilionidae)

The majority of the bats that occur in Washington and Oregon belong to the evening bat family. True to their name, most members of this fam-ily are active in the evening—and often again before dawn—when they typically feed on flying insects. A few species migrate to warmer regions for winter, but most of them hibernate in caves or abandoned buildings and mines.

Keen's Bat

Brazilian Free-tailed Bat
Tadarida brasiliensis

Total Length: 3½–4½ in.
Tail Length: 1¼–1¾ in.
Forearm: 1½–1¾ in.
Weight: ⁵⁄₁₆–⁷⁄₁₆ oz.

More than any other bat species, Brazilian Free-tailed Bats display the massiveness of their populations when they vacate their roosts for the moth-laden night skies. In the Carlsbad Caverns of New Mexico, for instance, the collective wingbeats of millions of free-tailed bats leaving their daytime roosts sound like the roar of a whitewater river, and the rising column can be seen at great distances. Colonies in southwestern Oregon do not reach the tremendous numbers that are seen elsewhere, but these bats are still fairly common. Non-migratory in Oregon, these bats hibernate in small colonies during winter.

DESCRIPTION: This small free-tailed bat is dark brown to grayish on the back and lighter on the underside. The ears are separated at the base. The upper lip is wrinkled. Little membrane connects the hindlegs and tail, thus the name "free-tailed."

HABITAT: In northern areas of their range in the western U.S., these bats are mostly found in pinyon-juniper woodlands.

FOOD: These bats forage primarily on such night-flying insects as beetles, ants and moths.

DEN: Individuals are known to roost in buildings in Oregon. Elsewhere, the bats roost in great numbers in caves. Large populations can carpet the walls and ceilings of caves and mines, and nursery colonies can have as many as 1500 pups to a square foot.

YOUNG: Females ovulate for a short period of time in March, and mating is spread out over a five-week overlapping period. One or two young are born in June. At birth, the young are two-thirds the length of their mothers; within three weeks they equal their mothers in mass.

SIMILAR SPECIES: The Brazilian Free-tailed Bat is the only free-tailed bat in this region. No other bats in Washington and Oregon have its noticeably protruding tail.

RANGE: The Brazilian Free-tailed Bat is one of the most wide-ranging mammals in the New World. In North America it occurs from Oregon to North Carolina and south through Mexico.

Fringed Bat
Myotis thysanodes

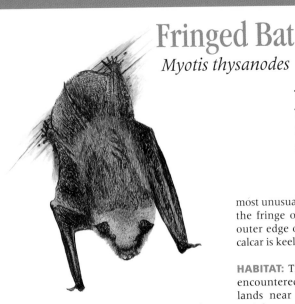

Total Length: 3⅜–3¾ in.
Tail Length: 1½–1¾ in.
Forearm: 1⅝–1¾ in.
Weight: ³⁄₁₆–⁵⁄₁₆ oz.

This bat can be found throughout most of Washington and Oregon. Of the *Myotis* bats, a small number belong to a group called the long-eared myotis bats, all of which have long ears and prefer high-elevation forests. The Fringed Bat belongs to this group, but it has shorter ears and is found at lower elevations than the others. A conspicuous fringe of stiff hairs along the outer edge of the membrane between the hindlegs and tail is a characteristic that usually distinguishes this bat from others, though it is useless as a field mark when the bat is in flight.

DESCRIPTION: This large bat, with a wingspan of up to 12 in., typically has pale brown fur that is darker on the back than on the undersides. The blackish ears are long and would extend well past the nose if pushed forward. The most unusual characteristic of this bat is the fringe of small, stiff hairs on the outer edge of the tail membrane. The calcar is keeled.

HABITAT: This bat is most frequently encountered in woodlands or grasslands near water sources. It occurs mainly at mid-elevations, but on the coast it ventures into low-elevation forests, and high-elevation forays are occasionally reported.

FOOD: Moths, flies, beetles, lacewings and crickets are commonly eaten. The presence of flightless insects in their diet has led to the speculation that these bats may glean some insects from foliage.

DEN: These bats roost in caves, mines and buildings. Up to several hundred Fringed Bats will cluster in maternal roosts in summer.

YOUNG: One or, uncommonly, two young are born in June or early July. The young bats reach adult size by three weeks, at which time they are capable of limited flight. Maternal colonies contain only females and the young of the year.

SIMILAR SPECIES: All the **mouse-eared bats** (*Myotis* spp., pp. 300–08) are generally indistinguishable when seen flying in dim light. It requires precise measurements and careful attention to detail to identify the species.

RANGE: The Fringed Bat is found from southern British Columbia southward through the western states and into Mexico.

Long-eared Bat
Myotis evotis

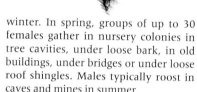

Total Length: 3¼–4¼ in.
Tail Length: 1⅜–1⅞ in.
Forearm: 1½–1⅝ in.
Weight: ⅛–⁵⁄₁₆ oz.

The dramatic nightly bat sagas that take place in summer skies are largely unknown to humans. In apparent silence, the bats of Washington and Oregon navigate and locate prey by producing ultrasonic pulses up to five times higher in pitch than our ears can detect and listening for the echoes of these sounds as they bounce off objects. In North America, bats are mainly insectivorous, and the aptly named Long-eared Bat appears to be well equipped for insect hunting.

DESCRIPTION: The wingspan of this medium-sized bat is about 11 in. The upperparts are light brown to buffy yellow. The undersides are lighter. This bat's black, naked ears are ¾–1 in. long. The tragus is long and narrow. The wings are mainly naked, and only the lower fifth of the tail membrane is furred. The calcar is keeled.

HABITAT: This bat occurs in forested areas with old-growth features that are adjacent to rocky outcroppings or badland landscapes. It occasionally occupies buildings, mines and caves.

FOOD: Feeding peaks at dusk and just before dawn. Moths, flies and beetles are the primary prey.

DEN: Both sexes of this mainly solitary bat hibernate in caves and mines in winter. In spring, groups of up to 30 females gather in nursery colonies in tree cavities, under loose bark, in old buildings, under bridges or under loose roof shingles. Males typically roost in caves and mines in summer.

YOUNG: Mating takes place in fall, before hibernation begins, but fertilization is delayed until spring. In June or early July, after a gestation period of about 40 days, a female usually bears one young; twins are uncommon. The young mature quickly and are able to fly on their own in four weeks.

SIMILAR SPECIES: The **Keen's Bat** (p. 302) has shorter ears, and its flight membranes are dark brown. All the **mouse-eared bats** (*Myotis* spp., pp. 300–08) are generally indistinguishable when seen flying in dim light. It requires precise measurements and careful attention to detail to identify the species.

RANGE: The Long-eared Bat can be found anywhere from southern British Columbia east to southern Saskatchewan and south to north-western New Mexico and Baja California.

Keen's Bat
Myotis keenii

Total Length: 2½–3⅝ in.
Tail Length: 1⅜–1¾ in.
Forearm: 1⅜–1½ in.
Weight: ⅛–³⁄₁₆ oz.

These uncommon and poorly studied bats are thought to have habits similar to those of the other *Myotis* bats (pp. 300–08). Keen's Bats are solitary and roost in trees or rock crevices, and during the night they fly out over waterbodies to feed. In forested areas you may be able to find individuals roosting under loose bark during the day. If you notice a roosting bat, be careful not to disturb it. During the day, a disturbed bat will start to fly away, but it will often be disoriented, and it may injure itself or bite people who touch it. The Northern Long-eared Bat (*M. septentrionalis*) and the Keen's Bat were long considered one species, but now it is known that their ranges do not overlap.

DESCRIPTION: This dark brown bat has a wingspan of 8¼–10 in. The fur is glossy brown with light undersides. Dark shoulder spots are usually visible.

The ears and flight membranes are dark brown. The long ears extend beyond the nose when laid forward. The long, slightly keeled calcar extends halfway from the heel to the tail.

HABITAT: This species seems to be restricted to temperate coastal rainforests.

FOOD: The Keen's Bat flies quite slowly but directly, taking high-flying insects along forest edges and over ponds and clearings.

DEN: Adults roost in tree cavities, rock crevices and caves and under bark.

YOUNG: In early June or July, each female in the nursery colony has one young. Little else is known about this species.

SIMILAR SPECIES: The **Long-eared Bat** (p. 301) has black flight membranes, and its ears extend more than ⅛ in. past the nose when laid forward. All the **mouse-eared bats** (*Myotis* spp., pp. 300–08) are generally indistinguishable when seen flying in dim light. It requires precise measurements and careful attention to detail to identify the species.

RANGE: This species has one of the smallest ranges of any North American bat—it is found west of the Cascades from southeastern Alaska to northwestern Washington.

California Bat
Myotis californicus

Total Length: 3–3¾ in.
Tail Length: 1¼–1⅝ in.
Forearm: 1¼–1⅜ in.
Weight: ⅛–³⁄₁₆ oz.

California Bats emerge shortly after sunset, and for a few minutes in the remaining twilight, they can be followed by eye as they fly erratically through the sky. As if surfing on invisible waves in the air, fluttering California Bats rise and dive at variable speeds in the pursuit of unseen prey. These activities appear disorganized and random, but they are actually deliberate and purposeful.

DESCRIPTION: This bat is small and yellowish brown. Its wingspan is about 9 in. The foot is tiny, and the calcar has a keel.

HABITAT: In the Pacific Northwest, this bat forages mainly over forested areas, shrub-steppe areas and arid grasslands.

FOOD: During the night, California Bats forage opportunistically in areas such as cliffs or poplar groves that concentrate night-flying insects or over water for emerging adult caddisflies and mayflies. Additionally, they can be observed in tree canopies feeding on moths, beetles and flies. Generally, California Bats fly 6–10 ft. above the ground or water when foraging.

DEN: California Bats are not too selective of their night roosts, and they have been found in both buildings and natural structures. Their day roosts are typically in rock crevices, but also in mine shafts, tree cavities and buildings, as well as beneath bridges and under loose tree bark.

YOUNG: A single young is born in late June to early July.

SIMILAR SPECIES: The **Western Small-footed Bat** (p. 306) has a dark "mask," but this feature does not help in identification at night. All the **mouse-eared bats** (*Myotis* spp., pp. 300–08) are generally indistinguishable when seen flying in dim light. It requires precise measurements and careful attention to detail to identify the species.

RANGE: The California Bat, truly a western bat, is found in coastal regions from southern Alaska south to California and Mexico. It ranges east into Montana, Colorado, New Mexico and Texas.

Little Brown Bat
Myotis lucifugus

On nearly every warm, calm summer night, the skies of Washington and Oregon are filled with marvelously complex screams and shrills. Unfortunately for people interested in the world of bats, these magnificent vocalizations occur at frequencies higher than our ears can detect. The most common of these nighttime screamers, and quite likely the first bat most people will encounter, is the Little Brown Bat.

Once the cool days of late August and September arrive, Little Brown Bats begin to migrate to wintering areas. Although it is not known where all of these bats spend winter, thousands of them travel to caves in the mountains and foothills. Large wintering populations are known to occur in certain large caves, and cave adventurers are advised to take special care not to disturb these hibernating animals. All bats may rouse on occasion during hibernation, and some may even fly out on warm nights. However, if a bat is disturbed too often, its increased metabolic rate can cause it to run out of fat reserves before insects are once again readily available in spring.

DESCRIPTION: As its name suggests, this bat is little and brown. Its coloration ranges from light to dark brown on the back, with somewhat paler undersides. The tips of the hairs are glossy, giving this bat a coppery appearance. The wing and tail membranes are mainly unfurred, though fur may appear around the edges. The calcar of this bat is long and unkeeled. The tragus, which is nearly straight, is half the length of the ear. The wingspan is 8¾–11 in.

HABITAT: Little Brown Bats are the most frequently encountered bats in much of North America. They are at home almost anywhere that has a waterbody nearby. They need a place to drink and a large supply of insects for their nightly foraging.

FOOD: Little Brown Bats feed exclusively on night-flying insects. In the evening, these bats leave their day roosts and swoop down to the nearest water source to snatch a drink on the wing. Foraging for insects can last for up to five hours. Later, the bats rest in night roosts, which are in a different place than their day roosts. Another short feeding period occurs just prior to dawn, after which the bats return to their day roosts.

DEN: These bats may roost alone, in small groups or in colonies of more than

RANGE: This widespread bat ranges from central Alaska to Newfoundland and south to northern Florida and central Mexico, though it is absent from much of the southern Great Plains.

Total Length: 2⅜–4 in.
Tail Length: 1–2⅛ in.
Forearm: 1⅜–1⅝ in.
Weight: ³⁄₁₆–⁵⁄₁₆ oz.

1000 individuals. Beneath a loose shingle, in an open attic or elsewhere in a building, under a bridge, in a hollow tree and beneath loose bark on a tree are all suitable roosts for Little Brown Bats. In winter, some bats may stay and hibernate in large numbers in caves and old mines, but most of them are believed to migrate to warmer climates.

YOUNG: Mating occurs either in late fall or in the hibernation colonies. Fertilization of the egg is delayed until the female ovulates in spring, and by June, pregnant females form nursery colonies in protected locations. In late June or early July, after about 50 to 60 days of gestation, each female bears one young.

The young are blind and hairless, but their development is rapid, and their eyes open in about three days. After one month, the young are on their own.

SIMILAR SPECIES: All the **mouse-eared bats** (*Myotis* spp., pp. 300–08) are essentially impossible to identify in flight. Even for specimens in hand, one needs a technical key.

DID YOU KNOW?

An individual Little Brown Bat can consume 900 insects an hour during its nighttime forays. A typical colony may eat 100 lb. of insects a year.

Western Small-footed Bat
Myotis ciliolabrum

Total Length: 3–3½ in.
Tail Length: 1³/₁₆–1¾ in.
Forearm: 1⅛–1⅜ in.
Weight: ⅛–¼ oz.

The Western Small-footed Bat is one of the region's "rock bats": it occupies daytime roosts in rocky habitats such as badlands, cliffs and talus slopes. Contrary to popular belief, the Western Small-footed Bat is not truly a creature of arid environments. Mammals that live in desert conditions have unique adaptations, mainly involving the kidneys and excretion, that prevent intolerable water loss. This bat lacks such adaptations, and though it may live among dry rocks, it never goes far from water.

DESCRIPTION: The glossy fur of this attractive bat is yellowish brown to gray or even coppery brown above, and its undersides are almost white. The flight membranes and ears are black, and the tail membrane is dark brown. This bat has a wingspan of 8–10 in., and some fur may be found on both the undersurface of the wing and the upper surface of the tail membrane. Across its face, from ear to ear, is a dark brown or black "mask." True to its name, this bat has noticeably small feet. The calcar is strongly keeled.

HABITAT: The Western Small-footed Bat prefers rocky or grassland regions, especially riverbanks, ridges and outcroppings with abundant rocks for roosting. It is sometimes found in rocky areas of ponderosa pine forests.

FOOD: Like most bats in Washington and Oregon, the Western Small-footed Bat eats primarily flying insects, including moths, flies, bugs and beetles.

DEN: In summer this bat roosts in trees, under loose bark, in buildings or in rock crevices. It hibernates in caves or mines in winter. Nursery colonies occur in bank crevices, under bridges or under the shingles of old buildings.

RANGE: The Western Small-footed Bat is found from southern British Columbia east to southwestern Saskatchewan and south through most of the western U.S. and well into Mexico. It is not present along the Pacific Coast of Canada or the U.S.

YOUNG: In small nursery colonies, each female will give birth to one young, sometime between late May and early June.

SIMILAR SPECIES: In dim light, you cannot see the Western Small-footed Bat's "mask"; a technical key to the bats of this region is needed to distinguish between the *Myotis* spp. (pp. 300–08).

Yuma Bat
Myotis yumanensis

Total Length: 3–3⅝ in.

Tail Length: 1¼–1¾ in.

Forearm: 1¼–1½ in.

Weight: ⅛–³⁄₁₆ oz.

Like most bats, Yuma Bats spend much of the summer days hanging comfortably in warm roosts, shifting slightly as temperatures rise and fall. They rest, relax and snuggle against one another until the moon rises and draws them outside. With nightfall, Yuma Bats fly out over the nearest wetland, snapping up rising insects in the cool, calm night air. Often, their stomachs are full within 15 minutes, and their foraging is finished for the night. They then return to their night roost, where they digest the evening meal before foraging again just before dawn.

DESCRIPTION: The medium-sized Yuma Bat has brown to black fur on the back, with a lighter color on the underside. The ears are long enough to extend to the nose when pushed forward. The tragus is blunt and only about half the length of the ear. The wingspan is about 9 in. The calcar is not keeled.

HABITAT: This bat tends to occur in grassland or shrub areas of the region, particularly in areas close to water; it usually forages over lakes and streams.

FOOD: Much of the Yuma Bat's diet consists of aquatic invertebrates, such as adult caddisflies, mayflies and midges.

DEN: Yuma Bats typically roost and form their maternal colonies in buildings, trees and caves and under south-facing siding and shingles. These structures must be within foraging distance of a suitable waterbody.

YOUNG: As with many types of bats, mating occurs during fall, with the sperm being stored within the female until fertilization in the spring. A single young is usually born in June or July.

SIMILAR SPECIES: All the **mouse-eared bats** (*Myotis* spp., pp. 300–08) are generally indistinguishable when seen flying in dim light. It requires precise measurements and careful attention to detail to identify the species.

RANGE: The Yuma Bat is found from west-central British Columbia south to California and Mexico and east to Colorado and western Texas; it is largely absent from the Great Basin.

Long-legged Bat
Myotis volans

Total Length: 3⅜–4 in.
Tail Length: 1⅜–2⅛ in.
Forearm: 1⅜–1¾ in.
Weight: ³⁄₁₆–⅜ oz.

The leg bones of this uncommon bat are responsible for its common name. However, the Long-legged Bat's leg bones are only fractionally longer than those of the very similar Western Small-footed Bat (p. 306), so they are not a good distinguishing characteristic in the field. Noticeable differences do occur in habitat selection. The Long-legged Bat always lives in or near coniferous forests, especially in the vicinity of water.

DESCRIPTION: Although this bat is the heaviest of the "little brown bats," it is heavier by an almost imperceptible amount. The wingspan is 10–11 in. The fur can be uniformly light brown to reddish to dark chocolate brown, but it is mainly dark brown. The calcar has a well-defined keel. The underwing is usually furred out to a line connecting the elbow and knee.

RANGE: The Long-legged Bat ranges from northwestern British Columbia southeast to western North Dakota and south through most of the western U.S.

HABITAT: This bat lives primarily in coniferous forests that are near waterbodies. It may forage along the shores of mountain lakes.

FOOD: The diet is composed primarily of moths, flies, bugs and beetles.

DEN: The Long-legged Bat spends winter hibernating in caves or mines. In summer it roosts in trees, buildings or rock crevices. Nursery colonies are located in bank crevices, under bridges or under south-facing shingles on old buildings.

YOUNG: Mating occurs in fall. Fertilization is delayed until spring, and the young are born in July or August, in large nursery colonies. Each female will bear just one young. The young mature quickly, flying on their own in about four weeks. The longest recorded life span for this species is 21 years.

SIMILAR SPECIES: All the **mouse-eared bats** (*Myotis* spp., pp. 300–08) are generally indistinguishable when seen flying in dim light. Precise measurements and careful attention to detail are required to identify the species.

Western Red Bat
Lasiurus blossevillii

Total Length: 3½–4¾ in.
Tail Length: 1⅜–2⅛ in.
Forearm: 1⅜–1¾ in.
Weight: ⅜–⅝ oz.

Considering that all other bats in Washington and Oregon have brownish fur, the Western Red Bat stands out and should be easy to recognize. This bat is not common, and the chances of seeing one are slim. It is virtually an unknown animal in the region, with stable populations only along the West Coast. The red bat begins foraging as late as two hours after sunset, at a time when it is too dark to recognize this bat's reddish hue.

DESCRIPTION: This colorful bat has orange or reddish fur with hairs up to ¾ in. long over the back, face and throat and around the ears. Males tend to be brighter than females, and some individuals may have a slightly frosted appearance. The wingspan is 11–13 in. The top of the membrane between the hindlimbs is densely furred on the anterior portion. The short, rounded, pale ears are almost hairless inside. *Lasiurus* bats are unique in this region in having four mammae; all other bats in these two states have two. As well, *Lasiurus* bats are migratory.

HABITAT: Low-elevation forests beside rivers appear to be favored.

FOOD: When it forages near farmlands, the Western Red Bat may feed heavily on agricultural pests. It primarily eats moths, planthoppers, flies and beetles, and it may sometimes alight on vegetation to pick off insects. The peak feeding period is well after dusk.

DEN: In summer, these solitary bats roost in foliage, which provides shade. The space beneath the roost must be free of obstacles to allow the bats to drop into flight.

YOUNG: Mating takes place in August and September, but ovulation and fertilization are delayed until spring. Gestation appears to take 80 to 90 days, and one to four young are born in June. They are thought to be able to fly when three or four weeks old, and they are weaned at five or six weeks. Age at sexual maturity is not known.

SIMILAR SPECIES: No other bat in Washington or Oregon has the color pattern and measurements of the Western Red Bat.

RANGE: The Western Red Bat ranges from South America north to extreme southern British Columbia.

Hoary Bat
Lasiurus cinereus

The Hoary Bat is one of the largest bats in Washington and Oregon, with a wingspan of about 16 in., but it weighs less than the smallest chipmunk.

This bat flies later into the night than any other bat in the region; once the last of the daylight has disappeared, the Hoary Bat courses low over wetlands, lakes and rivers in conifer country. It may not be as acrobatic in its foraging flights as the smaller *Myotis* bats (pp. 300–08), but no one who has ever witnessed a Hoary Bat in flight could fail to be impressed by its aerial accomplishments.

The large size of the Hoary Bat is often enough to identify it, but the light wrist spots, which are sometimes visible, confirm the identification. Many of the Hoary Bat's long hairs have brown bases and white tips, giving the animal the frosted appearance responsible for its common name. Though attractive, this coloration makes the Hoary Bat very difficult to notice when it roosts in a tree—it looks very similar to dried leaves and lichens.

Hoary Bats, as well as other tree-dwelling bats, have been the focus of recent scientific study to determine the importance of old roost trees in their habitat. These bats have complex requirements: though old trees may well be important, water quality and the availability of hatching insects in wetlands may be equally significant.

In May, these migratory bats usually return to Washington and Oregon from their wintering grounds further south. The males, it is thought, migrate only as far as the northern United States, where courting and mating occur. Although the males may remain at these sites for summer, some impregnated females seem to push farther north, where the young are born.

A few records from the northern mountains of Canada suggest that female Hoary Bats do migrate quite far north. Beginning in August or September, these bats migrate south again, sometimes in large flocks.

DESCRIPTION: The large Hoary Bat has light brown to grayish fur, and the white hair tips give it a heavily frosted appearance. Its throat and shoulders are buffy yellow or toffee colored. Its wingspan is 15–16 in. The ears are short, rounded and furred, but the edges of the ears are naked and black. The tragus is blunt and triangular. The upper surfaces of the feet and tail membrane are completely furred. The calcar is modestly keeled. Like the Western Red

RANGE: From north-central Canada, the Hoary Bat ranges south through most of southern Canada and almost all of the lower U.S. and into Mexico.

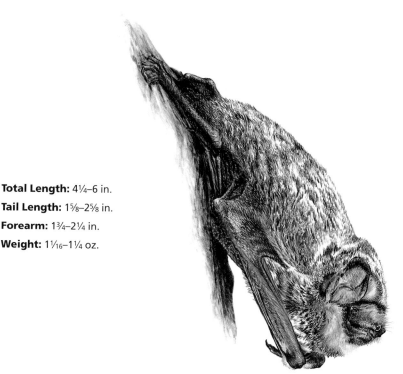

Total Length: 4¼–6 in.
Tail Length: 1⅝–2⅝ in.
Forearm: 1¾–2¼ in.
Weight: 1¹⁄₁₆–1¼ oz.

Bat (p. 309), the Hoary Bat has four mammae.

HABITAT: The Hoary Bat is often found near open, grassy areas in coniferous and deciduous forests or over lakes.

FOOD: The diet consists mainly of moths, planthoppers, flies and beetles, including many agricultural pests when this bat forages near farmlands. It sometimes alights on vegetation to pick off insects. Feeding activity does not peak until well after dusk.

DEN: During summer, this bat roosts alone in the shade of foliage, with an open space beneath the roost so that it can drop into flight.

YOUNG: Hoary Bats mate in fall, but the young are not born until late May or June, because fertilization is delayed until the female ovulates in spring. Gestation lasts about 90 days, and a female, though she has four mammae, usually bears two young. She places the first young on her back while she delivers the next one. Until they are able to fly, young bats roost in trees and nurse between their mother's nighttime foraging flights.

SIMILAR SPECIES: The **Silver-haired Bat** (p. 312) is black, with white-tipped hairs, and is slightly smaller. The **Big Brown Bat** (p. 313) is almost as large but does not have a frosted appearance.

DID YOU KNOW?

The Hoary Bat is the most widespread species of bat in North America, and it is the only terrestrial mammal native to the Hawaiian Islands.

Silver-haired Bat
Lasionycteris noctivagans

Total Length: 3⅝–4¼ in.
Tail Length: 1⅜–2 in.
Forearm: 1½–1¾ in.
Weight: ¼–⅝ oz.

back that give it a frosty appearance. The naked ears and tragus are short, rounded and black. The wingspan is 11–12 in. A light covering of fur may be seen over the entire surface of the tail membrane.

The handsome Silver-haired Bat flies slowly and leisurely throughout Washington and Oregon at twilight, first just after sunset (vesperal twilight) and again just before sunrise (auroral twilight). The feeding forays of this bat also happen twice a day. It usually flies fairly low to the ground, and it doesn't seem to be disturbed by the presence of an inquisitive human. If you chance to find one, either at night or in the very early morning, you may be able to watch it for some time as it dips and flops about the twilight sky catching insects. Listen closely as well, and you may hear the subtle *wicka-wicka-wicka* of its leathery wings.

DESCRIPTION: The fur is nearly black, with long, white-tipped hairs on the

HABITAT: Forests are the primary habitat, but this bat can easily adapt to parks, cities and farmland.

FOOD: This bat feeds mainly on moths and flies, and it forages over standing water or in open areas near water.

DEN: The summer roosts are usually in tree cavities, under loose bark or in old buildings. In winter these bats may hibernate in caves, mines or old buildings. Females form nursery colonies in protected areas, such as tree cavities, narrow crevices or old buildings.

YOUNG: Breeding takes place in fall or during a break in hibernation, but fertilization is delayed until the female ovulates in spring. In early summer, after a gestation period of about two months, one or two young are born to each female.

SIMILAR SPECIES: The Silver-haired Bat's white-tipped black hairs are unique among the bats of the region. The **Hoary Bat** (p. 310) has white-tipped brown or grayish hairs. The **Big Brown Bat** (p. 313) has glossy, mainly brown fur.

RANGE: This bat is found along the southeastern coast of Alaska, across the

southern half of Canada and south through most of the lower 48 states, but it is absent from the Gulf Coast, southern California, Nevada and southwestern Arizona.

Big Brown Bat
Eptesicus fuscus

Total Length: 3⅝–5½ in.
Tail Length: ⅞–2⅜ in.
Forearm: 1⅝–2⅛ in.
Weight: ⁷⁄₁₆–1 oz.

The Big Brown Bat is not overly abundant anywhere, but its habit of roosting and occasionally hibernating in houses and other human structures makes it a more commonly encountered bat. It is also the only bat that may be seen, though rarely, on warm winter nights, because it occasionally takes such opportunities to change hibernating sites. The relative frequency of Big Brown Bat sightings doesn't save this species from the anonymity that plagues most bats, however, because the "big" in its name is relative—this sparrow-sized bat still looks awfully small against a dark night sky.

DESCRIPTION: This big bat is mainly brown, with lighter undersides, and its fur appears glossy or oily. On average, a female is larger than a male. The face, ears and flight membranes are black and mainly unfurred. The blunt tragus is about half as long as the ear. The calcar is usually keeled.

HABITAT: This large bat easily adapts to parks, cities, farmland and buildings. In the wild, it typically inhabits forests.

FOOD: A fast flier, the Big Brown Bat feeds mainly on beetles and planthoppers, and rarely on moths or flies. Near farmland, it feeds heavily on agricultural pests. Foraging usually occurs at heights of no more than 30 ft., and the two peak feeding periods are at dusk and just before dawn.

DEN: In summer this bat usually roosts in tree cavities, under loose bark or in buildings. It spends winter hibernating in caves, mines or old buildings. Nursery colonies are found in protected areas, such as tree cavities, large crevices or old buildings.

YOUNG: This bat breeds in fall or during a wakeful period in winter, but fertilization is delayed until the female ovulates in spring. A female gives birth to one or two young in early summer, after about two months of gestation. As in most bats, the female has two mammae. The Big Brown Bat is quite long lived; one individual was known to be 19 years old.

SIMILAR SPECIES: The Big Brown Bat is not easy to distinguish from other large bats. The **Hoary Bat** (p. 310) has frosted brown or gray fur. The **Silver-haired Bat** (p. 312) has frosted black fur. The *Myotis* **bats** (pp. 300–08) are all smaller.

RANGE: This bat occurs from the southern tier of the Canadian provinces southward through most of the U.S.

Western Pipistrelle
Pipistrellus hesperus

In the grasslands and shrub-steppe communities of eastern Washington and Oregon, the Western Pipistrelle may be the first bat many people see—it begins foraging in the evening while the sun still shines, and in the morning it feeds well after dawn. During most of the night it rests, having ceased its activity by about 9:30 p.m. It forages heavily throughout summer to develop a layer of fat. In northern regions, the pipistrelles may migrate southward, and in some areas they hibernate. Whichever method the bats use to survive winter—hibernating or migrating—they require the fat layer for sustenance.

Like other bats, Western Pipistrelles are very clean. After foraging each night, they spend as much as 30 minutes grooming their fur and cleaning out debris or bugs that have accumulated. They use their tongues wherever they can reach. Otherwise, like cats do with their forepaws, these bats moisten their hindfeet to clean the remaining areas. Special attention is given to cleaning the ears. Because bats are dependent on their hearing to "see" the world through echolocation, a dirty ear would be intolerable. All bats have good eyesight, too, but for these nighttime fliers, hearing is more useful.

The flight of Western Pipistrelles is weak and erratic. Their slow flight is advantageous to them when enthusiastic naturalists are attempting to net them. Once they detect the net, they have enough time to turn in the air and avoid being caught. Being weak fliers, however, means they cannot cover great distances for food, shelter or water. Another downfall of their feeble flight is that a swift breeze nearly halts them, and strong winds force them back to their roosts.

DESCRIPTION: The Western Pipistrelle is the smallest bat in the U.S. Its wingspan is only 7½–8½ in. It is uniformly colored above, usually tawny yellow, grayish or even reddish brown, and whitish below. The wings, interfemoral membrane, ears, nose and feet are almost black, and it has a short, club-shaped tragus and a keeled calcar. The contrast of its dark face and light fur gives the appearance that it is wearing a mask.

HABITAT: Western Pipistrelles are most common in arid regions with rocky or scrubby areas. Sometimes found close to cities, they are usually the first bats out in the evening and may even be seen in broad daylight. One great threat to these miniature bats is dehydration. And yet,

RANGE: These bats are found mainly in the Southwest, but they occur all the way from southeastern Washington and eastern Oregon south to California and east to the Big Bend area of Texas.

Total Length: 2⅜–3⅜ in.
Tail Length: 1–1¼ in.
Forearm: 1–1¼ in.
Weight: ⅛–¼ oz.

some populations of Western Pipistrelles live in arid regions where no other bat species occur—far from suitable roosting sites, such as cliffs, rocky outcroppings, buildings or caves. These bats cannot fly the distances recorded between their locality and the nearest such sites. Because pipistrelles are unable to survive arid climates for long without shelter, one hypothesis suggests they may roost in the abandoned ground burrows of desert rodents, but it has not yet been substantiated. In just four instances, individual bats have been found underneath surface rocks in these desert areas.

FOOD: Western Pipistrelles feed on tiny insects, such as flies, some beetles, leafhoppers and planthoppers. Because of the small size of this bat, it cannot eat large insects.

DEN: When roosting or hibernating, these bats can be found in caves, mines, crevices and old buildings. Some bats in northern areas migrate southward instead of hibernating. Maternity colonies of Western Pipistrelles are found in crevices of rocky cliffs or in sheltered nooks of old buildings.

YOUNG: In June, females give birth to two young, usually in protected maternity colonies. These maternity colonies consist of not more than 12 females, and sometimes a female may roost alone to bear her young. The young require their mother's care for several weeks until they are mature and ready for independence. Females who are lactating are at great risk of dehydration, and they can be seen at any hour of the night at watering holes near their roost.

SIMILAR SPECIES: The combination of small size, pale fur and black ears, face and wing membranes makes this bat distinctive. Most *Myotis* **bats** (pp. 300–08) are larger and have a much longer tragus.

DID YOU KNOW?

The erratic and jerky flights of the pipistrelle bats in Europe encouraged the other general common name "flittermouse," or *Fledermaus* in German.

Spotted Bat
Euderma maculatum

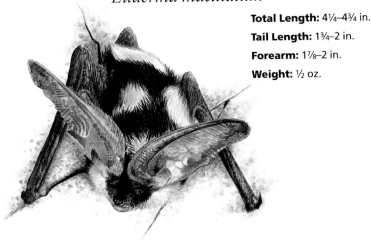

Total Length: 4¼–4¾ in.
Tail Length: 1¾–2 in.
Forearm: 1⅞–2 in.
Weight: ½ oz.

The Spotted Bat is an exhibitionist in a group of committed conformists. One glance at a Spotted Bat instantly reveals that it is no ordinary bat. The long, pink ears and the three huge, white polka dots that adorn its otherwise black back are sufficiently distinctive for this bat to stand out in a crowd, but its flair is not restricted to visual appeal. While feeding, the Spotted Bat gives loud, high-pitched, metallic squeaks that are easily heard by humans. Because most bats vocalize beyond our hearing, it is unusually pleasing to listen to the aerial drama of the rare Spotted Bat.

DESCRIPTION: The back is primarily black. A large, white spot marks each shoulder, with another on the rump and sometimes light-colored hairs behind the neck. The belly is whitish. The long,

pinkish to light tan ears project forward in flight but are folded back when the bat roosts. The wingspan is about 12 in.

HABITAT: These bats are found in highland ponderosa pine regions in early summer. They descend to lower-elevation deserts in August.

FOOD: Spotted Bats appear to be a specialized predator on noctuid moths, a large and diverse family of night-flying insects. A few beetles have also been found in their stomachs.

DEN: In summer, Spotted Bats seem to roost primarily in rock cracks and crevices on cliffs and in caves.

YOUNG: Usually one young is born in early summer. Even at a young age this bat has large ears, but the white spots on the back are absent on newborns.

SIMILAR SPECIES: The exceptionally large ears and large, white spots make the Spotted Bat distinctive among bats. The **Townsend's Big-eared Bat** (p. 318) also has large ears, but it lacks the black-and-white markings.

RANGE: This bat occurs from southern British Columbia, southern Idaho and southern Montana through to Arizona and New Mexico.

Pallid Bat
Antrozous pallidus

Total Length: 3¾–5⅜ in.
Tail Length: 1⅜–2 in.
Forearm: 1⅞–2⅜ in.
Weight: 9/16–1¼ oz.

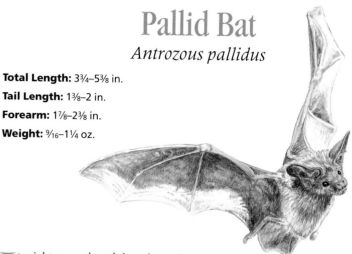

It might seem absurd that after millions of years of flight specialization, bats would be found foraging on the ground, but such is the case with Pallid Bats. These bats are still committed fliers, but they frequently land to take insects, other invertebrates and small vertebrates from the ground and from vegetation.

Although bats have few predators in the night skies, on the ground they are vulnerable to many threats. The light dorsal color of the Pallid Bat might be a protective adaptation that helps it blend in with the pale sands of its typically desert habitat.

DESCRIPTION: The back is light yellow. The underparts are pale creamy or almost white. Individual hairs are always darker at the tip than at the base, which is a reverse of the typical situation for bats. The broad, tan ears are extremely long, and if pushed forward they may extend past the muzzle. The median edge of the ears is not folded. With a wingspan of about 15 in., it is one of the largest bats in either the U.S. or Canada.

HABITAT: The Pallid Bat is typically associated with rocky outcroppings near open, dry areas, but occasionally it is found in evergreen forests.

FOOD: Insects are the main food, but some small vertebrates, such as lizards, have also been reported eaten. The bat may incidentally eat some fruits and seeds.

DEN: Pallid Bats gather in night roosts following foraging. These sites are generally in caves, overhangs or buildings. Their day roosts are nearby, typically in buildings or rock crevices.

YOUNG: These bats mate from October through December and occasionally into February. The sperm is stored in the female's reproductive tract until ovulation in spring. Young are born in May and June, and twins are common.

SIMILAR SPECIES: The smaller **Townsend's Big-eared Bat** (p. 318) is brown, has more prominent lumps on its nose and has larger ears that are joined at the base.

RANGE: The Pallid Bat ranges west of the Rockies from British Columbia, south to Baja California and eastward into Utah, Colorado, western Texas and central Mexico.

Townsend's Big-eared Bat
Corynorhinus townsendii

Few animals have ears to match the unusual Townsend's Big-eared Bat. In fact, the ears of this bat can be more than one-third the length of its body. If an elephant had the same proportions, a fully grown African Elephant, at up 25 ft. in length including the trunk, would have ears nearly 9 ft. long—dimensions approaching those of Dumbo, the famous Walt Disney character.

As humans, we tend to perceive the world primarily through our eyes, but the world can be explored just as effectively through other senses. Bats hold unquestionable aerial supremacy in the world of sound. Typically, the sounds that bats produce range between 20 kHz and 100 kHz. In contrast, the range of human hearing is generally considered to be from 20 Hz to 20 kHz. Each species of bat in Washington and Oregon echolocates at different frequencies, so a person equipped with a bat detector—these things actually exist—can often identify the species of bat from its ultrasonic nighttime calls. If you have good high-frequency hearing and a quiet night, you might hear the clicking sounds of bats in the air above you without the aid of equipment.

As well as catching flying insects directly in their mouths, bats also use the membranes of their wings and tail almost like a baseball glove. They deftly catch the insects and then pass them up toward the mouth. Typically, Townsend's Big-eared Bats forage only in the evening twilight. Only pregnant females forage again in the morning twilight, and when these females are lactating, they may venture out for a third feeding foray as well.

DESCRIPTION: This medium-sized brown bat's most noticeable features are its large, membranous ears, which can measure up to 1½ in. The ears are joined across the forehead at their bases. The median ear edges are double, and a prominent network of blood vessels is visible in the extended ears. At rest, the ears are curled and folded, almost resembling Bighorn Sheep horns (see p. 32). A set of conspicuous facial glands lies between the eye and nostril on each side of the snout. The belly is lighter brown than the back. This bat's wingspan is about 12 in.

HABITAT: This bat is found in open areas near coniferous forests and in arid areas.

FOOD: Townsend's Big-eared Bats emerge quite late in the evening, so they are seldom observed while feeding.

RANGE: The Townsend's Big-eared Bat ranges through all of western North America and south of central British Columbia, Montana and South Dakota.

Total Length: 3½–4½ in.
Tail Length: 1¼–2½ in.
Forearm: 1⅝–1⅞ in.
Weight: ¼–⅜ oz.

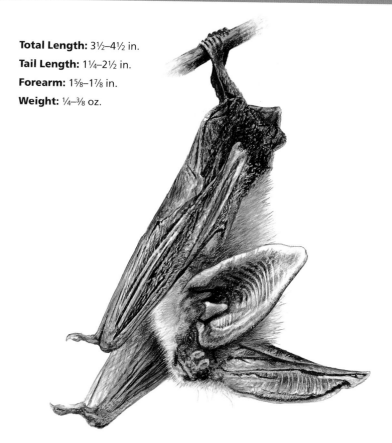

They forage along forest edges and are not thought of as gleaners. They catch mainly small moths in the air, but they also readily take beetles and flies.

DEN: Maternity colonies are found in warm parts of caves and abandoned mines. These colonies are not as large as those of many other bat species, and clusters of over 100 females and young are uncommon. Males in summer tend to be solitary. During winter hibernation, Townsend's Big-eared Bats tend to move deep into caves, where temperatures are constant.

YOUNG: Mating occurs following ritualized courtship behavior in October and November. The young bats are a quarter of their mother's weight when they are born, between May and July.

SIMILAR SPECIES: Because of its huge ears, this species can only possibly be confused with the **Pallid Bat** (p. 317), which is larger and paler and has smaller ears that are not joined at the base. The **Spotted Bat** (p. 316) also has huge ears, but its large, white spots make it unmistakable.

DID YOU KNOW?

Despite derogatory references to bats as "flying rats," they are actually more closely related to primates than they are to mice and other rodents.

INSECTIVORES & OPOSSUMS

This grouping, unlike the others in this book, actually encompasses two separate orders of mammals: shrews and moles belong to the Insectivora order; opossums are marsupials in the Didelphimorpha order (New World opossums).

Mole Family (Talpidae)

Moles spend the majority of their lives underground. They look a bit like large, rotund shrews, except their tails are proportionately shorter and their forelimbs are highly modified. Their streamlined shape makes moving in underground tunnels much easier. The forefeet appear enormous, with long claws, and they are turned outward like paddles, which enables moles to almost "swim" through soil. Their eyesight is poor, as you might guess from their tiny eyes, but their hearing is superb. Their most important sensory organ is the snout, which is flexible and usually hairless.

Townsend's Mole

Shrew Family (Soricidae)

Many people mistake shrews for very small mice, but shrews don't have a rodent's prominent incisors; they have minute ears, long, slender, pointed snouts, and many tiny teeth behind their incisors.

Because they are so small, shrews lose heat rapidly to their surroundings, and their metabolisms surpass those of all other mammals. These tiny mammalian furnaces use energy at such a high rate that they may eat three times their own weight in invertebrate and vertebrate food each day. Some shrews have a neurotoxic venom in their saliva that enables them to subdue amphibians and mice that outweigh them.

Of the shrews of Washington and Oregon, only the Marsh Shrew and Water Shrew are reasonably easy to identify visually, provided you can get a long enough look at them. The other species must be distinguished from one another on the basis of tooth and skull characteristics, distribution and, to some extent, habitat, though in many cases the ranges overlap.

Water Shrew

Opossum Family (Didelphidae)

As the only marsupial north of Mexico, the Virginia Opossum is the only mammal that carries its newborn young in a pouch. Marsupials get their name from the scientific name for this pouch, "marsupium." Because marsupials have a simple yolk-sac placenta, they bear extremely premature young that range from honeybee to bumblebee size at birth. Once in the marsupium, the young attach to a nipple and continue the rest of their development outside the uterus.

Virginia Opossum

American Shrew Mole
Neurotrichus gibbsii

Total Length: 4–5 in.
Tail Length: 1¼–1⅝ in.
Weight: ¼–³⁄₈ oz.

By its name alone, we can assume that this creature is more shrew-like than other moles found in this region. If you stumble across an American Shrew Mole in the western parts of Washington and Oregon, you may think you have found a shrew, because it has small forelimbs, it spends some time aboveground and it has a long, sparsely haired tail, as a shrew does.

The American Shrew Mole is the least subterranean mole in these two states. It is intermittently active throughout the day, pushing its way through leaf litter and decaying vegetation, instead of digging tunnels like other moles. As a shrew mole forages, it moves slowly and cautiously beneath the leafy debris, though it can move its forelimbs beneath the body and run with an agility impossible for other moles.

DESCRIPTION: This small, shrew-like mole is nearly black with a relatively long, hairy tail, tiny eyes, ear pinnae no more than ¼ in. long and large, scaly feet. The claws are long, but not flattened and broad as in other moles. The shrew mole may be blind—a pigmented layer of skin lies over the anterior surface of the eye lens.

HABITAT: American Shrew Moles prefer to live where there is abundant leaf litter, dead vegetation and rotting logs near streams, ravines or forested hillsides.

FOOD: Earthworms and sowbugs make up more than half of the shrew mole's diet. A wide assortment of other invertebrates and some vegetation are also eaten.

DEN: Commonly, shallow burrows are enlarged into chambers 3–5 in. wide. Nests in these chambers are made of dry leaves. Nests and all burrows are not built more than 12 in. below the surface.

YOUNG: Most mating occurs from March to May, but some individuals may breed as early as February or as late as September. Litter size varies from one to six extremely tiny young, which are about ¹⁄₃₂ oz. Females may have multiple litters in one season.

SIMILAR SPECIES: Other **moles** (pp. 322–24) have flattened claws and enormous forefeet. The **Marsh Shrew** (p. 334) and **Water Shrew** (p. 332) have longer, well-haired tails. **Shrews** (pp. 325–37) are smaller and do not have modified forelimbs.

RANGE: The American Shrew Mole is found from San Francisco up the coast to the Fraser River in British Columbia.

Townsend's Mole
Scapanus townsendii

Total Length: 7³/₄–9¹/₄ in.
Tail Length: 1¹/₄–2 in.
Weight: 2¹/₄–6 oz.

The stocky Townsend's Mole—the largest mole in North America—literally swims through the soil using its powerfully muscled forelimbs equipped with shovel-like claws. The "spoil" from building burrows is thrust vertically to the surface from below, and the resulting hemispherical mound of dirt is the proverbial "molehill." During its foraging at night, this mole may venture into lawns and leave a disfiguring series of soil mounds on the surface. Although some people may dislike the soil mounds for aesthetic reasons, they should remember that the mole's activities are beneficial for soil aeration, soil turnover, water absorption and pest control.

DESCRIPTION: This mole's rotund body is covered with short, black, velvety fur. The snout is long, the neck is short, the hindfeet are small and the tail is short and almost naked. The forefeet are enormously enlarged and cannot be rotated beneath the body; the claws are flattened and heavy. The minute eyes lie beneath the skin and are probably use-less. The nostrils at the end of the naked snout are crescent-shaped and point up.

HABITAT: Townsend's Moles prefer loose soil or cultivated fields, but they also occupy open brushlands in valley bottoms.

FOOD: Earthworms, insects of all stages and other invertebrates make up most of the diet, but some vegetation is also consumed.

DEN: This mole digs shallow surface tunnels—where most feeding occurs—as well as deeper tunnels with a nest chamber that is up to 8 in. wide. The two-layered nest consists of coarse, green grass with an inner layer of fine, dry grass, moss and leaves. Tunnels radiate out from the nest chamber to other parts of the burrow system.

YOUNG: Mating occurs in February with a single litter of one to four young born in late March. The hairless altricial young weigh about ³/₁₆ oz. at birth. At about 30 days, they are fully furred and weaned, and they leave the maternal burrows in May and June. They are sexually mature after their first winter.

RANGE: This mole is found west of the Cascades from near Huntingdon, British Columbia, south to northern California.

SIMILAR SPECIES: The **Coast Mole** (p. 323) is smaller—always less than 8 in. long. The **Broad-footed Mole** (p. 324) has a relatively hairier tail.

Coast Mole
Scapanus orarius

Total Length: 5³/₄–6⁷/₈ in.
Tail Length: 1–1⁵/₈ in.
Weight: 2–3 oz.

The mammalian equivalent to backhoes and bulldozers, moles toil about underground and bring subsurface soil to the surface. The surface deposits are known as "molehills," and a typical molehill of a Coast Mole is about 7 in. high. Between October and March, when the soil is moist and most digging occurs, one mole may push up 200 to 400 hills. The mole's activity aerates the soil, encourages water absorption and circulates nutrients.

DESCRIPTION: In winter, the upperparts of the Coast Mole are dark gray, sometimes with a silvery sheen. In summer, the fur often has a brownish tinge. The tail is pinkish and sparsely haired. The nose tip is naked and pink. Tiny, functionless eyes are beneath the skin. The feet are hairless, and the forefeet are enlarged and turned outward.

HABITAT: This mole inhabits a variety of soil types in meadows, deciduous woodlands, brush and even, if the soil is not too acidic, some coniferous forests.

FOOD: Earthworms make up more than three-quarters of the diet. Other invertebrates and some vegetation are also eaten.

DEN: The tunnels are 2 in. wide and may be 3 in. to 3 ft. beneath the surface. Chambers, which are 4 in. or greater in diameter, are expanded at regular intervals. Breeding nests about 7⁷/₈ in. wide are located about 6 in. beneath the surface. The nest is lined with coarse grass and has several connecting tunnels.

YOUNG: A single litter of two to five young is born each year in late March or early April following breeding in February.

SIMILAR SPECIES: The **Townsend's Mole** (p. 322) is larger and more rotund. The **Broad-footed Mole** (p. 324) has a relatively hairier tail.

RANGE: The Coast Mole is found from extreme southwestern British Columbia, down the coast into northern California and from northwestern Oregon slightly into Idaho.

Broad-footed Mole
Scapanus latimanus

Total Length: 5¼–7½ in.
Tail Length: ⅞–1¾ in.
Weight: about 2 oz.

Like all moles, the Broad-footed Mole is well suited to subterranean life—at one end it has a supersensitive snout and at the other end an equally sensitive tail. Its unique fur is velvety to prevent soil from sticking to it, and it is capable of lying both forwards and backwards over the body. With its sensitive tail and snout and its two-way fur, the Broad-footed Mole is ideally suited for moving forwards or backwards in its tunnel. The mole is unable to put its forefeet palm down against the ground; these feet are so well designed for "swimming" through the soil that they permanently stick out sideways, much like paddles with claws.

DESCRIPTION: The Broad-footed Mole is shiny gray with coppery highlights and slightly lighter undersides. The tail is short and has sparse, silvery fur. The eyes of a mole are greatly reduced in size

RANGE: This mole occurs from south-central Oregon throughout most of California.

and are essentially useless. The front feet of this mole are very close to the head, and they give the appearance that the mole has no neck.

HABITAT: These moles live in the soft, moist soils of a variety of different habitats, from low valleys to high mountain meadows.

FOOD: These moles primarily feed on earthworms, though other invertebrates, such as snails, slugs and insects, and some vegetation may also be consumed.

DEN: Moles spend most of their lives in their burrows. Special chambers are used for sleeping and raising young.

YOUNG: Mating occurs from February to late March, and a litter of two to six young are born in a grass-lined burrow chamber in April or May. The young are altricial and require several weeks of growth to reach full size.

SIMILAR SPECIES: Both the **Townsend's Mole** (p. 322) and the **Coast Mole** (p. 323) are much larger and have less hairy tails, and the **American Shrew Mole** (p. 321) is much smaller.

Masked Shrew
Sorex cinereus

Total Length: 2³/₄–4¹/₄ in.

Tail Length: 1–2 in.

Weight: ¹/₁₆–¹/₄ oz.

The Masked Shrew may be the most common shrew in much of Washington, but it is absent from Oregon. In spite of its abundance in Washington, it is unlikely that this shrew will be seen alive because it seldom lives longer than one year. You may see one dead in spring; starvation in late winter claims many of these shrews, leaving their tiny bodies to be recycled during the upcoming burst of life. This shrew follows its pointed nose and long whiskers through a world of underbrush and tall grass in both deciduous and coniferous forests.

ALSO CALLED: Cinereus Shrew.

DESCRIPTION: These medium-sized shrews have dark brown backs, lighter brown sides and pale underparts. The winter coat is paler, and the fur is short and velvety. It has a long, flexible snout, tiny eyes, small feet and a bicolored tail, which is dark above and light below. A few may have a dark patch on the nose—the "mask" for which the shrew is named.

HABITAT: The Masked Shrew favors forests, either coniferous or deciduous, and sometimes tallgrass plains or brushy coulees.

FOOD: Insects account for the bulk of the diet, but this shrew also eats significant numbers of slugs, snails, young mice, carrion and even some vegetation.

DEN: The nest, located under logs, in debris, between rocks or in burrows, is about 2–4 in. wide and looks like a woven grass ball. The nest does not have a central cavity; the shrew simply burrows to the inside.

YOUNG: Mating occurs from April to October, and, with a gestation of about 28 days, a female may have two or three litters a year. The four to eight young are born naked, toothless and blind. Their growth is rapid: eyes and ears open in just over two weeks, and the young are weaned by three weeks.

SIMILAR SPECIES: Most shrews look very similar. Without a specimen and a technical key, it is almost impossible to identify a shrew reliably.

RANGE: The Masked Shrew occurs across most of Alaska and Canada. Its range

extends south into northern Washington, through the Rocky Mountains and across most of the northeastern U.S., though it is absent from much of the northern plains.

Preble's Shrew
Sorex preblei

Total Length: 3³/₈–3³/₄ in.
Tail Length: 1³/₈ in.
Weight: ¹/₁₆–¹/₈ oz.

The very small and rare Preble's Shrew is probably the rarest and least studied shrew in the region. It is known only from a handful of localities in both Washington and Oregon, and researchers are not even sure if their range is continuous or scattered and patchy. Because most long-tailed shrews (*Sorex* spp.) are very similar, it can be assumed that the Preble's Shrew behaves much like other shrews. The areas where this shrew occurs are commonly inhabited by Yellow-pine Chipmunks (p. 244), Western Harvest Mice (p. 192), deer mice (pp. 193–97) and an assortment of voles and other shrews as well.

DESCRIPTION: The Preble's Shrew has a brownish-gray back that is lighter on the sides and underside. If you raise the upper lip on the side of the snout, four single pointed teeth can be seen behind the large, lobed first incisor. The third of these unicuspid teeth is not smaller than the fourth.

HABITAT: This tiny shrew seems to prefer dry sagebrush desert or grasslands with rocky areas. In Washington, it has been found in fir and pine forests.

FOOD: The Preble's Shrew is thought to eat mostly invertebrates, such as beetles, crickets, wasps, caterpillars and spiders.

DEN: The den is often found in soft soil, among rocks or under woody debris. The nest chamber is exceedingly small, and the entrance to the burrow is small and indistinct.

YOUNG: Little is known about this shrew's reproduction, but it is probably similar to other shrews. Mating likely occurs from April through July, with females having multiple litters a year.

SIMILAR SPECIES: The **Pygmy Shrew** (p. 337) is smaller. Range and habitat can help identify shrew species. Differences between most shrews are slight, and identification in the field is nearly impossible without a technical key and the animal in hand.

RANGE: The Preble's Shrew is found in extreme southeastern Washington, south  through eastern Oregon into California and Nevada, and east into Idaho, Montana and as far south as Colorado.

Vagrant Shrew
Sorex vagrans

Total Length: 3³/₈–4³/₄ in.
Tail Length: 1³/₈–1⁵/₈ in.
Weight: ³/₁₆–¹/₄ oz.

The Vagrant Shrew and the Montane Shrew (p. 328) may be the most difficult mammals in Washington and Oregon to distinguish from one another. Even experts have trouble telling whether the two tiny, medial tines on the upper incisors are located near the upper limit of the dark tooth pigment (Vagrant Shrew) or within the pigmented part of the incisor (Montane Shrew). Naturally, live shrews would never submit to such scrutiny, but luckily it is an issue only where the two ranges overlap.

ALSO CALLED: Wandering Shrew.

DESCRIPTION: This shrew is pale brown on the back and sides in summer. In winter, it is slightly darker over the back. The undersides vary from silvery gray to buffy brown. The tail is bicolored: whitish below, pale brown above.

HABITAT: The Vagrant Shrew favors forested regions that have water nearby. Sometimes it occurs in moister habitats, such as the edges of mountain brooks with willow banks.

FOOD: This shrew eats a variety of adult and larval insects, earthworms, spiders, snails, slugs, carrion and even some vegetation.

DEN: The spherical, grassy nest is usually built in decayed logs. It lacks a central cavity.

YOUNG: Mating begins in March, and litters of two to nine young are born from early April to mid-August. Females likely have more than one litter a year. The young are helpless at birth, and they must feed heavily from their mother to complete their rapid growth. Their eyes and ears open in about two weeks, and they are weaned soon thereafter.

SIMILAR SPECIES: The **Pygmy Shrew** (p. 337) is smaller. Range and habitat can help identify shrew species. Differences between most shrews are slight, and identification in the field is nearly impossible without a technical key and the animal in hand.

RANGE: The Vagrant Shrew extends from western Montana, Wyoming and Colorado west to the Pacific Coast and north into British Columbia and extreme southwestern Alberta.

Montane Shrew
Sorex monticolus

Total Length: 3³/₈–5 in.
Tail Length: 1³/₈–2 in.
Weight: ³/₁₆–¹/₄ oz.

The successful Montane Shrew is one of the most widespread members of its genus. It can be found from Alaska and the Yukon south to Mexico, in a variety of different habitats. As much at home on coastal islands as high mountaintops, this shrew is more of a generalist than other shrews. It is not even finicky about what it eats. Where the Montane Shrew coexists with other long-tailed shrews (*Sorex* spp.), this generalist is usually the most numerous.

ALSO CALLED: Dusky Shrew.

DESCRIPTION: This medium-sized shrew has a pale brown back and sides in summer. Its back is slightly darker in winter. The undersides are silvery gray to buffy brown. The bicolored tail is whitish below and the same color as the back above.

RANGE: The Montane Shrew is found from Alaska southeast to Manitoba and south into northern Oregon and along the Rocky Mountains to Mexico.

HABITAT: The Montane Shrew can be found in moist alpine meadows and wet sedge meadows, among willows alongside mountain brooks and in damp coniferous forests with nearby bogs.

FOOD: This shrew eats a variety of adult and larval insects, earthworms, spiders, snails, slugs, carrion and even some vegetation.

DEN: Montane Shrews usually build their spherical nests in decayed logs. The nest is a simple bundle of grass without a central cavity.

YOUNG: Mating occurs from March to August, during which time a female likely has more than one litter of two to nine young. The young are helpless at birth, and they must nurse heavily from their mother to complete their rapid growth. The eyes and ears open in about two weeks, and they are weaned soon afterward.

SIMILAR SPECIES: The **Pygmy Shrew** (p. 337) is smaller, but the differences between most shrews are slight, and identification in the field is nearly impossible without a technical key and the animal in hand.

Fog Shrew
Sorex sonomae

Total Length: 4¹/₈–7¹/₈ in.
Tail Length: 1³/₈–3³/₈ in.
Weight: ³/₁₆–¹/₂ oz.

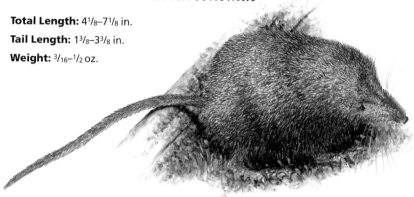

When naming a new species, the common name is often chosen to reflect certain qualities of the animal, its range or its habitat. Such is the case for the Fog Shrew. This large, brown shrew is found along the Oregon and California coastline, specifically in the active fog belt. Recent studies have revealed some information about this uncommon species, but it is much less studied then other shrew species. Observations of its grooming behavior show that it is meticulous about keeping clean. It cleans its face with moistened forefeet, much like a cat does.

ALSO CALLED: Sonoma Shrew.

DESCRIPTION: This large shrew is predominantly brown, with undersides darker than the back. Some individuals may be grayer than others. The long tail is the same color as the body. Its teeth can help distinguish it because the tine is lacking on the first upper incisor.

HABITAT: The Fog Shrew primarily inhabits moist forested areas, marshes or areas of dense cover near muddy streams. Alder, maple, hemlock and red cedar are the common overstory of this shrew's preferred habitat.

FOOD: Like other shrews, the Fog Shrew feeds on invertebrates, such as insect larva and adults, slugs, snails and earthworms.

DEN: Fog Shrews probably build spherical nests like other *Sorex* spp. These nests are usually in a sheltered area, such as in a decayed log or under a dense shrub. A spherical nest is a simple bundle of grass without a central cavity.

YOUNG: Virtually nothing is known about the reproductive behavior of the Fog Shrew. It probably has a gestation similar to other shrews, less than 20 days, and it likely mates and bears young in spring and summer.

SIMILAR SPECIES: The **Pygmy Shrew** (p. 337) is smaller. Most shrews are impossible to identify without a specimen and a mammal key.

RANGE: The Fog Shrew is found in moist coastal forests from southwestern Oregon through northwestern California.

Baird's Shrew
Sorex bairdii

Total Length: 3⁷/₈–5⁵/₈ in.
Tail Length: 1¹/₄–2¹/₂ in.
Weight: ³/₁₆–¹/₄ oz.

If you are walking through the moist coniferous forests of northwestern Oregon, you will probably find that you are in the prime habitat of the Baird's Shrew. In the Coast and Cascade ranges, where hemlock, yew and cedar thrive, a particular assortment of mammals will indicate the presence of the Baird's Shrew—even if you don't actually see one. Where there are Mountain Beavers (p. 282), Townsend's Chipmunks (p. 248) and Douglas' Squirrels (p. 277) there may also be this elusive shrew. This knowledge alone will have to be satisfying enough, because even biologists have trouble distinguishing this shrew from the more common Vagrant Shrew (p. 327).

DESCRIPTION: This small shrew is a medium brown color above and below, but the sides and belly are sometimes lighter than the back. In winter, it is slightly darker. The tail is faintly bicolored. The inside edge of the first upper incisor has a tine.

HABITAT: The Baird's Shrew favors very moist areas, such as marshes, streamsides and moist forests, wherever there is adequate cover.

FOOD: The exact diet of this shrew has not been well studied, but it presumably feeds on invertebrates, such as earthworms, slugs, snails and both adult and larval insects.

DEN: The reproduction and life history of the Baird's Shrew are not known. It may make a spherical grassy nest like other shrews, where females give birth and nurse their young. Grassy nests are found in sheltered areas like in rock crevices or under fallen logs.

YOUNG: Nothing is known about the reproduction of these shrews, but females probably give birth to several young in spring or summer. Like other shrews, Baird's Shrews probably do not live for more than one winter.

SIMILAR SPECIES: The differences between most shrews are slight, and identification in the field is nearly impossible without a technical key and the animal in hand.

RANGE: The Baird's Shrew is found only in northwestern Oregon.

Pacific Shrew

Sorex pacificus

Total Length: 5¹/₈–6³/₈ in.
Tail Length: 2¹/₈–2⁵/₈ in.
Weight: about ¹/₂ oz.

The unique Pacific Shrew is found only in Oregon and northern California and conducts its business in a manner unusual for shrews. While most shrews in North America are active throughout the day, the Pacific Shrew is mainly nocturnal. At night, this high-energy shrew hunts for insects, insect larvae, other invertebrates and even amphibians. The Pacific Shrew is a master of hunting low-flying insects. It can hear the insects flying, and it is fast enough to pluck them out of the air. When it is hunting terrestrial invertebrates or amphibians, it uses its keen sense of smell to locate its prey.

DESCRIPTION: The Pacific Shrew is a large, mainly reddish-brown shrew. Its coat is usually chestnut colored with a distinct reddish tinge. The tail may be the same color as the body or a light brown. In some individuals the tail is faintly bicolored. The feet are lighter than the body. A tine is on the inside edge of the first upper incisor.

HABITAT: Like many other shrews, the Pacific Shrew prefers moist environments with good protective cover. Grassy clumps under alder thickets, streamsides, wooded areas, moist ditches and damp forests are all suitable habitats.

FOOD: These nocturnal shrews feed on night-flying insects, insects larva, snails, slugs, centipedes, other invertebrates and several amphibians. It primarily uses hearing and smell to locate prey.

DEN: Pacific Shrews build a nest with loose, dry vegetation, such as grasses, mosses, lichens and leaves. It builds up the clump of material around itself until it is surrounded by the spherical nest. The nest is made in a sheltered space.

YOUNG: Mating occurs from March to August, during which time a female likely has more than one litter, each averaging four or five young. The young are helpless at birth, but the eyes and ears open in about two weeks, and the young are weaned soon afterward.

SIMILAR SPECIES: Although shrews are hard to identify in the wild, this one's large size, limited range and habitat, and reddish color help to distinguish it.

RANGE: The Pacific Shrew is found only in western Oregon and northwestern California.

Water Shrew

Sorex palustris

As everyone would agree, most of the shrews in Washington and Oregon have few distinguishing characteristics. Water Shrews, however, are an exception in the region's shrewdom—these finger-sized heavyweights are so unusual in their habits that they deserve celebrity status.

While other shrews prefer to wreak terror on the small vertebrates and invertebrates roaming on land, the Water Shrew takes the plunge to feed upon aquatic prey. The Water Shrew is a particularly fierce predator, ably seizing not only insect nymphs but even sticklebacks and other small fish. The shrew drags the catch onto land, where it is quickly consumed.

The Water Shrew is specially adapted for swimming: small hairs on the hindfeet widen the foot and create a flipper effect for propulsion. This shrew is very powerful and can easily out-swim most prey species. Once it is out of the water, this shrew's fringed feet serve as a comb with which to brush water droplets out of the fur.

Perhaps the easiest of all shrews to observe, the Water Shrew can be seen beneath overhangs along flowing waters, particularly small creeks and backwaters. If you are walking along these shorelines, it is not unusual to see a small, black bundle rocket from beneath the overhang into the water. The motion at first suggests a frog, but the Water Shrew tends to enter the water with more finesse, hardly producing a splash. Often, the shrew first runs a short distance across the surface of the water before diving in. Some voles and mice may also be scared into or across water in this way, but even at a quick glance you can distinguish this shrew from those rodents by its velvety, black color.

DESCRIPTION: This species and the Marsh Shrew (p. 334) are the largest shrews west of the Great Plains. The Water Shrew has a velvety, black back and contrasting light brown or silver underparts. The third and fourth toes of the hindfeet are slightly webbed, and a stiff fringe of hairs around the hindfeet aid in swimming. Males tend to be somewhat larger than females.

HABITAT: This shrew can be found alongside flowing streams with undercut, root-entwined banks, in sphagnum moss on the shores of lakes and occasionally in nearly dry streambeds or tundra regions.

FOOD: Aquatic insects, spiders, snails, other invertebrates and small fish form

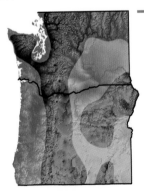

RANGE: This transcontinental species ranges from southern Alaska to Labrador and south along the Cascades and Sierra Nevada to California, along the Rocky Mountains to New Mexico and along the Appalachians almost to Georgia.

Total Length: 5$\frac{1}{2}$–6$\frac{3}{4}$ in.

Tail Length: 2$\frac{3}{8}$–3$\frac{3}{8}$ in.

Weight: $\frac{5}{16}$–$\frac{11}{16}$ oz.

the bulk of the shrew's diet. With true shrew frenzy, these scrappy water lovers may even attack fish half as large as themselves.

DEN: This shrew dens in a shallow burrow in root-entwined banks, in sphagnum moss shorelines or even in the wood debris of beaver lodges. The nest is a spherical mound of dry vegetation, such as twigs, leaves and sedges, and it is about 4 in. wide.

YOUNG: Water Shrews breed from February until late summer, and females have multiple litters each year. Females born early in the year usually have their first litter in that same year. Litters vary

in size from five to eight young, and, as with other shrews, the young grow rapidly and are on their own in a few weeks.

SIMILAR SPECIES: The **Marsh Shrew** (p. 334) is slightly larger, and has a limited range. Other smaller shrews lack the velvety, black fur of the Water Shrew.

DID YOU KNOW?

Both terrestrial and aquatic animals prey on Water Shrews. Weasels, minks and otters can catch them, and so can large trout, bass, walleye and northern pike.

Marsh Shrew
Sorex bendirii

Total Length: 5³/₄–6⁷/₈ in.
Tail Length: 2³/₈–3¹/₈ in.
Weight: about ¹/₂ oz.

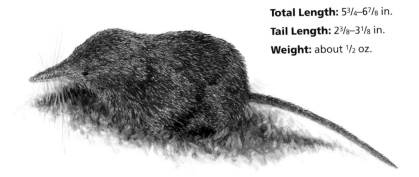

Little is known about this fascinating species. It captures much of its food in water and, like the Water Shrew (p. 332) and a few small rodents, it can even run across the surface a short distance before diving under. Beneath the water it appears silvery because of air trapped in the fur. This trapped air makes it so buoyant that, when it ceases swimming, it quickly pops to the surface like a cork.

The Marsh Shrew immobilizes its prey by a rapid series of bites, and these "frozen" creatures may be stored for a few hours. During rainy winter months, this shrew may move over half a mile from the nearest waterbody.

ALSO CALLED: Pacific Water Shrew.

DESCRIPTION: This large shrew has almost uniform velvety blackish or blackish-brown fur in winter; the pelage is somewhat browner in summer. The tail is dark above and below. The nose is pointed, and the hindfeet are fringed with stiff hairs, which help in swimming.

HABITAT: These shrews inhabit marshy areas along slow-moving streams and other wetlands.

FOOD: Both aquatic and terrestrial invertebrates are avidly devoured. Insects of all stages are eaten.

DEN: The nest is a ball of dry grasses, often beneath the loose bark of a fallen tree or within a rotted log or stump.

YOUNG: The typical litter size is four to seven young, and they are born in a bulky nest of grass. Virtually nothing is known of gestation or when the young become independent. Sexual maturity probably follows independence because maximum life span does not exceed 1¹/₂ years.

RANGE: From extreme southwestern British Columbia, this species follows the area west of the Cascade Mountains south as far as San Francisco.

SIMILAR SPECIES: The **Water Shrew** (p. 332) is about the same size, but it has silvery undersides and a bicolored tail. The **Trowbridge's Shrew** (p. 335) is much less than half the weight of the Marsh Shrew.

Trowbridge's Shrew
Sorex trowbridgii

Total Length: 4¼–5¼ in.
Tail Length: 1⅞–2⅜ in.
Weight: about ¼ oz.

The Trowbridge's Shrew tends to collect and store seeds, a behavior not reported in other North American shrews. Because its diet is diverse, it has an advantage over the Vagrant Shrew (p. 327) and the Montane Shrew (p. 328) where the ranges overlap.

Trowbridge's Shrews are active both day and night, but their periods of activity are short, followed by periods of quiescence. These shrews probably all die before they are 1½ years old, but during late summer their populations peak because of the early summer births.

DESCRIPTION: This velvety, dark gray (appearing black) shrew has undersides nearly as dark as the back. In summer, the body color is slightly brownish. The tail is sharply bicolored—dark above and light below. The tail of a young animal is hairy, but it tends to become less so in older individuals. The ears are nearly hidden in the hair, and the vibrissae are long and abundant. The feet are whitish to light tan.

HABITAT: Throughout its range, this shrew frequents mature forests with abundant ground litter. Generally, it appears to prefer dry ground beneath Douglas-fir, but when other shrew species are absent it occupies ravines, swampy woods and areas where deep grass borders salmonberry thickets.

FOOD: The diet is primarily small insects, spiders, centipedes, snails, slugs, earthworms and flatworms, but these shrews also often eat Douglas-fir seeds and seeds of other plants. They occasionally even eat subterranean fungi.

DEN: The nest of the Trowbridge's Shrew has not been described, but it is likely similar to that of other shrews.

YOUNG: Ordinarily, three to six young are born in spring and early summer. During this time adult females are continually pregnant.

SIMILAR SPECIES: Within its range, the **Marsh Shrew** (p. 334) is the only other species with dark undersides, but it is much larger and heavier with far fewer vibrissae.

RANGE: The Trowbridge's Shrew is found from southwestern British Columbia along the coast into central California.

Merriam's Shrew

Sorex merriami

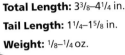

Total Length: 3³/₈–4¹/₄ in.
Tail Length: 1¹/₄–1⁵/₈ in.
Weight: ¹/₈–¹/₄ oz.

During archeological investigations at Mesa Verde National Park in Colorado, remains of Merriam's Shrews were found in pottery jars. The researchers concluded that the animals were collected intentionally by the Native American inhabitants. Although no full explanation exists for this unusual discovery, it seems unlikely that the shrews were intended for consumption—they are exceedingly small and smelly. The smell of Merriam's Shrews is particularly bad, and their noxious odor may have protected stored food from rodents.

DESCRIPTION: This shrew has grayish or brownish-gray upperparts and whitish underparts and feet. In winter it is brighter in appearance. The tail, though sparsely furred, is bicolored. The males have very large flank glands. If you lift the upper lip and view the four unicuspid teeth behind the upper incisor, the unicuspid teeth appear to be crowded together. The second one is the largest, and the third is larger than the fourth.

HABITAT: This shrew inhabits sagebrush flats, deserts, semi-deserts and sometimes dry grasslands. It seems to favor drier habitats than those habitats occupied by other *Sorex* spp.

FOOD: The Merriam's Shrew is thought to eat mostly insects, including beetles, crickets, wasps and caterpillars. Spiders are likely another seasonally common food source.

DEN: Merriam's Shrews make typical shrew nests, often under logs or in soft soil.

YOUNG: Mating occurs from April through July, with females having multiple litters of typically four to seven young in a year.

SIMILAR SPECIES: Without a technical key and the animal in hand, it can be impossible to identify which shrew you are looking at, but range and habitat should narrow the choices.

RANGE: The Merriam's Shrew has been found from Washington State to North Dakota and south to New Mexico and Arizona in appropriate habitat.

Pygmy Shrew
Sorex hoyi

Total Length: 2¹/₈–2³/₈ in.
Tail Length: 1–1¹/₄ in.
Weight: ¹/₁₆–¹/₄ oz.

Weighing no more than a penny, the Pygmy Shrew represents the furthest degree of miniaturization in mammals. It is considered to be one of the smallest of all North American mammals. The Dwarf Shrew (*S. nanus*)—found elsewhere in the United States—may weigh less, but it is longer than the Pygmy Shrew. In spite of its size, the Pygmy Shrew is every bit as voracious as other shrews; one female on record ate about three times her body weight each day for 10 days. The Pygmy Shrew may also be one of the rarest shrews in North America.

DESCRIPTION: This tiny shrew is primarily reddish to grayish brown. The color grades from darkest on the back to somewhat lighter underneath. It is usually grayer in winter. The third and the fifth unicuspid teeth are so reduced in size that they may go unnoticed.

HABITAT: The Pygmy Shrew lives in a variety of different habitats: moist to dry and forested to open, including deep spruce woods, sphagnum bogs, grassy or brushy areas, cattails and rocky slopes.

FOOD: These shrews feed primarily on both larval and adult insects, but earthworms, snails, slugs and carrion often make up a significant portion of the diet.

DEN: The spherical, grassy nest, 2¹/₂–4 in. wide, may be under logs, under debris or in rock crevices. Unlike the nests of many other mammals, there is no rounded cavity inside this grassy ball; instead the shrew simply burrows its way in among the grass.

YOUNG: Breeding takes place from May until August, and 4 to 10 young are born in June, July or August. Females generally have only one litter a year. Young born early in the year may have a late-summer litter, but most females do not mate until the following year.

SIMILAR SPECIES: Other shrews may be impossible to distinguish unless measurements are obtained; this shrew is the smallest in the region.

RANGE: The Pygmy Shrew occurs from Alaska east to Newfoundland and south to Colorado, the Appalachians and New England.

Virginia Opossum
Didelphis virginiana

Among the mammals of North America, the Virginia Opossum is unique because of its prehensile tail, maternal pouch, opposable "big toe" and habit of faking death. Famed by its portrayals in children's literature, the opossum is widely known but poorly understood. Few people realize that this animal is a marsupial, and that it is more closely related to the kangaroo and koala of Australia and to other marsupials of Central and South America than to any other mammal native to the United States or Canada.

Thanks to the many children's stories, we conjure up images of an opossum hanging in a tree by its tail. This behavior is not nearly as common as the literature suggests. An opossum's tail is prehensile and strong, but it is unlikely to be used in such a manner unless the animal has slipped or is reaching for something.

If a Virginia Opossum cannot scare away an intruder with fervent hissing and screeching, it rolls over, dangles its legs, close its eyes, lolls its tongue out and drools; the phrase "playing 'possum" is derived from this feigned death scene. Possibly, this death pose is so startling that the opossum will be left alone.

If you do much driving through the Virginia Opossum's range, it should not be long before you encounter one. Unfortunately, opossums are frequent victims of roadway collisions. They are slow-moving animals that forage at night and find the bounty of road-killed insects and other animals hard to resist. With an abundance of food, opossums may become very fat. They draw upon their reserves in winter in colder parts of their range, but much of Washington and Oregon is still too cold and dry for these creatures, with their naked ears and tails.

DESCRIPTION: This opossum is a cat-sized, gray mammal with a white face, long, pointed nose and long tail. Its ears are black, slightly rounded and nearly hairless. Its tail is rounded, scaly and prehensile. The legs, the base of the tail and patches around the eyes are black. Its overall appearance is grizzled from the mix of white, black and gray hairs. No other U.S. mammal resembles this opossum, and it is the only terrestrial mammal in the U.S. or Canada to have 50 teeth in total.

HABITAT: Moist woodlands or brushy areas near watercourses seem to be favored, but given a warm enough climate and access to permanent water, Virginia Opossums may be found almost anywhere, including cities.

RANGE: The Virginia Opossum is found in southern Ontario and most of the eastern U.S. It was introduced in the western U.S. and now ranges along the entire West Coast as far north as British Columbia and eastward along the Snake River into Idaho.

Total Length: 27–33 in.
Tail Length: 12–14 in.
Weight: 2$\frac{1}{2}$–3$\frac{1}{2}$ lb.

FOOD: A full description of the opossum diet would include almost everything organic. These omnivores eat invertebrates, insects, small mammals and birds, grain, berries and other fruits, grass and carrion.

DEN: By day, Virginia Opossums hide in burrows dug by other mammals, in hollow trees or logs, under buildings or in rock piles. In colder parts of the region, they may remain holed up in a den for days during cold weather, but they do not hibernate.

YOUNG: Up to 25 young may be born in a litter after a gestation of 12 to 13 days. The young must crawl into the pouch and attach to one of the 9 to 17 nipples if they are to survive. After about three months in the pouch, an average of eight to nine young emerge, weighing about 5$\frac{1}{2}$ oz. each. Females mature sexually when they are six months to a year old.

SIMILAR SPECIES: No other mammal shares the combination of characteristics seen in the opossum. Young, newly emerged from the pouch, might be mistaken for **rats** (pp. 204–05), but rats do not have naked, black ears.

DID YOU KNOW?

At about the size of a honeybee at birth, a Virginia Opossum begins life as one of the smallest baby mammals in North America.

Glossary

ALTRICIAL: describing offspring that are almost totally helpless at birth, usually being born without fur, with their eyes closed and unable to walk.

ARBOREAL: living in or pertaining to trees.

BOVID: a member of the cattle family (Bovidae).

BUFF: a dull, brownish yellow.

CACHE: a place in which food is hidden for future use; the food hidden in such a place.

CALCAR: in bats, a small projection from the inner side of each hindfoot into the membrane between the hindlegs.

CANID: a member of the dog family (Canidae).

CARNIVOROUS: flesh-eating (compare *herbivorous*, *omnivorous*).

CARTILAGINOUS: composed of cartilage (a translucent, somewhat elastic structural tissue).

CERVID: a member of the deer family (Cervidae).

CETACEAN: a member of the whale order (Cetacea); a whale, dolphin or porpoise.

COLONY: a group of animals living together and interacting socially.

CONIFEROUS: pertaining to needle-leaved, cone-bearing trees (e.g., fir, spruce, pine).

DECIDUOUS: pertaining to trees that shed their leaves in fall (e.g., oak, maple, elm).

DEWCLAW: a small toe, usually paired, located high on a hoofed mammal's leg, so that it typically touches the ground only in mud or snow.

DEWLAP: a loose fold of skin that hangs from an animal's neck.

DIURNAL: active during the day (compare *nocturnal*).

DORMANCY: a state of inactivity, with greatly slowed metabolism, respiration and heart rate.

DORSAL: pertaining to the back or spine (compare *ventral*). (See illustration below.)

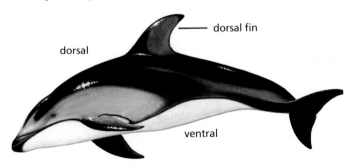

dorsal fin

dorsal

ventral

DREY: a spherical tree nest made of leaves, twigs and moss (see illustration).

ECHOLOCATION: the ability of some animals (including bats and cetaceans among mammals) to detect an object by emitting sound waves and interpreting the returning echoes, which are changed from bouncing off the object.

tree squirrel
drey

ENDANGERED: said of a species or subspecies that is facing imminent *extirpation* or *extinction*.

ESTIVATION: a state of summer dormancy that occurs in some mammals to conserve resources during extremely hot or dry periods (compare *hibernation*).

EXTINCT: said of a species that no longer exists anywhere.

EXTIRPATED: said of a species that no longer exists in a given geographic area but still survives elsewhere in the world.

FAMILY: a biological classification that ranks below *order* and designates a group of closely related *genera*.

FELID: a member of the cat family (Felidae).

FORB: a *herbaceous* plant other than a grass.

GENUS (PL. GENERA): a group of closely related *species* of organisms; if individuals from different species of a genus interbreed, their offspring are usually infertile.

GESTATION: the time of pregnancy, from conception to birth.

GREGARIOUS: preferring to live in large groups with other individuals of the same species; sociable.

GRIZZLED: said of mostly dark fur that is sprinkled or streaked with gray or another light color.

GUARD HAIRS: long, coarse hairs that help protect a mammal's *underfur* from the weather.

HABITAT: the environment in which an animal or plant lives.

HERBACEOUS: pertaining to plants that lack woody stems.

HERBIVOROUS: plant-eating (compare *carnivorous, omnivorous*).

HIBERNACULUM: the den in which an animal hibernates.

HIBERNATION: a state of winter dormancy in certain mammals during which the body temperature is lowered and all body processes are greatly reduced, thereby conserving resources and allowing the mammal to sleep through much of winter (compare *estivation*).

HIERARCHY: a social order; the ranking of individuals by social status.

HOME RANGE: the total area through which an individual animal moves during its usual activities (compare *territory*).

INSECTIVORE: a member of the order Insectivora (moles and shrews); any animal that depends on insects as its primary food source.

INTERBREED: for individuals of different species to mate with each other.

INVERTEBRATE: an animal that lacks a backbone, such as an insect, spider, earthworm or snail.

LAGOMORPH: a member of the order Lagomorpha (rabbits, hares and pikas).

MEMBRANE: a thin, flexible layer, such as the skin of a bat's wings.

MIDDEN: a storage pile of conifer cones and seeds or refuse pile of seed husks and cone debris on the ground (see illustration below).

MIGRATION: the journey that an animal undergoes to get from one region to another, usually in response to seasonal and reproductive cycles.

MUSTELID: a member of the weasel family (Mustelidae).

NOCTURNAL: active at night (compare *diurnal*).

OCHREOUS: an earthy yellow color.

OMNIVOROUS: feeding on both plant and animal material (compare *carnivorous, herbivorous*).

ORDER: a biological classification that designates a group of closely related *families* of organisms.

PALMATE: branching like the fingers of a human hand.

PAPILLA (PL. PAPILLAE): one of many small nubs projecting from the upper surface of the tongue; much more evident in certain mammals, such as cats.

PELAGE: the fur or hair of a mammal.

PERIANAL: located around the anus.

PINNA (PL. PINNAE): a part of the external ear that projects outward; made mostly of cartilage.

PINNIPED: a member of the subgrouping of the order Carnivora that encompasses all seals, sea-lions and walruses.

PRECOCIAL: describing offspring that are well developed at birth, usually having fur and opened eyes, and quickly being able to walk.

PREDATOR: an animal that kills its prey (compare *scavenger*).

Red Squirrel defending its midden

RUNWAY: a beaten path made by the repeated travels of small animals.

SCAT: a fecal pellet or dropping; feces.

SCAVENGER: an animal that feeds on animals it did not kill (compare *predator*).

SPECIES: a biological classification below *genus* that designates closely related organisms that are able to breed and produce viable offspring.

SUBNIVEAN: under the snow (but above the ground).

SUBSPECIES: a subcategory of *species* that designates a geographic population that is genetically distinct from other populations of that species, but is still able to successfully breed with them.

SUBTERRANEAN: underground.

TERRITORY: a defended area within an animal's home range.

TRAGUS: a lobe projecting upward from inside the base of the ears, as in bats (see illustration below).

UNDERFUR: a thick, insulating undercoat of fur.

UNGULATE: a hoofed mammal.

UNICUSPID: in shrews, any of the small teeth between the two front teeth and the large rear teeth.

UROPATAGIUM: the fold of skin that stretches from a bat's hind legs to its tail.

VENTRAL: pertaining to the belly (compare *dorsal*). (See illustration, p. 340.)

VERTEBRATE: an animal with a backbone, such as a mammal, bird or fish.

VIBRISSA (PL. VIBRISSAE): one of the stiff hairs that are situated about the nostrils or the face in many mammals; can serve as tactile organs; commonly called whiskers.

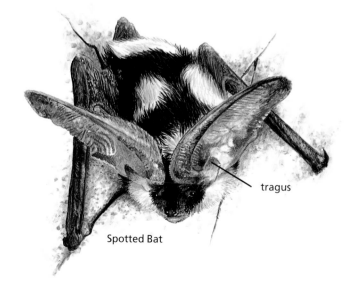

tragus

Spotted Bat

Index of Scientific Names

Page numbers in **boldface** type refer to the primary, illustrated species accounts.

Index of Common Names

Page numbers in **boldface** type refer to the primary, illustrated species accounts.